The Way of GRACE

BRUCE W. HUBBARD

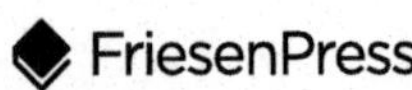

Suite 300 - 990 Fort St
Victoria, BC, V8V 3K2
Canada

www.friesenpress.com

First Edition — 2016

Edited by Marlene Hubbard

ISBN
978-1-4602-8602-9 (Hardcover)
978-1-4602-8603-6 (Paperback)
978-1-4602-8604-3 (eBook)

1. RELIGION, CHRISTIAN LIFE, SPIRITUAL GROWTH

Distributed to the trade by The Ingram Book Company

In the Word, the Lord speaks of the way in which we can walk. He speaks of the way of wickedness, the way of fools, and a way that seems right to a man but in the end it brings death. The Lord however, offers us another way. In fact if we want to find life, it is the only way. In Him we will discover the way of righteousness and the way of wisdom. Along this path of life we will find joy, peace, contentment, and the rest of knowing our service to Him in a way that brings Him pleasure. It is *The Way of Grace*. – Marlene Hubbard

Dedication

This book is dedicated to my mother, Ina Hubbard,
who is one of the most gracious women I have ever known.
She taught me a principle of grace one day,
when we were talking about forgiveness.
She told mc,
"Bruce, we need to let our soul heal quickly!"

" For the law was given by Moses, but grace and truth came by Jesus Christ."

Acknowledgements

I want to thank all those who helped me write this book:

The Lord Jesus Christ, Who has shown me His grace over and over.

My wife, Marlene, who has been such an encouragement to me and has been a close sister in daily fellowship. Also for her many hours of helping me edit, rethink, and rewrite my manuscript.

All my close brothers and sisters in Christ in Lethbridge who through our fellowship times together have shown me the way of grace. You are dear to me.

Harry Hubbard, who is not only my blood-brother, but a dear brother in Christ and a source of much encouragement in the Lord. Thank you for reading through my book as I was writing, and inspiring me to press on and publish.

John Stanley, of the church in Medicine Hat, for his time consuming proof reading and adding suggestions to the book.

All those people and situations that come my way each day to teach me about how to walk in God's ways and to respond using the power of His grace.

All the many people at FriesenPress who have given me many valuable suggestions in helping me put this work together.

Bless you all.

Forward

Book Cover Photograph:

This picture was taken on a beach in Australia approximately seven years before I came to know the Lord. We were lying on a sandy beach, and with darkness approaching, we lit a candle to help us see a little better. When I saw the beauty of the glowing candle standing upright in the sandal, I grabbed my camera and got ready to take a picture. Just as I lay there on the sand, ready, a little butterfly landed right on the side of the candle and spread its wings. 'Snap', the moment was captured.

Just as the butterfly was attracted to the light, God's grace draws us to Him, birthing in us new life and calling us to experience His grace. As we experience God in our life, the old passes away and is no longer our life's focus. In the same way as I laid there ready to snap a picture, we need to be ready for every path the Lord sends our way. It is often a path, which we never knew was there — even as you see the shadow of the butterfly's legs on its wings.

Why I Wrote This Book:

The way of grace is God's influence on our heart and its enablement in our life. It is the only way to experience life to its fullest. A human heart that allows God's grace to touch it will soon find a godly hungering and thirsting birthed within. A soul submitted to God's grace will find and experience His righteousness without limit. Even the smallest stone of care thrown into the Almighty's vast ocean of grace is felt by the Lord, resulting in a loving response and communion with Him. God's righteousness becomes a Christian experiencc.

We are all products of our past. Ever since my wife, Marlene, and I came to know Jesus Christ as Lord (in 1979), He has graciously worked within us, and showed us how to walk out our Christian lives. When looking back at the many things we have experienced, I am almost over-whelmed. I look at each step as a pathway, which the Lord has placed before us, fulfilling His purpose through us. As a trained teacher I have taught in many schools both in Canada and also abroad, mostly teaching and administrating in Christian Schools. I love to teach, not only young people, but anyone who is hungry to learn. One of my greatest joys is to share a truth with someone and to see a seed come alive in that person's heart. I take every opportunity that comes my way to share the Lord.

Grace touches all aspects of our life. It is the foundation upon which the Christian life rests. What is grace? How does it affect my life? As Marlene and I fellowship around Scripture, the Lord teaches us many new and interesting things about grace and its operation in our life. It took us a year and a half to complete this work, and it is undoubtedly one of the most fruitful things we have ever done together. We can only stand in awe and forever thank the Lord for His grace as He continues to work in our lives and in those around us as we fellowship in Him.

I give the Lord all the glory for so much that He has done. First and foremost that He drew me to come to know Him in a personal way. He recreated a marriage, which had fallen apart, and gave us a new love for each other. As new believers we became part of the church in Yahk, B.C. where we learned the concept of true fellowship among believers. By His grace, He carried us through the death of our youngest daughter, Chani. In 1986 to 1989, we spent time in Haiti as missionaries. The Lord protected us on several occasions where we had to be prepared to lay down our lives. At that time we learned so much about God's love and how to walk in His grace. It was there in Haiti in the midst of so much lawlessness that I published my first book – 'Laloua Bondie Pou Ayiti' (The Law of God for Haiti).

In 1999, we spent time in China and had the priceless privilege of fellowshipping with the underground church in the city of Daquing. How can this be done when a Chinese brother speaks Mandarin and I speak English? It can only be done by the Holy Spirit responding to the true love of one another in Christ. It was during our stay in China that I started to hear the bones of the Scriptures on grace rattling in the epistles of the Bible. The Lord helped me to find these bones, and then to put flesh on them, but it took the Holy Spirit to breathe life into them as my wife and I fellowshipped around each Scripture.

How To Use This Book:

The **Preface** explains how to come to know the grace of God in a personal manner. This is more important than knowing anything else. To get the most out of this book and experience His grace, it is imperative that one gets to know God personally.

Most Scripture in the book is quoted from the Amplified Bible, except for a few, which are noted as such. All scripture texts are written in italics, with discussed topics underlined. They are quoted in italics to make them easier to find and to emphasize God's word, rather than mine.

At the back of the book you will find the **Topical Index**. All words that are underlined within the book are found in this index with corresponding page numbers where the topic is discussed. As an example, on page 41, you will find *law of Christ*, within the Scripture. If you look in the Topical Index under "law", you will find "of Christ" and also you will find other related topics listed as well. You can also look under "Christ" and find the topic "law of". The Topical Index can also be used as a concordance to find Scripture.

Also at the back of the book is the **Scripture Index** containing a list of all Scriptures used within the book, along with their corresponding page numbers. Note that the page numbers in bold print are those that are fully written out in italics on that page. All other Scriptures listed are cross references.

My prayer is that as you read this book you will allow the scriptural truths to come alive in your heart. Let the Lord speak to you, let Him renew your vision, and most of all let Him manifest Himself through you as you walk out His truths in your life in new found freedom.

Recommended Further Reading:

Lawrence O. Richards, *Encyclopedia of Bible Words*, Grand Rapids, Zondervan

For Me

When I look upon Your cross
What do I see?
The greatest act of love
For me

You were dying
So that I could see
You were giving Your life
For me

Now when I look upon Your face
What do I see?
The very eyes of grace
For me

My friend, do you see the cross?
See His face so true?
Do you see His act of love?
For you

Words and music by Bruce Hubbard

Table of Contents

Preface

Standard for life was set by God, but broken by man — resulting in separation from God.

Intervention is required; it was initiated by God through grace, in Jesus Christ the Lord.

New life from God above is birthed in man through faith in Jesus Christ — resulting in restoration to God.

After the Lord created man and placed him in the Garden of Eden to tend it, He gave the command that he could eat of all the trees in the Garden except for the tree of the knowledge of good and evil. This command came with a consequence for disobedience — in the day that it was eaten the penalty was death (Gen. 2:15–17).

Now Adam's wife, Eve, was tempted to eat of the fruit of the tree of the knowledge of good and evil. The serpent beguiled her and lied to her about the consequence of disobedience. And when she saw the fruit as being good and pleasant to eat and nice to look at, and believing that it was going to make her wise and knowledgeable, she took the fruit and ate it. She also gave it to her husband to eat. Immediately they saw that they were naked and they tried to cover themselves and hide (Gen. 3:6–8).

All of mankind is born in sin and has a <u>sin nature</u> — a nature separated from God. This separation originated right after Creation, when man disobeyed God and fell under the penalty of disobedience (sin) and its wages of death.

This <u>original</u> <u>sin</u> (disobedience to God's will) is the source of the sin nature that we all possess today. As a result, death became the inheritance of all mankind (Rom. 5:12).

Before we knew Christ as our personal Saviour, we were spiritually dead, condemned under the penalty of our trespasses and sins. We routinely lived under the desires of our fallen nature. We were being dictated to by the prince of the power of the air (Satan) following the ways of unbelief and disobedience.

As we live under the impulses and passions of our carnal flesh (our fallen nature) we unknowingly find ourselves being obedient to that fallen nature, destined for condemnation and the wrath of God.

But the Lord God, Who is so rich in His mercy and Who loves us with pure love has provided a way out of this fallen condition of condemnation. He sent Jesus, the Son of God, to die for our sins and be resurrected from death. When we believe in this powerful act of God we have access to new life; we are delivered from judgement, and we are positioned in right standing with God (Eph. 2:1–5).

<u>Faith</u> and believing in God and the work of Christ come by accepting and receiving the Living Word of God. Believing <u>faith</u> comes by hearing this incredible message spoken by Christ Himself (Rom. 10:17). We must hear with our heart, not just our natural ear. If we believe in our heart and confess with our lips that Jesus is Lord and that God raised Him from the dead, we will be saved. It is with our heart that we believe God's message, and it is with our mouth that we speak out freely our faith confirming our salvation (Rom. 10:8–10).

To acquire <u>saving</u> <u>faith</u>, it is necessary to believe that God exists, and to have faith in what He has accomplished for us on the cross. It is impossible to be made right with God by any work or deed on our part — it is a free gift of God. <u>Faith</u> <u>pleases</u> <u>God</u> (Eph. 2:8–9; Heb. 11:6).

Before believing in Christ Jesus, God sees us as separated from Him by the barrier of our sin. Upon exercising our faith in Jesus Christ, we receive forgiveness of all our sin (past, present and future) and God forever destroys the barrier. He now sees us as righteous before Him; this allows us to approach God with freedom and without fear.

In Christ, we have been released from our position of condemnation. His blood has paid the price required for all sin. By faith in the death and resurrection of Christ, God's grace provides the mercy I require (Rom. 3:22–24). Sin brings death, but faith in Christ brings life.

In the world, we unknowingly were slaves to sin, but in Christ we become servants of God free to live a new life in obedience to Him (Rom. 6:16, 23).

Grace is entirely the work of Christ. It is never attainable by being a *good person*. Grace is the free gift of God and is only receivable by faith — believing and trusting in God's work, not our own. Beloved, grace is free and totally unmerited. Our natural mind finds this offensive because it believes that God should recognize that there is some good works found in all of mankind. The good works that we see in mankind have nothing to do with the attaining of salvation. It is only by God's grace that our spirit rejoices in the free gift of our salvation bringing us back into right relationship with God. We no longer need to hide from Him as in the Garden of Eden (Eph. 2:8–9).

By God's grace we become new creations — born again to a new life in Christ. This same grace enables us to operate in the kingdom of God here on earth where we can live our lives manifesting Christ as His children (John 3:3).

It is only in Christ that we become new creations. The old moral and spiritual condition passes away and the new has come. This is called the *Good News*, and for those who know Christ personally, they know why it is so called (2 Cor. 5:17).

Summary:

1. You must recognize that you are a sinner — you have fallen short of the goodness that God requires.

2. You must know that the wages of sin is death, but the free gift of God is eternal life in Jesus Christ.

3. You must believe that Jesus personally died for your sins and that God raised Him from the dead to newness of life. If you confess this faith with your mouth, you shall be saved.

4. Upon receiving Christ, you become a born again child of God. This grace of God makes you a new creation where old things pass away and behold, all things become new. He has given you His Spirit to dwell within you as a guarantee and guide of your new life in Christ Jesus.

Introduction

✞ POSITION/OPERATION OF GRACE ✞

Original sin in the Garden of Eden instantly touched the life of its victims — decreeing eternal death upon them. Original sin created a separation between God and man, leaving man in a position where he could no longer find rest in God's creation or in His presence (Gen. 3:7–8). Original sin also instantly imparted its bias or nature into all of creation. Creation now felt the impact of man's disobedience to God. Mortality was birthed and impregnated into all that God's hand had made. Death became the inheritance, and operated upon all of God's creation (Rom. 8:19–22; 1 Cor. 15:21–22).

Mankind now possessed an inherent sin nature, which made him slave to the grip of ungodliness as it produced its fruit of death. Sin (disobedience to God's command) now had power over man's newly acquired sin nature. The effect of original sin operated in the soul of mankind. He now lived out his mortal life from this newly acquired position of being separated from God (Gen. 4:7–8).

"Therefore, as sin came into the world through one man, and death as the result of sin, so death spread to all men [no one being able to stop it or to escape its power] because all men sinned" (Romans 5:12).

Sin gained its entrance into the world through the one man, Adam, and bequeathed death as the imminent condition and state of all things. Death now reigned through all of God's creation. Man lost his innocence and was now a wanderer in a world of death, unable to escape the power of its grasp. All of mankind had inherited the error of Adam's transgression.

"[To be sure] sin was in the world before ever the Law was given, but sin is not charged to men's account where there is no law [to transgress].

Yet death held sway from Adam to Moses [the Lawgiver], even over those who did not themselves transgress [a positive command] as Adam did. Adam was a type (prefigure) of the One Who was to come [in reverse, the former destructive, the Latter saving]" (Romans 5:13–14).

Death held sway; it exercised its governing power and influence, even holding power over those who did not transgress as Adam did. Original sin would have held man tight in its grasp for eternity had it not been for the grip of God's grace abounding even greater.

"But God's free gift is not at all to be compared to the trespass [His grace is out of all proportion to the fall of man]. For if many died through one man's falling away (his lapse, his offense), much more profusely did God's grace and the free gift [that comes] through the undeserved favour of the one Man Jesus Christ abound and overflow to and for [the benefit of] many.

Nor is the free gift at all to be compared to the effect of that one [man's] sin. For the sentence [following the trespass] of one [man] brought condemnation, whereas the free gift [following] many transgressions brings justification (an act of righteousness)" (Romans 5:15–16).

The trespass — the fall of man — is completely covered by the grace of God, which eradicates the effect or result of Adam's sin and the many transgressions that followed. The sentence for that one man's sin brings condemnation, but the free gift of the grace of Christ Jesus, brings us into the position of justification. Mercy triumphs over judgement (James 2:13)!

"For if because of one man's trespass (lapse, offense) death reigned through that one, much more surely will those who receive [God's] overflowing grace (unmerited favour) and the free gift of righteousness [putting them into right standing with Himself] reign as kings in life through the one Man Jesus Christ (the Messiah, the Anointed One)" (Romans 5:17).

Adam's deviation from truth established the reign of death in the world. However, when we receive grace, we are divinely destined and ordained to reign in life from the position of righteousness through Jesus Christ, the Messiah! As surely as death reigns in the world, it is with greater assurance that we ascertain our reign of righteousness in Christ Jesus. We are called to receive God's overflowing grace, taking hold of it and associating ourselves with it as an eternal companion. Grace is something to be taken hold of and held. We are to seize and apprehend that which has seized and apprehended us (Phil. 3:12). We are called to press on to make it our own, because Christ Jesus has made us His own. It is one thing for us to grasp grace, but it is even more blessed to be seized by grace itself.

"Well then, as one man's trespass [one man's false step and falling away] led to condemnation for all men, so one Man's act of righteousness [leads] to acquittal and right standing with God and life for all men.

For just as by one man's disobedience (failing to hear, heedlessness, and carelessness) the many were constituted sinners, so by one Man's obedience the many will be constituted righteous (made acceptable to God, brought into right standing with Him)" (Romans 5:18–19).

One man's transgression caused the condemnation of all mankind. One Man's act of grace set us free from this condemnation and positioned us in right standing with God. This one act of grace that brings salvation has appeared to all men. Our right relationship to God is not only dependent upon God's work of grace but our reception of the same (John 1:12).

"But the Law came in, [only] to expand and increase the trespass [making it more apparent and exciting opposition]. But where sin increased and abounded, grace (God's unmerited favour) has surpassed it and increased the more and superabounded" (Romans 5:20).

Grace did what the Law could not do. Being brought into right standing with God is an act that cannot be accomplished by man and his obedience to the Law. No amount of obedience to the Law and its sacrifices can perfect the conscience or cleanse and renew the inner man (Heb. 9:9). It takes a perfect sacrifice to cleanse the inner man; therefore, from our position as fallen man, all our sacrifices are imperfect.

Perfection is a position that can only be accomplished by God Himself — the perfect sinless sacrifice. Jesus, the perfect sinless Man offered Himself as the perfect Sacrifice. It was man's disobedience to God's word that caused the fall of man; it was God's obedience to His own word that avails and presents the righteousness of God as a free gift to fallen man — His grace.

The Word (Christ) became flesh and dwelt among us. The Word came into the world, and though the world was made by Him, the world did not recognize him from their position of their fallen nature. The Word, full of grace and truth, died on the cross, blotting out completely all the legal transgressions written against us — our sins — by nailing them to His cross. The Word, which embodies God's righteousness, can only be received by the grace of God through faith. It has absolutely nothing to do with our own goodness or works. Grace abounds beyond measure; it exceedingly overflows; it knows no bounds; it is eternal!

"So that, [just] as sin has reigned in death, [so] grace (His unearned and undeserved favour) might reign also through righteousness (right standing with God) which issues in eternal life through Jesus Christ (the Messiah, the Anointed One) our Lord" (Romans 5:21).

Sin reigned in death. Grace reigns through righteousness. The free gift that grace conveys is eternal life. It is not a conditional life dependent upon human effort to acquire it or to sustain it; it is a life that can only be secured and kept by the Eternal, Himself. Our position of rightcousness is obtainable *only* through faith in Jesus Christ the Lord.

When a believer comes to Christ, the effect of original sin is dealt a fatal blow. The believer is transferred from his position in the kingdom of darkness into his new position in the kingdom of the Son of God's love (Col. 1:13). The condemnation of eternal death is dealt with immediately and forever, by grace (Rom. 8:1–2, 33–34). Eternal life is given freely, and as many as receive it, they are given authority to become the children of God — believers in the Lord Jesus Christ (John 1:12).

Salvation occurs when the human heart repents — turns towards God, accepting Him as Saviour.

Repentance is an act of submission to God's grace and results in the reception of eternal life through the Lord Jesus Christ. Our position of righteousness is maintained in Christ Jesus. It is from our position of grace that we are seen as being holy, even as the Lord is Holy (Rom. 6:22). We now have a position where we actually become the righteousness of God, in Christ (2 Cor. 5:21). This grace is forever ours — never to be taken from us. It is totally unobtainable and impossible to be received by any human effort whatsoever. Oh the incredible, saving grace of God!

When man turns his life towards God and believes in Christ Jesus, he instantly receives eternal life. There are no conditions of work placed upon receiving eternal life; otherwise it would not be eternal life, and grace would not be grace (Rom. 11:6; Gal. 2:21). Our position of grace is entirely accomplished by believing in the cross of Christ, the blood of Jesus, and the grace of God. This is the position of every believer in Christ Jesus. No work on the part of man is called upon here. When we place our faith in the work of Jesus Christ and believe in Him, the power of original sin is forever broken and God's eternity is implanted into our heart — we move from the position of eternal death into the position of eternal life.

When a believer comes to Christ, the power of the sin nature within the soul is dealt a fatal blow. From our position of grace, we can now let grace operate and grow in our lives, as we increase in the knowledge of our Lord Jesus Christ (2 Peter 3:18). A believer now has the ability to let the grace of God train his senses and mental faculties to distinguish between what is morally good and noble and what is evil and contrary to divine law and order (Heb. 5:14). This is the training, teaching, and enabling of grace operating in our lives. Oh, the incredible grace of God!

Ungodly behaviour is not eliminated in our life by simply declaring it to be non-existent, or that God cannot see it. It is foolish to declare that God sees our sin as evil, before knowing Christ, but that He cannot see our sin after believing in Christ. Maturity comes to a Christian by having his senses and mental faculties trained by reason of use, to discriminate between what is morally good and evil, and then to do what is right.

God's grace does not blind God's eyes to seeing sin. To say that God does not know when a Christian acts in disobedience to His divine law is to make God out to be less than omniscient and even a fool. Grace is an ongoing, continuous act of God; it is part of His eternal nature. Repentance is intended to be an ongoing attitude of man — a lifestyle. When a Christian sins he does not need to ask Christ to die again for his sin; he merely needs to recognize the Truth — Jesus died for all his disobedience — and then to allow the grace of God to bring the renewing change into his life. This is the operation of grace bringing repentance and the renewing of our soul, as it produces the peaceable fruit of righteousness.

Both position and operation are common throughout Scripture and are evident in everyday natural circumstances. For example, I have fathered three children, therefore I am a father. My position of *father* is a work of God. It is done, it is finished and it is a fact — a fixed truth that cannot be changed or undone. However, to be a father is not just a position, it is also an operation. I need to *father* my children. The operation of me being a father is something temporary and mortal; it does not last forever. Both the position of father and the operation of fathering are accomplished by the grace of God.

At this moment in time, I am sitting in front of my computer writing about the position and operation of grace; however, Scripture tells me that I am not sitting at my computer, but rather that I am sitting in heavenly places, right now. This is my spiritual position in the realm of Truth. *"And He raised us up together with Him and made us sit down together [giving us joint seating with Him] in the heavenly sphere [by virtue of our being] in Christ Jesus (the Messiah, the Anointed One)"* (Ephesians 2:6). So my mortal man is sitting in front of the computer while my spiritual position is seated with Him in the heavenly realm. Both are happening at the same time. My spiritual position in the heavenly realm is eternal, but my operation here as a mortal man is temporary. Both are an expression of the grace of God.

An example of position and operation is seen even in salvation. I am saved now; and I am also being saved by God's grace. *"I write this to you who believe in (adhere to, trust in, and rely on) the name of the Son of God [in the peculiar services and blessings conferred by Him on men], so that you may know [with settled and absolute knowledge] that you [already] have life, yes eternal life"* (1 John 5:13).

"For the story and message of the cross is sheer absurdity and folly to those who are perishing and on their way to perdition, but to us who are being saved it is the [manifestation of] the power of God" (1 Corinthians 1:18).

"For we are the sweet fragrance of Christ [which exhales] unto God, [discernible alike] among those who are being saved and among those who are perishing;" (2 Corinthians 2:15).

The word of God is the will of God. The Spirit of God is the power of God. The Grace of God is the medium through which God's power expresses His will. It takes the grace of God to enable man to hear or see God. An ear that is not tuned by the grace of God cannot hear or receive the words of the Omnipotent. An eye that is not enlightened by the grace of God cannot see an act of God. Such mortal ears and eyes are deaf and blind before Him. Beloved, without God's grace surrounding us and allowing us to exist and move within it, we would never receive anything from God. God's grace is the medium through which God expresses Himself and inspires us. Without it we could not operate in the kingdom of God.

The grace of God is both positional and operational. Our position of grace is that we have obtained the forgiveness of sin and eternal salvation. This position of grace that God has bestowed upon us is a fact that cannot be reversed or added to by any effort on our part whatsoever. *"Giving thanks to the Father, Who has qualified and made us fit to share the portion which is the inheritance of the saints (God's holy people) in the Light. [The Father] has delivered and drawn us to Himself out of the control and the dominion of darkness and has transferred us into the kingdom of the Son of His love, In Whom we have our redemption through His blood, [which means] the forgiveness of our sins"* (Colossians 1:12–14). *"For it is by free grace (God's unmerited favour) that you are saved (delivered from judgement and made partakers of Christ's salvation) through [your] faith. And this [salvation] is not of yourselves [of your own doing, it came not through your own striving], but it is the gift of God"* (Ephesians 2:8).

This position that God has provided for us, is finished and complete. Nothing can be added to it or taken away from it. *"I know that whatever God does, it endures forever; nothing can be added to it nor anything taken from it. And God does it so that men will [reverently fear] Him [revere and worship Him knowing that He is]"* (Ecclesiastes 3:14).

The blood of Christ paved the way for both the position of grace and the operation of grace to affect our life. The position of grace is eternal; we cannot lose our eternal life — our heavenly home. The operation of grace in our life receives its authority and power from our position in Christ; grace enables our mortal man to operate in the kingdom of God here on earth. It teaches us to deny all ungodliness access to our life (Titus 2:12). It enables us to strip off and throw aside every encumbrance and sin that can cleverly cling to us and entangle us (Heb. 12:1). It allows Christ to perfect us and bring us into maturity (Heb. 12:2). It trains our mental faculties to discriminate between what is morally good and noble, and what is evil and contrary to God's law (Heb. 5:14).

The operation of grace in our life flows from our position of grace that we have in Christ (2 Cor. 12:9). It was by God's grace that the law was given — God identified Himself as a Gracious God when He gave the second set of tablets to Moses on Mount Sinai (Ex. 34:6). The law is not God's grace; grace comes to us independently from the law of God. The Law is an expression of God's will with respect to upright, moral and holy living. We all fall short of the holiness of God. The law, although holy in itself, cannot make us holy (Rom. 7:12; 8:3); it merely defines what holy/unholy behaviour is.

Christ has done what the law could not do. When I walk according to the flesh, the law of sin, which is in my flesh, has control over me and brings me under its sway. My ability to obey God is weakened by the flesh — the entire nature of man devoid of the Holy Spirit. I need to be born again — born from above by the Spirit — to have the power of my flesh subdued.

Christ came in the guise of sinful flesh and became an offering for sin. The power of sin in the flesh is deprived of its authority over all who accept the sacrifice of Christ (Rom. 8:3). The Spirit of God now abides in us (James 4:5–6); it is our guarantee of God's work in our life (Eph. 1:13–14). In Christ, I am a new creation (2 Cor. 5:17). I am prompted by the Spirit to obey God's word and allow the love of God and the grace of God to operate in my life on a moment by moment basis (1 John 2:1–6).

The Gospel has freed me from the curse of the law. In Christ, I now have continuous, gracious forgiveness as I learn to walk obediently to God by His grace, in His Spirit. The Holy Spirit of grace now directs my paths according to His law — I do not act lawlessly towards God; but I am especially committed to the law of Christ.

"For although I am free in every way from anyone's control. I have made myself a bond servant to everyone, so that I might gain the more [for Christ].

To the Jews I become as a Jew, that I might win Jews; to men under the Law, I became as one under the Law, though not myself being under the Law, that I might win those under the Law.

To those without (outside) law I became as one without law, not that I am without the law of God and lawless toward Him, but that I am [especially keeping] within and committed to the law of Christ; that I might win those who are without the law" (1 Corinthians 9:19–21).

The natural man tends to see sin in others much quicker than he sees it in himself. In truth, we should hate sin in ourselves with more zeal than we hate sin in others. As much grace as we show ourselves, we should show others. Beloved, it takes a vessel all cracked with imperfections to let the light of grace shine through. Any feeling of superiority or inferiority with respect to anyone else is an act of disgrace, not grace. *"Rejoice not when your enemy falls, and let not your heart be glad when he stumbles or is overthrown, lest the Lord see it and it be evil in His eyes and displease Him, and He turn away His wrath from Him [to expend it upon you, the worse offender]"* (Proverbs 24:17–18).

Grace-full eyes focus on forgiveness, not faults. Grace-full mouths speak words of love, not injustice. Grace-full fists beat not the flesh of others but rather the breast of self (Luke 18:10–14). Grace-full feet walk not arrogantly on a high way, looking down in superiority into the gutter; but rather they draw others by the fragrance of grace, in compassion, up onto the heavenly highway of hope.

A life that works up a high standard of ethics is not what fulfils the gospel of grace. We cannot merit God's love or grace by our works. We are able to love only because of God's grace working in our lives.

Let us now look at the position and operation of grace mentioned throughout the Epistles in Scripture. We will find that grace places us in an eternal position of righteousness. It is a work forever completed by God alone. We will also find that this same grace operates in our mortal soul, training and teaching us, as we sojourn here in this present world — as we, *"Await and look for the [fulfilment, the realization of our] blessed hope, even the glorious appearing of our great God and Saviour Christ Jesus (the Messiah, the Anointed One),"* (Titus 2:13).

"For the grace of God (His unmerited favour and blessing) has come forward (appeared) for the deliverance from sin and the eternal salvation for all mankind.

It has trained us to reject and renounce all ungodliness (irreligion) and worldly (passionate) desires, to live discreet (temperate, self-controlled), upright, devout (spiritually whole) lives in this present world," (Titus 2:11–12).

Here we see the two-fold nature of grace: our position of salvation, and the operation of grace training our soul.

"*But by the grace (the unmerited favour and blessing) of God I am what I am, and His grace toward me was not [found to be] for nothing (fruitless and without effect). In fact, I worked harder than all of them [the apostles], though it was not really I, but the grace (the unmerited favour and blessing) of God which was with me*" (1 Corinthians 15:10).

Here we see the two-fold nature of grace: the position of *I am what I am*; and the operation of grace working within. The word for 'grace' used in the New Testament is the Greek word '*charis*'. It is used over 120 times in Scripture. We will look at the scriptures listed below, as well as many others that talk about our position of grace and the work of grace in our life.

Beloved, all of the sunlight used to sustain life on earth is but a fraction of the total output of the sun. God's grace is sufficient to cover all sin, for all mankind, forever, and ever. Amen.

GRACE: *'charis'*

<u>Grace</u> (*charis*):

'the divine influence upon the heart, and its reflection in the life' (Abingdon's Strong's Exhaustive Concordance of the Bible).

- grace produces obedience to faith and makes disciples (Rom. 1:5)
- grace be yours (Rom.1:7)
- grace justifies (Rom. 3:24; Titus 3:7)
- grace not works (Rom. 4:4)
- faith by grace (Rom. 4:16)
- access to grace by faith (Rom. 5:2)
- grace abounds (Rom. 5:15, 17, 20)
- grace reigns through righteousness (Rom. 5:21)
- grace multiplies and overflows (Rom. 6:1)
- under or by grace (Rom. 6:14, 15)
- election or choosing by grace not works (Rom. 11:5, 6)
- grace warns (Rom. 12:3)
- speak through grace (Rom. 12:6)
- gifts according to grace (Rom. 12:6)
- boldness because of grace (Rom. 15:15)
- grace of Christ be with us (Rom. 16:20, 24; 1 Cor. 16:23)
- grace given to us (1 Cor. 1:4)
- grace actively lays the foundation (1 Cor. 3:10)
- partake by grace (1 Cor. 10:30)
- gifts of grace (1 Cor. 12:1–31)
- worked and laboured because of grace (1 Cor. 15:10)
- grace be to you (1 Cor. 1:3; 2 Cor. 1:2; Gal 1:3; Eph. 1:6; Philemon 1:3)
- grace conducts our lives, not the flesh (2 Cor. 1:12)
- grace is a benefit (2 Cor. 1:15)
- grace abounds to the glory of God (2 Cor. 4:15; 1 Tim. 1:14)
- do not receive grace in vain (2 Cor. 6:1)
- grace of giving (2 Cor. 8:1, 6, 7, 19; 2 Cor. 9:8)
- the grace of Jesus; through His poverty we become rich (2 Cor. 8:9)
- God is able to make grace abound (2 Cor. 9:8)
- long after and pray for you because of God's grace in you (2 Cor. 9:14)
- grace is sufficient (2 Cor. 12:9)
- grace as a blessing to you (Phil. 1:2; Col 1:2; 1 Thess. 1:1; 2 Thess. 1:2; Rev. 1:4)
- grace be with you as a benediction (2 Cor. 13:14; Eph. 1:2; 6:24; Col 4:18; 1 Thess. 5:28; 2 Thess. 3:18; 1 Tim. 6:21; 2 Tim. 4:22; Titus 3:15; Heb. 13:25; 2 John 1:3; Rev. 22:21)
- grace be with your spirit (Gal. 6:18; Phil. 4:23; Philemon 1:25)
- called into the grace of Christ (Gal. 1:6, 15)
- grace of ministry perceived (Gal. 2:9; Eph. 3:7)
- frustrate or set aside the grace of God (Gal. 2:21)
- fallen from grace (Gal. 5:4)
- the glory of His grace (Eph. 1:6)
- forgiveness according to the riches of His grace (Eph. 1:7)
- saved by grace (Eph. 2:5, 8)
- the exceeding riches of His grace (Eph. 2:7)
- stewardship of God's grace given to us (Eph. 3:2)
- grace a ministry worked by His power (Eph. 3:7)
- grace given to preach (Eph. 3:8)
- grace according to measure of gift of Christ (Eph. 4:7)
- our words should minister grace (Eph. 4:29)
- partakers together of grace (Phil. 1:7)
- know the grace of God in truth (Col. 1:6)
- sing with grace in your heart (Col. 3:16)
- speech be with grace (Col. 4:6)
- Christ glorified by grace in us (2 Thess. 1:12)
- consolation and hope through grace (2 Thess. 2:16)
- grace from God (1 Tim. 1:2; 2 Tim. 1:2; Titus 1:4; 2:11)
- called according to His purpose and grace (2 Tim. 1:9)
- be strong in grace (2 Tim. 2:1)
- Jesus tasted death by the grace of God (Heb. 2:9)

- come boldly unto the throne of grace (Heb. 4:16)
- insulting the Holy Spirit of grace. (Heb. 10:29)
- to fail or come short of the grace of God (Heb. 12:15)
- by grace we serve God acceptably (Heb. 12:28)
- the heart established or made firm with grace (Heb. 13:9)
- grace given to the humble (Jas. 4:6; 1 Peter 5:5)
- grace given in increasing measure (1 Peter 1:2)
- prophets prophesied of the grace (1 Peter 1:10)
- hope in the grace that is coming to us (1 Peter 1:13)
- husbands and wives heirs of the grace of life (1 Peter 3:7)
- stewards of the grace of God (1 Peter 4:10)
- God of all grace (1 Peter 5:10)
- we stand in the grace of God (1 Peter 5:12)
- grace multiplied unto you (2 Peter 1:2)
- grow in grace (2 Peter 3:18)
- pervert grace; turning it into immorality (Jude 1:4)
- grace be with all of us (Rev. 22:21)

In conclusion, it is imperative for Christians to know that grace and truth came through Jesus Christ (John 1:17). Christianity is the only religion that is founded on grace. Jesus died for the sins of all mankind, including Mohammed's sins, Buddha's sins, the Dali Lama's sins, etc., etc., etc., even the sins of men who do not believe that sin exists! Mohammed needed Jesus (grace and truth); Jesus does not need Mohammed.

Romans

✞ **POSITION OF GRACE:** (grace has made us unashamed of salvation through Christ; our righteousness comes from faith and leads to more faith)

"For I am not ashamed of the Gospel (good news) of Christ, for it is God's power working unto salvation [for the deliverance from eternal death] to everyone who believes with a personal trust and confident surrender and firm reliance, to the Jew first and also to the Greek,

For in the Gospel a righteousness which God ascribes is revealed, both springing from faith and leading to faith [disclosed through the way of faith that arouses to more faith]. As it is written, The man who through faith is just and upright shall live and shall live by faith" (Romans 1:16–17).

Grace does not produce shame, it eradicates it. How could such an incredible inheritance in the heavens ever produce shame? The question needs to be asked, "Why would we ever be embarrassed of the Gospel of Christ?" *"The fear of man brings a snare, but whoever leans on, trusts in, and puts his confidence in the Lord is safe and set on high"* (Proverbs 29:25). Righteousness delivers us from shame; unrighteousness makes us feel guilty. Trusting in the Lord brings us into the position of never being ashamed (Ps. 31:1).

The Gospel is God's power-tool that delivers us from eternal death; it both springs from faith and leads to more faith. It takes faith to obtain the position of salvation, but it does not stop there; faith then leads us on to more faith and thus grace leads to more grace (Rom. 5:20; 2 Cor. 9:8; 2 Peter 3:18). Faith has justified us and made us upright (position), and we shall not only live because of faith, but we shall live continuously *by* faith (operation). God's grace has saved us (our eternal position), and God's grace works through us as we live by faith (operation of grace). Our righteousness and our justification are eternal works wrought by the Gospel. We are positioned in heaven forever, because of them.

✞ **POSITION / OPERATION OF GRACE:** (not justified by works; the Law makes us conscious of sin; righteousness comes by belief in Christ Jesus; the Law attests to righteousness)

"For no person will be justified (made righteous, acquitted, and judged acceptable) in His sight by observing the works prescribed by the Law. For [the real function of] the Law is to make men recognize and be conscious of sin [not mere perception, but an acquaintance with sin which works toward repentance, faith, and holy character].

But now the righteousness of God has been revealed independently and altogether apart from the Law, although actually it is attested by the Law and the Prophets,

Namely, the righteousness of God which comes by believing with personal trust and confident reliance on Jesus Christ (the Messiah). [And it is meant] for all who believe. For there is no distinction," (Romans 3:20–22).

The law has nothing to do with justification, righteousness, or being accepted by God. It is God's grace alone that brings us into this position; it is His work and His work alone that has done this. There is nothing I can do to help our omnipotent God accomplish His work. The purpose of the law was to make men recognize and be conscious of sin. The function of the law is to make us aware of our sin and self-righteousness. It leads us to see our need for forgiveness. Only then can we receive the righteousness of God that is found only in Christ — His grace (Rom. 7:7; Gal. 4:1–5).

When we get saved and delivered from the eternal condemnation of the law, we do not lose our conscience — we do not move into a realm where sin does not exist anymore. It is not a cleared conscience but rather a seared conscience that claims to be unaware of sin, after having experienced salvation.

Righteousness is revealed independently and altogether apart from the law; the law testifies of righteousness — it gives clear proof of it (Rom. 7:12). God's righteousness in Christ is undiscriminating; it is obtainable by all men, Jew or Greek, circumcised, or uncircumcised. There is nothing in the New Testament that is contrary to the Old Testament — the New fulfils the Old. Christ accomplishes and makes available to believers the just and righteous requirements of the Law. In Him, we now live not by the dictates of our flesh, but rather by the dictates of the Spirit.

✞ **POSITION OF GRACE:** (justification comes by grace through redemption in Christ Jesus)

"Since all have sinned and are falling short of the honour and glory which God bestows and receives.

[All] are justified and made upright and in right standing with God, freely and gratuitously by His grace (His unmerited favour and mercy), through the redemption which is [provided] in Christ Jesus," (Romans 3:23–24).

Justification and right standing with God is given graciously as a free gift. It has nothing to do with our obedience to the law. The law does not determine whether God accepts us or loves us. God's love for us is total and perfect, even when we were totally disobedient to Him. Obedience to Him now, does not make Him love us more. There is not a righteous man on earth who does good and never sins (Eccl. 7:20).

Everybody needs God's grace. All have sinned and all have fallen short, but all can be justified by faith in the free grace of God through Christ Jesus.

✞ **POSITION OF GRACE:** (justification comes by faith independent of any works of the Law)

"It was to demonstrate and prove at the present time (in the now season) that He Himself is righteous and that He justifies and accepts as righteous him who has [true] faith in Jesus.

Then what becomes of [our] pride and [our] boasting? It is excluded (banished, ruled out entirely). On what principle? [On the principle] of doing good deeds? No, but on the principle of faith.

For we hold that a man is justified and made upright by faith independent of and distinctly apart from good deeds (works of the Law). [The observance of the Law has nothing to do with justification]" (Romans 3:26–28).

Being right with God is purely an act of grace. It has nothing to do with obedience to any set of rules or commands — either man's or God's. The only law that we need to tenaciously cling to now, is that we are saved by grace through faith in what the Son of God, Jesus Christ, has completed for us on the cross.

✞ **POSITION OF GRACE:** (the same faith justifies the circumcised and the uncircumcised)

"Since it is one and the same God Who will justify the circumcised by faith [which germinated from Abraham] and the uncircumcised through their [newly acquired] faith. [For it is the same trusting faith in both cases, a firmly relying faith in Jesus Christ]" (Romans 3:30).

The only faith that justifies anybody before God is faith in the Righteousness of God — the Lord Jesus Christ. The faith that Abraham had is the same faith that I have today. Abraham was born before the law was given to Moses.

"Because Abraham obeyed my voice, and kept my charge, my commands, my statutes, and my laws" (Genesis 26:5 KJV). Note, it was not Abraham's obedience to God's law that made him righteous before God, but it was his faith (Gen. 15:6; Rom. 4:3, 9, 18–22; Gal. 3:6; James 2:23). *"Jesus said unto them, Verily, verily I say unto you, Before Abraham was, I am"* (John 8:58 KJV).

✞ **OPERATION OF GRACE:** (faith confirms, establishes and upholds the Law)

"Do we then by [this] faith make the Law of no effect, overthrow it or make it a dead letter? Certainly not! On the contrary, we confirm and establish and uphold the Law" (Romans 3:31).

We cannot nullify the law of God — we cannot make it null and void. By walking uprightly and testifying to godly behaviour, we confirm, establish, and uphold the Law. This is the operation of grace in our life. From our perfect position of right standing with God, our inner man sees and approves of God's definition of perfect behaviour. Behaviour outside of the bounds of God's law is not perfect — it is sinful (1 John 3:4) — and will result in conviction by the Holy Spirit.

Abraham's righteous faith was demonstrated by a righteous action — an action in accordance with

God's command (Gen. 15:6; 22:11–18). Godly faith will never result in actions that contravene God's commands. Obedience to God demonstrates faith (1 John 4:9, 13; 5:3–4).

✞ **POSITION OF GRACE:** (justification comes through faith, not adherence to the law)

"For the promise to Abraham or his posterity, that he should inherit the world, did not come through [observing the commands of] the Law but through the righteousness of faith.

If it is the adherents of the Law who are to be the heirs, then faith is made futile and empty of all meaning and the promise [of God] is made void (is annulled and has no power).

For the Law results in [divine] wrath, but where there is no law there is no transgression [of it either].

Therefore, [inheriting] the promise is the outcome of faith and depends [entirely] on faith, in order that it might be given as an act of grace (unmerited favour), to make it stable and valid and guaranteed to all his descendants — not only to the devotees and adherents of the Law, but also to those who share the faith of Abraham, who is [thus] the father of us all" (Romans 4:13–16).

The Law came to Moses after Abraham had received God's promise. Abraham's promise came through faith and solely by the grace of God. This position of grace cannot be nullified by the giving of the Law. If it did, then faith is made futile and the promise of God is made void. If the Law overrides the promise, those who are without the Law (Gentiles), would perish because the Law would nullify the promise, and those with the law (Jews) would perish also, because the Law results in divine wrath.

God's grace was before the Law and is not frustrated by the giving of the Law. The faith that leads those outside of the Law to the promise (Jesus) is the same faith that is required to allow grace to cover the transgressions of those under the Law that they too might receive the Promise.

The Scripture above states that where there is no law, there is no transgression. We need to be careful that any motive for desiring to throw out God's law is not used as an excuse to continue in sin. If we dispose of the Law, there is a tendency to feel free to sin, because there is no longer any definition of transgression. We end up in a position of false freedom where we feel free to sin while under grace; this is not the essence of grace.

✞ **POSITION OF GRACE:** (Christ died for our misdeeds to secure our justification)

"But [they were written] for our sakes too. [Righteousness, standing acceptable to God] will be granted and credited to us also who believe in (trust in, adhere to, and rely on) God, Who raised Jesus our Lord from the dead,

Who was betrayed and put to death because of our misdeeds and was raised to secure our justification (our acquittal), [making our account balance and absolving us from all guilt before God]" (Romans 4:24–25).

Abraham's righteousness is the same righteousness we have today. It is only apprehended by faith and totally obtained outside of the law. Christ willingly laid His life down for our misdeeds; He does not need our help to make and keep us righteous. He was raised up from the dead to secure our justification by the power of God. He does not need our help to justify and keep us justified. It is arrogant to think that our flesh can — in any way — make us upright with God. *"Now the people stood by [calmly and leisurely] watching; but the rulers scoffed and sneered [turned up their noses] at Him, saying, He rescued others [from death]; let Him now rescue Himself, if He is the Christ (the Messiah) of God, His Chosen One"* (Luke 23:35)! Grace does not submit to its own desires, but rather it submits to the Father's desire (Matt. 26:39).

Through Christ's death and resurrection our account was balanced with God — forever absolving us from all guilt before the Eternal. Justification is found only in the fruit of faith, not the fruit of flesh! Faith produces life; flesh produces death.

✞ **POSITION OF GRACE:** (justified through faith)

"Therefore, since we are justified (acquitted, declared righteous, and given a right standing with God) through faith, let us [grasp the fact that we]

have [the peace of reconciliation to hold and to enjoy] peace with God through our Lord Jesus Christ (the Messiah, the Anointed One).

Through Him also we have [our] access (entrance, introduction) by faith into this grace (state of God's favour) in which we [firmly and safely] stand. And let us rejoice and exult in our hope of experiencing and enjoying the glory of God" (Romans 5:1–2).

Faith has given us access to God's grace. We have become God's people of favour where we have an eternal position that is forever firm and safe. From here we rejoice and exult in our hope of experiencing and enjoying the glory of God. Beloved, this has nothing to do with our works, or effort, or any intelligence on our part. This position of grace cannot be taken from us. It would take something stronger than God to take it from us, and there is nothing that exists that can do such, both now and forever!

✞ **POSITION OF GRACE:** (grace reigns through righteousness)

"But then Law came in, [only] to expand and increase the trespass [making it more apparent and exciting opposition]. But where sin increased and abounded, grace (God's unmerited favour) has surpassed it and increased the more and super-abounded,

So that, [just] as sin has reigned in death, [so] grace (His unearned and undeserved favour) might reign also through righteousness (right standing with God) which issues in eternal life through Jesus Christ (the Messiah, the Anointed One) our Lord" (Romans 5:20–21).

God's law came after sin had entered the world; it was given to define sin and to increase the awareness of sin. God's grace has always been here from the beginning of time and righteousness could be received by faith (as in Abraham).

Grace increased the more and super-abounded beyond all transgression. Beloved, the nature of evil is never greater than the nature of God. Sin causes death; grace reigns through righteousness and brings life eternal. Only in Christ does the word *eternal* have any true meaning.

When grace reigns through righteousness in our life, godly fruit is evident. Grace is present in everything the Lord does to enable and equip us to walk in life and be pleasing to Him. It is not our own works done in our attempt to please God, that are effective; it is grace working through us that delights Him.

Graceful workings are of an eternal nature even though they work through our natural man. As grace works through us, the eternal nature of God is manifest and becomes evident to the world around us. When sin is in control and works through us, it reveals a fallen nature — the nature of the prince of the power of the air (Eph. 2:1–3). As a Christian, my soul — that has previously been directed by my fallen nature — needs to be renewed by the operation of God's grace.

✞ **OPERATION OF GRACE:** (we are not to continue in sin; we have died to sin in Christ)

"What shall we say [to all this]? Are we to remain in sin in order that God's grace (favour and mercy) may multiply and overflow?

Certainly not! How can we who died to sin live in it any longer?

Are you ignorant of the fact that all of us who have been baptized into Christ Jesus were baptized into His death?

We were buried therefore with Him by the baptism into death, so that just as Christ was raised from the dead by the glorious [power] of the Father, so we too might [habitually] live and behave in newness of life.

For if we have become one with Him by sharing a death like His, we shall also be [one with Him in sharing] His resurrection [by a new life lived for God].

We know that our old (unrenewed) self was nailed to the cross with Him in order that [our] body [which is the instrument] of sin might be made ineffective and inactive for evil, that we might no longer be the slaves of sin.

For when a man dies, he is freed (loosed, delivered) from [the power of] sin [among men]" (Romans 6:1–7).

Christ was nailed to the cross and our old, unrenewed self with Him, in order that our body which is the instrument that sin uses might be made inoperative, ineffective, and inactive for evil. We are no longer slaves to sin. The power of slavery to sin has been overcome for us by the blood of the Lamb. We can now walk in freedom from this slavery and do that which is righteous before God. We are no longer compelled to obey the prompting of the flesh (which leads to sin), but we can obey the prompting of the Spirit which leads to righteousness (right doing before God).

Living uprightly can only come from our position of right standing before God. Our righteous works have nothing to do with obtaining our salvation, nor maintaining a righteous position before God. Christ — Himself —has made us righteous. We cannot become more righteous than that (Titus 3:5). It is by the grace of God that we are in right standing before God, and it is by the grace of God that we are able to do righteous works before God.

Grace is accessible by faith alone. Without faith the flesh and the mind cannot access the grace of God, but because of our position of grace, by faith we can allow God's grace to operate within and through us. We cannot operate *in* the Spirit *outside* of the Spirit; we cannot operate in faith outside of faith; and we cannot operate in grace outside of grace.

✝ **OPERATION OF GRACE:** (let not sin rule over you; we are under grace not the Law)

"Even so consider yourselves also dead to sin and your relation to it broken, but alive to God [living in unbroken fellowship with Him] in Christ Jesus.

Let not sin therefore rule as king in your mortal (short-lived, perishable) bodies, to make you yield to its cravings and be subject to its lusts and evil passions.

Do not continue offering or yielding your bodily members [and faculties] to sin as instruments (tools) of wickedness. But offer and yield yourselves to God as though you have been raised from the dead to [perpetual] life, and your bodily members [and faculties] to God, presenting them as implements of righteousness.

For sin shall not [any longer] exert dominion over you, since now you are not under Law [as slaves], but under grace [as subjects of God's favour and mercy]" (Romans 6:11–14).

Grace calls us to refuse sin and its cravings to operate or control our bodies any longer. By offering ourselves to the grace of God, we are empowered to operate righteously. Because we are no longer under the law, the power of sin no longer has any legal hold over us. In Christ, grace trains us to deny ungodly powers and attitudes from operating in our life, and hence, it teaches us to act in a righteous manner. It is our position of grace that keeps us in unbroken fellowship with Him and *guilt-free* from sin and its eternal consequences. We have now become subjects of God's mercy and favour; this is then manifested in our lives as we present ourselves to God as instruments of righteousness and yield ourselves to Him.

✝ **POSITION OF GRACE:** (freed from sin; servants of righteousness)

"And having been set free from sin, you have become the servants of righteousness (of conformity to the divine will in thought, purpose and action)" (Romans 6:18).

This Scripture describes the position that we have in Christ. God has freed us from the power of sin and has placed us in His righteousness. He did this by becoming sin for us that we would become the righteousness of God in Christ (2 Cor. 5:21). Christ does not violate our will when He saves us, neither does He violate our will in our daily walk with Him. He provides us freedom from sin by His grace. What He has done, He has finished, and He will not go back on His Word. Our will is still involved in our daily walk of righteousness. We can return to wallow in the mud — like a pig — anytime we choose (2 Peter 2:22), and yet His grace is still there to present us holy before the Father. It is not our works that make us upright before the Father; it is His only His grace that justifies us before God.

✞ **OPERATION OF GRACE:** (yield to righteousness; there is no benefit in unrighteousness)

"I am speaking in familiar human terms because of your natural limitations. For as you yielded your bodily members [and faculties] as servants to impurity and ever increasing lawlessness, so now yield your bodily members [and faculties] once for all as servants to righteousness (right being and doing) [which leads] to sanctification.

For when you were slaves of sin, you were free in regard to righteousness.

But then what benefit (return) did you get from the things of which you are now ashamed? [None] for the end of those things is death" (Romans 6:19–21).

Because grace does not have natural limitations, our flesh cannot limit the operation of grace in our life. Grace is ever present to encourage us and enable us to yield our bodies and faculties as servants of righteousness. This is the process of sanctification. Like grace, sanctification is both positional (1 Peter 1:2) and operational through the yielding of our members and faculties to the Holy Spirit (2 Thess. 2:13). When we were the slaves of sin (before we were saved) we were held under the eternal penalty of death and could not escape its grasp. But the Grace of God bought us and eternally placed us in His care. The price has been paid. We are no longer under the grasp of the legal death bond held against us. He wiped out the written code, which was in force and stood opposed to us. This legal note, which was hostile towards us, has been forever set aside. It has been cleared out of the way by the Cross of Christ — the Grace of God (Col. 2:14).

We are now bond servants of righteousness. The death penalty has been paid in full for me; it can never make demands upon me again! Sin can no longer enshroud me with the odour of eternal death, and by God's grace the works of sin have no have attraction to me. I have been made deathless. Is there any benefit to continue in the things that lead to death (disobedience to God's law)? The answer of course is, *"No!"*

Note that these Scriptures do not say that sin causes us to lose our salvation; nor do they say that *our* efforts are required to keep us upright before God. They merely state that there is no benefit whatsoever in works of death. Scripture declares that abounding in works of righteousness will keep us from being idle or unfruitful in our walk with Christ (2 Peter 1:8).

✞ **POSITION OF GRACE:** (set free from sin; slaves of God)

"But now since you have been set free from sin and have become the slaves of God, you have your present reward in holiness and its end is eternal life" (Romans 6:22).

In Christ, we are no longer the slaves of sin; but rather, we become the slaves of God. Beloved, the Holy Spirit will never lead a slave of God into disobedience to any of God's holy, righteous, and just commands. In Christ, our position is holiness, and this is obtained only by the grace of God. We have the privilege and reward of resting in His grace, and walking in His holiness. Our end-reward is eternal life, which we already possess (1 John 5:13).

✞ **POSITION / OPERATION OF GRACE:** (grace makes us dead to the Law; we now belong to Christ)

"Likewise, my brethren, you have undergone death as to the Law through the [crucified] body of Christ so that now you may belong to Another, to Him Who was raised from the dead in order that we may bear fruit for God" (Romans 7:4).

It is not the Law that died; it is we who have died to the Law's power, and though it defines sin, the Law no longer holds us. I have been crucified with Christ — I have shared His crucifixion — it is no longer I who live. It is now Christ who lives in me. My life is now lived through faith in the Son of God (Gal. 2:20).

We have been transferred from the dominion and control of darkness into the kingdom of the Son of His love (Col. 1:13). We now belong to God. His grace has given us this incredible eternal position, and from there it also equips and enables us to be followers of God's way.

We do not need to worry about our salvation — justification before God. This has been forever taken care of in heaven. The eternal consequence for our disobedience to God has been erased — as far as the east is from the west (Ps. 103:12). We are now free from the power of sin that condemned us, and are enabled by God's grace to walk in His newness of life — a life obedient to God. Obedience towards God in the kingdom of the Son of His love is a direct result of the grace of God operating in our life. Our obedience to Him now is because of love; it is a fruit of His love and mercy that has been graciously given to us.

✝ **POSITION / OPERATION OF GRACE:** (discharged from the Law, we now serve under obedience to the Spirit)

"But now we are discharged from the Law and have terminated all intercourse with it, having died to what once restrained and held us captive. So we now serve not under [obedience to] the old code of written regulations, but [under obedience to the promptings] of the Spirit in newness [of life]" (Romans 7:6).

We have been discharged from the Law, and it no longer has power to hold us. It is not the letter of the Law of God, which we serve, but the Spirit of God. In Christ, the Spirit prompts us to works of righteousness. The Law is no longer a guardian for us (Gal. 3:23–26). There is no longer any condemning power against us in the Law of God. We are now under the power of the Holy Spirit prompting us into obedience to God's holy way — attested to by the law of God.

The inheritance and blessings of God are released to us by faith — not law (Gal. 3:1–3). Faith has released us from the custody of the Law. We now serve God by being obedient to His Spirit, not obedient to His written regulations. Our freedom from the power of the law has given us a new birth — a newness of life. This newness is the result of the Spirit of God working in our life manifesting obedience, by the grace of God, not the flesh of man — obedience rooted in love rather than works.

Works brings death; faith brings life. *"And the very legal ordinance which was designed and intended to bring life actually proved [to mean to me] death"* (Romans 7:10). This is the same as the first command God gave in the Garden of Eden. That which was meant to bring life, actually proved to bring death to Adam and Eve (Gen. 2:16–17). This always has been the nature of Law and this is why justification is by grace and not works. The law did not cheat us; it was sin (disobedience to the Law) that cheated us. Grace brings us back into right relationship with God; it keeps us there, and it enables us to walk in newness of life in Christ. We can now delight in and endorse the law of God with our new nature (Rom. 7:22).

✝ **POSITION OF GRACE:** (no condemnation in Christ, walking after the Spirit; freed from the law of sin and death)

"Therefore, there is now no condemnation (no adjudging guilty of wrong) for those who are in Christ Jesus, who live [and] walk not after the dictates of the flesh, but after the dictates of the Spirit.

For the law of the Spirit of life [which is] in Christ Jesus [the law of our new being] has freed me from the law of sin and of death" (Romans 8:1–2).

In Christ, we can walk after the dictates and commands of the Spirit, rather than our flesh. Our condemnation has been forever erased for us because our sins have been dealt with by the work of the Cross of Christ. By God's grace we have been made new and now walk after the promptings of the Spirit. The adverse judicial sentence of condemnation to eternal death is no longer an issue to the Christian; this has been forever dealt with by the cross of the Lord Jesus Christ.

The fact that a Christian can feel conviction and be found guilty or act out of deceit or hypocrisy (sometimes translated condemned) even feeling mentally condemned before God, is evident in Scripture (Rom. 14:23; Gal. 2:11; Jas. 5:9, 12). The conviction and condemnation mentioned here has nothing to do with our position of eternal life, which we have in Christ Jesus. It is not a condemnation that carries with it the sentence of eternal death. That power has been dealt with forever by the blood of Christ on the cross.

However, if we as Christians do not deal with the conviction of sin properly, there will be a reaping of bondage and death in that area of our life. Repentance is the only way to deal with sin. When we cover our transgression we will not prosper. We must confess and forsake our sin (repent) in order to obtain mercy. If we do not uncover our sin, we rob ourselves of the life and freedom that mercy offers us. We block the life of the Spirit — the life of Christ — from working in us (Prov. 28:13). *"Destruction is certain for those who drag their sins behind them, tied with cords of falsehood"* (Isaiah 5:18 NLT).

Like a child adopted into a family, we have been forever placed into the family of God — this is eternally set. However, God can still correct His children and as His children we should feel conviction for our wrong actions. The purpose of conviction is never to sentence us to condemnation leading to death, but to direct us toward repentance and newness of life. The Spirit of God, by the grace of God, trains us to renounce and reject all ungodly, worldly, passionate desires in this present world (Titus 2:12).

We should respond to the promptings of the Spirit — not the promptings of self-condemnation (flesh) or of the accuser of the brethren (Rev. 12:10). When children receive correction from their father, it is love they are experiencing, not rejection. God is not rejecting us when He corrects and punishes us (Heb. 12:6).

Our freedom from the law of sin and death brings no condemnation of eternal death with it. That condemnation has been eradicated for us forever. The Law had condemned us to eternal death, but Christ, coming in the form of sinful flesh, made the perfect sacrifice and condemned sin in the flesh, bringing us eternal life. We can never be condemned for our sins again. When we bring correction to our brothers and sisters in Christ, it should not be in the form of condemnation. As a Christian we experience correction, not condemnation. There is no such thing as Christian condemnation — it is not from God — it is from the flesh. Condemnation from the flesh brings with it eternal death prompted by hate. Conviction from the Spirit brings with it eternal life prompted by love.

Within the body of Christ we are called to correct one another (Prov. 27:5–6; 28:23; Matt. 18:15–17; 1 Cor. 5:9–13; Gal. 2:12–14; 6:1; Heb. 12:5–11; 3 John 1:9–11). Our correction should be with the same attitude as the Spirit which convicts us of sin directing us towards repentance, which leads to life and restoration. Correction done by the Spirit of God never aligns itself with condemnation, which leads to death; it is always motivated towards reconciliation.

When we refuse to uncover our transgression and repent, we stand outside of the will of God by our own choice. Conviction opens the door for repentance, whereas condemnation holds us under bondage in that particular area of our life, and we will remain under that bondage until we turn and repent (Rom. 6:12–18; 8:13).

✝ **POSITION / OPERATION OF GRACE:** (Christ quickens our mortal bodies)

"But if Christ lives in you, [then although] your [natural] body is dead by reason of sin and guilt, the spirit is alive because of [the] righteousness [that He imputes to you].

And if the Spirit of Him Who raised up Jesus from the dead dwells in you, [then] He Who raised up Christ Jesus from the dead will also restore to life your mortal (short-lived, perishable) bodies through His Spirit Who dwells in you" (Romans 8:10–11).

The born-again, spiritual man is alive forevermore in Christ by the righteousness imputed to him by God Almighty.

Mortal man — on the other hand — has a temporary existence here on earth. My body is doomed to die and waste away; yet, the Holy Spirit is progressively restoring inner-life to my inner-self (2 Cor. 4:16). The grace of God is continually working in my body and soul. It renews and makes my body a vessel that submits itself to the Spirit rather than to the dictates of the flesh. The operation of grace in our life in this mortal body will terminate at the death of this perishable container.

✞ **OPERATION OF GRACE:** (habitually putting to death the works of the flesh)

"So then, brethren, we are debtors, but not to the flesh [we are not obligated to our carnal nature], to live [a life ruled by the standards set up by the dictates] of the flesh.

For if you live according to [the dictates of] the flesh, you will surely die. But if through the power of the [Holy] Spirit you are [habitually] putting to death (making extinct, deadening) the [evil] deeds prompted by the body, you shall [really and genuinely] live forever" (Romans 8:12–13).

The grace of God operating in our life makes us debtors to the Spirit, not to the flesh. Grace operating in our life constantly trains us to habitually deaden and make extinct the deeds prompted by the flesh. The power of the Holy Spirit, enabled by the grace of God, becomes the controlling factor in our mortal bodies. Before the grace of God came into our life we were obligated to obey our carnal nature — following the dictates of the prince of the power of the air (Eph. 2:1–3).

In Christ, by the grace of God, we can now be obligated to the promptings of the Holy Spirit and walk in the will of God, denying the rule of ungodliness. This power to walk in the ways of God came to us because of the grace of God poured out upon us, bringing with it, eternal life. This same grace growing within these clay vessels enables us to become slaves of God and walk in obedience to His word. It is the active operation of the grace of God in our life that enables us to avoid and extinguish the evil deeds prompted by our flesh.

✞ **POSITION / OPERATION OF GRACE:** (we are predestined, foreordained, called, justified and glorified by God)

"For those whom He foreknew [of whom He was aware and loved beforehand], He also destined from the beginning [foreordaining them] to be molded into the image of His Son [and share inwardly His likeness], that He might become the firstborn among many brethren.

And those whom He thus foreordained, He also called; and those whom He called, He also justified (acquitted, made righteous, putting them into right standing with Himself). And those whom He justified, He also glorified [raising them to a heavenly dignity and condition or state of being]" (Romans 8:29–30).

This heavenly position that we have in Christ is a direct result of the grace of God. We have been destined from the beginning of time to be justified and put into right standing with Him. By His grace, this same destiny will mold us into the image of the Son of God. This renewing of the soul takes place in our day to day life as we submit to Him. In this process He gives us heavenly dignity and glory, which is a fragrance of His likeness. When people see this reflection of Christ in us, they are seeing His glory being manifested.

We have been called, justified, and glorified by the grace of God. This is totally His work; it is accomplished without our help, whatsoever. The Grace of God, the Incarnate, has accomplished this for us, freely imputing His character into us.

✞ **POSITION / OPERATION OF GRACE:** (who can be against us if God is for us?)

"What then shall we say to [all] this? If God is for us, who [can be] against us? [Who can be our foe, if God is on our side?]" (Romans 8:31).

Our eternal position declares that God is for us. And now that God is for us, who or what can possibly be against us? If God, omnipotent, omniscient, and omnipresent, the Creator of the universe, is for us, what can possibly separate us from His love, which is in Christ Jesus our Lord? Our being in Him is a result of *His* work, not *our* effort. If God has put us in His hand, who or what can possibly remove us from this incredible position of grace?

The temporal operation of grace in this short-lived mortal body is founded in our position of grace, which eternally places us in God's care. What an honour!

Because of all this, our God is faithful to operate in our life — correcting, changing, renewing, and training us to habitually renounce ungodliness

— to walk in His ways. Beloved, if God be for us, nothing can stop Him from finishing His work in our life — no powers, principalities, or people can stop God!

✞ **POSITION OF GRACE:** (God acquitted us; nothing can separate us from His love)

"Who shall bring any charge against God's elect [when it is] God Who justifies [that is, Who puts us in right relation to Himself? Who shall come forward and accuse or impeach those whom God has chosen? Will God, Who acquits us?]

Who is there to condemn [us]? Will Christ Jesus (the Messiah), Who died, or rather Who was raised from the dead, Who is at the right hand of God actually pleading as He intercedes for us?

Who shall ever separate us from Christ's love? Shall suffering and affliction and tribulation? Or calamity and distress? Or persecution or hunger or destitution or peril or sword" (Romans 8:33–35)?

When it is God Who justifies us, how foolish it is for us to think that He will condemn us or even that we are able to condemn ourselves. There is nothing that can touch or even approach the position of grace that God has so freely given us. This is the hope of our calling in Christ Jesus. How arrogant and foolish it is to think that I can either help or hinder my God here. Our only task is to keep our eyes on Jesus as the Author and Finisher of our faith, allowing His grace to change us into His image — the perfect reflection of the Grace of God.

There is nothing in all creation that is able to separate us from the love of God, which is in Christ Jesus our Lord (Rom. 8:35–39) — not even the correcting, disciplining, punishing, and scourging that comes from His hand (Heb. 12:6). God's discipline is forever rooted in His love (Rev. 3:19).

Love is the fulfilling of the Law. When we love our neighbour as ourselves, we meet all the requirements of the Law. A loving action always fulfils the law of God (Rom. 13:9–14). As Christians, when we feel the conviction of sin in our life (Rom. 14:23; James 5:12), it does not mean that our gracious gift of eternal life is on the line; it simply means that the Father is graciously and lovingly disciplining us. *"The Lord hath chastened me sore: but he hath not given me over unto death"* (Psalm 118:18 KJV).

✞ **POSITION OF GRACE:** (eternal life is a gift of God's mercy only)

"So then [God's gift] is not a question of human will and human effort, but of God's mercy. [It depends not on one's own willingness nor on his strenuous exertion as in running a race, but on God's having mercy on him.]" (Romans 9:16).

Mercy — receiving eternal righteousness certified by the Father — has nothing to do with the recipient. We are the object of God's mercy, not the source of it. Is there any question in our heart about God needing our help to receive His mercy? Let it be forever banished from us.

When the mercy of God blows upon us, our own strength and even our willingness, disappear like mist in a dry wind. Beloved, jumping into the Pacific Ocean does not make waves in the Atlantic.

What an incredible rest waiting to be found in the mercy and grace of Almighty God. Our peace comes from this astonishing position of mercy that we have obtained in Christ Jesus our Lord and the peace that comes with it is ever-present as He faithfully operates in our life. Knowing this and believing in what He has done allows us to enter into His rest and to cease from our own works (Heb. 4:3).

✞ **POSITION OF GRACE:** (Christ is the end of the Law as a means of righteousness)

"For Christ is the end of the Law [the limit at which it ceases to be, for the Law leads up to Him Who is the fulfilment of its types, and in Him the purpose which it was designed to accomplish is fulfilled. That is, the purpose of the Law is fulfilled in Him] as the means of righteousness (right relationship to God) for everyone who trusts in and adheres to and relies on Him" (Romans 10:4).

The law is holy, just, good, and righteous; however, Christ is the end of the law of God as a means of righteousness. We have obtained a righteousness that is imperishable — a righteousness that is forever imputed to us by the grace of God.

Faith in Christ has forever birthed righteousness into our being; it supersedes the law. Our relationship with God is eternally fixed; it is an eternal fact. It is not something that I have to renew every year or millennium (Heb. 10:14).

✞ **POSITION OF GRACE:** (any work of the flesh makes grace meaningless)

"So too at the present time there is a remnant (a small believing minority), selected (chosen) by grace (by God's unmerited favour and graciousness).

But if it is by grace (His unmerited favour and graciousness), it is no longer conditioned on works or anything men have done. Otherwise, grace would no longer be grace [it would be meaningless]" (Romans 11:5–6).

The spiritual equation is quite simple here: [Grace + any human help = meaninglessness]. God's grace was abundantly poured out on me when I was a wretched, godless glob. How can I possibly add more meaning to something already perfect — that which God has completed by Himself? If I have been carefully and specially chosen by God when I was good-for-nothing, how can I believe my goodness *now* will help Him add to His love for me? If I am chosen, I am chosen; I cannot add to that. Wanting to add to God's perfect choice comes from a carnal desire to be recognized by God as being better than someone else because of our good works.

I need to constantly remind myself that God's grace is a free gift; it is not meaningless, and I cannot add to His perfection. Oh how great and unfathomable are the mercies of God!

✞ **OPERATION OF GRACE:** (live as a living sacrifice; do not conform to the world; renew your mind; walk humbly before God's calling)

"I appeal to you therefore brethren, and beg of you in view of [all] the mercies of God, to make a decisive dedication of your bodies [presenting all your members and faculties] as a living sacrifice, holy (devoted, consecrated) and well pleasing to God, which is your reasonable (rational, intelligent) service and spiritual worship.

Do not be conformed to this world (this age), [fashioned after and adapted to its external, superficial customs], but be transformed (changed) by the [entire] renewal of your mind [by its new ideals and its new attitude], so that you may prove [for yourselves] what is the good and acceptable and perfect will of God, even the thing which is good and acceptable and perfect [in His sight for you].

For by the grace (unmerited favour of God) given to me I warn everyone among you not to estimate and think of himself more highly than he ought [not to have an exaggerated opinion of his own importance], but to rate his ability with sober judgment, each according to the degree of faith apportioned by God to him" (Romans 12:1–3).

Having an understanding of God's grace is the springboard to confidently and decisively dive into the pool of life. Such a plunge presents our body as a living sacrifice — fully consecrated to God's call. In Christ, we are devoted to life, not death. God appeals to us to live accordingly, drawing our enablement from our position in grace. Our response to such a call draws us into our most reasonable service — this is called worship. This is not a worship service; it is a service of worship. Replacing our *service of worship* with a *worship service* is idolatrous. A person can attend a worship service and not even know God.

We do not worship God by violating His commands; we worship God in spirit and in truth (John 4:23). Romans 12:2, commands us not to be conformed to the world or fashioned after its ways. We are to be transformed — our nature changed. The position in Christ declares that we are changed, but the operation of this same grace in our life is transforming us daily. This renewal of our soul (mind, will, and emotions) is to prove and test what is good, acceptable, and perfect before God. When we are lacking, God gives us grace to bring that area of our life in line by laying it on the altar of His will. We are both perfect in His sight, and being perfected, at the same time.

This same grace then warns us not to think too highly of ourselves; it commands us to judge our abilities soberly and be honest in our estimate of ourselves. We are to be serious and in control, measuring our value in accordance with the degree of faith that God has given us. Our value is defined by God, not by us. For the whole body of Christ is made up of many individual parts with different functions; yet all parts are mutually dependent on one another (Rom. 12:5). Humility, gentleness, and forbearance — all fruit of the Spirit — are required to allow the grace of God to work His love into our lives, as He binds everything together in harmony (Col. 3:13–14).

✞ **OPERATION OF GRACE:** (sincere love hates evil and holds fast to good)

"[Let your] love be sincere (a real thing); hate what is evil [loath all ungodliness, turn in horror from wickedness], but hold fast to that which is good" (Romans 12:9).

Love that is not sincere (defined by God's reality) is not true love. We are to love in deed as well as word. It is through His grace that God loved us and it is this same grace that gives us eternal consolation and encouragement. This encouragement enables and strengthens our hearts, and keeps them unswerving in every good word and deed (2 Thess. 2:16–17). Perfect love hates what is evil; it also casts out all fear, because when you hate evil, you have nothing to be afraid of. Hating evil is like a protective shield for us because it places us right in the centre of God's grace.

The gracious position that we have eternally obtained in Christ is the source of perfect love operating in our life. It causes us to loath lasciviousness, wince at wickedness, and hate all ungodliness — you find iniquity absolutely irksome! The operation of this same grace in our life causes us to turn from these worldly attitudes. Godly repentance results in a turning *from* something and enables us to turn *to* something else. God's grace enables us to not only turn away from unrighteousness; it enables us to turn towards righteousness — right doing before God.

The hating of evil and the holding fast to what is good are both performed by the grace of God operating in our life. When these attitudes and actions are evident in our life, and abound, they manifest themselves as genuine and sincere love (2 Peter 1:2–7).

✞ **OPERATION OF GRACE:** (grace commands us not to repay evil for evil)

"Repay no one evil for evil, but take thought for what is honest and proper and noble [aiming to be above reproach] in the sight of everyone" (Romans 12:17).

Grace is incapable of being a source of evil. Evil action is not found within the operation of grace. From our position of grace, all evil actions on our part are atoned for, but far be it for us to claim that an evil action has been birthed by the grace of God (Rom. 6:2, 15). Evil actions cannot affect our position of grace.

The grace of God operating in our life continually enables us to love godliness, to loath ungodliness, to hold fast to goodness, and to hate evil — not to be overcome by evil, but rather to overcome evil with good (Acts 7:58–60; Rom. 12:21). It required the grace of God to overcome evil, bringing us into our eternal position of righteousness; it requires this same grace of God operating in our life to enable us to overcome evil with good. God's grace is always the source of godly actions, never evil actions (Phil. 4:8). Beloved, grace does not call us to avenge yourselves; we are called to let the Lord bring His judgement (Rom. 12:19).

✞ **OPERATION OF GRACE:** grace commands us to overcome evil with good)

"Do not let yourself be overcome by evil, but overcome (master) evil with good" (Romans 12:21).

If evil was unable to touch a Christian's life, we would have no need to overcome evil with good. However, Christians are warned to not let evil overcome them (Gen. 4:6–7). Beloved, evil does not have power over the holy gift of eternal life, which we have received. However it can sure spawn havoc on our mortal life here on earth, if we allow ourselves to indulge or partake in it (2 Cor. 6:15–16).

God has graciously provided an eternal position that is untouchable by evil — it is incorruptible

(Jas. 1:13). It is this same grace that teaches us to deny ungodliness, and it enables us to walk uprightly during our short sojourn here on earth. Overcoming evil with good is an operation of the grace of God in our life; it is this same grace that forever saves us.

✞ **POSITION / OPERATION OF GRACE:** (submission to government; God places government in power; resisting government is resisting God))

"Let every person be loyally subject to the governing (civil) authorities. For there is no authority except from God [by His permission, His sanction], and those that exist do so by God's appointment.

Therefore he who resists and sets himself up against the authorities resists what God has appointed and arranged [in divine order]. And those who resist will bring down judgment upon themselves [receiving the penalty due them]" (Romans 13:1–2).

Scripture clearly sanctions the existence of government authority; it is by the grace of God that governing authorities come into being (Dan. 2:20–21; Prov. 8:15–16). It is God that institutes civil government; therefore to resist any godly appointment (government authorities) is to resist God. As Christians, we are called to resist the devil, not God (James 4:7). We are no longer under the eternal judging or condemning power of the law of God, but we are under the judging and condemning power of God through the civil laws that govern our life here on earth. Government authority is instituted by God. To resist God ordained authority is to bring down God's judgement upon ourselves — whether we are Christian or not.

The only time we are allowed to be disobedient to the governing authorities where we live, is when those authorities demand an action that will violate our conscience towards God (Dan. 3:14–18; 6:7–10; Acts 5:28–29).

✞ **OPERATION OF GRACE:** (grace calls us to be subject to government for principle and for conscience sake)

"Therefore one must be subject, not only to avoid God's wrath and escape punishment, but also as a matter of principle and for the sake of conscience" (Romans 13:5).

Conscience is the issue here. When we violate any godly principle, our conscience — our sense of right and wrong — is the writing tablet upon which God communicates with us. The flesh feels fine when it avoids wrath, and escapes persecution, but the only way not to be overcome by disobedience to government and keep our conscience clear, is through humility, repentance, and godly obedience. We deny communication with God when we deny our conscience speaking to us (Rom. 2:14–15).

✞ **POSITION / OPERATION OF GRACE:** (judging; judgment seat of God)

"Why do you criticize and pass judgment on your brother? Or you, why do you look down upon or despise you brother? For we shall all stand before the judgement seat of God.

For it is written, As I live, says the Lord, every knee shall bow to Me, and every tongue shall confess to God [acknowledge Him to His honour and to His praise].

And so each of us shall give an account of himself [give an answer in reference to judgment] to God" (Romans 14:10–12).

We will all stand before the judgement seat of God (Rom. 2:6–7; 2 Cor. 5:10–11; Matt. 12:36–37; Acts 17:30–31; 1 Cor. 4:5). We escape eternal judgment only by being in Christ, but we shall still have to give an account to God.

Since we have been freed from the eternal judgment of God, we should not take on the role of a condemning judge over our brothers. We are to accept those whose faith is weak and not pass judgement on matters that are uncertain and debateable (Rom. 14:1). This is the essence of Chapter 14. Beloved, each one of us is going to stand before the judgement seat and give a personal account of himself to God. Our eternal position of salvation is never in question; otherwise God's grace would not be grace. The issue here is to make sure that we do not put a stumbling block before our brother.

We are admonished not to destroy or undo the work of God — a rather sobering thought. But rather, we are to pursue and aim at what makes for mutual harmony and edification (Rom. 14:19–20). When we operate from a position of grace, we bring grace to one another — that which is mutually up-building and maturing. Grace is not condemningly critical or judgmental. It is not designed to destroy the work of God in a brother who is weak in faith (has different convictions over disputable matters). Such destruction and division in the body of Christ is not the work of grace (Rom. 14:23).

✞ **OPERATION OF GRACE:** (wise to good, innocent to evil; Satan crushed under our feet)

"For while your loyalty and obedience is known to all, so that I rejoice over you, I would have you well versed and wise as to what is good and innocent and guileless as to what is evil.

And the God of peace will soon crush Satan under your feet. The grace of our Lord Jesus Christ (the Messiah) be with you" (Romans 16:19–20).

The grace of God is pronounced upon God's people as a blessing to be received and used to fight the good fight of faith. Our Lord Jesus Christ admonishes us to be well versed in wisdom and goodness and to be innocent to what is evil. Our position of grace gives us access to all of God's wisdom, and it proclaims our eternal innocence towards all condemnation due to sin. The operation of grace in our life enables us to walk in God's wisdom and to habitually put to death the deeds prompted by our flesh; we are to deaden all intercourse with lawlessness.

Guile is defined as 'clever deceit'. Even though our loyalty and obedience may be known to all, we are warned not be trapped by clever deceit, and fall into evil. Satan's position has been defeated totally by the grace of God. This work of God results in our eternal position of grace being found in Christ Jesus. Yet, Satan is also *being defeated* as our soul is in the process of being renewed daily. This work is accomplished by the operation of this same grace of God, enabling us to draw nigh to God and have power over the devil, not because of our goodness, but because of faith in God's goodness — His grace (James 4:6–7).

Being well versed and wise, results in us accurately and skilfully heralding and preaching the Word of Truth to those around us, enabled by the grace of God (2 Tim. 2:15; 4:1–5).

1 Corinthians

✞ **POSITION OF GRACE:** (grace forms the church; the church is made holy and consecrated as saints in Christ Jesus)

"To the church (assembly) of God which is in Corinth, to those consecrated and purified and made holy in Christ Jesus, [who are] selected and called to be saints (God's people), together with all those who in any place call upon and give honour to the name of our Lord Jesus Christ, both their Lord and ours:

Grace (favour and spiritual blessing) be to you and [heart] peace from God our Father and the Lord Jesus Christ.

I thank my God at all times for you because of the grace (the favour and spiritual blessing) of God which was bestowed on you in Christ Jesus.

[So] that in Him in every respect you were enriched, in full power and readiness of speech [to speak of your faith] and complete knowledge and illumination [to give you full insight into its meaning].

In this way [our] witnessing concerning Christ (the Messiah) was so confirmed and established and made sure in you" (1 Corinthians 1:2–6).

The pouring out of grace on a soul is a work, which establishes eternally Christ as the Lord of that life. When a soul is saved the church is birthed in that person, and he becomes part of the whole assembly of the body of Christ — the church.

Grace brings honour to the Lord Jesus Christ and it pronounces blessings upon the objects of His grace. It produces the fruit of thankfulness towards God and His people. Grace brings enrichment, power, and readiness to proclaim the good news. Grace begets grace. It illuminates and brings good judgement, discernment, and knowledge of the ways of God.

From our position of grace we are given the divine privilege of blessing others with that same grace. A blessing of grace enriches one's life and brings with it a readiness to testify of the grace of God to others (2 Tim. 4:2). Our calling of grace is to confirm and establish Christ (the Messiah) in one another. We are saints together with all who call on the name of the Lord Jesus Christ in any place and for all time (Heb. 11:38–40).

Grace is the God given ability that we have received to do whatever God has called us to do. It is boundless, and we now have the privilege of freely passing it on. There should be no conditions placed on our pouring out of grace towards others (2 John 1:9–11). We may find ourselves in a place of judgement as to whether a person is worthy of receiving grace from us. If that be the case beloved, we need to seriously question whether we as sinners were/are one wit deserving to receive anything from God.

The position of grace has bestowed upon us all things that pertain unto life and godliness (2 Peter 1:2–3). It is only by tapping into God's grace that this is manifested in every aspect of our life, resulting in a vessel established and fixed in the image of Christ. His grace never fails, never gives up, and never runs out.

✞ **OPERATION OF GRACE:** (grace operates in our soul by the Holy Spirit)

"That you are not [consciously] falling behind or lacking in any special spiritual endowment or Christian grace [the reception of which is due to the power of divine grace operating in our souls by the Holy Spirit], while you wait and watch [constantly living in hope] for the coming of our Lord Jesus Christ and [His] being made visible to all" (1 Corinthians 1:7).

Spiritual endowments are both received by grace and powered by grace through the Spirit of God. The power of the Spirit through the medium of divine grace operates in our soul — our mind, will and emotion. The operation of grace renews the mind, proves the will of God, and transforms our life into an acceptable sacrifice of worship to God. Grace takes an unworthy life and turns it into a life of worship. It grows as we wait upon the Lord and walk in obedience to His leading.

We all have a soul (mind, will, and emotion) that needs to be renewed. Before we knew Christ, our soul was under the power of the spirit of the world.

But now, as Christians, the Spirit of God has positioned Himself within our spirit bringing us under the power of God to renew our soul. Obviously, we have not yet arrived to Christ-like perfection as this is a progressive work in our life (Eph. 2:1–7; Phil. 3:12). It is a life-long process of humility, repentance, and submission to the Spirit of God as His grace, operating on our soul by His Spirit accomplishes this renewal and sanctification.

The Spirit of God is a searchlight penetrating the human spirit. It searches all the innermost thoughts, intents, and hidden motives of the heart. It is often our attitudes and the things that we are not conscious of that can trip us up and cleverly deceive us into believing that we are following after God. But in reality, we often follow after our own desires and belief systems. As we tap into this incredible power of grace for the saving and renewing of our souls, we find ourselves walking in more and more freedom in our life. Our souls become purified by welcoming and obeying the word of truth through the Spirit of grace (Heb. 12:1–2; James 1:21; 1 Peter 1:22).

The Corinthian church was falling behind in many things; they were just not conscious of their lack. Beloved, we need to see ourselves as not having arrived yet (Phil. 3:12), but that there are many things we believe about Christ, His church, and His kingdom that are in tainted with error. If this were not true, we would not see the multitude of factions in the church today. Disunity continues to hold its grip on the church as long as there is no admission of error and no repentance (Matt. 12:25). It is the Holy Spirit's job to bring unity of the faith. We are called to maintain the unity produced by the Spirit in the binding power of peace (Eph. 4:3, 13). Unity is a fruit that is found only when love is operating by the grace of God.

✞ **POSITION / OPERATION OF GRACE:** (grace establishes and guarantees our vindication)

"And He will establish you to the end [keep you steadfast, give you strength, and guarantee your vindication; He will be your warrant against all accusation or indictment so that you will be] guiltless and irreproachable in the Day of our Lord Jesus Christ (the Messiah)" (1 Corinthians 1:8).

Our vindication before God is complete, eternal and guaranteed; it has come to us by the grace of God. The grace of God is our warrant; He is our official authority giving us justification before God. It has been issued by God, signed by the Blood of the Lamb, and sealed by the Holy Spirit (Mark 14:24; Eph. 1:13). God guarantees to present us guiltless and irreproachable on the Day of our Lord Jesus Christ. It is from this incredible position of rest that we labour in the kingdom of God, allowing the Spirit of grace to direct us in all our affairs, establishing us to the end. The operation of grace establishes His kingdom in our life and keeps us on the narrow path (Matt. 7:13–14).

✞ **OPERATION OF GRACE:** (grace brings unity, not division in the church)

"For it has been made clear to me my brethren, by those of Chloe's household, that there are contentions and wrangling and factions among you.

What I mean is this, that each one of you [either] says, I belong to Paul, or I belong to Apollos, or I belong to Cephas (Peter), or I belong to Christ" (1 Corinthians 1:11–12).

The position of Grace declares that there is only one body of Christ — one church. Grace demands that the body of Christ be not divided. It was the Grace of God that birthed the body of Christ; hence, unity in the body is the identifying trademark of the body of Christ (John 13:34–35).

Unity is a fruit of the grace of God. It takes revelation to see the body of Christ as one. What you believe determines what you see, and what you see determines what you do. If you believe that the body of Christ is one, you will see it as one, and you will do things that build this oneness. You will not do things that enable division. From the Spiritual position of eternal grace, the body is seen as one, not broken into factions. The operation of grace works within the unity of the members of the body of Christ. A gracious work of God is never divisive; it always unifies. God is not interested in unifying two different factions under one roof;

He is interested, on a day to day basis, in building unity between each member of His body — the body of Christ.

We rend and tear the body of Christ by not discriminating and recognizing it with due appreciation (1 Cor. 11:24–32). Christ did not die for the Baptist Church, the Pentecostal Assemblies Church, the Full Gospel Church, the United Church, etc., etc., etc. Christ died for sinners that they would become His followers — the body of Christ — not followers of particular organizations, which have been started by men and their particular doctrines.

✝ **POSITION OF GRACE:** (unity is a fruit of grace; division is a fruit of the flesh)

"Is Christ (the Messiah) divided into parts? Was Paul crucified on behalf of you? Or were you baptized into the name of Paul" (1 Corinthians 1:13)?

Of all men, Paul could have claimed some pre-eminence here. He could have loved to take the lead, or be first here, but his disdain for such an ungracious attitude is evidenced by his words and actions. He rebuked people for trying to follow after him as the leader of part of the body of Christ. Such divisive attitude was evident and addressed in the early church (Acts 20:30; 3 John 1:9–11; Rev. 2:2).

Beloved, our position is in Christ alone, not in a faction of Christ. Our significance is found in Christ only; it should not be found in a position, which we have attained to in some local faction of the body of Christ. When we faction the church in the name of grace, we make grace a *disgrace*. The church becomes powerless and carnal — with little or no effect in the world — neither cold nor hot. It becomes *of the world* rather than *in the world* — not a testimony to Christ. Divisions in the church are a false witness and testimony of Christ to the world. We are not called to be a false testimony (Ex. 20:16; 23:1; Gal. 2:11–14; 3 John 1:9–11).

✝ **POSITION OF GRACE:** (grace makes Christ Jesus our Righteousness, Consecration, Redemption)

"But it is from Him that you have your life in Christ Jesus, Whom God made our Wisdom from God, [revealed to us a knowledge of the divine plan of salvation previously hidden, manifesting itself as] our Righteousness [thus making us upright and putting us in right standing with God], and our Consecration [making us pure and holy], and our Redemption [providing our ransom from the eternal penalty for sin]" (1 Corinthians 1:30).

Our life and our wisdom are founded in Christ, and this truth is revealed to us only by the grace of God. Our eternal position of grace has declared us righteous, consecrated, and redeemed by the blood of the Lamb. The eternal penalty for our sins has been dealt with forever. We have been brought into a place of holiness and righteousness totally by the work of Jesus Christ, not by our own effort.

As a Christian, the grace of God now operates in our life as we move and have our being in Him (Acts 17:28). The Wisdom of God — the revealing of His grace — is the motivation for all our glorying, boasting, and rejoicing. It has made us upright before God, made us holy, and paid the eternal penalty for our sin, all totally by His grace.

✝ **POSITION OF GRACE:** (spirit of the world does not understand grace; grace reveals spiritual truth by using spiritual language)

"Now we have not received the spirit [that belongs to] the world, but the [Holy] Spirit, Who is from God, [given to us] that we might realize and comprehend and appreciate the gifts [of divine favour and blessing so freely and lavishly] bestowed on us by God.

And we are setting these truths forth in words not taught by human wisdom but taught by the [Holy] Spirit, combining and interpreting spiritual truths with spiritual language [to those who possess the Holy Spirit]" (1 Corinthians 2:12–13).

The Spirit of God has been given to us for our realization of the grace so divinely poured out upon us. The Holy Spirit makes us fully conscious of and reveals to us the intimate knowledge of God's grace so richly lavished upon us. The spirit of the world knows nothing of the grace of God. It does not recognize it. But we have taken possession of the Spirit of God, that He may take possession of us for all eternity.

Truth takes possession of us as we enter into the grace of God. Truth does not have its source in human wisdom. It is spiritual — of the Spirit of God — and the world cannot receive it. Without the grace of God in our lives we cannot possible hope to receive or understand the things of God. This is why the fear of the Lord is the beginning of wisdom and knowledge, not the result of it.

The Word became flesh and dwelt amongst us bringing the revelation of God Almighty. Truth and grace are eternal. They are a part of the very nature of God. Spiritual language — the Word — needs the Spirit of God to reveal its meaning to us. Spiritual truth is the spiritual language of the Spirit of God. Falsehood is the mother tongue of the spirit of the world (John 8:42–59). As the children of God we are privileged to be recipients of God's Spirit and hence have access to His truth (Matt. 13:10–14; Luke 8:10; John 14:15–17, 23; 15:26–27; 16:13; 17:26).

It is the anointing of the Holy Spirit within us that teaches us, not someone else's anointing. Because the Holy Spirit is within us, we have no need for anyone to instruct us. It is our anointing within us that teaches us everything, and is true, and is no falsehood (1 John 2:27). The Spirit of God dwells within us to teach and guide us into all truth that we may give truth to others — the Gospel.

Fellowship occurs when we share truth with one another by the Holy Spirit. By the Spirit of God, the body of Christ feeds itself and edifies itself into maturity. Fellowship occurs when we lovingly express truth with one another, which causes us to grow up in all things in Christ. It is God's way of maturing His body. When each part of the body of Christ is functioning in the Spirit of God, the body brings itself into maturity (Eph. 4:15–16). Fellowship occurs when spiritual truths are expressed in spiritual language to one another as the Holy Spirit guides and directs and controls His body — the church.

The natural ear hears the same words as the spiritual man; however, they need to be spiritually discerned and the natural man cannot comprehend the spiritual truth behind those words (John 9:1–41). The living word of God is a foreign language unless the Holy Spirit opens the eyes of our heart and understanding (Eph. 1:18; Phil. 1:9–10; Col. 1:9).

✞ **OPERATION OF GRACE:** (grace is hidden from the natural man; grace brings revelation to the spiritual man)

"But the natural, nonspiritual man does not accept or welcome or admit into his heart the gifts and teaching and revelations of the Spirit of God, for they are folly (meaningless nonsense) to him; and he is incapable of knowing them (of progressively recognizing, understanding, and becoming better acquainted with them) because they are spiritually discerned and estimated and appreciated" (1 Corinthians 2:14).

The natural man cannot receive or approve of the things of God. Truth and grace are not welcomed or admitted entrance into the heart of natural man. From the carnal heart, they are heard and seen as foreign, but to us in Christ, the grace of God has provided the Interpreter to live within us.

We increase in the understanding and use of God in our life as we grow in the understanding of His grace. It teaches us as we learn and walk in the things of God by His Spirit. To us who believe, our life-driven purpose is to become more intimately acquainted with Jesus and the power out-flowing from His resurrection. As grace operates in our life, it leads us to walk in things that are good, pleasing, and acceptable to God. This includes, by necessity, sharing in His sufferings, with the end result of being transformed into His likeness (Rom. 12:2; Phil. 3:10).

Beloved, be not discouraged when the world refuses to receive the things of God — it is foolishness to them. It is only those who have the Spirit who can understand spiritual truths. Because the world does not have the Spirit of God they are incapable of knowing the things of God — only God's children have this ability. Things pertaining to the kingdom of God are nonsense to people of the world — meaningless folly, a target of mockery and distain. If we were of the world, it would love us, but because we are not of this world, it hates us. The world hates the children of the Word even as it hates the Word of God (John 15:19; 17:14, 16, 18; 18:36). The kingdom of God and the grace of God are not from this world. Neither should our life be sourced in this world, or be directed by the spirit of the world. We are not called to judge the world; the world stands condemned already. Judging is God's job (1 Cor. 5:12–13).

✝ **POSITION OF GRACE:** (spiritual man; judgment; mind of Christ)

"But the spiritual man tries all things [he examines, investigates, inquires into, questions, and discerns all things], yet is himself to be put on trial and judged by no one [he can read the meaning of everything, but no one can properly discern or appraise or get an insight into him].

For who has known or understood the mind (the counsels and purposes) of the Lord so as to guide and instruct Him and give Him knowledge? But we have the mind of Christ (the Messiah) and do hold the thoughts (feelings, and purposes) of His heart" (1 Corinthians 2:15–16).

Our spiritual man is born-again (born from above) and renewed by the power of the Spirit of God. This enables us to examine and investigate all things. Yet, no one can appraise or get insight into the spiritual man because its power resides in God, and who can know the mind of the Spirit of God? Who can instruct Him? It is the living word of God that effectively works in our soul and spirit, exposing, analysing, and judging the thoughts and intents of our heart (Heb. 4:12).

In our eternal position of grace, we have the mind of Christ (1 Cor. 2:16). With the operation of grace in our lives, we progressively recognize, understand, and become better acquainted with the workings of the Spirit of God as it reveals the thoughts, purposes, and intents of the heart of Christ. Grace has given us access to the very mind of God! Glance at the cross of Christ and you will catch a glimpse of our Father's heart — our source of all grace.

Having possession of the thoughts of God is not just for our benefit personally, or corporately as the body of Christ; it is to manifest the love and grace of God to the world. Having the feelings and purposes of God in our heart divinely influences our life and affects the lives of those around us. With the purpose of God working in our life, we have a life driven by grace as we conform more and more unto the image of His likeness.

✝ **POSITION / OPERATION OF GRACE:** (grace ministers to our carnality when we act like infants in Christ)

"However, brethren, I could not talk to you as to spiritual [men], but as to nonspiritual [men of the flesh, in whom the carnal nature predominates], as to mere infants [in the new life] in Christ [unable to talk yet!]" (1 Corinthians 3:1).

Possessing the mind of Christ does not mean that you automatically walk in the Spirit in all that you do. When we allow the desires of the flesh and our carnal nature to predominate, we act as mere infants in Christ. The carnal nature cannot communicate spiritually. It can discuss and give philosophical opinions about spiritual matters, but it cannot talk spiritually — it is unable to. Infants in Christ require others to constantly feed them with milk and change their diapers. An infant is quite oblivious to the real issues in life, and they fuss when they are uncomfortable. It takes the grace of God operating in our lives to draw us into and mature us in Christ where we are able to distinguish between good and evil. Fellowship enables us to constantly exercise our spiritual senses (Heb. 5:14).

The grace of God operates in our lives; it disciplines us to discriminate between what is morally good and what is evil or contrary to God's law. It enables us to deny lawlessness — sin (Is. 5:20; Titus 2:12). Because of our position in Christ, we are continually covered by His grace as it teaches and matures us.

The church at Corinth had many good workings of the Spirit of God. Nonetheless, Paul still addressed them as immature, nonspiritual, carnal Christians — unable to talk yet! Most Christians who have known the Lord for a few years would find it offensive to be called nonspiritual, immature, and carnal. Beloved, maturity is measured and evidenced in spiritual depth of character, not in length of time. Whenever asks me, "How long have you known the Lord?" My response is, "Fifteen fathoms!"

One has to question as to how mature a Christian really is, if he has known the Lord for many years and still feels inadequate to lead someone to Christ, baptize them in the Lord's name, and teach them to observe everything Jesus has commanded (Matt. 28:18–20; Heb. 5:13) — *unable to talk yet.* Fellowshipping is where we learn to talk. Fellowship is when we assemble spiritually; it is when we continuously watch over and admonish one another, and stir up and incite one another to godly deeds and activities (Heb. 10:24–25). Listening to preaching is not what matures us in Christ; fellowshipping (learning to talk spiritually) is God's way of maturing His body. Beloved, let us not forsake or neglect the spiritual assembling of the body!

The Great Commission is for all Christians; it is not just for a few so called professionals. Maturity is measured in depth of obedience to Christ, not in attaining to some position in an institution that claims to represent Christ.

The fruit of jealousy, strife, and lauding one person over another in the body of Christ (factions), is the result of carnality — men following the spirit of the world rather than the Spirit of God. Factions and divisions are the result of spiritual civil war.

✝ **OPERATION OF GRACE:** (grace ministers to the unspiritual, fleshy factions of the church)

"For you are still [unspiritual, having the nature] of the flesh [under the control of ordinary impulses]. For as long as [there are], envying and jealousy and wrangling and factions among you, are you not unspiritual and of the flesh, behaving yourselves after a human standard and like mere (unchanged) men?

For when one says, I belong to Paul, and another, I belong to Apollos, are you not [proving yourselves] ordinary (unchanged men)" (1 Corinthians 3:3–4)?

Note that the Christians living in the city of Corinth had the mind of Christ. They were justified, redeemed, consecrated, and made righteous. They were made holy in Christ. They were selected and called to be saints. They were in every respect enriched in full power and readiness of speech. They were not consciously falling behind any special spiritual endowment or Christian grace. Yet through all this, what was a sign of their lack of spirituality? In spite of having all these spiritual gifts, what was the thing that revealed their spiritual immaturity?

The Christians living in Corinth were dividing the church in Corinth. Some were saying that they belonged to Paul's church, or Apollos' church, or Peter's church, or Christ's church. This dividing of the church was being promoted by the people, not by the aforementioned leaders. Paul rebuked the tolerance of such factions in the church; he neither encouraged it, nor celebrated it. God warned the Christians not to get involved with such men who would be called leaders and draw disciples after them to their own following (Acts 20:29–30; Rom. 16:17; 3 John 1:9–10; Jer. 5:30–31). We are called to turn aside and avoid such persons — faction leaders — who would divide the precious body of Christ.

All Christians, including leadership, are admonished not to do anything from motives that produce, encourage, or maintain factions (Phil. 2:3). Selfishness, conceit, and empty arrogance — carnality — forms the foundation of the factions in the church today. Most Christians (including faction leaders) do not even see the division in the body of Christ. They just shrug it off as being normal and believe that the church will never be unified. Beloved, when you start believing the church is one, you will start seeing the church as one, and you will start doing the things that show the church truly is one. If you do not believe the church is one, you will never see it as one and never act as one.

Grace calls us in the true spirit of humility and lowliness of mind to esteem and see others as better and superior to ourselves. We are to think more highly of others than we do of ourselves (Phil. 2:4). This is the mind of Christ that has been made available to us by the grace of God! This grace enables us to see the body of Christ the way the Spirit of God sees it, and it also enables us to operate as representatives of Christ, through His body.

Beloved, we must not just give lip service to the body of Christ; we must do the work we have been called to do. Grace never acts divisively. Faction leaders use spiritually corrupt words to draw disciples away after themselves to their own party — dividing the body of Christ (Jer. 5:20–31; Acts 20:30). The spirit of the world, operating through man's flesh, divides the church (1 Cor. 11:17–19).

✝ **POSITION / OPERATION OF GRACE:** (grace does not recognize heads of factions; grace plants, and waters, all the while recognizing Christ as the Foundation)

"What then is Apollos? What is Paul? Ministering servants [not heads of parties] through whom you believed, even as the Lord appointed to each his task:

I planted, Apollos watered, but God [all the while] was making it grow and [He] gave the increase.

So neither he who plants is anything nor he who waters, but [only] God Who makes it grow and become greater.

He who plants and he who waters are equal (one in aim, of the same importance and esteem), yet each shall receive his own reward (wages), according to his own labour.

For we are fellow workmen (joint promoters, labourers together) with and for God; you are God's garden and vineyard and field under cultivation, [you are] God's building.

According to the grace (the special endowment for my task) of God bestowed on me, like a skilful architect and master builder I laid [the] foundation, and now another [man] is building upon it. But let each [man] be careful how he builds upon it.

For no other foundation can anyone lay than that which is [already] laid, which is Jesus Christ (the Messiah, the Anointed One)" (1 Corinthians 3:5–11).

Servants are not heads or leaders of their own church. God does not call anyone to start another church in a city where the church already exists. Grace does not call and appoint people to establish or maintain factions of the church. Grace gives glory to God, and growth to the church. Growth and maturity will only come by the operation of grace bringing revelation of the body of Christ, to the body of Christ.

Those who labour in the perfecting and equipping of the saints are equals; they are co-workers. They are joint labourers — one in purpose and objective. They are submitted one to another. It is the spirit of the world today that distorts God's word with worldly, deceptive logic and philosophy, which declares that somebody needs to be first among equals. Beloved, each labourer's work will receive its own reward. God's building — the church — is the only *building* that won't burn when Christ comes the second time.

The operation of grace in Paul's life made him a master builder — a builder used by the Master. God laid the foundation of Jesus Christ using Paul. He was like a tool in the hand of God as God did His work. Then God used Apollos to build some more upon the foundation, which He had built. Apollos was not greater than Paul, and Paul was not greater than Apollos; they were co-workers, neither one of them was first among equals.

It is the carnal mind that asks, "How big is your church?" *Bigger is better* is a carnal cliché, not a spiritual truth. Builders, used by God, need to humbly recognize the body of Christ and let God do the building and get the glory. The church — God's consecrated people — needs a revelation of the body of Christ. There is only one church (Eph. 4:4–5). It takes God's grace operating in our life to believe, see, and do the work of ministering toward building up the body of Christ (Eph. 4:12).

Note that the apostles always planted the church in local areas; they never planted *a* church. Beloved, if *a* Christian is present, *the* church is there; and God never calls anyone to plant *another* church. If all Christians mimicked the faction leaders of the church today, we would all have our own buildings and programs. If we mimicked the apostle Paul today, we would see the church being built on the only foundation, Jesus Christ, the Messiah, the Anointed One.

✞ **OPERATION OF GRACE:** (grace builds on the Foundation of Truth)

"But if anyone builds upon the Foundation, whether it be with gold, silver, precious stones, wood, hay, straw,

The work of each [one] will become [plainly, openly] known (shown for what it is); for the day [of Christ] will disclose and declare it, because it will be revealed with fire, and the fire will test and critically appraise the character and worth of the work each person has done.

If the work which any person has built on this Foundation [any product of his efforts whatever] survives [this test], he will get his reward.

But if any person's work is burned up [under the test], he will suffer the loss [of it all, losing his reward], though he himself will be saved, but only as [one who has passed] through fire" (1 Corinthians 3:12–15).

When Paul left the leaders of the church of the city of Ephesus for the last time, he committed them to God and to the Word of His grace (Acts 20:32). Paul did not shrink from telling all things that were beneficial and true — the whole purpose, plan, and counsel of God (Acts 20:20, 26).

The operation of God's grace builds us up and edifies us. Such building is evidenced not in the amount or size of physical structures but in the working of His grace by His Spirit in our lives — spiritual sanctification and character, not gifts. The size of a person's *ministry* is never mentioned in Scripture because it is irrelevant to God and should be irrelevant to His body today. Paul calls the idolatry of ministry, carnal. *"After this Paul lived there for two entire years [at his own expense] in his own rented lodging, and he welcomed all who came to him, Preaching to them the kingdom of God and teaching them about the Lord Jesus Christ with boldness and quite openly, and without being molested or hindered"* (Acts 28:30–31).

Because of our position of grace and our rightful inheritance among God's consecrated people, we will experience the transformation of our soul. We need to be diligent to build with gold, silver, and precious stones — the building materials of the kingdom. A godly response to the circumstances of life that come our way will build a work that will stand firm in days of trial. Such a work shows evidence of the operation of grace, and the leading of the Spirit in our lives.

The character and worth of God's work is not related in any way to the size of buildings, the greatness of programs, the number of members of a faction of the church, or even the number of 'sister factions', which have been planted throughout the world. It is only evidenced in the acts of grace in individual lives revealing Christ in His body, as it lives in unity.

The division we see in the church today is a false testimony of the body of Christ. Much has been built in times past and done in the name of Christ that has long since passed away. There are many remains of so-called past *visions* and *callings* of God throughout the world today that are being maintained by people who believe they are working for God.

If a person's work is burned up under the test, he loses his reward, though he himself will be saved as one who has passed through the fire. (I sometimes think that there is going to be a rather large smoking section in heaven!)

✞ **POSITION OF GRACE:** (grace makes us His temple, collectively and individually)

"Do you not discern and understand that you [the whole church at Corinth] are God's temple (His sanctuary), and that God's Spirit has His permanent dwelling in you [to be at home in you,

collectively as a church and also individually]" (1 Corinthians 3:16)?

The grace of God allows us to experience the indwelling of the Holy Spirit both individually and collectively; it is a permanent, eternal, and ongoing event. We are automatically placed into the body of Christ at our re-birth. This position of grace is only discerned and understood as we experience the operation of this same grace revealing who God is, what He has done, and what He is doing, both individually and collectively.

Our spiritual knowledge of God is both personal and corporate. We do not come to know God through another person's acquaintance — a vicarious experience or relationship. We must personally come to know God ourselves. From our personal position of grace, we come to be more intimately acquainted with Him through our life's circumstances. With the leading of the Spirit both personally and corporately in the body of Christ, we experience the operation of grace in our new life in Christ.

Corporately, from our position in the body of Christ, we have the privilege of operating in and through the Spirit of God as He moves in and through His people — loving, edifying, teaching, correcting, and encouraging each another. This is the essence of fellowship and it is God's way of maturing His church.

✞ **POSITION / OPERATION OF GRACE:** (grace warns against corrupting the temple of God)

"If anyone does hurt to God's temple or corrupts it [with false doctrines] or destroys it, God will do hurt to him and bring him to the corruption of death and destroy him. For the temple of God is holy (sacred to Him) and that [temple] you [the believing church and its individual believers] are" (1 Corinthians 3:17).

The warning here is two-part. It warns teachers, and it warns listeners. God's temple is sacred to Him. It is better to poke a tiger than to trifle with God's temple. All of our work for our Father needs to be saturated in the knowledge of God's grace and the body of Christ. For someone to set themselves up against the grace of God is to skirt disaster — he who has ears to hear, let him listen to and give heed to what the Spirit is saying to the church. It is a warning like this that graciously nourishes the fear of God in our heart!

✞ **POSITION / OPERATION OF GRACE:** (grace is not boastful or proud about one leader over another)

"So let no one exult proudly concerning men [boasting of having this or that man as a leader], for all things are yours,

Whether Paul or Apollos or Cephas (Peter), or the universe or life or death, or the immediate and threatening present of the [subsequent and uncertain] future — all are yours,

And you are Christ's, and Christ is God's" (1 Corinthians 3:21–23).

When the grace of God is operating, pride is not present. All works of God are authored by Him alone and accomplished by Him alone; thus there is no room for pride in a saved soul. How can we ever be proud of our salvation or even something God has done in our life? We are certainly blessed by it, but we cannot be proud of something given to us so freely and undeservedly. Pride is a feeling of elation or satisfaction founded when we have too high an opinion of ourselves or in what we have done or accomplished. How could we ever be proud of any work of God? Humbled, yes, but proud, certainly not! Pride, arrogance, and the evil way are things that God hates; conceit is never condoned (Prov. 8:13).

Pride feels natural to the carnal man working under the influence of the spirit of the world. The church at Corinth was manifesting the fleshly fruit of pride by dividing the church into factions. They were also demonstrating it in their condoning of sexual sin (1 Cor. 5:1–2). Beloved, works built by the flesh will not stand in the day of the Lord, no matter how many religious trappings cover them (Is. 31:3). God so loved the world that He died to save it and deliver it from the power of the evil one. God hates worldliness and its fruit, which manifests through our flesh (John 3:16; Gal. 5:19–21).

✞ **POSITION / OPERATION OF GRACE:** (grace does not go beyond what is written; it does not foster factions in the church; it does not boast of one work of God over another)

"Now I have applied all this [about parties and factions] to myself and Apollos for your sakes, brethren, so that from what I have said of us [as illustrations], you may learn [to think of men in accordance with Scripture and] not to go beyond that which is written, that none of you may be puffed up and inflated with pride and boast in favour of one [minister and teacher] against another.

For who separates you from the others [as a faction leader]? [Who makes you superior and sets you apart from another, giving you the pre-eminence?] What have you that was not given to you? If then you received it [from someone], why do you boast as if you had not received [but had gained it by your own efforts]" (1 Corinthians 4:6–7)?

It is pride and arrogance that demands one person to be pre-eminent over another. Such pride and rivalry amongst leadership is quickly transferred to its followers (Jer. 5:31; Matt. 15:14). Pre-eminence declares that there be a first among equals, or that only one can drive the bus, or that the buck stops here, etc. This pre-eminent comparing one with another is unwise and foolish (2 Cor. 10:12); it is not a work of the Spirit of God. It is founded on the flesh — the carnal nature. It is from the world. That is why Scripture declares that the factions in the church are founded on carnality, not the Spirit of God. Adherents of such division prove themselves to be unchanged men under the control of worldly impulses — men in whom the carnal nature predominates (Rom. 16:17–18).

God's grace has given us all things that are prerequisite for living a godly life in Christ Jesus, our Lord. He has blessed us with all spiritual blessings. Pride and the desire to be more or have more than someone else are a result of the fleshy, mortal nature of man being unable to see and receive the things of God. Such pride and the desire for pre-eminence results in what Scripture calls: a *faction leader*, not a "Pastor".

What could possibly make one work of God better than another work of God? Pride and arrogance are like twin brothers that exalt the flesh; they do not glorify the Spirit (2 Chron. 25:19; Ps. 123:4; Prov. 8:13; 21:24; Is. 9:9; Jer. 48:29).

Beloved, God has never told anyone to start another church in the midst of His church. The God of grace never instructed Paul to start *a* church where *the* church already existed. If *a* Christian is present anywhere in the world, *the* church is present; and there is no calling by the Spirit of God to plant another church in its midst. Revelation of God's church is revelation of God (Eph. 3:10). The body of Christ does not need another church; it needs revelation of *the* existing church — *the* body of Christ. We do not go to *a* church; we have come to *the* church (Rom. 1:7; 1 Cor. 1:2; 2 Cor. 1:1; Eph. 1:1; Phil. 1:1; Col. 1:2; 1&2 Thess. 1:1; Heb. 12:22–23).

We are called to think and live in accordance with Scripture, not by standards set by others who believe and preach what is between the lines of Scripture, which perverts the Truth (Prov. 30:5–6; Rev. 22:19).

✞ **POSITION / OPERATION OF GRACE:** (grace brings correction in the church)

"For the kingdom of God consists of and is based on not talk but power (moral power and excellence of soul).

Now which do you prefer? Shall I come to you with a rod of correction, or with love and in a spirit of gentleness" (1 Corinthians 4:20–21)?

The kingdom of God is not about the natural man's eating and drinking, but rather it is about our spiritual man — our righteousness, peace and joy in the Holy Spirit (Rom. 14:17). The kingdom is not based upon nor does it consist only of words and talk, but of doing (James 1:22–25; 2:15–16). The power we have available to us by the grace of God is sufficient to produce moral power and excellence in our soul. The developing of this excellence or goodness is a progressive operation of the grace of God (2 Peter 1:5–9). Maturing in Christ is a process that takes time and is only accomplished as we exercise the operation of God's grace in the renewing of our soul.

Because of our eternal position of grace we have obtained by the blood of the Lamb, God can now bring the operation of grace to us, correcting us without consuming us.

✞ **OPERATION OF GRACE:** (grace works holiness into our life, not immorality)

"It is actually reported that there is sexual immorality among you, impurity of a sort that is condemned and does not occur even among the heathen; for a man has [his own] father's wife" (1 Corinthians 5:1).

Sexual immorality and impurity are actions that are not appropriate for Christians. From our position of holiness (1 Cor. 1:2), we are not to be involved with sexual immorality (1 Thess. 4:3–5). Our position of eternal life is not at stake here. In fact, it is because of our position of eternal righteousness that God will bring the operation of grace into our midst when we need correction. Grace will train us to deny ungodliness in our bodies — these holy vessels. Grace will discriminate between good and evil, and lead us to a renewing of the mind — putting off the old, and a putting on the new nature. Beloved, we are not to be overcome by evil, but rather we are to overcome evil with good (Acts 16:22–28; Rom. 12:21).

✞ **OPERATION OF GRACE:** (grace calls for discipline; pride and arrogance have no part of grace; grace does not fellowship with immorality)

"And you are proud and arrogant! And you ought rather to mourn (bow in sorrow and in shame) until the person who has done this [shameful] thing is removed from your fellowship and your midst" (1 Corinthians 5:2)!

Here we see that the person who has done this shameful thing is to be put out of fellowship. The church is the people of God. Fellowship is a spiritual action where the people of God allow the Spirit of God to work through them. It is a cleansing operation of the grace of God (1 John 1:7). The church is the position that God has eternally placed us into and no person can remove us from it.

Scripture here shows that we can remove one another from fellowship, but we cannot remove someone from the position of grace that he has been eternally given us in Christ Jesus — His body, which is the church (Col. 1:24). The Corinthian believers were doing a shameful thing here. They were operating predominantly in the carnal nature, not discerning the body of Christ correctly and hence were responding in a proud and worldly manner.

Sin in their midst should have filled them with grief and shame until the person who was guilty of this sin repented, or was removed from their fellowship. This is an example of the operation of grace in the midst of the church. Discipline is not to be administered with a condemning spirit or an attitude of *I am holier than thou.* Grace and love are the driving force and power that are used to remove a person from fellowship. The purpose of removal is for restoration. From an eternal perspective, it is better to be removed in love and truth, than to be received in pride and deception (Prov. 27:5–6; 28:23). Beloved, everybody in Christ is just as holy as everyone else in Christ — our position of grace guarantees this.

The perpetrator of this sin was not being removed from salvation in Christ — no human can do that. He was being removed from the fellowship of the saints. Varying degrees of holiness, which are only seen by the carnal eye, is not the issue here. The issue was redemption, restoration, and maintaining the wholeness of the body of Christ.

✞ **POSITION / OPERATION OF GRACE:** (grace provides correction in the church; grace allows us to be present in the spirit; it takes the grace of God to deliver a brother over to Satan)

"As for my attitude, though I am absent [from you] in body, I am present in spirit, and I have already decided and passed judgment, as if actually present,

In the name of the Lord Jesus Christ, on the man who has committed such a deed. When you and my own spirit are met together with the power of our Lord Jesus,

You are to deliver this man over to Satan for physical discipline [to destroy carnal lusts which prompted him to incest], that [his] spirit may [yet] be saved in the day of the Lord Jesus" (1 Corinthians 5:3–5).

Judging one another in the body of Christ is an operation of grace with the power of God. It does not throw a member into eternal hell; its purpose is to save him from temporal hell here on earth. This spiritual action is only possible because of the unity between the Holy Spirit and the spirits of God's people. Being in Christ produces a unity that is spiritual and eternal. Unity is evidenced when God's love is operating; disunity is evident when the spirit of the world is operating. Unity in the Spirit is redemptive; disunity is destructive.

An assembly in Christ is not just a natural assembly; it is a spiritual assembly (Heb. 10:25). A jig saw puzzle sitting in its box is not assembled. Putting the pieces into various colour groups or in neat rows does not mean that the puzzle is assembled. When each part is linked together and doing just what it is called to do, the puzzle is assembled. So it is with the body of Christ. When the parts are joined together and doing what the Spirit is calling them to do, you have true assembly. This is the essence of Christian fellowship and is sadly lacking in the church today. Note that we can be present with one another in spirit even though we are not present in the body (2 Kings 5:26).

The unity to be found in Christ is not limited by place or time; this is the fundamental nature of the one body of Christ. If we look at the body of Christ with the natural/carnal eye, we divide it up into convenient doctrinal groups, often even proud of our group. Groups then tend to focus on natural unity, with the hope that this will bring about spiritual unity. The church is called to focus on spiritual unity, with godly peace and love being the binding factors (Eph. 4:3). The carnal mind of man sees factions as a 'convenient choice', but they thwart and make of no effect the working of disciplinary grace (love) within the body of Christ.

In the church at Corinthian, the deliverance of this man over to Satan was an operation of the grace of God. The graceful purpose of turning one over to Satan is to bring about restoration and repentance — the changing of one's mind. The disciplining of the flesh results in carnal lusts being destroyed, that the spirit and soul may be saved on the day of the Lord. This operation of grace is a blessing, not a curse. Our spirit found its birth in the position of grace, it finds its life in the operation of God's grace, and it will find its eternal rest in this same grace of God.

This disciplinary operation of grace was carried out by the body of Christ; it was not relegated to leadership. It is a spiritual operation done by the Spirit of God, not by man. We wrestle not against flesh but against spiritual wickedness in high places (Eph. 6:12). This spiritual judgement is initiated by the Spirit of God and carried out through the body of Christ. It is designed to heal the body and restore it to the completeness, which is found only in Christ. Note how the spiritual realm is not bound by distance — *"When you and my own spirit are met together with the power of our Lord Jesus."* This statement sounds almost 'spooky' to the carnal mind but it is living truth to our spiritual man. The power of the Lord Jesus unites with the body of Christ and accomplishes a work of the Lord Jesus Christ.

The nature of Christ demands that church discipline be carried out and fulfilled by the body under the direction of the Spirit of God. Many times church discipline attempted in the factions of the church today only results in more division. New factions are often started from a disgruntled saint that's being disciplined. When the body of Christ is divided into so many separate pieces with each piece accountable only to its self, godly discipline within the body of Christ vanishes like a vapour, and its function and purpose is made of little or no effect.

✝ **POSITION / OPERATION OF GRACE:** (grace never boasts; grace commands us to purge out the old leaven in the body of Christ)

"[About the condition of your church] your boasting is not good [indeed, it is most unseemly and

entirely out of place]. Do you not know that [just] a little leaven will ferment the whole lump [of dough]?

Purge (clean out) the old leaven that you may be fresh (new) dough, still uncontaminated [as you are], for Christ, our Passover [Lamb], has been sacrificed.

Therefore, let us keep the feast, not with old leaven, not with leaven of vice and malice and wickedness, but with the unleavened [bread] of purity (nobility, honour) and sincerity and [unadulterated] truth" (1 Corinthians 5:6–8).

Our Christian walk can be likened to the feast of Christ. Our Passover Lamb has been sacrificed, and we have been made into new, fresh, uncontaminated dough. The grace of God directs us to purge out the old leaven of vice, malice, and wickedness; we are to walk in the pure, sincere, and unadulterated truth — the pure unleavened dough that we are in Christ. This is the operation of grace working in our life drawing its continual source of power from our eternal position of pure unadulterated grace. Let us keep this feast by the grace of God, not by submission to the flesh. Oh, how the uncontaminated blood of the Lamb continues to cleanse us and keep us cleansed for all eternity!

It is the grace of God that has made us His very own. There is no room for boasting here. Boasting is not good; it is unseemly and entirely out of place. Pride is a fruit of the flesh, not a fruit of the Spirit of grace. Pride prevents us from being intimately acquainted with the grace of God. It blinds us to the knowledge of sin in our members and keeps the intimacy of God from flowing freely within the body of Christ.

Tolerance of sin within the body of Christ is not the message of the cross. God dealt with sin and He expects us, by the grace of God, and walking in His spirit, to follow in His steps. Sin that is left ignored and undisturbed never results in the growth of the body of Christ; it will always bring desolation. Sin left unchecked and free to roam will always beget more sin. Beloved, when you are born in a barn, you cannot smell it.

The sin of dividing the church into factions is so well accepted as normal, and even regarded as birthed by the Spirit, that few spiritual noses detect this carnality. Often, it is even celebrated as people pride themselves in another year's accomplishment for their denomination. Any division of the church is founded on carnality and worldliness. When the foundation is worldly, how can the fruit be truly spiritual and glorify God?

Just being sincere is not enough in itself as many times we can be sincerely wrong. The feast of fellowship in the body of Christ is to be partaken in purity, sincerity, and unadulterated truth. There is no room for changing or bending the word of God to meet our individual desires. There is danger in using worldly terms to describe spiritual concepts. The word 'denomination' is not found in scripture; however, it is often used to justify division or factions. The essence of our sanctification is in our recognition of untruth in our life and repenting of such, not ignoring or celebrating it.

✝ **OPERATION OF GRACE:** (grace is the source of disciplinary judgment within the body of Christ)

"I wrote you in my [previous] letter not to associate [closely and habitually] with unchaste (impure) people —

Not [meaning of course that you must] altogether shun the immoral people of this world, or the greedy graspers and cheats and thieves or idolaters, since otherwise you would need to get out of the world and human society altogether!

But I write to you not to associate with anyone who bears the name of [Christian] brother if he is known to be guilty of immorality or greed, or is an idolater [whose soul is devoted to any object that usurps the place of God], or is a person with a foul tongue [railing, abusing, reviling, slandering], or is a drunkard or a swindler or a robber. [No] you must not so much as eat with such a person.

What [business] of mine is it and what right have I to judge outsiders? Is it not those inside [the church] upon whom you are to pass disciplinary judgment [passing censuring sentence on them as the facts require]" (1 Corinthians 5:9–12)?

There is more to bearing the name of Christ than just saying you are a Christian. When you bear the name of Christ, you are carrying within you the Name above all names — this is not a trivial thing. The grace of God admonishes us not to associate closely and habitually with Christians who act untowardly in Christ; we are required not to even eat with them. This is an operation of the grace and love of God that requires us to walk in the Spirit, accomplishing His plans and purposes in His time, His way.

Our position in Christ commands a complete separation from worldly attitudes and actions. It takes the operation of the grace of God in our life to accomplish this. Grace positions us in the arena of perfection, and then as it operates in our life, it draws us towards that same perfection.

Those outside of the body of Christ are already judged and they stand in a position of eternal condemnation. Lord Jesus, help the body of Christ to hold out the Word of truth to them that they may see where they stand. Help them confess their sin and come under the position of protection found in Your eternal grace. Salvation in Christ Jesus places us on the redeemed side of judgement.

Judgment outside of the church is not our concern; but we are mandated by the grace of God to judge within the church. Grace has given us our position of eternal salvation and from this placement it trains and corrects us. A Father's love for his children includes discipline. When we feel the disciplinary grace of God in our life, we can rest assured that it comes from eternal love, not from temporal abandonment — even that was taken care of on the cross (Mk. 15:34).

Beloved, our position of grace is never withdrawn from us; it is eternal. Gracious judgment can only come from the position of grace that we have in Christ Jesus; and it always draws one closer to God — love begets more love. Lord Jesus, help us to draw near to embrace the disciplinary grace mandated in the body of Christ. All discipline in the church should be purposed to restore, rather than condemn. It is to be exercised only in matters that are clearly identified as sin in Scripture. Doctrinal issues and '<u>disputable convictions</u>' are never a basis for church discipline (Rom. 14:1–13). Christians need not judge the world, which is already judged. However, we are called to evaluate and judge issues in our life. Judgement motivated by the grace that is found on the cross of Christ is restorative, not condemning.

✞ **<u>POSITION / OPERATION OF GRACE</u>:** (grace should be used to apply discipline in the body of the Christ)

"God alone sits in <u>judgment</u> on those who are <u>outside</u>. Drive out that wicked one from among you [expel him from your church]" (1 Corinthians 5:13).

We have been judged and declared eternally innocent by the precious blood of the Lamb of God; this is an eternal fact. God poured out His grace upon us even while we were yet sinners. To point a finger at anyone in the world is merely to point a finger at our own shadow — when we did not know the grace of God. Grace of Christ was not given to discipline the world (Isaiah 26:10); the discipline of grace is meant to be applied to a person who is living in the position of grace.

✞ **<u>OPERATION OF GRACE</u>:** (grace should be used to judge disputes in the body of Christ)

"I say this to move you to <u>shame</u>. Can it be that there really is not one man among you who [in action is governed by piety and integrity and] is wise and competent enough to decide [the private grievances, disputes, and quarrels] between members of the brotherhood,

But brother goes to <u>law</u> <u>against</u> <u>brother</u>, and that before [Gentile judges who are] unbelievers [without faith or trust in the Gospel of Christ]?

Why, the very fact of your having <u>lawsuits</u> with one another at all is a <u>defect</u> (a <u>defeat</u>, an evidence of positive <u>moral</u> <u>loss</u> for you). Why not rather let yourselves <u>suffer</u> <u>wrong</u> and be deprived of what is your due? Why not rather be <u>cheated</u> (<u>defrauded</u> and <u>robbed</u>)?

But [instead it is you] yourselves who wrong and defraud, and that even your own brethren [by so treating them]" (1 Corinthians 6:5–8)!

The grace of God should move us to shame when we cannot judge grievances with piety, integrity, and wisdom. Affairs amongst the brotherhood should be judged by the brotherhood, not by those outside the church. Righteousness is meant to judge the affairs of the righteousness (1 Cor. 6:1–8), and it is shameful to believe that you need unrighteous men to judge members of the body of Christ. Such an action is sure evidence of the fact that one has already been defeated.

The kingdom of God affects this world greatly, but it is not *of* this world. The kingdom of God has come into the world to bear witness to the Truth. The world and its ways have nothing in common with Christ whatsoever, and nothing in Christ is given to the world except His offering of salvation.

The world has no power or jurisdiction over/in the kingdom of God. When Jesus stood before Pilate with His life being on the line, He told Pilate that if His kingdom were of this world, His followers would be fighting to prevent Him from being handed over to the authorities (John 18:36). He knew that His life was not under the authority of the world; it was under the authority of Him Who sent Him (John 19:10–11). As Christians, we need to take a lesson from this.

When we as Christians feel we have been wronged and then look to worldly authorities to declare our righteousness, we have just lost our testimony of Christ's righteousness. Trusting in the world for our vindication is evidence of defeat and moral loss. It is neither a position nor an operation of grace. Christians should rather count it all joy, be glad to suffer wrong, and be deprived of their rights here on earth (Heb. 10:34). It is better to be cheated and robbed, rejoicing in the kingdom of God, than to lose kingdom heritage by haranguing our oppressors in heathen law courts.

The question needs to be asked, "Why would we as Christians, who have the Spirit of God, go to worldly authorities to settle our disputes, instead of to the brotherhood where the Spirit of God dwells?" Would it be because we ourselves know in our hearts that we are also in the wrong, and do not want this exposed before the brotherhood? By going to worldly authorities, we feel we can safely hide our wrongs while at the same time point out the wrong in our brother. We are foolishly afraid of the Spirit of God searching deeper into our own soul and exposing the wrong within our own life (John 3:20).

If we are willing, He will show us where the log is in our own eye when we are worried about the sliver in our brother's eye (Matt. 7:1–5). Jesus uses the word *hypocrite* and as stated above, such a person has already been defeated and has lost morally. With this type of worldly behaviour, one loses the intimacy of the body of Christ and the accountability that resides there. Beloved, discipline happens within the context of fellowship, by the leading of the Spirit of God; it is not delegated to a church service.

✞ **OPERATION OF GRACE:** (unrighteousness does not partake of the kingdom of God)

"Do you not know that the unrighteous and the wrongdoers will not inherit or have any share in the kingdom of God? Do not be deceived (misled); neither the impure and immoral, nor idolaters, nor adulterers, nor those who participate in homosexuality,

Nor cheats (swindlers and thieves), nor greedy graspers, nor drunkards, nor foulmouthed revilers and slanderers, nor extortioners and robbers will inherit or have any share in the kingdom of God" (1 Corinthians 6:9–10).

Beloved, if this Scripture was talking about our salvation, we would all be in trouble. The kingdom of God is righteousness, peace, and joy in the Holy Spirit. What is being clarified here is that a person who indulges in such immoral activities will not experience the righteousness, peace, and joy of the Holy Spirit here in this mortal life.

This Scripture does not mean that a person loses his position of eternal life because of these actions — otherwise grace would not be grace. Our position of grace cannot be undone by sin. However, sin is never sanctioned to accomplish the operation of grace. Anyone who has such improper fruits in his life should reflect as to whether he is truly living in the knowledge of Christ, and the freedom found in Christ's redeeming power. Before we knew grace we lived and conducted ourselves in the passions of our flesh. Now that we know Christ, we are obligated to bear fruits of righteousness.

✞ **POSITION OF GRACE:** (grace purifies us; frees us from guilt; and justifies us in Christ Jesus)

"And such some of you were [once]. But you were washed clean (purified by a complete atonement for sin and made free from the guilt of sin), and you were consecrated (set apart, hallowed), and you were justified [pronounced righteous, by trusting] in the name of the Lord Jesus Christ and in the [Holy] Spirit of our God" (1 Corinthians 6:11).

Christ has washed us clean. He purified, consecrated, and justified us eternally when we trusted in the name of the Lord Jesus Christ — a work of the Holy Spirit. When man cleans something, it always gets dirty again, but when God cleans something, it is eternally pure. The holy qualities of God have been imputed into us, and they are so pure that they cannot be overcome or reversed by our actions. It is this pure gift of God's grace that continually covers us, teaches us, and enables us to operate in the character and Spirit of God that has been so richly given to us and increasingly abounds in us (2 Peter 1:8). The gift of the grace of God keeps us from becoming unfruitful, unproductive, and ineffective. It operates in our lives, forming progressively the likeness of Christ in our inner being. The grace of God reveals to us what we were, and it shows us what we eternally are as it trains and enables us to follow in Christ's steps as we sojourn through our life here in these temporary tents (1 Peter 1:2–4; 2:21).

✞ **POSITION / OPERATION OF GRACE:** (under grace, everything is permissible; grace warns us to not become slaves of or be brought under the power of anything outside of Christ)

"Everything is permissible (allowable and lawful) for me; but not all things are helpful (good for me to do, expedient and profitable when considered with other things). Everything is lawful for me, but I will not become the slave of anything or be brought under its power" (1 Corinthians 6:12).

From our position of grace, nothing can remove or nullify our eternal life that we have obtained in Christ Jesus. Beloved, grace is able to keep and hold us eternally blameless. This grace is an extension of the character of God; it is from the hand of God Himself. It operates in our life warning us not to become slaves to things that are not good, not expedient, or not profitable (Rom 6:16). If we choose to permit things to have power over our lives in our day to day walk, we will reap consequences here and now. The operation of grace can keep us from coming under the powers that desire to enslave us. Grace enables us to deny these things a foothold in our life.

Note that a child of grace can come under bondage to things that are unrighteous. Beloved, our body was not made for immorality, but rather was created for the habitation of the Lord. In Christ, we are new creations and God would have our life reflecting Christ in us — grace allows us to come under new management. Whoever commits and practices sin is a slave to sin, but the Lord's purpose is to save, sanctify, and raise our body again (1 Cor. 6:13). As Christians, we cannot afford to give any area of our being to the devil. Our freedom (authority) in Christ allows the grace of God to root out all falsity and replace unbelief with belief in the work of God — we cease believing a lie and open our ears to truth (John 8:45–47).

✞ **POSITION / OPERATION OF GRACE:** (our body is a part of Christ; grace demands us not to join it together with a prostitute)

"Do you not see and know that your bodies are members (bodily parts) of Christ (the Messiah)? Am I therefore to take the parts of Christ and make [them] parts of a prostitute? Never! Never" (1 Corinthians 6:15)!

From our eternally pure and holy position as a member of the body of Christ, the grace of God cries out for us not to take the parts of our body and join them with a prostitute. Never! Never! Such a fervent plea can only come from the position of eternal grace — grace that saw the passion in the Garden of Gethsemane, the completion on the Cross by our Lord Jesus, and then birthed at Pentecost by the Spirit. Beloved, the words 'never' and 'forever' only have true meaning from our position of being in the name of the Lord Jesus Christ.

✞ **OPERATION OF GRACE:** (grace is pleading with us not to become one with wickedness)

"Or do you not know and realize that when a man joins himself to a prostitute, he becomes one body with her? The two, it is written, shall become one flesh" (1 Corinthians 6:16).

We have become one body with Christ, should I therefore now take the parts of Christ and make them parts of sexual immorality? Never! Never! Thank God for His grace that keeps us pure. We are not to celebrate the festival of Christ by intimately joining ourselves to wickedness. Never! Never! What fellowship has Christ with wickedness? None! Our position of grace commands us to let the grace of God operate within our bodily members, training them to deny becoming one with ungodliness.

✞ **POSITION OF GRACE:** (grace joins us to the Lord making us one in the spirit)

"But the person who is united to the Lord becomes one spirit with Him" (1 Corinthians 6:17).

The grace of God has made us one spirit with Him. This is an act that is wholly accomplished by God. We are one in spirit with God. What an incredible eternal position in Jesus Christ our Lord! It is this oneness that draws us deeper and deeper into the fear of the Lord, the only place we find true rest. The fear of God draws us and makes us run towards Him, not away from Him. The fear of God draws you out of danger and into His protection, unlike fear in the world, which kills and destroys.

As in a marriage, we are personally united to Christ and together we are the body of Christ. This union is complete, perfect, and indissoluble, by the virtue of God. It is the spirit of a dog that returns to the vomit, and the spirit of a pig that returns to the mire (Prov. 26:11; 2 Peter 2:22). As the bride of Christ, we should not be letting anything replace or usurp the position of Christ in our heart.

✞ **OPERATION OF GRACE:** (grace trains us to shun immorality; sexual sin is against one's own body)

"Shun immorality and all sexual looseness [flee from impurity in thought, word, or deed]. Any other sin which a man commits is one outside the body, but he who commits sexual immorality sins against his own body" (1 Corinthians 6:18).

Enabled by the grace of God, we are to avoid and flee from sexual immorality. This includes all impurity in thought, word, and deed. Something is made impure when it is combined with something that is not of the same nature. The position of grace in our life is holy, perfect, and pure. It takes the operation of this same grace to enable us to shun impurity and allow His nature to continually cleanse us and keep us in His will.

Sexual immorality is the only sin that is directed against one's own body. There is a spiritual significance in sexual immorality; it is not just an act of the flesh that carries no consequences with it. We are members of the body of Christ, and as such, we are commanded to shun all such lascivious looseness in our lives.

✞ **POSITION / OPERATION OF GRACE:** (grace makes our body the temple of the Holy Spirit; we are not our own; grace commands us to glorify God in our body)

"Do you not know that your body is the temple (the very sanctuary) of the Holy Spirit Who lives within you, Whom you have received [as a Gift] from God? You are not your own.

You were bought with a price [purchased with a preciousness and paid for, made His own]. So then, honour God and bring glory to Him in your body" (1 Corinthians 6:19–20).

Beloved, you are not your own, you have been made His; you have been bought at a very precious price, a very dear dowry. The grace of God commands us to honour God in our body. This is our reasonable service of worship to God. The sanctuary of God (our body) is not created for sexual sin, but rather it is a temple of worship in life to God.

The grace of God continually calls us to recognize that our life is based in our eternal position of grace in Christ. We are not our own; we do not have to be slaves to our fleshy desires. We are called to do as God desires, as the Spirit of grace teaches and leads us in His holy ways, bringing glory to Him in our body.

The eye of grace allows us to see that the price that God has paid for us is no small affair. The Word of God's power became flesh and blood. It fulfilled all the requirements necessary to pay for all the debts we would ever owe to the Author of life. God's purchase price is perfect and complete; it lacks nothing. It is God that set the price, and it is God that fulfilled the price when He declared, "It is finished:" (John 19:30; Rom. 6:22–23).

✞ **POSITION / OPERATION OF GRACE:** (grace leads us into the ways and principles of God)

"For circumcision is nothing and counts for nothing, neither does uncircumcision, but [what counts is] keeping the commandments of God" (1 Corinthians 7:19).

From our position in Christ, the word of grace tells us to keep the commandments of God. Keeping the commandments of God has nothing to do with our position of eternal life; it has to do with all the aspects of our spiritual life here on earth (1 Cor. 7:1–40).

Beloved, the law of God has nothing to do with our justification before God and our gracious position of eternal life. The law of God defines right and wrong actions; it brings definition to works of righteousness, and it identifies ungodliness. Grace teaches us to deny and shun actions contrary to divine law — ungodliness. The keeping of divine commands carries with it no penalty of debt, but it does bear with it great reward of grace, bringing peace of mind, and the presence of God. A lawful walk of grace is not a contradiction; it is a fruit of grace, evidence of faith, and of our new creation in Christ Jesus (Rom. 7:22). Beloved, ungodliness is never profitable; godliness is always profitable. The New Covenant — the law of God written on our heart — brings with it a confirmation as to whether our actions and attitudes in our life line up with the word of God (Jer. 31:33; Rom. 2:15; Heb. 8:10, 10:16).

✞ **OPERATION OF GRACE:** (grace desires marriage to be in the Lord)

"A wife is bound to her husband by law as long as he lives. If the husband dies, she is free to be married to whom she will, only [provided that he too is] in the Lord" (1 Corinthians 7:39).

When a believer is yoked together with an unbeliever, it is a mismatch (Dan. 2:43; Eccl. 7:26–28; 2 Cor. 6:14). The god of this world is never in unity with the God of Creation; it is just not in the devil's nature to submit to the Almighty. His nature is to promote disobedience to God's commands (Gen. 3:1); he is the father of lies (John 8:44) and his work is to kill, steal and destroy (John 10:10). The operation of grace here tells us that it is better to marry a believer, and as deep calls to deep, grace calls to grace. To grow in grace requires submission to the grace of our Lord. Thank you Lord for Your grace that forever covers all our misgivings in our life; it continually receives us where we are at, and patiently works in our life, in-spite-of our mistakes.

✞ **POSITION OF GRACE:** (grace identifies life principles for us to follow)

"Do I say this only on human authority and as a man reasons? Does not the Law endorse the same principle?

For in the Law of Moses it is written, You shall not muzzle an ox when it is treading out the corn. Is it [only] for oxen that God cares?

Or does He speak certainly and entirely for our sakes? [Assuredly] it is written for our sakes, because the plowman ought to plow in hope, and the thresher ought to thresh in expectation of partaking of the harvest" (1 Corinthians 9:8–10).

The principles found in the law are not contrary to the principles of grace. They have been written for our sake to be used in our life. The only way God's commands can effectively be applied to our life is from our position of grace in Christ Jesus our Lord. Grace has brought us out from under the condemnation of the law; however, it has not abolished the principles of righteousness upon which the law is based and written for our sakes (Rom. 7:12). The law can never make us righteous, only the grace of God does that. The principles found in God's commands give us divine direction and boundaries for our walk of grace. The law points us to grace, and this same grace teaches us in turn to deny ungodliness. The Holy Spirit will never lead you into sin (disobedience to the commands and law of God).

✝ **POSITION OF GRACE:** (grace is not under the law)

"To the Jews I became as a Jew that I might win Jews; to men under the Law, [I became] as one under the Law, though not myself being under the Law, that I might win those under the Law" (1 Corinthians 9:20).

In Christ, we become servants to everyone, in order to bring them to Christ. To those who follow the law, we do the same, even though we ourselves are not subject to the law — our position of eternal life is obtained only by the grace of God. Our purpose of becoming as one under the Law is to win these people to Christ so that they might find justification in the grace of God — to be reconciled to God. The main ministry that God has given us is reconciling the world to Christ.

✝ **OPERATION OF GRACE:** (grace does not act lawlessly towards God)

"To those without (outside) law I became as one without law, not that I am without the law of God and lawless toward Him, but that I am [especially keeping] within and committed to the law of Christ, that I might win those who are without law" (1 Corinthians 9:21).

To the Gentiles, we become as one without the law of God, not that we ourselves are without the law of God. Grace places us outside of the condemnation of the law of God, yet we are not lawless towards God. The grace of God operating in our life will teach and train us to follow the principles found in the commands of God.

Our righteous position of grace does not teach us to live in a manner that is contrary to God's righteous law. Beloved, we are free, but we are not our own. Our position of grace in Christ covers all our iniquity; it trains us to do justly, to love mercy, and to faithfully walk in humility with God (Micah 6:8; Matt. 23:23). Grace never leads us into iniquity. In Christ, we become all things to all men for the purpose of winning people into the grace of God, not for the purpose of indulging our flesh. If you continually surrender yourself to anything, you become the slave of that thing (Rom. 6:16).

✝ **POSITION / OPERATION OF GRACE:** (grace warns us not to fall into sin)

"Do not be worshippers of false gods as some of them were, as it is written, The people sat down to eat and drink [the sacrifices offered to the golden calf at Horeb] and rose to sport (to dance and give way to jesting and hilarity).

We must not gratify evil desire and indulge in immorality as some of them did — and twenty three-thousand [suddenly] fell dead in a single day!

We should not tempt the Lord [try His patience, become a trial to Him, critically appraise Him, and exploit His goodness] as some of them did — and were killed by poisonous serpents;

Nor discontentedly complain as some of them did — and were put out of the way entirely by the destroyer (death).

Now these things befell them by way of a figure [as an example and warning to us]; they were written to admonish and fit us for right action by good instruction, we in whose days the ages have reached their climax — their consummation and concluding period.

Therefore let anyone who thinks he stands [who feels sure that he has a steadfast mind and is standing firm], take heed lest he fall [into sin]" (1 Corinthians 10:7–12).

The grace of God warns us here to be careful not to follow after the same sins that the people of God fell into in the Old Testament. Their demise is a warning to us who are under God's grace today. They were written both to admonish us and to fit us for right action. It is only by the grace of God that we can discern these things, and it is only by the grace of God that He continually works in our life teaching us to deny ungodliness, which so cleverly can work its power over our life. We are told to take heed lest we fall into sin.

Many antichrists have arisen; they oppose Christ in the guise of Christ. The use of religious rhetoric and pious presentation of doctrines not of God have bombarded the church from the beginning of its existence. False teachings, bringing false definition and meaning to the church, have confused and divided it since its inception. Anything and everything that displaces God and truth in our life will leave us with a substitute that brings desolation.

Beloved, anything that denies truth will replace truth with its own definition (Gen. 3:1). For example, 'church division' is scripturally wrong, yet we find churches celebrating and attempting to give God the glory for the development of their 'denomination'. Beloved, golden calves have plagued God's people for a long time (1 Kings 12:25–33).

✞ **POSITION / OPERATION OF GRACE:** (grace sets us free in all things)

"All things are legitimate (permissible), [and we are free to do anything we please], but not all things are helpful (expedient, profitable, and wholesome). All things are legitimate, but not all things are constructive [to character] and edifying [to spiritual life]" (1 Corinthians 10:23).

All things are legal and legitimate with respect to our position in Christ. Yet, all things are not constructive to building the character of Christ in my life. All things are not edifying to my spiritual life. From our position of grace in Christ we have been set free from the power of condemnation under the Law. However, this does not mean that we can continue to live in sin. If we continue to sin we are choosing to be held in bondage by sin. When a Christian disobeys God, he does not lose his position of eternal life in Christ; however he does lose life in the Spirit, and he fails to produce kingdom fruit in that area of his life.

We are the slaves of whomever or whatever we obey. The grace of God delivers us from the power of sin; it never leads us into wilful disobedience to God (Rom. 6:15–18). When grace operates in our life, it will always lead us in the direction of godliness, not ungodliness. Grace will always train us to deny ungodliness and will lead us to walk wisely in our spiritual life.

✞ **POSITION / OPERATION OF GRACE:** (grace will not lead people into sin)

"Do not let yourselves be [hindrances by giving] offense to the Jews or to the Greeks or to the church of God [do not lead others into sin by your mode of life];" (1 Corinthians 10:32).

Because of our position in Christ, we become all things to all men for the purpose of bringing others to Christ. The grace of God operating in our life will never cause us to lead others into sin. Grace trains us not to be a hindrance to the Jews, to the Greeks, or to the church of God.

Beloved, a mode of life that is filled with the grace of God is a life that lives uprightly. Grace trains us to abstain from the passions and fleshy desires of our lower nature. These desires war against the soul, but grace trains us to be servants of the Almighty.

✞ **POSITION / OPERATION OF GRACE:** (by grace we have communion — remembrance of Christ; new covenant — the body and blood of Christ, proclaiming the Lord's death)

"And when He had given thanks, He broke [it] and said, Take, eat, This is My body, which is broken for you. Do this to call Me [affectionately] to remembrance.

Similarly when supper was ended, He took the cup also, saying, This cup is the new covenant [ratified and established] in My blood. Do this as often as you drink [it], to call Me [affectionately] to remembrance.

For every time you eat this bread and drink this cup, you are representing and signifying and proclaiming the fact of the Lord's death until He comes [again]" (1 Corinthians 11:24–26).

The only way we can truly partake of the blessings found in the body of Christ is by His grace. Because of what He has done for us we can eat with the Lord's body and affectionately remember Him. Drinking of the cup of the new covenant is a drink of grace. The blood of the Lamb of God obtains for us a position that allows us to drink of the cup of grace and affectionately remember Him.

Communion proclaims truth; it presents the fact of the Lord's death and gives us access to real spiritual benefits. His death, resurrection, and His imminent return are a cornerstone of the Christian faith. They are eternal facts that we proclaim to the world as part of the Good News. Our position of grace in Christ Jesus allows the act of communion to be an operation of grace with power to bring healing and health to the body of Christ.

✞ **OPERATION OF GRACE:** (grace does not allow unworthy participation in communion)

"So then whoever eats the bread or drinks the cup of the Lord in a way that is unworthy [of Him] will be guilty of [profaning and sinning against] the body and blood of the Lord" (1 Corinthians 11:27).

Outside of the grace of God, we are unworthy. It is only by His grace that we have been authorized to approach the throne of God. His nail-pierced hands and His wounded side display the love of God towards us. When we celebrate communion with one another, we are acknowledging the work of grace accomplished on the cross of Christ, bringing Him affectionately to our remembrance — we bow down to the Worthy One, the Holy One, sacrificed for us. His eternal, unchanging grace has been richly poured out upon us and His unfathomable goodness has been made accessible to us.

Our worthiness is found only in continuous self-inspection in recognition of the grace of Jesus Christ. Any other approach makes us unworthy and guilty of sinning against the body and blood of the Lord.

✞ **OPERATION OF GRACE:** (grace brings judgment and discipline at the communion table)

"But when we fall short and are judged by the Lord, we are disciplined and chastened, so that we may not [finally] be condemned [to eternal punishment along] with the world.

So then, my brothers, when you gather together to eat [the Lord's supper], wait for one another" (1 Corinthians 11:32–33).

When we fall short, God's grace disciplines and chastens us. Correction is an act of grace. It is the very fact that we are not our own anymore — not a part of the world and its ways — that we come under the gracious, loving correction and discipline of the Lord. Beloved, to be chastened under the grace of God is so much better than being woefully ignorant of the hand of God, and falling under condemnation with the world. To surrender all to the Lord is not a grievous, burdensome task; it is a gracious, glorious operation of God, worked into our life because of the position of the grace we have obtained in Christ Jesus. Love and correction go together; they are companions.

Let us learn to wait on the Lord and on the body of Christ. As we allow the grace of God to draw us close to Him, it will enable us to let His power operate in and through our lives as we delight in His presence in one another.

✞ **POSITION / OPERATION OF GRACE:** (grace works in our life)

"But by the grace (the unmerited favour and blessing) of God I am what I am, and His grace toward me was not [found to be] for nothing (fruitless and without effect). In fact, I worked harder than all of them [the apostles], though it was not really I, but the grace (the unmerited favour and blessing) of God which was with me" (1 Corinthians 15:10).

When the grace of God works within us, it produces righteous fruit. As we release ourselves to Him, He will manifest Himself in our life. A life disciplined by the Lord does not continue in a display of debauchery; it produces the fruit of the Spirit. The works of grace are evident throughout Scripture:

- gifts of grace (1 Cor. 12:1–31)
- works of grace (1 Cor. 15:10)
- grace of giving (2 Cor. 6:1–7; 9:8)
- grace of ministry (Gal. 2:9; Eph. 3:7)

- speech of grace (Col. 4:6)
- glorified grace (2 Thess. 1:12)
- strong in grace (2 Tim. 2:1)
- grace strengthens (Heb. 13:9)
- grace of life (1 Peter 3:7)
- grace gifts (1 Peter 4:10)
- grace and humility (1 Peter 5:5)
- God of all grace (1 Peter 5:10)
- persevere in grace (1 Peter 5:12)
- grow in grace (2 Peter 3:18)
- pervert grace (Jude 1:4).

"And with great strength and ability and power the apostles delivered their testimony to the resurrection of the Lord Jesus, and great grace (loving-kindness and favour and goodwill) rested richly upon them all" (Acts 4:33).

Grace is not only a position that we have obtained in Christ; it is God's strength, ability, and power manifesting itself through the works done in our life. Grace *is* something (position), and grace *does* something (operation).

✞ **POSITION OF GRACE:** (grace causes faith to be founded in the death and resurrection of Christ)

"And if Christ has not been raised, your faith is mere delusion [futile, fruitless], and you are still in your sins [under the control and penalty of sin];" (1 Corinthians 15:17).

The foundation of our faith rests upon the fact that Christ has been raised from the dead. Without the resurrection of Christ, the Gospel would become a delusion and we would still be under the control and penalty of sin — lawlessness. But by Christ being raised from the dead, we are vindicated and justified before God and the bonds of sin in our life have been broken. It is His resurrection life that enables us to apprehend and live our life abundantly in Christ. Faith is never fruitless when it is founded in the resurrection life of Christ. This incredible position of grace so freely found through faith enables us to move and have our being in Him, resulting in our life expressing the fruit of righteousness.

✞ **OPERATION OF GRACE:** (grace warns us not to be deceived and misled, to sin no more)

"Do not be so deceived and misled! Evil companionships (communion, associations) corrupt and deprave good manners and morals and character.

Awake [from your drunken stupor and return] to sober sense and your right minds, and sin no more, For some of you have not the knowledge of God [you are utterly and wilfully and disgracefully ignorant, and continue to be so, lacking the sense of God's presence and all true knowledge of Him]. I say this to your shame" (1 Corinthians 15:33–34).

The grace of God warns us not to be deceived or lead astray from the truth. It also warns not to deceive ourselves in thinking that evil companions will not affect our life. Our life should not display the symptoms of sin. Grace teaches us to deny ungodliness — not allow it to take root in the delicate, compassionate soil of our heart. Our heart needs to be hardened against sin and softened towards things of God (Prov. 4:23). Scripture warns us not to be deceived (Luke 21:8; John 7:47; Rom. 7:11; 1 Cor. 6:9; 2 Cor. 11:3; Gal. 6:7; 1 Tim. 2:14; 2 Tim. 3:13; Titus 3:3; James 1:16; Rev. 13:14; 20:10). Disobedience to God very cleverly conceals itself and deftly takes us by the hand, laying hold of our soul and motivating our actions to produce works that lead to spiritual death (Rom. 7:11). The devil's cunning can corrupt and induce us to be lead astray from the righteous way — wherein we are called to abide (2 Cor. 11:3; Rev. 13:14; 20:10).

The grace of God admonishes us to awake from ignorance of the knowledge of God. Where such ignorance exists, there is a lack of the sense of the presence of God in our life. When we do not walk by faith, we end up walking by external or outward appearance — unable to see God (2 Cor. 5:7; Heb. 11:6). It is not that God is not there; it is that we lack the knowledge of His presence and grace, and hence act without Him. Grace makes 'unable' become 'enabled'; it makes 'disgrace' become 'grace'.

✞ **POSITION / OPERATION OF GRACE:** (grace reveals that sin exercises its power through our abuse of the Law)

"Now sin is the sting of death, and sin exercises its power [upon the soul] through [the abuse of] the Law" (1 Corinthians 15:56).

The strength of sin is found in disobedience to the Law. Because of the inherent power of God's word, disobedience to that word promotes death. This death is produced and created by the very word of God itself. *"But of the tree of the knowledge of good and evil and blessing and calamity you shall not eat, for in the day you eat of it you shall surely die"* (Gen. 2:17).

Grace places us into the Word of God Himself. Having paid the price for our justification, the Word freely releases us from the power of sin and death. To be in the Word is life; to be outside of the Word is death. To be in Christ is life; to be outside of Christ is death. Beloved, this is why we have no need of anyone to teach us, because the Word is dwelling within us and by the Spirit we will never be led into error as we are taught by Him (1 John 2:27).

Note that sin exercises its power upon the soul. Our mind, will, and emotions are the targets of attack for our enemy. In Christ, the power of sin has been broken and dealt with and we are no longer under the condemning power of the law. We have been crucified with Christ. We are dead; nevertheless, we live by faith in Christ.

What shall we say then, now that we are under grace, shall we continue abusing the law that grace may abound? God forbid! Disobedience to God's law never has and never will bring power, blessing, or goodness to the soul of man. The operation of grace in our life enables us to be obedience to God through the renewal of our soul. Grace is not divinely intended to be walked out through our ignorant, habitual disobedience to God's ways.

✞ **POSITION OF GRACE:** (grace brings us victory through our Lord Jesus Christ)

"But thanks be to God, Who gives us the victory [making us conquerors] through our Lord Jesus Christ" (1 Corinthians 15:57).

Victory and 'being in Christ' are synonymous. The word 'Lord', carries with it ownership — a Possessor who has power of decision and control. When Jesus is our Lord, His decisions carry with it the power and sovereignty of God Almighty to enable us to walk as His servants. It is only through His lordship that we find victory. Such victory begins and ends with thanksgiving.

Christ makes us conquerors, yes, even more than conquerors. This is not gained by *our* own ability; it is *God's* ability working through us. When we realize that we wrestle not against flesh and blood but against spiritual wickedness in high places, we see the necessity of making Jesus Christ our Lord. It is our position of grace that makes us over-comers. Any action of victory on our part must come from the operation of grace working through our lives. An action is only victorious if is has been fought from the position of grace in God; it is never defined by the outcome, or the circumstances. All victories outside of Christ are temporary, and perish with time (Acts 7:58–60).

✞ **OPERATION OF GRACE:** (grace accomplishes work that is never futile or to no purpose)

"Therefore, my beloved brethren, be firm (steadfast), immovable, always abounding in the work of the Lord [always being superior, excelling, doing more than enough in the service of the Lord], knowing and being continually aware that your labour in the Lord is not futile [it is never wasted or to no purpose]" (1 Corinthians 15:58).

When grace operates in our life, the work of the Lord abounds. When our eyes are glued on God's grace, we are immovable, steadfast, and firmly fixed on His work. When we have the grace of God operating in our life, *our* labour is *His* labour; it bears the seal and stamp of God's approval — a work of the Holy Spirit.

Discouragement is designed to frustrate a work of God. But, when we are continually aware of the grace of God operating through us, we will not be distracted in our work for the Lord. A work of grace is *always* profitable; it is *always* successful. It is *never* barren or ineffectual. A work of grace cannot be enhanced by the flesh, and it is never devoid of truth.

When our mind, will, and emotions are enabled by the grace of God, we produce a work of the Lord — a work not determined by our definition of success. Grace enable us to find the success of resting in Him — His definition of success. Successful outcome is found only by arriving at the place where He has called you, by the way He has called you (Joshua 1:8).

The littlest work of God is insurmountably larger than the largest work of man. An eye that calls one work of God better than another, is an eye ruled by the flesh, not inspired by the grace of God. Beloved, God's grace operating through our life is a work of God. Oh what joy to realize that a work of grace is never futile, never wasted, and never purposeless! Grace drives our life and gives it eternal purpose; it gives us a life driven by God's purposes here and now.

2 Corinthians

✞ **POSITION / OPERATION OF GRACE:** (grace produces a clear conscience and pure motives in our conduct in the world)

"It is a reason for pride and exultation to which our conscience testifies that we have conducted ourselves in the world [generally] and especially toward you, with devout and pure motives and godly sincerity, not in fleshly wisdom but by the grace of God (the unmerited favour and merciful kindness by which God, exerting His holy influence upon souls, turns them to Christ, and keeps, strengthens, and increases them in Christian virtues)" (2 Corinthians 1:12).

The grace of God operating in our soul causes us to distinguish between what is morally good and morally wrong. It enables our behaviour to be free from pretence and hypocrisy, and to be generous in God as He works through our life. Godly devotion and sincerity is not a work forged by our flesh; it is a work that is enabled by the Spirit of grace, bringing forth the corresponding fruit.

God's favour and loving-kindness exerts influence over our souls, keeping, strengthening, and enabling Christian virtue to find increase in our life. Such work is only possible when a soul finds its position within the bounds of grace. Both a clear conscience and a seared conscience declare a righteousness — one the righteousness of Christ, the other the righteousness of self. Grace produces the fruit of God's righteousness (the fruit of the Spirit); the flesh manifests its *own* righteousness and fruit. Grace is a holy influence that turns us to Christ, then keeps us, strengthens us, and matures us in Christ-likeness.

There is an air of confidence that we acquire in God; it is not arrogance or presumption. In our position of grace, we find confidence that God will work out all things for the good in our lives. The more confident we are in our position of grace the more confident we are in the operation of it in our lives and the less likely we will be tossed and turned like the waves of the sea — we will not be operating in the doubtful, double mind of our own works.

✞ **POSITION OF GRACE:** (grace gives us the Holy Spirit as a seal and guarantee of God's promise)

"But it is God Who confirms and makes us steadfast and establishes us [in joint fellowship] with you in Christ, and has consecrated and anointed us [enduing us with the gifts of the Holy Spirit];

[He has also appropriated and acknowledged us as His by] putting His seal upon us and giving us His [Holy] Spirit in our hearts as the security deposit and guarantee [of the fulfilment of His promise]" (2 Corinthians 1:21–22).

Grace was revealed and sealed into our life by the Holy Spirit. The seal of God is not a temporary 'keep it and maintain it if you can' type of seal; it is an eternal seal, guaranteeing our eternal position of grace, which has been freely bestowed upon us. We have been purchased by Him and are eternally His; He acknowledges us as His children. This position is freely given and cannot be earned or improved upon by any effort on our part. God has left *Himself* as a deposit in our hearts, thus guaranteeing that He will fulfil His promise (John 14:16–17; 1 Cor. 3:16)). He will dwell with us and be in us, forever!

It is only from this incredible position of grace that we have the privilege of experiencing God's pruning and perfecting, as He produces the fruit of the Spirit in our life. In order for us to operate in grace, our position must be founded in grace. The operation of grace is an operation of God; it is not a manipulation of man's flesh. God is not interested in manipulating our flesh; He is interested in changing our heart. We cannot bring about a work of the Spirit in our lives by trying to manipulate our flesh — Christ has done what the law could not do (Gal. 3:3).

A seal has been placed upon us by God, keeping us eternally free from Satan's grasp. We have been marked by God, and His mark proves, confirms, and attests to His faithfulness. It places us in a position beyond the grasp of doubt and despair. It provides us with the hope that He is who He professes to be.

It is God that gives us the ability and the unction to stand firm. The more confident I am in my position of grace, the more confident I am able to stand firm in fellowship with Christ.

✞ **POSITION / OPERATION OF GRACE:** (grace corrects)

"For if I cause you pain [with merited rebuke], who is there to provide me enjoyment but the [very] one whom I have grieved and made sad" (2 Corinthians 2:2)?

Disciplining grace does not drive our soul away from God; it draws us towards the ways of God. God's discipline is not designed to destroy the soul; it is designed to draw the soul away from destruction. Godly grief guarantees the impartation of God's goodness into our soul; this operation of grace deposits the very character of God into our life.

A soul pained and grieved by the Spirit of God is a soul that will repentantly finish in a position of rejoicing at the goodness and graciousness of God. Pain, administered by God, cleanses us from all the unrighteous things in our life that do not conform to God's will in thought, purpose, and action.

A soul pained by worldly grief is a soul that propagates death (2 Cor. 7:10). Beloved, it is better to be 'grieved in God' than 'happy in hell'. Godly grief works repentance — a change of mind and purpose. It does not batter the soul; it builds it; it makes us better, not bitter.

Commands, admonitions, reproofs, and punishment delivered by the hand of God do not destroy; they heal and build up the object of God's care and love. Merited rebuke is an edifying experience; it operates within the bounds of grace. Reproofs and discipline are the way of a godly life (Prov. 6:23).

✞ **OPERATION OF GRACE:** (correction because of grace)

"But if someone [the one amongst you who committed incest] has caused [all this] grief and pain, he has caused it not to me, but in some measure, not to put it too severely, [he has distressed] all of you" (2 Corinthians 2:5).

Grace is greater than any power of sin. Note that the effects of sin are to be felt by all who are under the grace of God. Disobedience to God causes righteous pain, and it is only because of the grace of God that we can feel this type of pain and distress. Our position of being in Christ allows us to feel the arrows and darts of devilish deeds inflicted on other members in the body of Christ. To ignore or disclaim the work of sin in any member of the body of Christ is a celebration of the flesh, not a celebration of the Spirit.

God's grace enables us to deny works of darkness in our life. It allows us to feel the consequences of the work of sin in other members of the body of Christ. If the work of grace, which convicts us and calls us away from sin, is ignored or set aside and made of no effect, we turn our back on the very thing that can heal us and restore righteousness in our life. To ignore or be unreceptive to such grace is to court death in those areas of our life and to refuse to let the righteousness of God to touch us. A mere opening of our heart to the work of grace is enough to heal horrendous scars of sin, both now and forever. The more we walk in this truth, the more we experience the freedom of it.

✞ **OPERATION OF GRACE:** (correction because of grace)

"For such a one this censure by the majority [which he has received is] sufficient [punishment]" (2 Corinthians 2:6).

When we refuse to allow the grace of God to denounce ungodliness in our life, this same grace of God will eventually manifest its work of discipline towards us through the body of Christ. Such censure only operates because of the position of grace operating in the lives of those involved. Godly censure operates in opposition to ungodliness and is solely enacted out of reverence towards God and His will.

Note that godly censure imposed upon any part of the body of Christ comes directly from the body of Christ itself, not from an institutionalized, authoritative structure. Godly censure, like God's grace, must be received in order for it to leave its effect. "*My grace is sufficient*" is the voice that echoes in the hallways of godly censure. It is not a show of man's authoritative power or up-manship; it is recognition of the grace of God operating within the body of Christ. Such censure draws a wayward heart into the place of knowing the sufficiency of grace. Grace is the work of the Spirit manifesting the love of God.

✝ **OPERATION OF GRACE:** (correction because of grace)

"So [instead of further rebuke, now] you should rather turn and [graciously] forgive and comfort and encourage [him], to keep him from being overwhelmed by excessive sorrow and despair" (2 Corinthians 2:7).

The grace of God consoles, encourages, and strengthens; it brings comfort. It summons the needy soul back to the side of fellowship — living in the love and grace of Christ. The voice of grace operating through the majority, guides the receiving soul to the place of forgiveness and reconciliation. It brings peace to the repentant soul, lest it be destroyed and swallowed up by despair.

A repentant soul does not need rebuke or condemnation as it is renewed in the grace of God. Grace is not designed to devour a soul; it is designed to swallow up a soul in the everlasting loving-kindness and mercy of God. The operation of such grace brings life to any soul that receives it; not death. Death comes by rejecting the operation of grace in our life.

✝ **OPERATION OF GRACE:** (correction of offenders by grace)

"I therefore beg you to reinstate him in your affections and assure him of your love for him;" (2 Corinthians 2:8).

The grace of God exhorts us to reinstate our affections to a censured soul before God. We are to make valid and to publicly confirm our love towards him — a love that is not really ours but in reality is Christ's love flowing through us by the grace of God. We are called to reassure one another of God's affection; this can only be demonstrated by our actions. Grace begs us to reaffirm our love towards the censured. This reaffirmation is for the building up of the whole body of Christ.

God's love is always there and it is never withheld, but it is *our* affection that needs to be reinstated. The receptive heart needs to drink fully of the experience and knowledge of God's love. God's grace operating through the body of Christ can now publicly declare the completion of this work of grace through His body, as it operates and reinstates in love.

A father's love is always present even in the correcting of his child. During the disciplining of the child, the father is not showing affection; however, he definitely is showing love. Proper discipline always finishes by reaffirming one's affection. Beloved, let us not confuse love and affection.

✝ **POSITION / OPERATION OF GRACE:** (grace causes forgiveness to break the bonds of Satan, and builds the body of Christ)

"If you forgive anyone anything, I too forgive that one; and what I have forgiven, if I have forgiven anything, has been for your sakes in the presence [and with the approval] of Christ (the Messiah),

To keep Satan from getting the advantage over us; for we are not ignorant of his wiles and intentions" (2 Corinthians 2:10–11).

The presence of the Spirit of Christ is the identifying mark of any work being done within the bounds of grace. Presenting forgiveness to a receptive soul is a work of grace accomplished within the body of Christ. When a part forgives, the whole forgives, because we are all of the same Spirit — the same body. The authority by which something is done or not done must always come by the approval of the Messiah and His grace. Disregarding sin is a work of the spirit of the world; forgiving sin is the work of the Spirit of grace.

Grace is superior to and surpasses any work of iniquity or any human, worldly authority. It is only because of our position in Christ that we have the advantage over all the wiles of Satan (Eph. 6:11; 2

Tim 2:24–26). The grace of Christ can overreach and over-power any devilish boundary/bondage. As members of the body of Christ, we are not to be ignorant of, nor to misunderstand the working of the grace of God in one another's life. To go wrong in either the estimation or application of God's grace in one another's life produces disgrace.

Any work of grace brings wholeness to the body of Christ. God's goal is the redemption and renewal of the whole body, with each part realizing its mutual dependence upon every other part. The body of Christ is a living, self-healing body, directed by the head — the Messiah.

✞ **POSITION OF GRACE:** (Christ — the aroma of grace — brings life)

"But thanks be to God, Who in Christ always leads us in triumph [as trophies of Christ's victory] and through us spreads and makes evident the fragrance of the knowledge of God everywhere,

For we are the sweet fragrance of Christ [which exhales] unto God, [discernible alike] among those who are being saved and among those who are perishing:

To the latter it is an aroma [wafted] from death to death [a fatal odour, the smell of doom]; to the former it is an aroma from life to life [a vital fragrance, living and fresh]. And who is qualified (fit and sufficient) for these things? [Who is able for such a ministry? We?]" (2 Corinthians 2:14–16).

It is only because of our position in Christ that we make visible or make known what has been previously hidden and unknown. It is by the grace of God that we expose to view and bring to one another's recognition both the will and character of God. Any recognition of God's grace revealed to us helps us to define who and what we are in Him. This same grace carries with it the smell of life to those who know life, and the smell of death to those who do not know life (the unrepentant). Grace makes known the fragrance of the knowledge of God wherever it goes.

We are merely redeemed vessels holding out and dispensing grace. We are a vital fragrance, living and fresh to those who know life. Yet we are a fatal odour, a fragrance of doom to those who do not know life.

Possessing proper credentials or qualifications is never a question when it comes to grace. Who is qualified to receive grace? Who is qualified to dispense it? None, no not one, but by the grace of God! The only qualification required to handle grace is to know that you are in grace. The knowledge of God's grace is something that is alive and grows within us as we live our lives in Him.

✞ **POSITION OF GRACE:** (the letter of law kills, but the Spirit of grace gives life)

"[It is He] Who has qualified us [making us to be fit and worthy and sufficient] as ministers and dispensers of a new covenant [of salvation through Christ], not [ministers] of the letter (of legally written code) but of the Spirit; for the code [of the Law] kills, but the [Holy] Spirit makes alive" (2 Corinthians 3:6).

Our ministerial qualification came to us by the grace of God. A minister of grace is never a minister of the legal code of God, but rather a minister of the Spirit of God. It is not legal code that brings us life. It is only the Spirit of God that conveys the gracious gift of eternal life to us.

Though the Spirit never works contrary to or in defiance to the law of God, it is not the law that makes us the dispensers of the New Covenant; it is the Spirit of God that does this. Grace endows us with such honourable titles as 'ministers' and 'dispensers'. This is our position in Christ regardless of our actions. We don't earn the title nor can we obtain it through works of performance (or credentials earned at a Bible school). We are who we are, by the grace of God. Beloved, there is no other position that exists that is greater than this!

God has made us His representatives on this earth (2 Cor. 5:20). Just as one who gives life insurance is called an agent, God calls us agents of salvation. *"Your priests will be agents of salvation; may your loyal servants sing for joy"* (Psalm. 132:9 NLT).

✞ **POSITION OF GRACE:** (grace removes the veil; the Old Covenant is done away with)

"In fact, their minds were grown hard and calloused [they had become dull and had lost the power of understanding]; for until this present day, when the Old Testament (the old covenant) is being read, that same veil still lies [on their hearts], not being lifted [to reveal] that in Christ it is made void and done away.

Yes, down to this [very] day whenever Moses is read, a veil lies upon their minds and hearts.

But whenever a person turns [in repentance] to the Lord, the veil is stripped off and taken away" (2 Corinthians 3:14–16).

Grace opens our eyes to the Old Testament's testimony of Christ. Without grace, we cannot see Christ in the Old Testament. God's grace lifts the veil that hinders the knowledge of God where the Old Covenant requirements have been fulfilled for us in Christ.

An unregenerate mind and heart is covered with the thick callousness of unrighteousness. A hard heart is unteachable; it will not submit or listen to things spoken by the Spirit, and its power to understand has been desensitized. Only the grace of God can soften and renew such a heart and mind. The eyes of grace are not veiled; they see beyond flesh, and time. As they gaze at the glory of God, they change us into His very likeness from one degree of glory to another. This is the work of repentance — the grace of God operating in our life revealing the will of God and enabling us to grasp the power of forgiveness and grace.

Revelation only comes by repentance and reverence for the grace of God. The law of God has been written on our heart and the old Covenant has been completely fulfilled and done away with. We now serve God in the newness of the Spirit, not in the written letter of the law.

✞ **OPERATION OF GRACE:** (grace is changing us into His image)

"And all of us, as with unveiled face, [because we] continued to behold [in the Word of God] as in a mirror the glory of the Lord, are constantly being transfigured into His very own image in ever increasing splendour and from one degree of glory to another; [for this comes] from the Lord [Who is] the Spirit" (2 Corinthians 3:18).

The Grace of God that brings salvation has appeared to us; it has only given us an eternal inheritance and position in Christ, and it also operates in our life. It teaches us to deny ungodliness and worldly desires, and it trains us to live with a sound mind, temperately and discreetly beholding the glory of God, allowing it to transfigure us into His very own image — a truly glorious work of God. Our position in Christ has removed the veil, and now allows that same grace to operate continually on our saved souls. This is the work of the Spirit of God.

When we gaze through the eyes of grace, as in a mirror, the Word of God which is sharper than a two-edged sword, exposes our motives, our inward thoughts, and feelings; it then graciously transforms us into the image of our blessed Saviour. Grace operating in our life makes us not only a seer of the truth, but a transformed doer of the word of truth. It teaches us to renounce all worldly passions that are not of God, and to live upright, godly lives in this present world. Such a work of God is grounded in grace; it is not founded on the fancy of man's flesh. As we continue to behold the Word, He continues to work.

✞ **POSITION OF GRACE:** (our ministry of grace is not discouraging)

"Therefore, since we do hold and engage in this ministry by the mercy of God [granting us favour, benefits, opportunities, and especially salvation], we do not get discouraged (spiritless and despondent with fear) or become faint with weariness and exhaustion" (2 Corinthians 4:1).

Our ministry of grace to the world is a direct result of the gracious position that we have in Christ Jesus. Eternal grace does not get discouraged or become faint and weary with exhaustion. Our position of grace in Christ places us in a fearless fortress that is untouched by fatigue and powered by a forgiveness that dispels all fears. We are blessed with benefits, endowed with opportunities, and secured in our salvation. We are oppressed, but not forsaken; downtrodden, but not destroyed. Exhaustion and burnout is a work of the flesh, not a work of the Spirit of God.

✞ **OPERATION OF GRACE:** (grace calls us to renounce shameful ways; not to adulterate the Word of God; and to commend ourselves to every man's conscience)

"We have renounced disgraceful ways (secret thoughts, feelings, desires and underhandedness, the methods and arts that men hide through shame); we refuse to deal craftily (to practice trickery and cunning) or to adulterate or handle dishonestly the Word of God, but we state the truth openly (clearly and candidly). And so we commend ourselves in the sight and presence of God to every man's conscience" (2 Corinthians 4:2).

The grace of God operating in our life enables us to speak out in contradiction of ungodliness; it enables us to set forth and declare through our life and testimony, the righteousness of God in Christ. A life enabled by grace will forbid worldly desires to gain a foothold; it will cause us to give up deceit and to renounce all the ways of wickedness in our daily life. Such a work can only be enabled by the grace of God; it can never be a presentation of the power of our flesh, which when tested by enough time, is always doomed to failure.

Grace causes us to accept the word of God, rather than adulterate it. Adultery is a work of the flesh and when we try to accomplish the word of God in the power of the flesh, we adulterate the word of God. It is by the Spirit of God that we are enabled to present truth clearly and openly. Our lives are living epistles written by the grace of God, operating continuously in our souls. It is this gracious manifestation of truth that presents and introduces the presence of God to a hurting, graceless world. Grace adjures us to declare and live a life demonstrating that we can do nothing *against* the truth, but only *for* the truth (2 Cor. 13:8).

✞ **POSITION OF GRACE:** (the treasure of grace, in an earthen vessel, for the glory of God)

"However, we possess this precious treasure [the divine Light of the Gospel] in [frail, human] vessels of earth that the grandeur and exceeding greatness of the power may be shown to be from God and not from ourselves" (2 Corinthians 4:7).

Heavenly grace cannot be manufactured by an earthen vessel. At best, we merely possess and have the priceless privilege of containing this heavenly treasure. Unlike the world, it is not the vessel that keeps the contents; it is the contents that keep the vessel. It is the exceeding greatness and grandeur of God that flows through these frail vessels to a wanting world. Though we have it as our possession, in truth, it has apprehended us in its eternal grip.

We possess it in the sense of being joined by the bonds of blood or marriage. Our claim of ownership is merely a reflection of its ownership of us. We are vessels of grace because He first 'graced us' that we might be the grace of God toward one another.

✞ **OPERATION OF GRACE:** (grace does not discourage; it renews our inner being daily)

"Therefore we do not become discouraged (utterly spiritless, exhausted, and wearied out through fear). Though our outer man is [progressively] decaying and wasting away, yet our inner self is being [progressively] renewed day after day" (2 Corinthians 4:16).

Our position of grace is untouched by fear and fatigue. The operation of grace working on these frail vessels can make them weary if they look to themselves as their source of strength. The flesh is weak and is progressively wasting away, and it can be made fragile through fear. However, our inner man rejoices at the workings of grace in our life; we experience progressive renewal as gracious forgiveness dispels all our fears.

Our position in Christ is an eternal source of strength that encourages and feeds these fragile vessels. A jar glazed with grace and fired by trials is a vessel that truly reveals the glory of God. The outer man is mortal; the inner man is eternal.

✟ **OPERATION OF GRACE:** (grace makes us earnestly ambitious to please God)

"Therefore, whether we are at home [on earth away from Him] or away from home [and with Him], we are constantly ambitious and strive earnestly to be pleasing to Him" (2 Corinthians 5:9).

The grace of God purposefully compels us to strive to be pleasing to Him. There is nothing we can do to merit our salvation or please Him from our position of grace in Christ Jesus; yet, this same grace, operating in this vessel of clay, drives our life with purpose and endeavour. However, there will still be areas in our soul that refuse to respond to grace, where we end up substituting God's way with our own solutions. Our vessel (soul) needs to be continually renewed in order to properly respond to the righteousness (grace) that has been poured into it.

Any substitute for His grace only brings about fatigue, frustration and failure; it breeds and builds self-significance, self-reliance and self-righteousness. Such substitutes seek growth outside of the nurture of faith in Christ's righteousness. We end up seeking our own righteousness and often even religiously ask God to bless our fleshly affairs.

✟ **POSITION OF GRACE:** (grace declares and defines the essence of a new creation)

"Therefore if any person is [ingrafted] in Christ (the Messiah) he is a new creation (a new creature altogether); the old [previous moral and spiritual condition] has passed away. Behold, the fresh and new has come" (2 Corinthians 5:17)!

Upon the reception of God's grace, our life becomes reborn and redefined as a new creation. This work of God is only accomplished in Christ. The old moral and spiritual situation passes away. What is left is new — recently made. Renewing is not accomplished by human effort; it is only accomplished by faith and acceptance of the work done by the Lord Jesus Christ. Beloved, note, it is a new *creation* not an old thing that has been made over.

Being grafted into the Vine allows the life of Christ to flow into our life and bring forth new growth with it. The finished product is a work of God — a work of grace. When God declares that something is finished, it is finished. When God declares that something has come, it has come (Rev. 3:8). Our position of grace has come to us, and the work of this grace produces a new creation — a work achieved by the hand of God.

This new creature has new values and new morals. It required Christ's death and resurrection to bring this grace to us and it requires our old nature to pass away allowing the newness and freshness to become ours (Gal. 2:20–21). This is a work that has been accomplished by the Spirit, but it is also a work in progress as this same grace continually renews our soul and brings us into alignment with that perfect position, which we have in Christ. Repentance and faith are the only tools a person requires to allow God's handiwork to be accomplished.

✟ **POSITION OF GRACE:** (grace makes us ministers of reconciliation)

"It was God [personally present] in Christ, reconciling and restoring the world to favour with Himself, not counting up and holding against [men] their trespasses [but cancelling them], and committing to us the message of reconciliation (of the restoration to favour)" (2 Corinthians 5:19).

The Grace of God hanging on the cross for our sins has restored and reconciled us to God. This limitless grace of Christ has brought us to Himself. It is His limitless grace, which has commissioned us and committed us to the message of reconciliation — the message of the restoration of God's favour towards mankind.

The position of Jesus on the cross purchased our position of grace in heaven. The commission of Christ's grace authorizes our work of grace — the message of reconciliation.

There is no greater authority in heaven or earth that exists that can purchase our position in Christ. God's grace has commissioned us to be ministers of His message of grace. It is the grace of God that empowers and enables us to go into the whole world and make disciples, baptize, and teach them all the things that grace has taught us — that by grace all our sins have been forever cancelled.

✞ **POSITION / OPERATION OF GRACE:** (grace introduces us into the reality of possessing all things)

"As grieved and mourning, yet [we are] always rejoicing; as poor [ourselves, yet] bestowing riches, on many; as having nothing, and [yet in reality] possessing all things" (2 Corinthians 6:10).

The grace of God is our all sufficient joy; in it we possess the riches of God. The significance of what we have in the natural is nothing; yet because of the grace we have received in Christ, we are always rejoicing and bestowing riches on many — from our position of possessing all things.

Beloved, if we already possess all things in Christ, how much more do we need? A soul governed by the grace of God does not fix its affections on temporary things. When eyes are fixed on grace, all else becomes secondary.

A heart trusting in the grace of God will neither be ashamed nor abandoned. It receives God's best, not just a mere beggar's morsel. Even a scrap from God's table of grace is sufficient to feed a million. In contrast, a million gathered from the world's table still leaves a soul in want. When eyes do not focus on the grace of God, they miss the possession of God. There is nothing to be compared to it.

✞ **POSITION OF GRACE:** (grace fellowships with grace)

"Do not be unequally yoked with unbelievers [do not make mismated alliances with them or come under a different yoke with them, inconsistent with your faith]. For what partnership have right living and right standing with God with iniquity and lawlessness? Or how can light have fellowship with darkness" (2 Corinthians 6:14)?

In Christ, all believers are equal. Here the grace of God admonishes us to not attempt fellowship with one who is not an equal — an unbeliever. In Christ, our position of grace does not make one person better than another — it equalizes them. However, people who are unbelieving, and without trust in God, are found to be on a different foundation than a believer. Unbelievers have their foundation of life built on iniquity and lawlessness; they are in darkness. God's position of grace is a position of light. How can light commune with darkness? When we walk in the light, we have fellowship one with another and we experience a godly intimacy in the Spirit of Christ.

Fellowship is not a natural phenomenon; it is a spiritual operation. Darkness socializes with darkness, but light fellowships with light. Light cannot fellowship with darkness. Fellowship is a submission of spirit one to another in Christ — a spiritual intimacy. Truth does not bow its knee to a lie, nor does the Spirit bow its knee to the flesh. In truth, every knee must bow itself to Christ.

Our gracious position in Christ is the source of all fellowship that we have with one another. Fellowship is the fruit of grace operating in our lives towards one another. Grace fellowships with grace, not darkness. When a righteous soul attempts fellowship with darkness, it becomes like a muddied fountain or a polluted spring that yields, falls down and compromises its integrity (Prov. 25:26).

✞ **POSITION OF GRACE:** (grace dwells in God's people)

"What agreement [can there be between] a temple of God and idols? For we are the temple of the living God; even as God said, I will dwell in and with and among them and will walk in and with and among them, and I will be their God, and they shall be My people" (2 Corinthians 6:16).

God walks in, with, and among His people. How could God give approval or assent to working cooperatively with other gods? God does not even agree to disagree with the devil; there is no agreement whatsoever (Jude 1:8–9).

Truth exposes the lie; it does not agree to give it a foothold. God's grace has been poured into His temple and it leaves no room for other gods. The fear of the Lord is to hate evil, not make allowance for it, or even give it a right to exist in our life.

God's love and God's hatred are not contradictory; they define truth.

The grace of God will dwell in us for all eternity. This same grace operating in our life constantly influences our being and our works. We are now the temple of the living grace of God. We have become a nation made up of the same stock and language; the stock and language of grace. It is this grace poured into our lives that has made God our God. We are who we are because of God's grace. This position cannot be taken from us, neither can our efforts increase it; it originates *in* Him, and is forever kept *by* Him.

✞ **POSITION / OPERATION OF GRACE:** (grace separates, cleans, and treats with favour in Christ)

"So, come out from among [unbelievers], and separate (sever) yourselves from them, says the Lord, and touch not [any] unclean thing; then I will receive you kindly and treat you with favour," (2 Corinthians 6:17).

The grace of God calls us to come out. Our response is to leave or sever any influence that unbelievers have on our spiritual integrity. We depart by our own accord, but not by our own power; it is the grace of God that enables us to depart from the land of compromise. This same grace enables us to mark off the limits and boundaries of godliness that set us apart for God's purposes and righteousness.

In the midst of fellowship, the Holy Spirit allows us to touch truth. As truth fastens itself to us, it becomes an odour to those around us. Whatever adheres or clings to us is what we present to others as we touch their lives. A foul odour indicates the deportment of death or uncleanness. We are to be celibate towards death and intimate towards Life. Our position of cleanness calls us to operate in cleanness; it is the eternal condition of our life. The cleansing operation of God's grace in our life is the trademark of His ownership upon us. It always leaves the fragrance of Life, filling the air with every touch of His hand.

Grace is something that needs to be received. We receive our position of eternal life by receiving the grace of God. The operation of God's grace works in our life as we continue to receive and grow in God's grace. We are accepted by God when we receive His grace. We experience the hand of God taking our hand when we agree to put our hand in His. It is His grace that keeps us and is forever with us. This same grace works in us as we cease from our own working and allow Him to enable us.

✞ **POSITION OF GRACE:** (grace makes us sons and daughters)

"And I will be a Father to you, and you shall be My sons and daughters says the Lord Almighty" (2 Corinthians 6:18).

It is the grace of God that has made God our Father, and we, His sons and daughters. This is a work of God alone and our calling is merely to receive it. The Almighty has made us acceptable to God, and now as His children, we rejoice in God's peculiar care and protection so graciously poured out upon us. As sons and daughters we have acquired a position in the family of God, totally without any effort on our part. Behold what manner of grace the Father has bestowed upon us that we should be called the children of God — the children of His eternal grace (1 John 3:1).

✞ **POSITION / OPERATION OF GRACE:** (grace cleanses and consecrates us in the fear of God)

"Therefore, since these [great] promises are ours, beloved, let us cleanse ourselves from everything that contaminates and defiles body and spirit, and bring [our] consecration to completeness in the [reverential] fear of God" (2 Corinthians 7:1).

Having obtained the promises of God so freely given, grace begs a response to such a position. It calls us to cleanse ourselves from contaminates and to consecrate ourselves to completion, in the fear of God. We are called to respond to the operation of God's grace in our lives by letting it enable and empower us to cleanse ourselves from things that defile the body and spirit — all untruth and falsity (Prov. 3:1–4). Beloved, it is because we have these blessings that we can unreservedly resist the defilement of ungodliness with the authority of God's grace (James 4:6–8).

Filthiness of the flesh and the soul has no right to the temple of God. The same grace that has created the temple now works to cleanse and consecrate it. This is done only in the fear of God, not the fear of man. The fear of man tries to improve itself for its own selfish purposes. Cleansing done in the fear of God, and by the power of God, works out *His* purposes and plans. We are the vessels; we are not the scrub brushes. We are the branches, we are not the trimmers. By the grace of God, I am not the same vessel that I was when I first received the eternal cleansing touch of God's grace. His grace is changing me — moment by moment — into the person He wills me to be (2 Cor. 3:18).

✞ **POSITION / OPERATION OF GRACE:** (gracious grief works repentance)

"For even though I did grieve you with my letter, I do not regret [it now], though I did regret it; for I see that that letter did pain you, though only for a little while;

Yet I am glad now, not because you were pained, but because you were pained into repentance [that turned you to God]; for you felt a grief such as God meant you to feel, so that in nothing you might suffer loss through us or harm for what we did" (2 Corinthians 7:8–9).

The grace of God, operating through Paul, nurtured a soulful sadness and caused grief to the brethren at Corinth. They were thrown into sorrow by the grace of God. Paul at first did feel regret; yet he no longer regretted when he could see that it was a work of grace, designed only to bring godly sorrow with a divinely appointed purpose — repentance.

This pain, procured by grace, was but for a moment, but it wrought an eternal work in the hearts of its recipients. Paul was not glad about the fact that this gracious work had brought grief and pain, but rather that it had brought a change of mind that had worked the purpose of God into the hearts of its receivers. This gracious grief accomplished God's purpose and plan; it wrought life and reconciliation, not death and division.

The Holy Spirit, working the things of God into the believers' hearts by grace, prevented a loss that could only be seen through the eyes of grace. Pain is not the purpose of God, restoration/reconciliation is. The goal of grace is to keep us from being damaged, injured, or lost. Grace made the Corinthian believers feel a grief that God purposed them to feel. It turned them towards God, not away from Him. The fear of man drives us from God in arrogance; the fear of God draws us towards Him in repentance and humility.

✞ **POSITION / OPERATION OF GRACE:** (godly grief graciously brings life)

"For godly grief and the pain God is permitted to direct, produce a repentance that leads and contributes to salvation and deliverance from evil, and it never brings regret; but worldly grief (the hopeless sorrow that is characteristic of the pagan world) is deadly [breeding and ending in death]" (2 Corinthians 7:10).

Godly grief and righteous pain begotten by the grace of God, produces a repentance that is founded on faith and furthers our deliverance from evil. Salvation is the present eternal position of all Christians. This same grace that begets our salvation also delivers and preserves us from the consequences of being molested by evil. It does not carry with it the side effects of regret, but rather it brings with it the effects of righteous joy, freedom, and life.

Worldly grief leaves a soul in a state of hopelessness — a characteristic of worldly abandonment. Such grief leaves its victim in the stupor of death — a position enveloped in the depressing darkness of ignorance and sin. There can never be enough worldly grief to atone for sin; it always leaves deeper regret and demands more grief — a cycle of hopelessness, misery, and death.

Beloved, the grace of God operating in our life will germinate and bring to maturity the fruit of God in our life. Grace does all that is sufficient to bring forth godly results. Walking in the ways of the world feeds the flesh and produces works, which are contrary to the fruit of the Holy Spirit (Gal. 5:16–25).

It is only because of our position of grace that we experience the operation of grace in our life. Grace teachers the wise in heart to accept and obey the commands of the Lord. It teaches us to heed and receive instruction and correction, and in doing so it brings life both to the receiver and to those around them.

✞ **POSITION / OPERATION OF GRACE:** (godly sorrow is a work of the grace of God)

"For [you can look back now and] observe what this same godly sorrow has done for you and has produced in you; what eagerness and earnest care to explain and clear yourselves [of all complicity in the condoning of incest], what indignation [at the sin], what alarm, what yearning, what zeal [to do justice to all concerned], what readiness to mete out punishment [to the offender]! At every point you have proved yourselves cleared and guiltless in the matter" (2 Corinthians 7:11).

The gracious reality of godly sorrow produces earnestness in our life to accomplish, promote, and strive after the will of God. Grace enables us to give all diligence to the things of God. From our position in Christ, grace now teaches us, and the unction of the Spirit draws us upwards unto godliness. Grace compels us to clear ourselves of all complicity and the condoning of sin. It teaches us to renounce all ungodliness. Grace rings a righteous alarm when sin is sanctioned. Our souls yearn after the goodness and righteousness of God as we yield ourselves to the working of grace.

Grace produces zeal to do justice to all concerned. It creates a readiness within us to dispense godly discipline as we allow ourselves to be tools in the hand of the Sprit. Only correction done by the grace of God can bring about the working of God's will, and can reproduce the righteous character of God in one's life. The work of godly sorrow causes one to clear oneself before God, to be indignant towards evil and to yearn to do justice to all concerned. We become ready to embrace gracious orders to mete out punishment, enacted within the bounds of God's Spirit — His will. Self-righteousness is defined and powered by our own goodness and efforts; the righteous alarm of grace has nothing to do with self-righteousness.

Grace enables us to stand with one another in Christ — showing, proving, establishing, and exhibiting the will of God. Grace places no one outside of the church (outside of fellowship, yes, but not outside of the church). Godly inspired grief will only draw the church together and strengthen it. It introduces and positions Christ into each and every work of grace within His body. Grace calls us to be partners of righteousness, not partners with unrighteousness.

"Whoever is partner with a thief hates his own life; he falls under the curse [pronounced upon him who knows who the thief is] but discloses nothing" (Proverbs 29:24). Being an accomplice to the overlooking of sexual sin is a position that needs to be repented of. It takes the grace of God to see our position, and it takes this same grace to draw us out of it into His light. When it comes to sin, fence-sitting is never an option for a Christian.

✞ **POSITION / OPERATION OF GRACE:** (grace reveals God's caring love, working within the body of Christ)

"So although I did write to you [as I did], it was not for the sake and because of the one who did [the] wrong, nor on account of the one who suffered [the] wrong, but in order that you might realize before God [that your readiness to accept our authority revealed] how zealously you do care for us" (2 Corinthians 7:12).

The motivation and demonstration of a work of grace is always demonstrated with an attitude of 'care for one another'. Our Lord's earnestness and unction in accomplishing our salvation is the same passion that produces the promoting and striving after godliness in our own life. It is by the enabling power of the grace of God that we diligently care for and earnestly nurture the character of Christ in one another. Grace gives us an intimate acquaintance with God's zealous love for us, and it enables us to express it towards one another.

Acceptance of the authority of the grace of God working through others enables the power of God to conform us into the image of His dear Son — this is God's plan and purpose for His body. A work of God's grace is always a caring work that brings wholeness to the body of Christ. We need to be constantly reminded that God is love and that love should be both the motivation and the resultant fruit of any and all gracious correction.

✞ **POSITION / OPERATION OF GRACE:** (grace does not make us slaves living in the fear of man)

"For you endure it if a man assumes control of your souls and makes slaves of you, or devours [your substance, spends your money] and preys upon you, or deceives and takes advantage of you, or is arrogant and puts on airs, or strikes you in the face" (2 Corinthians 11:20).

God is not addressing some cult here; He is addressing the church of God which is at Corinth. God's authority, exercised through man, is never used to control others. The only control a Christian is called to be under is the control of the Holy Spirit. Worldly authority is hierarchical where one person or position is higher than another (Mk. 10:42; 2 Cor. 1:24; Gal. 2:6). God's authority frees us where we can chose the life of Christ and share what God is doing in our life with one another (John 7:17–18; 1 Cor. 14:26); it makes us slaves of Christ, not man (Rom. 6:18, 22).

Man-ordained authority controls men through prophets and programs and men who like to take the lead — to assume control (Jer. 5:30-31; 3 John 1:9–10). When we see authority as being in a position, we blindly follow the person in that position rather than being responsible to discern for ourselves whether something is from God or not (John 7:17–18).

God's control works through the Holy Spirit and it is our responsibility to discern and test the spirits to see if they are of God (Acts 5:4–10; 1 John 4:1). Christians are never required to submit to something they do not believe to be of God (John 5:30; 7:17). This is a good thing; otherwise man would have control of the church instead of God.

Positions of man are not important to God (Gal. 2:6). The statement, "You should do this because I am a church leader!" is a carnal statement; it is not from the Spirit of God. Such an attitude is assuming control of your soul. It assumes that one person's hearing from God is divinely designed to direct your affairs. Beloved, we are called upon to warn, encourage, and correct one another, but never to control others. Having begun our new life in Christ by surrendering the control of ourselves over to the Holy Spirit, how can we now reach perfection by coming under man's control again? This is a silly and thoughtless attitude.

Such control, because it is founded in the flesh, not the Spirit, will enslave your soul devouring your significance in Christ. It will also demand a percentage of your resources to maintain itself. If this control is questioned there will be a quick response of slapping you in the face with guilt. This fleshly control is fuelled by pride not the Spirit of God. Such pride preys on unsuspecting souls, enslaving them, and demanding loyalty to men and institutions. Up-man-ship is often camouflaged by religious declarations that noncompliance to the system means you are backslidden, or even are a wolf in sheep's clothing, etc., etc.

When pride powers the actions of men, it finds its authority in the self-perpetuated world of seeing others as less than they are, and seeing themselves as greater than others. Such pride can even prey on saints in the church (1 Cor. 5:1–2; 2 John 1:10). God hates pride; He judges it (Job 40:11–12; Prov. 8:13; 21:4; 1 John 2:16).

The world and its ways operate on the authority of man and man's pride; the kingdom of God operates in the authority of the Lord Jesus Christ and humility. The Greek word 'exousia' translated 'authority' means 'freedom of choice', not power or control over someone. An ear listening to the Spirit of God can never blame someone else for deceiving them. We are responsible for our own salvation and our walk with the Lord (John 7:17; James 1:14).

A prideful man wrestles against flesh and blood threatening to strike others in the face (Matt. 26:67–68; 27:30). Passing out guilt and making demands for selfish purposes is a spiritual slap in the face; it is not rooted in love. On the contrary, the man of God should aim at and pursue righteousness (1 Tim. 6:11–14).

Grace equips the man of God to manifest truth in love (2 Tim. 3:16–17). It is a blessing to be struck lovingly in the face by grace; there is no motivation of pride in such a blow "*Let the righteous man smite and correct me — it is a kindness. Oil so choice let not my head refuse or discourage; for even in their evils or calamities shall my prayer continue*" (Psalms 141:5).

✝ **POSITION / OPERATION OF GRACE:** (grace causes us to pour ourselves out for one another)

"*But I will most gladly spend [myself] and be utterly spent for your souls. If I love you exceedingly, am I to be loved [by you] the less*" (2 Corinthians 12:15)?

Being spent for one another is the expected economy of the kingdom of God. The joy of being spent can only be accomplished by the inspiration of grace working through our life. The state of another soul is of paramount importance and concern for a Christian, and such love is only manifested under the influence of the grace of God.

Just as grace is not always received, love is not always received. Only a fool wags his head and believes that Jesus and His followers are losers (Matt. 27:39–44; John 19:15–18). Lord, help us repent of any such attitude in our own life.

✝ **POSITION / OPERATION OF GRACE:** (gracious correction confronts sin within the body of Christ)

"*I have already warned those who sinned formerly and all the rest also, and I warn them now again while I am absent, as I did when present on my second visit, that if I come back, I will not spare [them],*" (2 Corinthians 13:2).

The grace of God does not cease from warning and admonishing us to depart from sinful activities after we are saved and sanctified by the blood of the Lamb on the cross. It is the grace of God that warned us about the outcome of sin with respect to eternal life. This warning introduced us to the saving grace of God when we first believed. It is this same grace that continues to warn us to abstain from sinful activities as we mature and grow in Christ.

Grace produces an overpowering hunger and thirst in our souls, which desires the best for the body of Christ. It is not motivated by revenge or pride; but rather is founded on love — the jealous love that God has for his people. Grace hates evil; it never hates people — it loves them unto repentance.

Christ always upholds His standard of righteousness. He brings gracious correction to us causing us to judge ourselves and confront our sin (John 8:1–11; 9:1–41). If received, the outcome of this correction will lead to repentance, resulting in a changed life. However, grace at times reaches a point where it becomes determined not to spare, but to use its power to punish. Oh, the blessing of God's gracious punishment (Ps. 141:5; James 5:19–20).

Galatians

✞ **POSITION OF GRACE:** (grace rescues and delivers us according to God's will)

"Who gave (yielded) Himself up [to atone] for our sins [and to save and sanctify us], in order to rescue and deliver us from this present wicked age and world order, in accordance with the will and purpose and plan of our God and Father —" (Galatians 1:4).

It is God alone who delivered Himself up and gave Himself over to death on the cross. God instituted and carried out the entire work of salvation; it has nothing to do with our own prowess or purity. He plucked us out of the hand of Satan; He chose us, rescued us, and delivered us from the grip of sin. He delivered us from this present evil world, according to His will. This incredible plan and purpose was not championed by the power of man, but rather the will of God.

Our position of grace in Christ is totally a work of God; it happened even before we were born. We have been drawn and rooted out of this present wicked age and world order. We are now stationed in an order of godliness and righteousness in Christ Jesus. The same grace that drew us out is the same grace that works and operates in our life, enabling God's order to function within us here in this present time (Eph. 2:1–5).

For God to turn His back on us when we are in His grace would be for God to turn His back on Himself. Though we are ungracious, yet He remains gracious — for He cannot deny Himself. If God be for us who can be against us? God has placed His Spirit in us as a guarantee of His eternal grace in our life. When we are delivered, we are given over into God's power for His use. His grace is now able to keep, use, take care of, and manage our life according to His designs and purposes.

✞ **POSITION OF GRACE:** (when grace is recognized it finds fellowship and understanding)

"And when they knew (perceived, recognized, understood, and acknowledged) the grace (God's unmerited favour and spiritual blessing) that had been bestowed upon me, James and Cephas (Peter) and John, who were reputed to be pillars of the Jerusalem church, gave to me and Barnabas the right hand of fellowship, with the understanding that we should go to the Gentiles and they to the circumcised (Jews)" (Galatians 2:9).

Our position of grace in Christ authorizes, equips, and commissions us to do God's work. When we see God's grace working in and through a person's life, we will always find fellowship with God's people of grace. It is not a charisma that is founded in the flesh and brings glory to the flesh; it is a spiritual anointing that is personified in truth and gives God glory. Grace is an enablement of God, not an empowerment by man. Grace commissions us with His calling and then equips and enables us to complete it. Any true work or ministry in our life has only come about because of the position of grace, which we have received in Christ Jesus, our Lord.

✞ **OPERATION OF GRACE:** (Paul rebuked Peter who stood condemned in grace)

"But when Cephas (Peter) came to Antioch, I protested and opposed him to his face [concerning his conduct there], for he was blameable and stood condemned" (Galatians 2:11).

The grace of God blamed and condemned Peter for attempting to go back under the law for justification. Peter was blameable. Our position of grace does not eradicate all blame in our life. It is imperative to note that Peter's salvation was not on the line here, but his conduct was not becoming of grace, and hence, it needed to be reproved. The grace of God enabled Paul to oppose and protest against Peter's conduct. Peter stood blamed, accused, and condemned for his actions even though he was under God's grace. Our position of grace that we have obtained in Christ causes its operation to correct, admonish, and draw us closer into His presence. Grace does not call us to live a life contrary to the Gospel (Truth) of grace; it calls us to a life of blameless conduct.

✝ **POSITION OF GRACE:** (we are justified by grace, not law)

"[Therefore, I do not treat God's gracious gift as something of minor importance and defeat its very purpose]; I do not set aside and invalidate and frustrate and nullify the grace (unmerited favour) *of God. For if justification* (righteousness, acquittal from guilt) *comes through [observing the ritual of] the Law, then Christ* (the Messiah) *died groundlessly and to no purpose and in vain. [His death was then wholly superfluous.]"* (Galatians 2:21).

The grace of God is not to be set aside or invalidated. Justification by works nullifies the grace of God. It is not our actions that make us upright with God; it is only the action of Christ Jesus that has eternally justified us. The foundation of our entire life rests upon the fact that we have obtained grace in Christ Jesus. This grace of God is divinely purposed and we are not allowed to nullify it by self-righteous justification. If the Law can justify anyone before God, then Christ died for nothing and we would still be in our sin — a wretched place.

To treat the very purpose of Christ's death on the cross as being vain is to turn our back on God's provision. We revile Him and reproach Him abusively when we tell Him, "...*Descend now from the cross that we may see and believe...*" (Mark 15:32b KJV). Beloved, He saved us by *not* saving Himself — a kingdom principle. We need not attempt to save ourselves by adding to a salvation furnished so costly and graciously. It is arrogant, egotistic, and abortive to the grace of God to believe that our own works merit us receiving anything from His hand. How can we possibly add anything to divinely designed, eternal favour? The only work of man we will see in heaven is the scars on our Saviour's body.

✝ **POSITION OF GRACE:** (we love by faith)

"Now it is evident that no person is justified (declared righteous and brought into right standing with God) through the Law, for the Scripture says, The man in right standing with God [the just, the righteous] shall live by and out of faith and he who through and by faith is declared righteous and in right standing with God shall live.

But the Law does not rest on faith [does not require faith, has nothing to do with faith], for it itself says, He who does them [the things prescribed by the Law] shall live by them [not by faith].

Christ purchased our freedom [redeeming us] from the curse (doom) of the Law [and its condemnation] by [Himself] becoming a curse for us, for it is written [in Scriptures], Cursed is everyone who hangs on a tree (is crucified);" (Galatians 3:11–13).

A man is justified by faith apart from any works of the law. Our boasting in Christ is not founded upon the principle of our works, but rather on the principle of faith in Him. It was necessary for Christ to fulfil the Law (as the perfect sacrifice) that we might be declared righteous. The foundation of the grace of God in our life has not been imputed to us as a result of our obedience to the Law of God. The Law always demands more works, whereas grace is free. If adherents to the law are justified before God, then faith is nullified and salvation by grace is without meaning — Christ would have died in vain and He would not be Lord of lords!

We know that a man is not justified by works of the law but only through faith in Christ Jesus. Belief in Christ is an operation of faith; faith supersedes the principle of law. Our life is sustained by this faith, not by the law. Our position of grace, obtained by faith in Christ Jesus, now exercises a vital power upon our soul. This strong, living conviction and belief in Jesus Christ is the only salvation afforded to mankind by God. Grace and its operation is the only foundation of salvation and purpose for our life, because, *"For in Him we live, and move, and have our being..."* (Acts 17:28a KJV).

The price Christ paid for us redeemed and recovered us from the dominion of the Law. This has nothing to do with any effort or striving on our part. We were under the damning curse pronounced upon all sin by the Law of God. The purpose of Christ was for Him to be made sin for us; the purpose of man is to receive and live in that grace. The purpose of the Law is to point out our own unrighteousness (sin) in order that we can receive His righteousness — purely by the grace of God. The fulfilling of righteousness is only found in the resting position of Christ on the cross. Faith in Christ fulfils all the righteous requirements of God. He died on behalf of, and for the sake of me, and there is nothing I can do to add to His sacrifice. Self-righteousness has no place in God's providential righteousness.

Law has nothing to do with faith and those who live by it do not require faith. Hence, religious laws that abound within the church cause many to follow them, even without needing the saving knowledge of Christ by faith (Col. 2:6–8). Such church laws and traditions creep into a person's heart and either prevent or stifle the operation of faith required for Christian life to flourish (Mk. 7:13; Rom. 4:14; 1 Tim. 4:7; 6:10–11; 2 Tim. 3:5). Such laws create self-righteousness

✞ **POSITION / OPERATION OF GRACE:** (the yoke of grace calls us to love)

"For you, brethren, were [indeed] called to freedom; only [do not let your] freedom be an incentive to your flesh and an opportunity or excuse [for selfishness], but through love you should serve one another.

For the whole Law [concerning human relationships] is complied with in the one precept, You shall love your neighbour as [you do] yourself" (Galatians 5:13–14).

The call to freedom is the mark of grace. Our authority in Christ bestows upon us liberty to choose our way of life. True liberty is only experienced when we live as we should, not as our evil desires dictate. In Christ, we are forever freeborn, unrestrained, and liberated from the yoke of justification by works of the Law.

The grace of God is not a license for sin, neither does grace redefine sin. Any activity that God has defined as sin was wrong before we knew Christ and is still wrong after we know Christ. The difference Christ makes is that we no longer are condemned to eternal death because of our sin. The freedom that we have in Christ is not freedom to continue in sin but rather freedom to deny sin its foothold in our life. We have been called to liberty and this liberty is not to be used as an opportunity for our flesh; but rather, through love, we are called to serve one another. The law of God does not impute or empower us with righteousness, but it does define righteous actions and attitudes. Love is defined as the fulfilling of the law and when we are acting in love, we will not find ourselves violating God's commands (Matt. 22:37–40; Rom. 3:21).

Grace calls us to the authority of God and its freedom. Our liberty cries out, "Father, not my will, but Yours be done." Liberty is defined as living as we should, not as we please. Desires birthed in Christ are not fleshy desires; they are desires that hunger and thirst after righteousness. Grace gives us license to do as Christ pleases, not as our flesh demands. Grace teaches us to omit things that have no relationship with righteousness and our new bond servant life in Christ Jesus.

We have been made free and exempt from the obligation of obedience to the Law for our justification. We are no longer a slave to that which held us (the Law); we are emancipated and unrestrained — yet slaves of the Living God. Our obligation to serve God now is seen as a reasonable service of worship — fulfilling the requirements of God. Grace enables us to deny ungodliness — both its actions and its attitudes (Rom. 12:1).

Freedom is *only* found in Christ. We experience the yoke of grace on our life because of the love of God leading us and teaching us. Just as a father holding his little son's hand as they cross a busy street, Christ's grace leads and guides us through the distractions of the world around us (Heb. 12:1; 2 Peter 2:20). Grace has placed our hand in the Father's hand and we now follow His will not because we are a 'good little boy', but rather because He is our good Father, teaching and showing us the boundaries of freedom. We follow because of His love, not because of our goodness. Our restraint or yoke in Christ Jesus is a consequence of His love. When we are walking in love, we are not breaking any of His laws; we fulfil them just as Christ did and still does today.

Authority from God gives us freedom of choice, and when we choose to operate in the will of the Father, we always find ourselves positioned in His absolute freedom. Authority founded in the world places people under another person's power where rulers lord it over them (Matt. 20:25). Pilate thought that he had power and authority over Jesus. Jesus explained to him that he would have no power over Him if God had not given it to him from above (John 19:11). Our authority in Christ gives us freedom from the control of man.

✞ **OPERATION OF GRACE:** (grace reveals the conflict of the flesh and the Spirit)

"But I say, walk and live [habitually] in the [Holy] Spirit [responsive to and controlled and guided by the Spirit]; then you will certainly not gratify the cravings and desires of the flesh (of human nature without God).

For the desires of the flesh are opposed to the [Holy] Spirit, and the [desires of the] Spirit are opposed to the flesh (godless human nature); for these are antagonistic to each other [continually withstanding and in conflict with each other], so that you are not free but are prevented from doing what you desire to do" (Galatians 5:16–17).

Grace commands us to live habitually in response to the Holy Spirit. The Spirit, which is Holy, will never lead us to walk in ways that are unholy and ungodly — things that gratify the cravings and desires of the flesh, things that disobey God's righteous commands. Christ did not fulfil the law to enable us to fulfil the works of the flesh. The grace of God has made us the righteousness of God in Christ.

Because of our position in Christ, we are enabled by the grace of God to be controlled by something that is holy, not fleshy. Our life is now regulated by holiness. We now conduct our life in an enablement that is sourced from the hand of God Himself. Christ has forever satisfied the justice of God by dying for our sins. Our disobedience never needs to be eternally punished again — that would violate God's principle of justice. Our sins have been paid for by God Himself and need not be paid for again by our efforts, works, or goodness.

The Holy Spirit commands us not to 'fulfil the lust of the flesh'. If you set your affections on the things of the flesh, the Holy Spirit is there to oppose you. If you wish to live according to the Spirit, our flesh will always be there to create conflict. Beloved, the issue is choice, not strength. The strength of the Spirit versus the strength of human flesh need not be debated. I have been crucified with Christ; it is no longer I living through this soul, but Christ who is living in me. My life is now habitually lived by faith in Christ Jesus, Who in the likeness of sinful flesh, condemned sin in the flesh (Rom. 8:3). Grace declares that when we suffer in the flesh, we have ceased from sin. Grace is not a fleshy celebration; it is a spiritual declaration of holy dedication. Grace calls us to be holy as He is holy (1 Peter 1:15–16; 4:1).

Outside of Christ, one does not comprehend the conflict between the Spirit and the desires of the flesh. We sense a battle and the symptoms of sin, often not knowing what we are stumbling over (Prov. 4:19).

In Christ, the grace of God discloses this conflict to us and enables us to do spiritual battle, *"For we wrestle not against flesh and blood but against principalities, against powers, against the rulers of the darkness of this world, against spiritual wickedness in high places"* (Ephesians 6:12). A victorious walk is a walk in obedience to the Spirit of grace. As we allow His Spirit to work in our life, it renews our soul and imparts new attitudes and actions into our being allowing our life to manifest His grace.

✞ **POSITION OF GRACE:** (God's all sufficient grace enables us to be led by the Spirit)

"But if you are guided (led) by the [Holy] Spirit, you are not subject to the Law" (Galatians 5:18).

The grace of God leads us by accompanying us. It attaches itself to us as an indwelling attendant, compelling us, and influencing our soul. We become subject to its leading — subject to the Spirit rather than the letter of the Law (John 6:63; 2 Cor. 3:6). It is the grace of God leading us by the Spirit of God that makes us approved of God — righteous.

It is not observance of the Law that brings approval because without faith it is impossible to please God. It is the seal of the Holy Spirit that marks us as divinely approved. We are citizens of the kingdom of God, not subjects of the kingdom of darkness. 'If we are led' is a condition of choice relegated to the soul of man. The enabling power of grace covers our insufficiencies as our soul finds its sufficiency in the work of Christ on the cross. This sufficiency is totally and eternally capable of covering all our inadequacies.

✝ **<u>OPERATION OF GRACE</u>:** (grace reveals the fruits of the flesh)

"Now the doings (practices) of the <u>flesh</u> are clear (obvious): they are immorality, impurity, indecency,

Idolatry, sorcery, enmity, strife, jealousy, anger (ill temper), selfishness, divisions (dissensions), party spirit (<u>factions</u>, sects with peculiar opinions, heresies),

Envy, drunkenness, carousing, and the like. I <u>warn</u> you beforehand, just as I did previously, that those who do such things shall not <u>inherit</u> the <u>kingdom of God</u>" (Galatians 5:19–21).

The works of the flesh are not difficult to identify. Outside of the grace of God, one does not even know what ungodliness is. The nature of man without God is fleshy, sensuous, and subject to cravings that incite sin. These fleshly works are spiritually discerned because they are in opposition to the Spirit of God.

As we walk in the Spirit of grace, we are enabled to uncover and identify the practices of the flesh. The grace of God teaches us to deny and depart from such works and it affirms that if we do not do so, we will not participate in the kingdom of God. We cannot be partakers of the kingdom of the flesh and the kingdom of God simultaneously. Grace working in our life calls us to come out from such activities and attitudes.

Note that factions and divisions in the body of Christ are a work of the flesh, not the Spirit. Such works will not be profitable in the kingdom of God. Any work founded on the flesh may look large, religious, and pious but will lack the true power of Christ working in its midst (Matt. 13:58). If we do not follow the way God asks, we end up living out our own desires unto desolation and destruction (Prov. 1:29–32).

✝ **<u>POSITION OF GRACE</u>:** (grace has crucified our flesh)

"And those who belong to Christ Jesus (the Messiah) have <u>crucified</u> the <u>flesh</u> (the godless human nature) with its passions and appetites and desires" (Galatians 5:24).

The grace of God has placed us in the position where our flesh has been crucified. Our godless human nature has been deprived of its reigning power. This has been accomplished not by our own strength, but by the enablement of the grace of Christ, through the power of the Holy Spirit. By our own strength (the strength of our flesh), we are not even able to grapple with one corruption. It is not our life that we now live, but rather it is the life of Christ and His resurrected power that lives and operates through us by the grace of God.

Depraved, vile, passionate deeds are powered by the desires of the flesh. The affections of our mind, our will, and our emotions have been delivered from the dominion of darkness. We have been transferred into the kingdom of the Son through the work of Jesus Christ, not through our own efforts. From our position of grace, we belong to the Spirit of God, not godless human, carnal appetites; the operation of grace works this truth into our soul on a day to day basis.

Either we covet after the Spirit or we submit ourselves to the cravings, longings, and desires of the flesh — that which is at enmity to the Spirit of God. It was necessary for Jesus to come in the likeness of flesh that God could accomplish the work required in our flesh.

"For God has done what the <u>Law</u> could not do, [its power] being <u>weakened</u> by the <u>flesh</u> [the entire nature of man without the Holy Spirit]. Sending His own Son in the guise of sinful flesh and as an offering for sin, [God] <u>condemned</u> <u>sin</u> in the <u>flesh</u>

[subdued, overcame, deprived it of its power over all who accept that sacrifice]," (Romans 8:3).

We have begun our new life spiritually by the power of God's grace working in our life. We now need to let this same grace enable us to continue living in grace and not in dependence upon the strength and wisdom of our own flesh.

Our nature without the Holy Spirit is not able to obey God. The flesh with its inherent disobedience to God — begotten in the Garden of Eden — was not, is not, and never will be able to obey God. The power of the flesh needed to be crucified and supplanted by the power of the Holy Spirit. Our inborn nature needed to die and our life needed to be re-born. The life we now live is powered by faith in the work of grace, which God has accomplished for us. It now bears fruit of the Spirit, not fruit of the flesh (Rom. 8:6–9; Gal. 6:8).

✝ **POSITION / OPERATION OF GRACE:** (grace first calls us then commands us to walk by the Spirit of grace)

"If we live by the [Holy] Spirit, let us also walk by the Spirit. [If by the Holy Spirit we have our life in God, let us go forward walking in line, our conduct controlled by the Spirit.]

Let us not become vainglorious and self-conceited, competitive and challenging and provoking and irritating to one another, envying and being jealous of one another" (Galatians 5:25–26).

Disciples of Christ should be living by the power of the Holy Spirit. This is true for every believer who has been positioned in Christ. Grace admonishes us that since we now have our very existence or being in the Spirit of God, let us then let our life be controlled by this same Spirit. Our very breath of life is graciously given to us by God Himself. Let us therefore now go forward with our walk accompanied by conduct that is controlled by this same Spirit of life.

Eyes that are fixed on grace cannot succumb to self-conceit. Gracious eyes do not precipitate provocation or radiate irritation. Eyes fixed on flesh incubate envy and jealousy. The grace working in and through one another is not led astray by outward things, but rather it fixes its focus on eternal, unseen things. Such grace is always a benefit to others and a corresponding blessing to us as well.

✝ **OPERATION OF GRACE:** (grace restores and reinstates offenders to God and godliness)

"Brethren, if any person is overtaken in misconduct or sin of any sort, you who are spiritual [who are responsive to and controlled by the Spirit] should set him right and restore and reinstate him, without any sense of superiority and with all gentleness, keeping an attentive eye on yourself, lest you should be tempted also" (Galatians 6:1).

When the divine standard between good and evil — the law of God — is overstepped, the grace of God is required to restore and set right. Grace reinstates a lost soul back to its Creator, and positions it on the path of righteousness. There is no 'holier-than-thou' attitude allowed in the grace of God. A work of grace cannot be proud; it can only be humbly subservient to its newly acquired position. Pride comes before a fall; grace walks in humility. It is grace and grace alone that can restore a person to uprightness. A gracious eye judges itself and sees itself as a servant, not a superior. Superiority causes stumbling, like the blind leading the blind; grace lifts the humble and brings sight to blind eyes (John 9:39–41).

In Galatians 6:1, 'any person' makes it clear that there is no person exempt from falling into sin. For the unsaved, grace is needed to bring the assurance of God's eternal love. For the saved, grace is needed to teach and train tarnished souls, nurturing and bringing them to spiritual maturity. We all need faith in God's grace to meet the divine standard of righteousness. As God's holy people, we need to be wary of our self-will dabbling into the realm of divine authority. Grace is only apprehended when we are in submission to God, not when we are being a helping hand or an assistant to the Divine. God is not my co-pilot; He is my pilot and my flight plan. Pride and arrogance are not found in gracious submission to God.

✞ **OPERATION OF GRACE:** (grace fulfils the law of Christ)

"Bear (endure, carry) one another's burdens and troublesome moral faults, and in this way fulfil and observe perfectly the law of Christ (the Messiah) and complete what is lacking [in your obedience to it]" (Galatians 6:2).

The grace of God commands us to carry and sustain one another by upholding each other at all times. Christians are both perfect (position in Christ), and they are being made perfect (the operation of grace in our life). When we support one another, it does not mean that we condone or participate in one another's sin. To love one another, even in the midst of troublesome moral faults, is what fulfils the law of Christ. Grace helps us to enable a brother to stand; it never enables sin.

A support adds strength to a structure. Gracious support strengthens, encourages, and helps hold a brother up; it does not augment ungodliness. Discipline and the removing of ungodliness in the body's midst can only add strength to the body as a whole. Troublesome moral faults can only be handled by the grace of God working through us and applying it to another's lives. It requires the law of loving one another to manifest the grace of God. Loving one another is not an option; it is a commandment of God (John 13:34–35).

Grace calls us to carry and bear one another's heaviness and troubles. We are to rejoice with those who rejoice and we are to weep with those who weep. We are not to be found lacking in obedience to the law of grace (Christ). The law of grace brings life (Rom. 8:2), and redemption (1 Cor. 9:21), not neglect and abuse. To live in grace and to hold out the word of grace to others that they may appropriate it, is our calling in Christ (Phil. 2:16).

✞ **OPERATION OF GRACE:** (grace gives us eyes to see deception)

"Do not be deceived and deluded and misled; God will not allow Himself to be sneered at (scorned, disdained, or mocked by mere pretensions or professions, or by His precepts being set aside), [He inevitably deludes himself who attempts to delude God.] For whatever a man sows that and that only is what he will reap" (Galatians 6:7).

The grace of God warns believers not to be misled or deceived. Delusion — a fixed belief maintained in spite of presented truth — is the device of the devil. It does not allow the word of God to make progress in our life, and it does not allow it entrance or find any place in our life (John 8:36–38, 43–45).

Revelation is God disclosing Himself in truth, having the eyes of our heart flooded with light (John 3:19–21; Acts 26:18). This is the work of the Spirit of God. It is only within the boundaries of the grace of God that we can see as God sees. Pretensions, professions, and the setting aside of God's precepts draw us away from the right path. Though still in our position of grace in God, straying causes us to wander from the way of virtue and entangles us in sin. Grace never causes us to mock God's precepts or act pretentiously. The god-of-self distains the ways of God; it always ends up deluding itself in the end.

Beloved, the Omniscient and Omnipotent cannot be ridiculed or humiliated. Anyone who attempts to set aside truth will find himself operating outside of truth, and deluded (Gen. 4:9). God's precepts and principles are not set aside by grace; they are fulfilled by grace. The seed that we scatter is the seed that we shall harvest. Seeds sown by grace are seeds sown to the Spirit, not the flesh. Through the Spirit we glean life; through the flesh we reap corruption and death.

✞ **OPERATION OF GRACE:** (grace enables us to sow to the Spirit)

"For he who sows to his own flesh (lower nature, sensuality) will from the flesh reap decay and ruin and destruction, but he who sows to the Spirit will from the Spirit reap eternal life.

And let us not lose heart and grow weary and faint in acting nobly and doing right, for in due time and at the appointed season we shall reap, if we do not loosen and relax our courage and faint" (Galatians 6:8–9).

Seeds planted by the flesh will yield decay, ruin and destruction. Seeds planted by the Spirit produce life in the will of the Father. Even the word of God when sown by the flesh (for personal gain) will not produce life in the Spirit (Matt. 4:6; 2 Peter 3:15–16). The letter kills but the Spirit gives life. Things of the flesh affect the flesh. When we sow in sensuality, we reap fleshy returns. Grace teaches us to deny the flesh and sow in the Spirit. It enables us to walk and live in the Spirit — both now and forevermore. The flesh is subject to corruption and moral decay. Grace is not corruptible and it does not tempt us to do evil (James 1:13).

Grace commands us not to be wearied out, exhausted, or found spiritless. We are always to be busy about our Father's business, actively working the works that are approved by God and honouring Him. When we receive the grace of God, we come to know the incredible honour that God has bestowed upon us. This same grace now manifests godly honour to others as it operates through us.

Grace calls us to reasonable service and worship to God. It enables us to do right and keeps us from being despondent and faint hearted. Its source is resurrection power, not reconstituted human effort. The strength of flesh, which perishes with time, is subject to corruption and will never stand in glory before God. The spirit is willing and the flesh is weak, but grace brings courage and strength to us in our weakness.

✝ **OPERATION OF GRACE:** (grace opens eyes of opportunity to exercise goodness to others)

"So then, as occasion and opportunity open up to us, let us do good [morally] to all people [not only being useful or profitable to them, but also doing what is for their spiritual good and advantage]. Be mindful to be a blessing, especially to those of the household of faith [those who belong to God's family with you, the believers]" (Galatians 6:10).

Grace gives us eyes that see opportunity. As we see the signs of the times, *our* time becomes God's time. We are often graciously blown into the presence of a sin-weary soul caught in a storm of crisis and decision. We become the bearers of that which is spiritually good and advantageous to those around us. We are used by God for the profit of others — vessels of clay holding out blessings to a weary world. Our cargo of grace is to be freely lavished upon all people. Note that grace that is not received is never lost. Beloved, we cannot run out of God's provision; it is endless and eternal.

✝ **POSITION OF GRACE:** (grace exposes carnality, it does not nurture it)

"Those who want to make a good impression and a fine show in the flesh would try to compel you to receive circumcision, simply so that they may escape being persecuted for allegiance to the cross of Christ (the Messiah, the Anointed One)" (Galatians 6:12).

Good impressions and fine shows are founded in the flesh. The carnal eye compels the head to turn toward works that fulfil selfish desires. This is what gives false religion its incentive; religious ceremony driven by the flesh, which does not need to have its dependence upon God.

The eyes of grace turn not from the persecuted path of God's righteousness; they are fixed on Jesus, the Leader and Source of our faith, and He is also the Finisher, bringing our faith to maturity and perfection (Heb. 12:2). Grace is found only by faith, and operates when we are willing to bear the cross of Christ, walking in His steps. The mind of Christ is resolved and purposed to please the Spirit. It takes pleasure and delights in the things of God, not in things of the flesh. It rejoices when right and truth prevail (1 Cor. 13:6).

The compulsion for worldly things is a sign of carnality (1 John 2:15–17). Many of the things we see and participate in to support the 'status quo' of what is often called 'church life' are in reality, just a fine show of the flesh. A head turned by the eye of fleshy circumcision (an outward show of godliness) cannot see the things of spiritual circumcision. This same verse (Gal. 6:12) could be restated with any activity that demands obedience to law, for example, 'offering sacrifices, paying tithes, being in church every Sunday', etc.

Approaching God through the flesh never produces the fruit of the Spirit; it attempts to avoid the persecution encountered by a soul that is 100% dead to itself and 100% alive to Christ. The works of the flesh will never help us accomplish the Great Commission (Matt. 28:18–20).

Carnality is not a seed to be planted in the flower bed of grace. Our new birth in Christ was graciously given to us so that we would be a sample of what He was created to be. Grace equips us to be a reflection of Him. We have been circumcised by the Spirit of God and our new life is a spiritual life, hidden with Christ in God.

The natural eye does not see the oneness that we are in Christ. This oneness is divinely designed to present truth to the world. Our new nature now endorses and delights in things of the Spirit, not things carnal (Ps. 1:2; Rom. 7:22). Eyes looking down from the cross of Christ are eyes that see through the glass of eternity — though darkly — and are not fixed on the glory of temporary earthly things like new buildings and programs (1 Cor. 13:12; James 1:22–25). Gracious eyes are little affected by the world with its luring and compelling charms; they seek first the kingdom of God.

Ephesians

✞ **POSITION OF GRACE:** (grace reveals sainthood)

"Paul, an apostle (special messenger) of Christ Jesus (the Messiah), by the divine will (the purpose and the choice of God) to the saints (the consecrated, set-apart ones) at Ephesus who are also faithful and loyal and steadfast in Christ Jesus:" (Ephesians 1:1).

The divine will of the Almighty is opened up for us like a gift by the gracious hand of God. The will of the Omnipotent and what He has determined, defines the path set before us and where we should tread (Prov. 16:9; 20:24). When the Omniscient makes a choice, it reveals His desire and pleasure, and should be received with utmost reverence and sincerity on our part. Just as Paul was chosen by divine will, the Lord's will and purpose for our life is revealed to us through the personage of Jesus Christ.

Only God can determine and define what is set apart and holy. Holiness is not a fabrication of human hands; it is a revelation of the righteousness of God graciously imputed unto us. What God has considered clean, cannot be declared unclean by any human authority. Our position in the grace of God commands us not to call *unclean* what He has made and determined to be *clean* (Acts 10:15).

Anyone who is saved is considered a saint in God's eyes. Sainthood is not a title given to good men; it is a blessing graciously given to men who have humbled themselves and recognized a good God. They have been made holy by the blood of Christ — the grace of God. Becoming a saint has nothing to do with any good works we have done. Sainthood, our most holy position in Christ, was accomplished and finished many years before our birth; it was accomplished by the eternal God outside of the constraints of time (Eph. 1:4).

Faith has imputed to us today, the salvation, which was accomplished by Christ on the cross over 2,000 years ago. Faith takes us from the *now* and transfers us into the *eternal*. Faith activated by grace develops in us a life of loyalty and steadfastness in Christ Jesus. It gives us hope, purpose, and significance both in our life here and in the hereafter (Rom. 8:16–18).

✞ **POSITION OF GRACE:** (grace benefits us with spiritual peace)

"May grace (God's unmerited favour) and spiritual peace [which means peace with God and harmony, unity, and undisturbedness] be yours from God our Father and from the Lord Jesus Christ" (Ephesians 1:2).

Tranquillity is the fragrance of grace. The soul becomes secure in its salvation through Christ, and it fears naught from God. Grace produces contentment in all present circumstances, and a reverberant joy in eternal matters. Undisturbed by the world and its ways, grace makes us eternally exempt from the goad of ungodliness round about us. We find ourselves secure, safe, and prosperous in the realm of God.

✞ **POSITION OF GRACE:** (grace blesses us with every spiritual blessing in the heavenly realm)

"May blessing (praise, laudation, and eulogy) be to the God and Father of our Lord Jesus Christ (the Messiah) Who has blessed us in Christ with every spiritual (given by the Holy Spirit) blessing in the heavenly realm" (Ephesians 1:3)!

Grace invokes blessings upon those within its grasp. All blessings that come from God are designed to prosper us in the things of God. A voice rooted in grace is a voice enabled to speak living words; it is a voice empowered by Life. An utterance of God spoken through a willing vessel will proclaim the purposes and plans of God — plans for good, not harm. Blessings are fragments of grace that are able to sustain and nourish the weariest soul as it receives the living Word.

It is only in Christ that we acquire this grace of God, and God does not hold back when He portions blessings to us abundantly. The crumbs that fall from the Master's table are sufficient to bring life to any situation. Better a heavenly crumb than a whole, man-made loaf.

✞ **POSITION OF GRACE:** (grace operated on our life even before the beginning of time)

"Even as [in His love] He chose us [actually picked us out for Himself as His own] in Christ before the foundation of the world, that we should be holy (consecrated and set apart for Him) and blameless in His sight, even above reproach, before Him in love" (Ephesians 1:4).

Our assurance of salvation is not founded by our actions and though we experience it now, it was founded in the eternities. He chose us before the world even existed — long before we were created. God's love reached through time and blessed us; it set us apart for His use. We do not achieve holiness by bearing our own yoke; we receive holiness by taking *His* yoke upon us (Matt. 11:28–30).

Being picked or chosen by God is not a small thing. We are not only chosen *by God*, we are chosen *for God*. We have been embraced by the Eternal, designated as disciples, and identified as saints to manifest the wisdom and glory of God. It is not our fitness that makes Him choose us, but rather it is His choosing that makes us fit. Grace has separated us from the rest of mankind to be peculiarly His own. Our purpose in life originates from the virtues found in Christ, and grace continually watches over us as it operates from the power of the cross.

His holiness has been given to us freely; we are now without blemish, without blame, and without spot or wrinkle. We are found faultless before the Father of lights. This treasure of God has been placed in these earthen vessels, to show that the power and glory come from above, not from below (John 3:19–21; 2 Cor. 4:7). This has all been accomplished by the grace of God.

✞ **POSITION OF GRACE:** (grace operated in our life before we were even born)

"For He foreordained us (destined us, planned in love for us) to be adopted (revealed) as His own children through Jesus Christ, in accordance with the purpose of His will [because it pleased Him and was His kind intent] —

[So that we might be] to the praise and the commendation of His glorious grace (favour and mercy), which He so freely bestowed on us in the Beloved" (Ephesians 1:5–6).

The grace of God — appointed before the beginning of time — foreordained our adoption. The Almighty predetermined according to His purpose for us to become His children. Our position of grace was established eternally even before the inception of time, so how could we possibly ever make it more perfect?

God's purposes are pure, issuing from a will that is eternal. God is love, and all His purposes and plans are motivated by love. It is through this love that grace allows us to encounter and enjoy His family (the saints) together with Him (Gal. 6:10). This grace operates in our soul enabling us to live a life that demonstrates the grace of God to the world around us. The body of Christ — the church — is seen as the family of God's grace.

✞ **POSITION OF GRACE:** (grace saves and delivers in a practical way)

"In Him we have redemption (deliverance and salvation) through His blood, the remission (forgiveness) of our offenses (shortcomings and trespasses), in accordance with the riches and the generosity of His gracious favour,

Which He lavished upon us in every kind of wisdom and understanding (practical insight and prudence)" (Ephesians 1:7–8).

Grace not only took the bad, it gave the good. The blood of the Beloved has delivered us from death and saved us from our shortcomings and trespasses. It then bestows lavishly upon us wisdom and understanding, all by the love of God.

The gracious favour of God has freely given us practical insight into His divine plans; it gives us prudence to walk out His purposes. The riches of God provide an abundance, a plenitude of heavenly possessions, all of which are found resident in Christ — His body (Eph. 3:14–21; Col. 1:18–19). Beloved, God's plan is for fellowship to unlock these blessings; fellowship equips us to use them for His glory.

The benevolence of the Beloved exerts His holy influence upon our soul, bringing a practicality to God that cannot be accessed outside of the cross of Christ. When we believe that we receive blessing from God because of our own works or goodness, we short-circuit the meaning of grace. We hinder the very power of His resurrection from working in and through our life.

Wisdom and understanding are not just a 'religious' affair, they are practical. Grace is not just a religious concept; it is a functional reality — it shows us the way of life. Jesus really did die for our complete justification before the Father, and we really do partake of this rich, generous grace as we lovingly walk in the works He has ordained for us (Acts 7:58–60).

✞ **POSITION OF GRACE:** (grace makes us God's heritage, and appoints us to live to the praise of His glory)

"In Him we also were made [God's] heritage (portion) and we obtained an inheritance; for we had been foreordained (chosen and appointed beforehand) in accordance with His purpose, Who works out everything in agreement with the counsel and design of His [own] will,

So that we who first hoped in Christ [who first put our confidence in Him have been destined and appointed to] live for the praise of His glory" (Ephesians 1:11–12)!

It is God who has made us; it is not our own doing or wisdom that has forged us. The glory goes to God, not to earthen vessels. In Christ, we have been recreated as heavenly vessels, designed according to His will and purpose. Grace has been set forth, placing God's design and purpose in view. Our position of grace is the foundation for the working out of this same grace, appointing us to live for the praise of His glory. We are a private possession of the Almighty, drawn to Him by hope in Christ (Prov. 3:32). Our confidence placed in Christ enables us to live according to His design and will, by the grace of God. Our confidence is not a fading worldly wish; it is an eternal hope, sealed by the Holy Spirit, and empowered by the Eternal Himself.

It is by His will that He has purchased us as His own; His grace has given us His counsel for our mortal walk and our eternal hope. Such confidence in the counsel of God destines and appoints us to the praise of His glory. A vessel that has been made His heritage cannot help but be a glorious vessel. There are not enough words to express this work of the glorious grace of God that makes us His heritage!

✞ **POSITION OF GRACE:** (God's rich grace is motivated by His intense love)

"But God — so rich is He in His mercy! Because of and in order to satisfy the great and wonderful and intense love with which He loved us,

Even when we were dead (slain) by [our own] shortcomings and trespasses, He made us alive together in fellowship and in union with Christ; [He gave us the very life of Christ Himself, the same new life with which He quickened Him, for] it is by grace (His favour and mercy which you did not deserve) that you are saved (delivered from judgment and made partakers of Christ's salvation)" (Ephesians 2:4–5).

Love longs to be satisfied. God's love, intense and wonderful, demands grace to be showered on the unlovely. When the dew from the wealth of grace precipitates on a parched and weary soul, its refreshment transforms and softens the hardest of hearts. Death is swallowed up and loses its sting when grace is received by a thirsty soul. God's love raises the dead to life. His mercy, blown upon dry bones, brings new life even to the most impossible situations. Sin deceives the mortal soul and produces death, but God's grace quickens and produces victorious immortality — eternal life. A dead soul that feels the grasp of God's grace is lifted far above and beyond any boundaries imposed upon mortality. Our new life is the same quickened life that was given to Christ Himself. Our undeserved deliverance from judgment becomes our victory.

God's mercy brings eternal strength to impoverished souls. We were dead men walking

— doomed to eternal death — but mercy has bought us and brought us into the presence of the Almighty, with confidence birthed by Him.

Being made alive is enough in itself, but He has eternally lavished upon us the fellowship with Christ both here in His body — the church — and eternally in heaven. Such communion starts with faith in the blood of the Lamb of God and continues throughout eternity. Life is only found in fellowship and union with Christ — His body.

✝ **POSITION OF GRACE:** (grace raises us up and sits us down with Christ Jesus) *"And He raised us up together with Him and made us sit down together [giving us joint seating with Him] in the heavenly sphere [by virtue of our being] in Christ Jesus (the Messiah, the Anointed One).*

He did this that He might clearly demonstrate through the ages to come the immeasurable (limitless, surpassing) riches of His free grace (His unmerited favour) in [His] kindness and goodness of heart toward us in Christ Jesus" (Ephesians 2:6–7).

The grace of God has raised us up from the position of eternal death to the position of eternal life — a new life birthed by, and dedicated to God. Grace has also caused us to sit down together with Him in the heavenly realm. Such a lofty position cannot be attained by any effort on our part. Immeasurable grace cannot be measured, obtained or maintained by the works of man. God's grace manifests the inexhaustible kindness and goodness of the heart of God. It is only by virtue of being in Christ Jesus that this is revealed to us. His goodness of heart has come to us, down through the ages, by the power of God Himself, giving us joint seating with the Almighty.

✝ **POSITION OF GRACE:** (grace is applied to our life by the Spirit of God through the operation of faith)

"For it is by free grace (God's unmerited favour) that you are saved (delivered from judgment and made partakers of Christ's salvation) through [your] faith. And this [salvation] is not of yourselves [of your own doing, it came not through your own striving], but it is the gift of God;

Not because of works [not the fulfilment of the Law's demands], lest any man should boast. [It is not the result of what anyone can possibly do, so no one can pride himself in it or take glory to himself.]" (Ephesians 2:8–9).

Salvation is only conceived and secured within the bounds of the covenant of grace. It is applied to the soul of man by the Spirit of God through the operation of faith. Faith is the way or means which God has appointed for the receiving and enjoying of salvation and deliverance from judgement. Faith is not the product of man's free will and power, but rather it is the free gift of a gracious God. The only works that are acceptable to God are works of grace (Rom. 4:4).

Faith, grace, and salvation are not made available to us because of our deserving them, or by our performance of good works; they are birthed *by* God, not *from* man. Faith (a divinely inspired conviction) is the footpath to grace (a divinely conferred condition) resulting in salvation (a divinely formulated emancipation). Only in Christ Jesus do we receive freedom from the eternal judgement of God.

No one can pride himself in, or take any glory for a work of grace. Man's boasts and glory are to be in the Lord only (Ps. 20:7; 34:2; Jer. 9:24; 1 Cor. 1:31; 2 Cor. 10:17). Pride is the product of our own striving (working) — doing what we can possibly do. Grace is not so. It is the product of God's handiwork, freely bestowed upon undeserving, unworthy, and wayward souls.

✝ **POSITION / OPERATION OF GRACE:** (God's workmanship produces works of grace)

"For we are God's [own] handiwork (His workmanship), recreated in Christ Jesus, [born anew] that we may do those good works which God predestined (planned beforehand) for us [taking paths which He prepared ahead of time], that we should walk in them [living the good life which He prearranged and made ready for us to live]" (Ephesians 2:10).

What the hand of God has done, no human hand can undo. A spiritual re-birth is not facilitated by the flesh. That which is born of the Spirit, is of the will of God, but that which is born of the flesh, is of the will of the flesh. The grace of God has touched our life in order for us to do good works and to walk in them. "Doing God" (walking in the Spirit) is the purpose of God's handiwork. We are made a habitation *for*, and have become the property *of*, our manufacturer — God. What we do *with* and *in* this habitation becomes our works (Ps. 94:17; 132:13–14; Jas. 4:5–6).

God has placed before us, paths of progress, not wanderings of wantonness, or ditches of dissipation (Prov. 16:9; 20:24). A path planned by God is a privilege to walk on; it is life. Direction decreed by the world brings drudgery and death. Grace has not only recreated us, it enables us to walk freely on divinely decreed paths of purpose.

✞ **POSITION OF GRACE:** (grace decrees citizenship with the saints)

"Therefore you are no longer outsiders (exiles, migrants, and aliens, excluded from the rights of citizens), but you now share citizenship with the saints (God's own people, consecrated and set apart for Himself); and you belong to God's [own] household.

You are built upon the foundation of the apostles and prophets with Christ Jesus Himself the chief Cornerstone" (Ephesians 2:19–20).

The grace of God has accorded us rights of citizenship in the kingdom of God. Before we knew Christ, we were foreigners and strangers — without the knowledge of God. We did not share in the things of God; we were aliens, excluded from the household of the Almighty. However, God's ultimate plan for us is that we would be inside of His will as His own precious possession (Ps. 132:13–14).

We are built upon the foundation of the apostles and prophets with Christ Jesus Himself being the chief Cornerstone. All truth is founded only in Christ; He is our foundation. Christ is set as the farthest boundary, the uttermost beginning, and the end of all that exists in the kingdom of God. He is seen as the corner from which all else is set, and is found to be a secret place, a refuge, and a security for all who put their trust in Him (Ps. 9:10; 91:2; Prov. 3:5–6; 18:10).

As fellow citizens with all the saints we are to give attention to developing a constant increase in Christian knowledge, and a life conformed to the image of the Source of our citizenship — Christ Jesus. Citizenship in the kingdom of God is not affected by anything of this world. Grace has translated us from darkness to light, from the position of God's indignation and wrath into the kingdom of His dear Son of is love — from the world and its ways, into God and His ways.

✞ **POSITION OF GRACE:** (grace literally places us in His sanctuary, we become His sanctuary)

"In Him the whole structure is joined (bound, welded) together harmoniously, and it continues to rise (grow, increase) into a holy temple in the Lord [a sanctuary dedicated, consecrated, and sacred to the presence of the Lord]" (Ephesians 2:21).

It is God who has fitly joined us together. The grace of God has created and is building a structure — the church, the body of Christ, a holy temple. The eye of flesh cannot see this work of grace. All the saints — the people of God — are placed together under the hand of the Master Builder (Heb. 11:39–40).

Growth and increase are the nature of this structure; it is a living structure, which is holy, dedicated, and filled with the presence of the Lord. It is the carnal, worldly nature of man, which attempts to duplicate and represent the Living God through buildings, programs and organizations (1 Cor. 3:1–4).

Such organizations are always doomed to failure because Jesus (a living being) cannot be represented by a non-living organization no matter how hard it tries. God is not interested in filling a man-made structure with His presence; this is idolatry of a high degree. God is building His church, not churching a building.

The bond we have with God is experienced through our intimate relationship with Him and His body, not through a man-made structure. Man-made bonds are harmonious for a season — they cater to the flesh (Gal. 6:12–13). God's bond is harmonious forever — it is a product of the Spirit. A work welded together by man will at best last a life-time; God's weld endures forever.

✝ **POSITION / OPERATION OF GRACE:** (grace builds)

"In Him [and in fellowship with one another] you yourselves also are being built up [into this structure] with the rest, to form a fixed abode (dwelling place) of God in (by, through) the Spirit" (Ephesians 2:22).

The grace of God is busy constructing an eternal, living temple. We are being positioned together by God that we would become a manifestation of Him — the revelation of God. Being in Christ automatically means that we are to have fellowship with one another, because we are the body of Christ. Christ is a living body with life flowing from one part to another — fellowship. If fellowship is not functioning properly, the body is dysfunctional.

We are an abode that is eternally fixed by God Himself. The Holy Spirit is the instrument used to accomplish this gracious work. The operation of grace in our life by the Holy Spirit causes us to see the true temple of God and to be willing vessels in this living-stone structure. When we walk in the Spirit of grace we have true fellowship with one another and this action causes us to grow and increase in the presence of God, cleansing us from all sin and guilt (1 John 1:7).

✝ **POSITION / OPERATION OF GRACE:** (ministry by/of the grace of the Gospel)

"Of this [Gospel] I was made a minister according to the gift of God's free grace (undeserved favour) which was bestowed on me by the exercise (the working in all its effectiveness) of His power" (Ephesians 3:7).

The gift of grace given by God calls us ministers of God. To be a minister *of* grace you have to be a minister *by* grace. A ministry is bestowed by the exercise of God's power; it is not a credential of intelligence. God is not just interested in a mind, well versed in Scripture; He is interested in a heart well-grounded in grace. Jesus found most of His disciples on the wharf, not the local Scripture school.

A minister is one who serves others (Num. 11:28). Christians are servants of the King of kings — God Himself. We are ministers of the Gospel — the good news. We proclaim the grace of God made manifest and begotten in Christ.

Our life presents Jesus Christ as having suffered death on the cross to secure eternal salvation for all mankind in the kingdom of God. We share in the power of His resurrection — the truth that Jesus has been restored to life and exalted to the right hand of God in heaven. We preach that this same Jesus will return in just the same way He left to consummate the kingdom of God (Acts 1:9–11). As ministers of the Gospel we live our life knowing that Jesus Christ is the Way, the Truth and the Life (John 14:6).

✝ **POSITION / OPERATION OF GRACE:** (grace dispenses treasures of glory)

"May He grant you out of the rich treasury of His glory to be strengthened and reinforced with mighty power in the inner man by the [Holy] Spirit [Himself indwelling your innermost being and personality]" (Ephesians 3:16).

From the treasury of God's glory, grace imparts strength and power to our inner man. This is accomplished by the Holy Spirit indwelling our innermost being. There is not a corner in our life that is inaccessible to the Spirit of God. There is no place in our entire being or personality that He neglects to reinforce truth, out of His glorious treasury. Our treasure of imparted glory manifests itself as it works through our life. Man was created in God's image before the fall; man is recreated in God's image after his redemption. Strengthened by God's might, we are enabled to dispense grace to all who cross our path — the ministry of reconciliation (2 Cor. 5:18).

In Christ, God's righteousness becomes our righteousness and thus we are brought into relationship with Him. This imparted righteousness instills into our life the peace and prosperity that the world does not know (John 14:27). Just as

His righteousness guides us, His glory protects us (Is. 58:8).

✞ **POSITION / OPERATION OF GRACE:** (by faith, grace abides in the human heart)

"May Christ through your faith [actually] dwell (settle down, abide, make His permanent home) in your hearts! May you be rooted deep in love and founded securely on love,

That you may have the power and be strong to apprehend and grasp with all the saints [God's devoted people, the experience of that love] what is the breadth and length and height and depth [of it];" (Ephesians 3:17–18).

Faith in Christ, the divine gateway to grace, opens the human heart to be a habitation for God (Psalm 132:13–14). We are rooted in love; we are strengthened and made firm in the affections of God. To be fixed in God's love is to be thoroughly grounded and made secure in brotherly love. Grace places us in a position of power, making it possible to grasp and experience the breadth, length, and height of God's love. To know God's grace is to dispense God's grace. To grow in God's grace is to grow in God's love. God's power can be used for the enhancement of physical strength (1 Kings 18:46; Judges 16:3); however in Christ, it seems to be primarily for the manifestation of His kingdom (Acts 7:55–60).

Beloved, it is the carnal man who wants to walk in power for its own glory (Acts 5:1–10). God's love rooted deep in our heart will bring persecution, not worldly glory (Acts 8:1; Rom. 8:16–18).

✞ **POSITION / OPERATION OF GRACE:** (grace enables us to be doers of the Word)

"[That you may really come] to know [practically, through experience for yourselves] the love of Christ, which far surpasses mere knowledge [without experience]; that you may be filled [through all your being] unto all the fullness of God [may have the richest measure of the divine Presence, and become a body wholly filled and flooded with God himself]" (Ephesians 3:19)!

Grace presupposes action and experience, not thought and theory. The grace of God inspires us to perform the word of God. It incites us to be a producer — a doer of the Word. With grace operating through us, we present the word of God as a practical reality to the world around us. Grace allows us to experience God and to be intimate with His love. A vessel that is full of God is a vessel that radiates the presence of God, and imitates His love.

Christ is the eternal reality for all of creation. He is not just a thought or concept. He is tangible truth that is only found through faith. For us to be wholly flooded with God is not just an idea, it is the goal of God. The abundance of the Almighty is busy building Himself a habitation; an abode He desires to fill and flood with His glory (Psalm 132:13–18). Our Creator is committed to this purpose and end; His plan is far beyond all our highest imaginings, hopes, and dreams. May the church glory in God Almighty for ever and ever! May the presence and glory of God be our portion and our life.

✞ **POSITION / OPERATION OF GRACE:** (grace is given individually; gifts to the church are individual, they are to be used to equip the saints who are to minister to and build up the body of Christ)

"Yet grace (God's unmerited favour) was given to each of us individually [not indiscriminately, but in different ways] in proportion to the measure of Christ's [rich and bounteous] gift.

Therefore it is said, When He ascended on high, He led captivity captive [He led a train of vanquished foes] and He bestowed gifts on men" (Ephesians 4:7–8).

God calls each one of us to individually apprehend and experience His grace. A personal relationship is required for salvation, and a personal response is required for grace to do its work in our heart. A grain of grace from God is enough to fill the largest expanse of any needy heart.

A 'measure' is defined as a vessel used to determine a quantity — the required or due amount. Our prayer needs to be, "O Lord let this vessel be filled with your grace abundantly and overflowing." Beloved, it is never God's measure that lacks; it is the willingness of the vessel that lacks.

God's gifts to the church are a direct result of the work of His grace, given to men. A gift of grace is not something we possess or a position that we hold; it is something that is endowed upon us as the need arises. It is an equipping of the Spirit that flows through our vessel to equip others.

These gifts have been given for the equipping of the saints:

– apostle (one sent forth with orders, a delegate or messenger) equips by: putting in order, arranging, and making complete.

– prophet (one to instruct, comfort, encourage, rebuke, convict, and stimulate) equips by: revealing, repairing and adjusting.

– evangelist (one who brings good news or tidings, a herald of salvation) equips by: fitting others out with sound principles of the Gospel.

– pastor (one to care for others) equips by: mending what has been broken or hurt, strengthening what is weak, sick or lost.

– teacher (one who teaches concerning the things of God) equips by: preparing the saints, completing what is lacking, imparting knowledge for the work of the ministry.

A gift is not a position or an office that men hold in a church or receive a salary for. A gift is given by God and empowered by Him for His purpose and glory; it is not something you attain to by putting in a required number of hours of study. It is not something you can receive from any man or institution or group of people. A gift is not something you can retire from, nor step down from, nor step up to. A gift given by God is not something God ever takes away (Rom. 11:29). It is not something man can vote in or vote out; you cannot withdraw from it, nor can it be withdrawn from you. You cannot give your gift to anyone else or inherit it from your relatives.

A gift is to be used anytime and place, whereas a position is relegated to a certain place, and other positions from other localities do not have authority to operate outside of their defined place. Positions like this are worldly and operate like the world. (The C.E.O. of Walmart does not operate in the Canadian Tire locality.) However, gifts from God are independent of any place. All gifts operate by authority of the Holy Spirit and He is not limited to a particular neighbourhood. A person with the gift of *encouraging* can *encourage* anywhere, anytime; he does not need to be authorized by the C.E.O. of some organization. Beloved, it is best to let the blind lead the blind.

To do violence to any gifting is to do it to our own hurt (Prov. 13:13; 15:32). *"For God's gifts and His call are irrevocable. [He never withdraws them when once they are given, and He does not change His mind about those to whom He gives his grace or to whom He sends His call.]"* (Romans 11:29).

All of these gifts mentioned here in Ephesians are given by God's grace and are divinely designed to supply the saints with all of the tools required for: making disciples, baptizing them into the name of the Father and of the Son and of the Holy Spirit, and teaching them everything that Jesus has commanded. Mature, equipped Christians should be busy about their Father's business — ministering to the body of Christ.

✞ **POSITION / OPERATION OF GRACE:** (grace ordains the believer to ministry)

"His intention was the perfecting and the full equipping of the saints (His consecrated people), [that they should do] the work of ministering toward building up Christ's body (the church)" (Ephesians 4:12).

God's intention is to furnish and equip His saints completely. We are responsible for the work of building up the body of Christ. The ministry of building up Christ's body, the church, is the work of the saints, not just a few select leaders.

The phrase, 'one another', is mentioned nearly fifty times in the New Testament. The act of promoting one another's Christian growth is a divine commission delegated to the saints; it is not the 'job' of a 'leader'. It is God who has authorized His saints to do the work of ministering toward building up the living body of Christ; our position of grace in Christ is our mandate to minister. Ministry ordained *by grace* is the only foundation for effective ministry *of grace*, which will result in maturity of the body of Christ.

Authority to work in the kingdom of God is a personal passion that comes directly from the Spirit of God; it is not a passion authorized by the carnal nature of man. God's authority is given to every member of the body of Christ. Learning to respond to the Holy Spirit is vital as one matures in Christ. We must respond to what the Holy Spirit is authorizing us to do. God's authority is liberating, not controlling.

✞ **POSITION / OPERATION OF GRACE:** (grace brings us to the measure of the fullness of Christ)

"[That it might develop] until we all attain oneness in the faith and in the comprehension of the [full and accurate] knowledge of the Son of God, that [we might arrive] at really mature manhood (the completeness of personality which is nothing less than the standard height of Christ's own perfection), the measure of the stature of the fullness of the Christ and the completeness found in Him" (Ephesians 4:13).

The grace of God never gives up. Maturity is the goal of saintly ministry. The grace of God has brought us into the body of Christ and it now operates in our life through the Holy Spirit. It promotes and ministers to us through one another, bringing us to maturity. Grace will draw us into the very stature of fullness and completeness found in Him.

To grow in grace is to grow in maturity. This requires precise and correct knowledge of God. It is a process, a progressive revelation where we maintain a continual attitude of "*...forgetting those things that are behind and reaching forth onto those things which are before"* (Phil. 3:13c KJV).

Our goal is the prize of the upward calling of God in Christ Jesus. Here on earth we have a glimmering view of the kingdom of God's grace as through a glass dimly. Grace keeps our gaze fixed on Jesus as it draws us on to the eternity written in our hearts. The kingdom of grace to which we are called and which is implanted in us, can only be found in Christ.

✞ **OPERATION OF GRACE:** (grace calls us to separate from perverseness)

"So this I say and solemnly testify in [the name of] the Lord [as in His presence], that you must no longer live as the heathen (the Gentiles) do in their perverseness [in the folly, vanity, and emptiness of their souls and the futility] of their minds" (Ephesians 4:17).

The grace of God solemnly commands us not to live in godless perverseness. Grace teaches us to deny ungodliness, not embody it. Are we to persist in and tarry in sin now that grace has abounded to us? Is the grace of God potent enough to change our position in the eternities, but impotent when it comes to our mortal walk here on earth? Certainly not! Beloved, that same grace that moves the heavens for us is the same grace that can order our affairs on earth too. Grace is not a fabricator of folly or vanity. The grace of God that has moved the mountain of sin and condemnation for us, desires to work through us fulfilling the will of the Father.

Grace is a formulator of wisdom and a motivator of humility which flows forth from a soul that is full and overflowing with the presence of God. Grace is not futile; it is active and effectual in the daily renewing of a human soul. To persist in perverseness, under the guise of grace, is neither the plan nor the purpose, which the life God has so freely provided for us through the suffering of Christ Jesus (1 Peter 2:21–24).

✞ **OPERATION OF GRACE:** (grace provides our new nature in God)

"Strip yourselves of your former nature [put off and discard your old unrenewed self] which characterized your previous manner of life and becomes corrupt through lusts and desires that spring from delusion;

And be constantly renewed in the spirit of your mind [having a fresh mental and spiritual attitude],

And put on the new nature (the regenerate self) created in God's image, [Godlike] in true righteousness and holiness" (Ephesians 4:22–24).

The grace of God has positioned us in the place of procuring a new nature. The stripping off of our former nature can only be done by the operation of grace. We are commanded here to cast off the manner of life and conduct that we once habitually walked in — a life of ungodly motivations and manifestations. Life outside of the grace of Christ is a life led by lusts and desires that have sprung from the springboard of delusion. To live outside of grace is to live a lie. Lusts and corruption are not birthed from truth; they are brought about by the deceitfulness of sin — disobedience to God.

Delusion is an unreality or lie that cannot birth truth; but truth, in a renewed mind and attitude, will expose and reveal what is destructive to the human soul. A regenerated self, recreated by the operation of grace, takes on the nature of God. Such nature is not steeped in actions of self-destruction, but rather it operates in works of righteousness and holiness. Godly behaviour and attitude is the product of gracious renewal. In this process of renewal, God's grace targets the ungodly biddings in our life and replaces them with righteous desires. God's grace works inwardly towards godliness; it never produces the fruits of unrighteousness.

Newness comes only by repentance and faith in the work of Christ's grace. Fresh mental and spiritual attitudes come not from man's efforts, but they are imparted into a receiving, repentant heart by the Spirit of grace. Our new nature has been recreated in God's image. It is brought about by our change of heart towards God, allowing Him to recreate within us His nature. Our part is to strip and discard our old self along with all its deluded desires and lusts. As we present this to Him, He then recreates the new nature within us. We are to disrobe deceitful delusions and let Jesus clothe us with His pure white garments of righteousness (Rev. 3:18).

✝ **OPERATION OF GRACE:** (grace stands for truth; it protects us from the source and the effect of sin)

"Therefore, rejecting all falsity and being done now with it, let everyone express the truth with his neighbour for we are all parts of one body and members one of another.

When angry, do not sin; do not ever let your wrath (your exasperation, your fury or indignation) last until the sun goes down.

Leave no [such] room or foothold for the devil [give no opportunity to him]" (Ephesians 4:25–27).

We are required to reject all falsity and to be done with it. Grace demands a truthful expression. Any part of the body that does not deal truthfully (according to God's design or purpose) is like a cancerous growth, slowly destroying its relationship with the very body from which it obtains its life. Grace does not whitewash over ungodliness leaving it intact. It exposes ungodliness and provides opportunity for repentance to allow grace to do its work.

Grace dealt a fatal blow to the power of death over our life by placing us in a position of eternal life in Christ Jesus. It then operates on our life, instructing and enabling us to put off and reject any relationship with ungodliness.

It renews our soul as it promotes a new mind of truth that sees sin as an abnormality to the spiritual man. To put on a new nature means that the old is done away with. A new nature created in God's image is the object of the operation of grace in our life. The ointment of grace cures a sick soul by rejecting sin and eradicating it by the blood of the Lamb. It gives us God's authority to be done with it.

We are exhorted to reject and be finished with all falsity and deception because we are all parts of one another. We are reciprocally and mutually dependent upon one another. We belong to one another; we are members of one another (Rom. 12:5; Eph. 4:16).

The church system teaches us that we need to find a faction of the church where we feel comfortable and then become adherents or members of it. This falsity needs to be repented of. We need to be done with this deception and recognize the truth that I belong to you and you belong to me. We are members one of another; God does not call us to be members of a church organization with a government tax number (sometimes promoted so that you can give to God even more). Give unto

Caesar what is Caesar's and give unto God what is God's.

Anger, when it is not directed by the Spirit of God, can lead to sin. The degree that we love the Lord is the degree that we hate evil. The very fear of the Lord is defined by the hatred of evil (Prov. 8:13). Godly hatred and godly anger are founded in God and thus are redemptive in nature. Any ungodly motivation leading towards wrath needs to be dealt with quickly or else it will leave a crack for the devil's toe to acquire a place to hold on to. Grace warns us here to leave no room or opportunity for such devilish grip on your soul.

✞ **OPERATION OF GRACE:** (grace helps us to hate what is evil and love what is good)

"Let all bitterness and indignation and wrath (passion, rage, bad temper) and resentment (anger, animosity) and quarrelling (brawling, clamour, contention) and slander (evil-speaking, abusive or blasphemous language) be banished from you, with all malice (spite, ill will, or baseness of any kind).

And become useful and helpful and kind to one another, tender-hearted (compassionate, understanding, loving-hearted), forgiving one another [readily and freely], as God in Christ forgave you" (Ephesians 4:31–32).

Bitterness and bad temper is to be exiled from our life. Lips touched by the gracious forgiveness of God should only evidence loving-kindness. Nothing short of the measure of Christ's grace is to be the standard of our interaction towards one another. Such divine standard can only be achieved *by* and *through* the grace of God. The compassion of God, graciously manifested through a willing vessel, displays the excellence of the heart of God.

Our foundation for work in the kingdom of God is built upon forgiveness. It takes a kingdom heart to cry out with a loud voice, "*...Lord, lay not this sin to their charge...*" (Luke 23:34; Acts 7:60b KJV). Forgiveness has been authorized by grace. Compassionate, tender-hearted loving-kindness, rooted in the soil of forgiveness, produces its finest fruit when blown on by the winds of persecution from a hate-filled world.

Being useful to one another is the call of grace. We are never truly useful when we allow anything but the Spirit of God to motivate us. 'Forgiving our trespasses as we forgive others who trespass against us' is the teaching of God's grace. Being overcome by anything that is not of God never manifests the kingdom of God. Sin will not manifest the purposes of God, and it is never a manifestation of Christ. The world is constantly trying to figure out how it can keep on sinning while trying to avoid or ignore the consequences of sin. To try and find a cure for the symptoms of a disease without recognizing the cause of the disease is pure foolishness.

✞ **POSITION OF GRACE:** (grace places us in the love of the Omnipotent and it calls us to imitate this same love)

"Therefore be imitators of God [copy Him and follow His example], as well-beloved children [imitate their father].

And walk in love, [esteeming and delighting in one another] as Christ loved us and gave Himself up for us, a slain offering and sacrifice to God [for you, so that it became] a sweet fragrance" (Ephesians 5:1–2).

God is love, and to walk in His steps is to walk in love. The fragrance of God's grace should flow from a walk of love. To imitate God does not require a talent or gift on our part; it requires the gift of His eternal grace enabling us to walk by His ability (authority). An offspring imitates its parent; grace enables us to imitate our Parent. We have been positioned in a love that knows no limit; a love that eternally embraces us and forever fancies us.

Christ's love has not been bequeathed to people who deserve it. It has been freely given solely by the grace of God. It desires to work through devout vessels, spreading the fragrance of His grace upon all mankind — displaying the divine love of the cross of Christ. The odour of the Omnipotent is sweet to the spirit, but foul to the flesh. A sweet smell, a sacrifice acceptable and well pleasing to God bears the scent of the cross; it is not readily received by unrepentant hearts. Grace's call of replicating God's love, one towards another, is the distinguishing mark of a disciple. We are to be imitators of Christ, offering forgiveness, compassion, and self-sacrifice.

✞ **OPERATION OF GRACE:** (grace calls us to morality and purity, and thankfulness to God)

"But immorality (sexual vice) and all impurity [of lustful, rich, wasteful living] or greediness must not even be named among you, as is fitting and proper among saints (God's consecrated people).

Let there be no filthiness (obscenity, indecency) nor foolish and sinful (silly and corrupt) talk, nor coarse jesting, which are not fitting or becoming; but instead voice your thankfulness [to God]" (Ephesians 5:3–4).

Immorality and impurity have no habitation in a God-fearing heart. Wasteful living can be defined as any time spent outside of the will of God. The grace of God calls us to handle our time wisely. Our longing should be for God — as a deer in the desert panting for water. Grace calls us to hunger and thirst after righteousness; it is the purpose of grace (Matt. 5:6; 6:33).

Our bodies and our mouths are members of our God-filled vessel. We are receptacles of righteousness — consecrated containers of Christ's riches. Such vessels give glory and thankfulness to God. The dung of the world cannot remain for long under the cleansing power of God's grace. Grace declares the stench of the world as not fitting — not becoming or proper for a saint sanctified by the blood of the Lamb (1 John 2:15–17; 3:13; 5:19).

✞ **OPERATION OF GRACE:** (grace is the foundation of our security)

"For be sure of this: that no person practising sexual vice or impurity in thought or in life, or one who is covetous [who has lustful desire for the property of others and is greedy for gain] — for he [in effect] is an idolater — has any inheritance in the kingdom of Christ and of God" (Ephesians 5:5).

There is a direct relationship between walking in righteousness and manifesting the kingdom of God in our day to day life. None of us is perfect, as we all can fall into sin from time to time. *"As it is written, There is none righteous, no, not one:"* (Rom. 3:10 KJV). This is why we need the grace of God. This scripture in Ephesians unveils the urgency for the gift of grace to be operating in our life in order that we do not practice these carnal, idolatrous things.

Godly inheritance comes by the free favour of God, through the death of Jesus Christ (Gen. 22:8). Just as it took divine life to breathe life into man, it took divine death to deliver mankind from the grip of sin and death.

An inheritance is a possession received by right of the giver, not the receiver. The right of possession is passed on and received as a free gift upon the death of the giver. As inheritors of the kingdom of Christ, we now have the privilege to do the works of God — works of righteousness. Each man's work is to be revealed by fire, which will test the motive behind each work. *"If any man's work shall be burned, he shall suffer loss: but he himself shall be saved; yet so as by fire"* (1 Cor. 3:15 KJV).

✞ **OPERATION OF GRACE:** (grace calls us to be aware of deception; grace commands us not to be sharers and associates with the sons of rebellion)

"Let no one delude and deceive you with empty excuses and groundless arguments [for these sins], for through these things the wrath of God comes upon the sons of rebellion and disobedience.

So do not associate or be sharers with them" (Ephesians 5:6–7).

Delusion and deception are the work of the devil (Gen. 3:1). Revelation and restoration are the work of the Spirit of grace. Empty excuses and fallacious arguments are the fruit of rebellious, disobedient, and impenitent hearts. When we are deceived we are cheated out of something that was ours. Deception often does its work through the mind, in the guise of reason and logical argument (Col. 2:8).

Worldly philosophy has the innate ability to soil and spoil what it touches. It boasts of faith that bears no fruit; it is like empty clouds, never bringing life or refreshment to a barren soul. The grace of God warns us not to be cheated by it, or become its prey. Worldly philosophy seems sensible to the mind of man. Hence, anyone concerned more with traditions than truth, easily falls victim to its wiles.

The spirit of the world desires to draw us into rebellious and disobedient activities — things that the wrath of God targets. The Spirit of grace positions us in a place where we are eternally free from the wrath of God. It then trains us and operates in us making us willing to do the work of God's good pleasure. It is not by our own strength that we are effectual; it is by the strength of the Omnipotent, working in us, causing us both to desire and to display the works of God through our life in Christ (Prov. 16:3).

The grace of God commands us to avoid being partakers with the sons of rebellion and disobedience. To join together with a partaker of perversion is to be cheated from bearing the marks of Christ and to become an object of God's wrath. We are not to be participants of the Lord's Table and the table of demons. Grace calls us to be members of God's promises and sufferings; it never trains us to be partakers of sin. The principles of God are manifested through the outward workings of the Spirit of grace. The principles of the world are spread by the spirit of the world; they are anti-Christ.

✝ **<u>POSITION / OPERATION OF GRACE</u>:** (grace makes us heirs of the Light and produces the fruit of the Spirit in our life)

"For once you were <u>darkness,</u> but now you are light in the Lord; <u>walk</u> as <u>children</u> of <u>Light</u> [lead the lives of those native-born to the Light].

For the <u>fruit</u> (the effect, the produce) of the <u>Light</u> of the Spirit [consists] in every form of kindly goodness, <u>uprightness</u> of <u>heart</u>, and <u>trueness</u> of <u>life</u>" (Ephesians 5:8–9).

The grace of God instructs us to live as children of Light. It is only by being born again that we are able to walk as children of the Light. Wrongdoers hate the Light and will not expose themselves to the light because they love the darkness. They do not want their evil deeds to be uncovered and reproved. The practice of deceit is exposed by light. The practice of truth displays what is right, and is perceived as being founded in light — truth draws us towards light. Truth manifested by any vessel brings glory to God. Darkness will always shirk away from the Light; it lies unprotected and exposed before the Light (John 3:19–21).

Before we knew Christ, we were habitually under the sway of the demon spirit that constantly worked in us, making us sons of disobedience. We were positioned as heirs of God's wrath and indignation (Eph. 2:1–3). Grace has justified us and translated us from the kingdom of darkness into the kingdom of Christ. We are now heirs of eternal life and the blessings found only in Christ Jesus, our Lord. We are positioned in God's eternal favour.

The fruit of the light of the Spirit is founded in God's grace. It manifests itself in every form of goodness, uprightness, and truth. These are the godly characteristics produced by the operation of the Spirit of grace in our life. Grace brings rightness — a correctness of thinking, feeling, and acting — as it operates on our mind, our will, and our emotion. A soul inundated by the grace of God is dispelled of darkness and lifted into the eternal Light of God.

From such a lofty position, godly change is birthed into our being. This is only possible by having faith in the work of the cross of Christ, and personally receiving the Grace of God as our Saviour. This super-natural intervention of God's grace is in opposition to our natural, human reason and wisdom. Grace births a personal excellence into our soul, furnishing it with a renewed mind with a desire for discipline and direction from God. In Christ we have power to deal with any darkness that confronts our soul.

✝ **<u>OPERATION OF GRACE</u>:** (grace does not produce fruitless deeds of darkness; grace exposes and convicts and reproves the conduct of darkness)

"And try to <u>learn</u> [in your experience] what is <u>pleasing</u> to the <u>Lord</u> [let your lives be constant proofs of what is most acceptable to Him].

Take no part in and have no fellowship with the fruitless deeds and enterprises of darkness, but instead [let your lives be so in contrast as to] expose and reprove and convict them" (Ephesians 5:10–11).

As we experience and grow in the grace of God, we unveil the Lord's pleasure. Our lives are to be proofs of what is acceptable to God. Our deeds are the result of His acceptance of us; they are not what make us acceptable to Him. Exploits of iniquity are always exposed and reproved by works of righteousness. We are to test, examine, and prove actions and attitudes to see if they are genuinely ordained by God. Our life is to be in contrast to a life founded in the world.

There is nothing good that comes from our own righteousness — self-righteousness. It is only His righteousness imputed into our souls that has any significance. Righteousness is meant to be manifested through us, and in turn, it produces pleasure for the Lord.

Pleasing the Lord is a fruit of the grace of God working in our life. It is not necessary to please God to receive His grace; it is necessary to have faith in His grace to please God (Heb. 11:2, 6). His eternal provision of grace towards us is not effected by whether our actions and attitudes please Him (Eph. 4:30). Our actions and attitudes do not affect God, they affect us. God is not a puppet to our whims of pleasure or grief. He is the very Creator of these emotions. God's grace is not dispensed to us in proportion to the amount of pleasure or grief we could possibly cause the Lord, otherwise grace would not be grace.

✝ **OPERATION OF GRACE:** (grace causes God's purpose to become our purpose)

"Look carefully then how you walk! Live purposefully and worthily and accurately, not as the unwise and witless, but as wise (sensible, intelligent people),

Making the very most of the time [buying up each opportunity], because the days are evil" (Ephesians 5:15–16).

Any time spent outside of the will of God, is a waste of time. God's purposes, imputed into us, give us a divine mission and a divine function. There is nothing outside of God that carries any eternal significance. Purpose for life is only found in Christ. A walk that has been purposed by the grace of God is a walk that has a divine destiny. With God's plans and intentions imparted into us, we can cleave unto the Lord and recognize our calling in Christ Jesus. God's purposes stand forever; they are not thwarted by man. They give us an eternal inheritance in Christ, and this eternal salvation reflects God's holy purposes that are expressed in our manner of life.

"...For this purpose the Son of God was manifested, that He might destroy the works of the devil" (1 John 3:8c KJV). God has resolved, made ready and prepared all things for us. He has appointed and ordained us to declare and execute the commission that He has given us. We are ordained to be ministers of reconciliation, and that makes us ministers of grace. God's eternal grace has made us redeemers of time so that we can make the most of every opportunity for doing good, knowing that all things are ours in Christ Jesus. His grace is always sufficient to enable us to see all circumstances as opportunities to manifest His will. Beloved, when we see our time as sacred, our actions become sacred.

✝ **OPERATION OF GRACE:** (grace demands wisdom in the will of the Lord)

"Therefore do not be vague and thoughtless and foolish, but understanding and firmly grasping what the will of the Lord is" (Ephesians 5:17).

Grace tells us not to be without purpose or reason; not to be senseless or slack in our grasp of the will of the Lord. It demands us to continually seek His will and to have a firm grip on it, that we may learn to seek what is vital and prize what is of real value. God wishes His grace to be manifested through us to the lost and to be a blessing to all mankind through Christ.

The desire and pleasure of God is manifested through our obedience to His commands. God's will is for us to choose His way, not our way. Grace is not a license for foolishness or thoughtlessness.

Grace trains us to be wise in the ways of God; grace is always inclined towards good. It is never unclear or without purpose; it never commands evil actions or stands in self-righteousness.

✞ **OPERATION OF GRACE:** (we are to be filled with the Spirit of grace, not intoxicated by the spirit of alcohol)

"Do not get drunk with wine, for that is debauchery; but ever be filled and stimulated with the Holy Spirit" (Ephesians 5:18).

We are not to be become inebriated with alcohol and act unrestrainedly. The grace of God calls us to be filled with and controlled by the Holy Spirit, not the spirit of alcohol. Intoxication and immoderation cause us to abandon our grip on the will of God; it impedes our ability to act according to the mind of Christ; it destines us to a self-indulgent life (Prov. 31:4–5).

It is never by our efforts that we maintain the grace of God in our life, and fortunately, our position of grace never abandons us. As we live by the Spirit of God, our actions and attitudes should manifest that same grace in our life. Even when we lose our grip, God's grip is ever present. Walking on the water at the command of God, one moment; and calling out for salvation, the next moment, depends entirely upon God's grip on our life, not our grip on God's life (Matt. 14:29–31).

✞ **POSITION / OPERATION OF GRACE:** (grace enables us to be strong in the Lord)

"In conclusion, be strong in the Lord [be empowered through your union with Him]; draw your strength from Him [that strength which His boundless might provides]" (Ephesians 6:10).

It is only through our union with Christ that we are empowered. Because dominion has been decreed for the people of God, the grace of God in Christ enables us to do divine deeds. God's ability is only accessible by His grace; God's work is not accomplished by the force or strength of man. Empowerment is boundless in Christ and meaningless outside of Christ. It is only when we rejoice in our own weakness that the power of Christ truly is manifested through us (2 Cor. 12:10).

We are strong in the Lord when we define our significance in Him. The knowledge of God does not manifest God's strength if it is not administered by the Spirit of God. The letter kills but the Spirit gives life. Knowledge puffs up but the Spirit of love and grace edifies and builds up. Grace flowing from the Almighty is dispensed to us to manifest God's will in all situations that we encounter in our daily life. Being strong in the Lord should be the concluding position of all the circumstances in our life as we grow in grace.

✞ **POSITION / OPERATION OF GRACE:** (God's armour is found in His grace)

"Put on God's whole armour [the armour of a heavy-armed soldier which God supplies], that you may be able successfully to stand up against [all] the strategies and the deceits of the devil.

For we are not wrestling with flesh and blood [contending only with physical opponents], but against the despotisms, against the powers, against [the master spirits who are] the world rulers of this present darkness, against the spirit forces of wickedness in the heavenly (supernatural) sphere" (Ephesians 6:11–12).

As children of God, we are called to put on and clothe ourselves with the full and complete armour of God. Goliath was not beaten by the armament and skill of man; he was beaten by the armament and will of God. David had to put off the notion of man's ways and faithfully trust in and rely on God's ways. In any battle of the Lord, it is God who supplies the weapons of our warfare — albeit a stone or a song (1 Sam. 17:40, 49; 2 Chron. 20:20–22; Acts 16:25). It is only when we are found bearing the accoutrements of God's armour that we find success (1 Sam. 25:29; Acts 7:58–60).

Standing up against deceitful strategies can only be accomplished by wearing the mighty weapons of our warfare. These weapons are not carnal — not natural — because we do not fight against flesh. We wrestle despotisms. We grapple with powers and spar with dark spiritual forces of wickedness in the heavenly places. The weapons of our warfare are mighty, through God, for the destruction and demolition of demonic devices, and satanic strongholds. God's weapons will accomplish God's work.

A stronghold is anything relied upon for safety or significance. When you place your security in anything outside of Christ, it becomes an idolatrous stronghold in your life. It will start feeding you and teaching you to believe in lies. It will make you weak in faith and instead of trusting in God, releasing the weight of the battle to Him, it demands you to use your own strength to hang on to that stronghold. This only leaves room for more footholds of bondage.

As we discover these carnal castles in our life, we need to deal with them ruthlessly, or we will find ourselves weak in our walk with God. We need to sincerely seek God's wisdom on how to wield spiritual weapons in this matter that we might be set free. All our warfare is to be governed by the Spirit of grace, operating through our new, godly nature, not by our human nature.

Philippians

✞ **POSITION OF GRACE:** (grace is a blessing proclaimed to all of God's people)

"Paul and Timothy, bond servants of Christ Jesus (the Messiah), to all the saints (God's consecrated people) in Christ Jesus who are at Philippi, with the bishops (overseers) and deacons (assistants);

Grace (favour and blessing) to you and [heart] peace from God our Father and the Lord Jesus Christ (the Messiah)" (Philippians 1:1–2).

Being a bond servant of our Lord Jesus Christ is a gracious calling on our life. We are known as peculiar people who willingly give themselves up into God's hand. We display ourselves as devoted to Him, without regard to our own interests (Matt. 6:33; Phil. 2:3; 1 Peter 4:3–4).

Saints are not loved by the spirit of the world (John 15:18–19; 1 John 3:13); we are loved by God. We have been made holy by the blood of the Lamb, not by the sweat of our brow. Our calling of sainthood implies a special relationship with God. All of our trespasses toward God have been atoned for; we are now called to live in harmony because of the divine nature, which is residing within us. The gracious calling of sainthood is one that inspires humble reverence and awe within us. Sainthood is a relationship made sacred by God; it is not a position secured by man's goodness.

All saints in Christ Jesus, along with overseers and deacons, are joint recipients of grace and peace from God. The grace of God, poured out from the Great Shepherd and Bishop of our souls, garrisons all of God's saints — His consecrated people. We, as God's saints, are charged with the duty of watching over each other and encouraging the Spirit's work in our midst. We are to convey grace and peace to all those around us, especially the family of God.

✞ **POSITION / OPERATION OF GRACE:** (He Who has started a work of grace will finish it; grace is to be shared)

"And I am convinced and sure of this very thing, that He Who began a good work in you will continue until the day of Jesus Christ [right up to the time of His return], developing [that good work] and perfecting and bringing it to full completion in you.

It is right and appropriate for me to have this confidence and feel this way about you all, because you have me in your heart and I hold you in my heart as partakers and sharers, one and all with me, of grace (God's unmerited favour and spiritual blessing). [This is true] both when I am shut up in prison and when I am out in the defence and confirmation of the good news (the Gospel)" (Philippians 1:6–7).

Our confidence rests complete in the fact that He who has begun a good work in us will not neglect it, but will bring it to full completion. A work of grace is never a temporary solution applied to a transient problem; it is an eternal application of the power and wisdom of God resulting in a change of heart, which leads to a change in our life. Confidence in the world will eventually bring disappointment and discontent, but confidence in the Lord is a mark of our appointment to divine grace; we are never overcome, or put to shame (Ps. 25:2; Isaiah 54:4; Acts 7:58–60; 1 Peter 2:6).

Our heart is the centre of our spiritual being and all activities that issue from our life. Because we hold one another in our hearts, grace appoints us to partake and share the favour and blessings of God with each other. Grace is not bound by prison walls, nor restrained by chains of iron; however, a heart fettered by fear casts aside its confidence in the Almighty and misses the operation of grace and mercy in its midst.

A heart inside the grace of God is free even in prison, but a heart outside of God's grace is not free even outside of prison. The Gospel of grace opens the doors to freedom in the deepest dungeons of every heart. The freedom found in the kingdom of God is not a temporary natural freedom; it is an eternal freedom founded outside of this temporary passing world.

Grace is divinely designed to be partaken of and shared; it is not designed to collect dust on the shelf of selfishness. Grace is meant to be experienced and shared, and as we do this we are actively involved in the operation of God's love. We are not to hang God's grace up on a rack of religion keeping it at arm's length. Grace is practical, touchable, usable, and of eternal effect on our being.

✞ **OPERATION OF GRACE:** (to grow in grace is to grow in love; growth in love is a display of our acquaintance with God)

"For God is my witness how I long for and pursue you all with love, in the tender mercy of Christ Jesus [Himself]!

And this I pray: that your love may abound yet more and more and extend to its fullest development in knowledge and all keen insight [that your love may display itself in greater depth of acquaintance and more comprehensive discernment]" (Philippians 1:8–9).

As we partake and share in the grace of God, the love of God unveils itself within us. The grace of God causes us to testify of the tender mercies of Christ Jesus. Grace enables us to pursue others with love; it empowers us to apprehend that, which has apprehended us. With God being our witness, who can stand against us and defeat us? His very Spirit witnesses that we are His.

To grow in God's grace is to grow in the knowledge of God and His love (2 Peter 3:17–18). This love apprehends us and causes us to long for and actively pursue fellowship in the body of Christ. It also instils within us the need to pray for others to be fully developed in His ways of knowledge, insight, and discernment. Oh, the incredible joy of being acquainted with God!

Longings and desires birthed by grace flow from the heart of God and flood our soul making our knees of flesh bow to His loving kindness. Grace draws us toward perfect love, a love meant to be displayed as a garment on our life, revealing our acquaintance with God and His ways (Col. 3:12–14). It is His abundance that causes us to abound in His character. The grace of God operates through righteousness and abounds all the more when the ways of the world besiege us. The operation of grace is a display of God's love in our life, and it dispenses divine discernment as we grow in acquaintance with His ways (Prov. 1:1–5).

Having God as our witness is not a light thing, yet it is most comforting. Calling on God to be our witness is not to be used to wield self-righteousness or self-justification. The Omnipotent knows all things and to call on Him is to recognize His grace and mercy, which has been abundantly shed towards us. In order to call on Him, in love, it takes a heart submitted to God. The heart of God responds to a broken spirit and a contrite heart in man (Ps. 51:17).

✞ **OPERATION OF GRACE:** (grace reveals real value; grace enhances our moral discernment)

"So that you may surely learn to sense what is vital, and approve and prize what is excellent and of real value [recognizing the highest and the best, and distinguishing the moral differences], and that you may be untainted and pure and unerring and blameless [so that with hearts sincere and certain and unsullied, you may approach] the day of Christ [not stumbling nor causing others to stumble]" (Philippians 1:10).

Grace reveals the Divine's definition of 'true value'. Our approval by God brings with it the very character of God Himself. His grace equips us to sense what is vital — enabling us to distinguish moral difference. Grace does not camouflage the issue of morality; it enhances our perception of it. Before our encounter with God's grace, we knew not what morality was. From our position in grace we approve and prize what is excellent, untainted, pure, and blameless. It is grace that opened the eyes of our understanding to enable us to see what is unerring and vital in all of our life's affairs.

It is our position of grace obtained by the blood of the Lamb, which enables us to approach the day of Christ with confidence. It is the operation of this same grace, which keeps us from stumbling and causing others to stumble, as we trek onward towards the day of Christ.

Our value must be placed solely upon the work accomplished by the cross; it is the foundation of our very significance. Our value has nothing to do with what we do; it is only found in what Christ has done for us. If we lose confidence in what Christ did on the cross, or begin to rely on our own works, our value is compromised. Salvation by the cross is always an offense to the flesh; albeit, it is the work of the cross that equips us to examine, test, and prove what is genuine and Christ-like.

✝ **POSITION / OPERATION OF GRACE:** (grace fills us with the fruits of righteousness; grace manifests the glory of God)

"May you abound in and be filled with the fruits of righteousness (of right standing with God and right doing) which come through Jesus Christ (the Anointed One), to the honour and praise of God [that His glory may be both manifested and recognized]" (Philippians 1:11).

Being filled with the fruits of righteousness is a work achieved by the grace of God. The Spirit of God dwelling and working within us enables us to develop dispositions and habits which reflect His righteousness. We are called to abound *in* and be filled *with* fruit that exemplifies God. Our right standing *with* God enables us to practically demonstrate right doing *in* God. Our position of grace brings His honour and glory into our life. The operation of grace in our life practically exhibits this same honour and glory to those around us, and presents our life as being founded *in* and *with* God.

✝ **POSITION OF GRACE:** (grace gives us the mind of Christ)

"Let this same attitude and purpose and [humble] mind be in you which was in Christ Jesus: [Let Him be your example in humility:]" (Philippians 2:5).

As we live in one accord with one another — being one in mind and purpose: not being motivated by strife or contention, thinking more highly of one another than we do of ourselves, not looking out only for our own interest, but being concerned for the interests of others, we manifest the mind of Christ (1 Cor. 2:16). This divinely inspired, humble attitude and mind is to be manifest in God's glorious saints. The understanding, knowledge, and wisdom of Christ should conduct all of our life's affairs. It is only by being placed in the grace of God that the attitudes of the Almighty can be made manifest in our life.

✝ **OPERATION OF GRACE:** (grace is a calling to obedience)

"Therefore, my dear ones, as you have always obeyed [my suggestions], so now, not only [with enthusiasm you would show] in my presence but much more because I am absent, work out (cultivate, carry out to the goal, and fully complete) your own salvation with reverence and awe and trembling (self-distrust, with serious caution, tenderness of conscience, watchfulness against temptation, timidly shrinking from whatever might offend God and discredit the name of Christ)" (Philippians 2:12).

Our precious Saviour has shown us the perfect way — the way of humility. He stripped Himself of all divine privileges and rights, and He assumed the employ of a servant. As a man, He then obediently humbled Himself even further, to the call of suffering death on the cross. Such limitless obedience has been exemplified for us so that we should also follow in its divine shadow. Grace is a calling to loving obedience.

Enthusiastic obedience to God is the calling of all saints. Actions fired by the zeal of God are actions that accomplish the work of God. Grace calls us to work out our salvation with fear and trembling. Our life is to enthusiastically display the life of Christ. Fear and trembling are the close companions of such a high calling. They do not make us slaves to dread, but rather they make us slaves to hope and love, setting us free. Godly fear and trembling, fired by the coals of hope, and burning with flames of love, produce a grace that is unquenchable.

A work of grace is not a means to win the affections *of* man; it is a divine demonstration of God's affection *for* man. The pleasing of man is a selfish snare, but the pleasing of God is a divine delight.

Our confidence is not to be founded in the flesh; it is to be established in the Spirit of Christ, making us timidly shrink from all that would sully our walk with our Saviour. Our confidence reflects what Jesus Christ has done.

✞ **POSITION / OPERATION OF GRACE:** (grace enables us both to desire and to do God's good pleasure)

"[Not in your own strength] for it is God Who is all the while effectually at work in you [energizing and creating in you the power and desire], both to will and to work for His good pleasure and satisfaction and delight" (Philippians 2:13).

Human strength does not power a work of grace. Because of our position in Christ Jesus, we embody the grace of God as it effectually operates in us. As we commit our ways to the Lord, He causes the thoughts and intents of our heart to become agreeable to His will, making *our* ways become *His* ways (Prov. 16:3). The will of our flesh can neither receive nor achieve the will of God. The Spirit of grace dwelling within us creates and energizes the will of God within our soul. Work powered and enabled by the Spirit of grace, births saintly satisfaction and divine delight within us. God delights in working through His people.

✞ **OPERATION OF GRACE:** (grace enables us to shine as lights in a dark world)

"That you may show yourselves to be blameless and guileless, innocent and uncontaminated, children of God without blemish (faultless, unrebukable) in the midst of a crooked and wicked generation [spiritually perverted and perverse], among whom you are seen as bright lights (stars or beacons shining out clearly) in the [dark] world" (Philippians 2:15).

Saints — those who have been crucified with Christ — should be unaffected by the world. The grace of God, like a consecrated cleanser, trains us to deny wickedness to operate in our life. A sanctified soul, living in the midst of a wicked world, is sure to shine as a star in a world that constantly distorts and opposes the plans and purposes of God. Before we became acquainted with the grace of God, we were under the control of the god of this world; we were obedient to the prince of the power of the air (Eph. 2:2). However, grace has now positioned us outside of the devil's powerful grasp, and this same grace now works in us enabling us to be obedient and responsive to the will of God. Beloved, what is fashionable to the world is not fashionable to God, and what is fashionable to God, is not fashionable to the world. Wickedness is an abomination to the righteous, and righteousness is an abomination to the wicked (Prov. 29:27).

To be obedient to the world is to deny the grace of God. But we, as bright shining beacons of grace, are to offer to all men, the Word of Life; holding it out to them as the light in a dark and perverted world without hope.

✞ **POSITION OF GRACE:** (grace deadens our confidence in the flesh)

"For we [Christians] are the true circumcision, who worship God in spirit and by the Spirit of God and exult and glory and pride ourselves in Jesus Christ, and put no confidence or dependence [on what we are] in the flesh and on outward privileges and physical advantages and external appearances —" (Philippians 3:3).

The grace of God has marked us with a divine circumcision that identifies us as worshippers of the Almighty. It is only in Christ Jesus that we can worship God in the Spirit. It is a gracious position where we have no confidence in what we can accomplish in the flesh. The eyes of grace gaze not on outward appearance, but rather they gaze upon the inward man, applying God's power to the inward parts of our being. Though we cannot be proud of our salvation, we can pride ourselves in our Saviour. When we pride ourselves in Jesus Christ, we put no faith in our flesh. All of our advantages and privileges in Christ Jesus are rooted and founded in the Spirit of grace, not the flesh or works of man.

True circumcision is a work of God. It is the hand of Christ performing a spiritual operation, cutting off our whole corrupt, carnal nature, and leaving in its place a new nature, which does not submit to the power of carnal passions and lusts. Now that we are circumcised, we no longer put confidence in our own talents or abilities (on what we are able to do in the flesh). We now depend upon the Source of truth and grace, resulting in true fellowship with one another. This is a distinguishing mark of Christians (1 John 1:3).

✞ **POSITION / OPERATION OF GRACE:** (grace gives us all things in Christ; it progressively teaches us and manifests the life of Christ)

"Yes, furthermore, I count everything as loss compared to the possession of the priceless privilege (the overwhelming preciousness, the surpassing worth, and supreme advantage) of knowing Christ Jesus my Lord and of progressively becoming more deeply and intimately acquainted with Him [of perceiving and recognizing and understanding Him more fully and clearly]. For His sake I have lost everything and consider it all to be mere rubbish (refuse, dregs), in order that I may win (gain) Christ (the Anointed One)," (Philippians 3:8).

The grace of God has positioned us to know Christ intimately, seeing all else as refuse and rubbish. The essence of grace makes things of the world smell of the offensive odour of excrement. The preciousness of Christ makes all other things worthless and incomparable in value (Job 28:12–19; Prov. 8:11). Oh, that we would see everything as rubbish, rather than act as collectors and hoarders of things of no value in Christ! The privilege of knowing Christ is priceless, but eyes set on the subtleties of the world are deceived by a heart seeking its own desires. To have Christ is to have all things, what more can we need?

Doing the will of God should be the focus of our life and should not be used as a means of acquiring material goods. Neither should it be used as a means of trying to twist God's arm to give us spiritual gifts or blessings, simply because we think we deserve it by having completed certain spiritual activities.

Paul even considered all his training and credentials, which he obtained through study and devotion to God, as rubbish compared to just knowing Christ. The credentials that he now had in Christ were not obtained by any effort or study on his part; it was purely the grace of God that Paul boasted in (2 Cor. 10:17–18).

Knowing Christ raises us above the affairs of the world and places us in a position of prominence and power — a position not observable by the eye of flesh. The eyes of Christ are set on doing the Father's will — things eternal — not on things of the earth (John 5:19; 12:49–50). Eternal things are superior in rank and authority, far above things of the earth. We as saints and rulers in the kingdom of God are to respond to the cries of the world with, "Silver and gold have I none; but such as I have give I thee."

Progression in Christ is never measured by material value. Godly maturity identifies itself with Christ's suffering (Phil. 2:17–18; Col. 1:24; 1 Peter 4:12–19). It is manifested by the sharing of this same suffering, which causes our transformation into His likeness. Our gain is Christ, not gold. God's wisdom is far more valuable than gold or silver. God's wisdom is not manifest to the world by idols of silver and gold — the work of men's hands. God does not require *our* money to do *His* work. Eyes fixed on material wealth rather than godly suffering, become tepid temples, claiming richness, yet knowing not the wretchedness, and pitiable, poor, blindness of their naked state. True riches are the gold of God, refined and tested by the Almighty Himself. A heart that prefers material wealth over godly suffering is destined to be spewed out of the mouth of God. Relationship with Christ is measured by fellowship and intimacy with His sufferings, not gold (Rev. 3:14–19).

✞ **POSITION OF GRACE:** (Christ is the foundation of grace)

"And that I may [actually] be found and known as in Him, not having any [self-achieved] righteousness that can be called my own, based on my obedience to the Law's demands (ritualistic uprightness and supposed right standing with God thus acquired), but possessing that [genuine righteousness] which

comes through faith in Christ (the Anointed One), the [truly] right standing with God, which comes from God by [saving] faith" (Philippians 3:9).

The righteousness of God cannot be attained by human sweat. When we gain Christ, we are founded on God's grace, not our own self-achieved righteousness. Our obedience to God is not what makes us righteous; our obedience is a fruit of our position in Christ. Our right standing with God is found only through the work of Christ, not the work of man. To be founded in Christ, is to be recognized by God as being upright through the work of Christ — our character or state is shown to be Christ-like.

To be known as 'Christians' first came to the church at Antioch (Acts 11:26). To be known as being 'in Him' is an honour that grace bestows upon us. (It is not much of a testimony of Christ for two Christians to work together for a year and not even know that the other is a Christian — this is a shame, not an honour.) To be found 'in Christ' is accomplished only by being in right standing with God by faith. The workings of Christ in our midst should show the fruit of righteousness and should bring about a great awe (Acts 5:11, 13). Christ's righteousness is something birthed by God and imparted into His people to display to the world an invitation and a warning to not regard His grace lightly.

✝ **POSITION / OPERATION OF GRACE:** (grace identifies us with Christ — both His power and His sufferings; it is our suffering in grace that transforms us)

"[For my determined purpose is] that I may know Him [that I may progressively become more deeply and intimately acquainted with Him perceiving and recognizing and understanding the wonders of His Person more strongly and more clearly], and that I may in that same way come to know the power outflowing from His resurrection [which it exerts over believers], and that I may so share His sufferings as to be continually transformed [in spirit into His likeness even] to His death," (Philippians 3:10).

The regulating rule of our life, the pronounced purpose of our being, is to know Christ. Our position in Christ is fixed and eternal; our submission to the operation of grace in our life makes us progressively become more acquainted with Him, in an increasingly intimate way. Just as in a marriage relationship, being more acquainted with one another does not mean you are more married, our increasing acquaintance with God's grace does not mean that we are more saved.

Our ambition and goal is to recognize and realize Christ in our life. An acquaintance with the grace of Christ cannot but forever change those who allow it to affect their lives. Only those who distrust their own efforts can benefit from the touch of grace. The personage of Christ becomes stronger and clearer to the eye fixed on the grace of God. Eyes set on grace can even observe wickedness and still receive direction and wisdom from God. Whatever the eye is fixed upon, is what enters the heart and soul of man (Matt. 6:21).

The wonder of Christ's person inevitably leads us to His sufferings and His glory. It is only when we embrace His suffering that we share in the glory and power found in the cross of Christ. Suffering in Christ causes the heart to rejoice and hence the glory of God to be seen by men.

One needs to participate in His suffering in order to know His suffering (1 Peter 4:12–19). Padded pews are designed to alleviate suffering. The grace of God has not delivered us from suffering; it has changed our position and hence our perspective of it. Suffering in the world carries a curse with it, but suffering for righteousness holds the blessing of God within it. Suffering for Christ transforms us.

Our position of grace opens the door to blessed suffering, which transforms the soul of man into the likeness of Christ. The allure of this transformation is a work of the grace of God operating in our soul. Grace so captivates us and charms us, that suffering is no longer something to be avoided, but rather something to be embraced, because it brings with it the character of Christ. Grace cries out, *"Father forgive them for they know knot what they do!"* and *"Father, not my will but Thy will be done"* (Luke 22:42; 23:34; Acts 7:60)!

Christians should expect that being mistreated and misunderstood is a part of the normal Christian life. It takes the grace of God to find joy in such treatment, and it takes grace's enablement coming from the power out-flowing from His resurrection, to transform us into His likeness. Jesus' resurrection required His death, and the riches requited from His death contain the power to transform us into the likeness of His grace. This is never appealing to our flesh. Advantages that appeal to the flesh will not lead to righteousness. They are not the riches of grace; they are founded on the love of the world (1 John 2:15–17). It takes the realization of our death in Christ to access God's gracious power to transform our lives (Gal 2:20).

✝ **POSITION / OPERATION OF GRACE:** (grace draws us into resurrection life)

"[in the hope] that if possible I may attain to the [spiritual and moral] resurrection [that lifts me] out from among the dead [even while in the body].

Not that I have now attained [this ideal], or have already been made perfect, but I press on to lay hold of (grasp) and make my own, that for which Christ Jesus (the Messiah) has laid hold of me and made me His own" (Philippians 3:11–12).

Oh, the calling of the power of grace! A heart abandoned to grace is captivated by the allure of its calling. Turning cursing into blessing, and death into life, grace cries out for the impossible to be possible. Grace doesn't call heaven down but rather it begs for the soul, even while in this body, to experience resurrection power here in this life. A life abandoned to grace carries little earthly attachment or worldly attraction; things of the earth hold no eternal value.

Our perfection is not yet complete, but grace beckons us to press onward and upward as we submit to its call (Heb. 11:40). Grace gives us both a desire and an ability to grasp the purpose for which Christ has laid hold of us. Grace commands us to make Him known to others that others might have communion with Him. Even as Christ has been brought to us, we are to bring Christ to others and hence others to Christ. We need to be grasped by grace and empowered to stand in the gap of suffering, abuse, ridicule, and scorn. We are called to be a bridge of grace for others to cross over on. We have been made His own, so that He would become our all in all; our sufficiency is to be found in Christ (Phil. 4:11–13).

✝ **POSITION / OPERATION OF GRACE:** (grace draws us upward; it teaches us to forgive the past, and press on towards the future — Christ-likeness)

"I do not consider, brethren, that I have captured and made it my own [yet]; but one thing I do [it is my one aspiration]; forgetting what lies behind and straining forward to what lies ahead,

I press on toward the goal to win the [supreme and heavenly] prize to which God in Christ Jesus is calling us upward" (Philippians 3:13–14).

We have not yet appropriated perfection, yet the lure of God's love draws us upward and sets our focus on one attitude: forgetting the past and straining forward, toward to the future. It is this attitude that gives us the purpose and vision of Christ in our life. As we let His holy power and influence take hold of our soul, He will both prompt and govern it. The only way to capture Christ is to let Him capture us — like a piece of metal drawn by a magnet only to become a magnet itself. It is only by being in Christ that we live, move, and have our being (Acts 17:28).

The goal or prize is the heavenly reward of Christian character — Christ-likeness. Problems of the world pale and dissipate in the presence of God's grace. Our calling is upward, not earthly. Our saintly sojourn here on earth is to manifest this upward, eternal glory in these earthly bound bodies. These temporary tents are to be used for the glory of God here on earth, till such time as they expire and free us to receive our heavenly bodies (Phil. 1:21–24). Our lives are to be presented as living sacrifices, holy and acceptable to God (Rom. 12:1–2).

✞ **POSITION OF GRACE:** (grace makes heaven our homeland; it transforms us by the power that holds the universe together)

"But we are citizens of the state (commonwealth, homeland) which is in heaven, and from it also we earnestly and patiently await [the coming of] the Lord Jesus Christ (the Messiah) [as] Saviour,

Who will transform and fashion anew the body of our humiliation to conform to and be like the body of His glory and majesty, by exerting that power which enables Him even to subject everything to Himself" (Philippians 3:20–21).

The grace of God transforms us from earthly residency to heavenly citizenship. This divine citizenship is the foundation from which we patiently await the coming of our blessed Lord and Saviour. Our position in Christ guarantees our forthcoming transformation. He will fashion anew the body of our humiliation to make it conform to the body of His glory. Mortality will take on immortality and majesty; even death will be swallowed up and shall be no more (1 Cor. 15:52–55; Rev. 20:14). All this gracious work is enabled by the same power that the Almighty uses to subject everything unto Him.

Our homeland is in heaven, and from this position we await His coming and His transforming power — power enough to create, sustain, and dispose of the universe. He does not need man's muscles to assist Him. Such magnificence and graciousness can only make us bow our knees in awe, and cause us to rest securely before our Lord and Saviour, Jesus Christ.

✞ **POSITION / OPERATION OF GRACE:** (God's grace is our sufficiency; God's sufficiency is our grace)

"I have strength for all things in Christ Who empowers me [I am ready for anything and equal to anything through Him Who infuses inner strength into me; I am self-sufficient in Christ's sufficiency]" (Philippians 4:13).

Our source of strength is found only in Christ; there is nothing that can overpower God's will for our life. In Christ, our strength is sufficient for all things, whether it be stones, swords, or the mouths of lions (Acts 14:19; 2 Cor. 11:25; 2 Tim 4:17). Our strength lies not in realizing our own desires, but rather in submitting to the will of the Almighty (Act 7:58–60). The strength that we have in Christ is ever present, ever ready, and more than equal to anything, which comes our way. Grace infuses inner strength into us making us totally sufficient in Christ.

The boundaries of our limitations are set by the will of God, not our own personal will or desire. God does not empower us to do as we desire, but rather to co-live with His will. We dare not dictate to God, but rather we are to roll our ways upon the Omnipotent, entrusting them entirely to Him, submitting them to His active will. He will then cause our will and desires to come into line with His will, defining and establishing success in our life. God's success is sufficient, and in God's sufficiency is where we find our success.

Colossians

✞ **POSITION OF GRACE:** (grace places us in a hope that brings true joy and manifests itself in true love)

"For we have heard of your faith in Christ Jesus [the leaning of your entire human personality on Him in absolute trust and confidence in His power, wisdom, and goodness] and of the love which you [have and show] for all the saints (God's consecrated ones),

Because of the hope [of experiencing what is] laid up (reserved and waiting) for you in heaven. Of this [hope] you heard in the past in the message of the truth of the Gospel," (Colossians 1:4–5).

We express our faith in Christ Jesus by placing our entire life in His hands, trusting in His goodness and wisdom, not our own. Faith births within us a revelation of God's grace and loving-kindness, which we in turn spread abroad to those around us.

The grace of God inundates us with an irrepressible joy, which awakens within us as we consciously perceive His presence. The reality of God's presence fills us with a joy and hope that is based in reality, and is eternal. Though now we see through a glass darkly, our hope founded in faith is not shrouded (2 Cor. 3:13–18). Hope in the Lord is more real than worldly assuredness, for all heaven and earth shall pass away, but truth remains forever.

Divinely birthed hope causes us to rejoice in trials knowing that pressure produces patience and a maturing of character, which develops and forges the habit of joyful and confident hope in eternal life. *"Such hope never disappoints or deludes or shames us, for God's love has been poured out in our hearts through the Holy Spirit Who has been given to us"* (Romans 5:5).

Hope founded in Christ does not disappoint, nor does it leave scars of shame on any heart resting in the grace of the Almighty. The power of the Holy Spirit causes us to abound as the God of all hope fills us with joy and peace. Grace lifts us above worldly sorrow; we are not as others who have no hope, without God, lost in the world (Eph. 2:1–3). His abundant mercy has begotten us to a living hope that is ever ready to account for the reason it resides within us (1 Peter 1:3).

✞ **OPERATION OF GRACE:** (grace positions us in a place of intimacy with God)

"Which has come to you. Indeed, in the whole world [that Gospel] is bearing fruit and still is growing [by its own inherent power], even as it has done among yourselves ever since the day you first heard and came to know and understand the grace of God in truth. [You came to know the grace of undeserved favour of God in reality, deeply and clearly and thoroughly, becoming accurately and intimately acquainted with it.]" (Colossians 1:6).

Grace brought the truth to us through the Gospel. From our new position of truth, this same grace continues to train us to deny worldly hope and grow in godly hope. *"And every man that hath this hope in him purifieth himself, even as he is pure"* (1 John 3:3 KJV).

Beloved, grace bears fruit; it grows in our midst as we become intimately acquainted with it — as it becomes the very love of our life. From the time we come to know God's grace, it works in us effectually, making truth an intimate companion. Intimacy with God's grace, changes us; it is never imputed in vain. Our bodies are members of Christ and our intimacy with Christ makes us one with Him, and with one another (Gal. 3:28).

Grace teaches us to shun immorality and honour God with our bodies in everything we do because it affects the whole body of Christ (Joshua 7:1, 5, 10–13; 2 Cor. 11:29). From our position of righteousness in Christ, we are called to operate in righteousness in order that the body of Christ manifests the reality of our intimacy with God.

✞ **OPERATION OF GRACE:** (grace causes us to pray unceasingly for the betterment of others; it draws us into a pleasing and fruitful walk in God.)

"For this reason we also, from the day we heard of it, have not ceased to pray and make [special] request for you, [asking] that you may be filled with

the full (deep and clear) knowledge of His will in all spiritual wisdom [in comprehensive insight into the ways and purposes of God] and in understanding and discernment of spiritual things —

That you may walk (live and conduct yourselves) in a manner worthy of the Lord, fully pleasing to Him in all things, bearing fruit in every good work and steadily growing and increasing in and by the knowledge of God [with fuller, deeper and clearer insight, acquaintance, and recognition]" (Colossians 1:9–10).

It is the grace of God operating in our life that causes us to perpetually pray for one another. It incites and seduces us unto love and good works; it does not encourage us to dodge our duty of prayer for one another, nor to be lazy, or unfruitful in the affairs of the Spirit. God's grace is real; it is not just a concept. All things from God have the inherent ability to affect our life in a very tangible way.

Unceasing prayer is powered by the Spirit of grace; it encourages us in the remembrance of God's people. This same grace working within us desires God's best to be at work in others, which will always result in the best for us, too. Beloved, because of the inherent nature of the body of Christ, it is for our own benefit to have others filled with a deep and clear knowledge of the will of God. It can only benefit us to have brothers, sisters, and even enemies around us to be filled with spiritual wisdom and insight into the ways and purposes of God. It is always to our own advantage for others (especially our enemies) to have godly understanding and discernment of spiritual things. This is why we pray for our enemies, and do good deeds towards them (Prov. 25:21–22; Matt. 5:43–44; Rom. 12:17–20).

When our flesh is puffed up with pride, it sees itself as superior in knowledge and ability over those around it. God's grace does not act in such a manner; it desires God's best even upon its enemies. Evil is never overcome with evil; it is always overcome with good (Rom. 12:21). The nature of grace causes us to rejoice when others around us are blessed, and to pray unceasingly for the benefit of others, because grace recognizes our mutual dependence upon one another in the body of Christ (Rom. 12:5, 15).

Grace ordains us to a life conducted in a manner that is worthy of the Lord (Phil. 1:27). Such worthiness can neither be obtained nor powered by the flesh and efforts of man. A walk that is conducted by the Spirit of grace operating in our life is pleasing to God, and it bears godly fruit in all that it does. A walk of grace builds within us a deeper acquaintance with God (Heb. 5:14). God's grace, operating in our life, progressively draws us closer and closer to His likeness, and it always brings glory to Him.

✝ **OPERATION / POSITION OF GRACE:** (grace invigorates us and gives us joyful endurance in trials; we have gratitude for what He has done)

"[We pray] that you may be invigorated and strengthened with all power according to the might of His glory, [to exercise] every kind of endurance and patience (perseverance and forbearance) with joy,

Giving thanks to the Father, Who has qualified and made us fit to share the portion which is the inheritance of the saints (God's holy people) in the Light" (Colossians 1:11–12).

The power of God vested in us by the prayers of others, gives us endurance and patience as we persevere and bear up under all the trials and circumstances of life (Acts 8:24; 10:30; 2 Thess. 3:1–2). When grace operates in our life in the midst of the fiery flames of trial, it produces a joy and thanksgiving directed towards our heavenly Father, and hence a blessing towards others (Dan. 3:16–30; 4:1–3; 6:14–21; Acts 7:58–60). Only by the grace of God can a trial be transformed into a joy for us, and a blessing towards others.

Qualifications are heavenly ordained, not earthly appointed; it is God Who has qualified us as saints and made us fit to share in His eternal salvation. It is not our own efforts and accomplishments that have qualified us; all our very best efforts and accomplishments lie pallid before the grace of God (Luke 8:38–39).

Whether we acknowledge it or not, there is never a moment in our life when we are not entirely dependent upon the grace of God. Our inheritance is eternally provided for us by Christ. Saints are people of truth and knowledge, and they are eternally surrounded by the spiritual purity associated with it. Our portion is in the Light; it is an inheritance that is shared with God's holy people who live in the Light. God is light and there is no darkness to be found in Him (John 3:19–21).

Living in the light is a requirement for fellowship — a distinguishing mark of Christians (1 John 1:3). We have not yet arrived to perfection. However, in true and unbroken fellowship, we allow God's light to shine upon us, and darkness is dealt with. When we apply the light to the darkness, the blood of Jesus Christ cleanses and removes us from all sin and accompanying guilt (1 John 1:7).

✝ **POSITION / OPERATION OF GRACE:** (grace has drawn us out of darkness and placed us in light)

"[The Father] has delivered and drawn us to Himself out of the control and the dominion of darkness and has transferred us into the kingdom of the Son of His love,

In Whom we have our redemption through His blood, [which means] the forgiveness of our sins" (Colossians 1:13–14).

The grace of God has translated us from darkness to light, and has made us the righteousness of God in Christ (2 Cor. 5:21). The dominion of darkness has been deposed and overcome by the light of God's love. Darkness blinds the minds of those who do not believe, leaving them unable to even see their captivity. Being born blind, they do not know what they are doing, where they are going, or over what they stumble (Prov. 4:19). In this unregenerate state, man is unknowingly positioned in eternal darkness, and is blindly walking about in it. Nothing less than the power of grace can deliver man from his position of eternal death and condemnation.

We have been redeemed out of the dominion of darkness and placed into the kingdom of Christ. Our eyes are now opened revealing the life of Christ before us, and the powers of darkness must flee (Jas. 4:7). The regenerated soul becomes an inheritor of the kingdom and nature of God and is divinely assigned to righteous conduct — a worker of light in the midst of a dark and degenerate world. We have been bought by the blood of Christ and have freely received forgiveness for all our sins. It is the grace of God that now works the nature and life of that same divine blood into our life.

✝ **POSITION OF GRACE:** (grace presents us blameless before God, it is our calling)

"Yet now has [Christ, the Messiah] reconciled [you to God] in the body of His flesh through death, in order to present you holy and faultless and irreproachable in His [the Father's] presence.

[And this He will do] provided that you continue to stay with and in the faith [in Christ], well-grounded and settled and steadfast, not shifting or moving away from the hope [which rests on and is inspired by] the glad tidings (the Gospel), which you heard and which has been preached [as being designed for and offered without restrictions] to every person under heaven, and of which [Gospel] I, Paul, became a minister" (Colossians 1:22–23).

It was necessary for Christ to die in order to pay for our sin, so that we could be made holy and faultless before God (Rom. 3:21–24). We have been reunited with God through Christ; His death and resurrection together present us before the Father, irreproachable and unimpeachable. Though once we were estranged and hostile towards God because of our evil deeds, Christ has now appeased God's wrath towards us and placed us in His favour — positioned faultless before Him. *"For our sake He made Christ [virtually] to be sin Who knew no sin, so that in and through Him we might become [endued with, viewed as being in, and examples of] the righteousness of God [what we ought to be, approved and acceptable and in right relationship with Him, by His goodness]"* (2 Corinthians 5:21).

Beloved, this is the work of eternal grace, not a temporary work of mortal man. It is impossible for man to do any work of eternal significance outside of the grace of God. The only eternal work that man can do is to refuse reception of the grace of God, and hence, live eternally in hell (outside of God's presence). The Law was temporary (requiring regular sacrifices over and over again); grace is eternal, and by His one sacrifice, He forever fulfilled all the Law's demands on our life (Heb. 7:28; 9:25–28). Here, 'forever' and 'once for all' indicate all past sins, all present sins, and all future sins.

Through the Gospel, God guarantees our inheritance as we stand steadfast in the faith, not swerving away from the hope of eternal life. We are called in one hope, and that hope is found in Christ Jesus — the hope of glory. The Father, Who has loved us and given us everlasting hope by the grace found in Christ Jesus, will never forsake us (Heb. 13:5). Our calling is to hold fast to our hope without wavering, for He who promised is faithful. Such a promise was founded before time even began, and it does not need human effort to sustain it.

✞ **POSITION / OPERATION OF GRACE:** (grace was founded on suffering and it is revealed through suffering)

"[Even] now I rejoice in the midst of my sufferings on your behalf. And in my own person I am making up whatever is still lacking and remains to be completed [on our part] of Christ's afflictions, for the sake of His body, which is the church" (Colossians 1:24).

One cannot help but feel reverence for God at our privilege of suffering when we see it in the light of completing what remains of Christ's suffering, for His body — the church. It is part of the fullness of the message of the Gospel of Jesus Christ. Suffering is a part of the full Gospel, and is the message, which is revealed to God's holy people, for His glory.

When we suffer for Christ, we suffer for the body of Christ, and this is to be counted as a joy and a point of rejoicing. Grace puts within us an attitude whereby we truly become torn between two desires: to live and be a blessing for others, or to die and be with the Lord which is far better for ourselves (Phil. 1:20–23). Suffering in accordance with God's will gives us the opportunity to reflect His righteousness. As we commend our soul to Him, He is faithful to give us the grace to endure. Suffering within the will of God, works righteousness in our life — our calling as the church (1 Peter 3:12–16). Self-inflicted suffering fosters self-righteousness.

✞ **POSITION / OPERATION OF GRACE:** (grace presents Jesus as Saviour and Lord)

"As you have therefore received Christ, [even] Jesus the Lord, [so] walk (regulate your lives and conduct yourselves) in union with and conformity to Him" (Colossians 2:6).

It is only in Christ that the divine wisdom of the ways and purposes of God are progressively revealed to us. We come to Christ through faith, and by the grace of God we are to continue living in the same manner as we conduct all of our life's affairs.

We have been re-birthed in our position of grace in Christ and this same grace continues to teach and train us to conduct and normalize our life to conform to His will. Jesus is to be both our Saviour and our Lord. It is because of our position of salvation that His grace can operate in our life, enabling Jesus to be Lord of all our affairs (Rom. 12:1–2).

✞ **POSITION OF GRACE:** (grace gives us all things in Christ)

"And you are in Him, made full and having come to fullness of life [in Christ you too are filled with the Godhead — Father, Son and Holy Spirit — and reach full spiritual stature]. And He is the Head of all rule and authority [of every angelic principality and power]" (Colossians 2:10).

Christ contains the fullness of Deity, and as such, we who are 'in Christ' are made full and have come to the fullness of life; we are made complete and reach full spiritual stature. Christ takes us from nothingness and gives us everything; there is no greater position possible than knowing Christ.

Oh, the boundless riches of Christ that lifts impoverished souls to the throne of God so freely, and unreservedly gives all things into their hands (1 John 3:1–3)!

As soon as a soul perceives its possession of all things in Christ, it is immediately without want, and it is endless in gratitude. Saints powered by gratitude will rule over all other powers and principalities. We become vessels of authority when we place ourselves at Christ's disposal, and when we open our heart to Him (Prov. 28:14; 2 Peter 1:4–7). Such eternal bounties can only be administered by the Spirit of God; they cannot be comprehended or apprehended by our flesh.

✝ **POSITION OF GRACE:** (grace transfers us from death to life; it completely clears our transgressions before God)

"And you who were dead in trespasses and in the uncircumcision of your flesh (your sensuality, your sinful carnal nature), [God] brought to life together with [Christ], having [freely] forgiven us all our transgressions,

Having cancelled and blotted out and wiped away the handwriting of the note (bond) with its legal decrees and demands which was in force and stood against us (hostile to us). This [note with its regulations, decrees and demands] He set aside and cleared completely out of our way by nailing it to [His] cross" (Colossians 2:13–14).

Before we knew Christ, we were dead men walking — our flesh controlling us and our sensuality knowing no restraints (Eph. 2:1–3). The grace of God has crucified our flesh with Christ; nevertheless, we now live by faith in the Son of God (Gal. 2:20). Our spirit which once was dead to God is now alive, and our flesh which once was alive to self has now been crucified with Christ. Now, we are not to live as debtors to our fleshly desires, but rather as debtors to the Spirit, which has been quickened in us (Rom. 8:10–13).

In Christ, we have no tag-a-long transgressions, which have any authority to hold us down; we have been *forever* set free from *all* our transgressions. We have been made alive together with Christ, and as such, our actions and conversations of life will be divinely ordered. Christ did not die to justify us to continue partaking in sin (Rom. 6:1–2). He died to remove our sin, and deliver us from its power. Having done this, He now teaches and trains us to deny ungodliness access to our life as He renews our soul. Pigs, not saints, have a natural tendency to return to the mire.

Like paying someone else's legal costs and penalty, Christ has completely cleared out all the demands and decrees, which were held against us due to our sin. This includes all our sin — past, present, and future. Beloved, when Christ wipes something clean, no streaks are left behind. We are called to respond in like mind (Philem. 1:17–18).

✝ **OPERATION OF GRACE:** (grace enables us to eradicate evil desires in our life)

"So kill (deaden, deprive of power) the evil desire lurking in your members [those animal impulses and all that is earthly in you that is employed in sin]: sexual vice, impurity, sensual appetites, unholy desires, and all greed and covetousness, for that is idolatry (the deifying of self and other created things instead of God)" (Colossians 3:5).

This is a sanctifying work that requires the operation of the grace of God in our life; it is not possible to overcome such powers outside of the enablement of the Spirit of grace. Our bodies are called to be temples of the Holy Spirit, and are not to be turned over to powers that work iniquity. We are not to be tents and temples of transgression (Rom. 12:1–2; 1 Cor. 3:16–17; 6:16–20).

The grace of God calls us to control the evil desires dictated by our flesh. We are to deprive of power and destroy the strength of the animal impulses within us; we are to slay all that is earthly within which is employed in sin. If we choose to feed evil desires, it will increase their power over us. God calls us to assassinate sensual appetites, destroy unholy desires, kill covetousness and greed, slaughter sexual vice, and exterminate impurity, all by His grace.

When God's searchlight shines on our soul, it reveals evil desires — idols (Prov. 20:27). No amount of our own will-power will eradicate the root of these desires. At our best effort, our own will-power obeys the law — an outward show of control. At worst, it fails miserably in self-righteousness, and does nothing to change the nature of our heart.

The only thing that changes our heart is repentance; it allows Christ to crucify evil desires and birth new godly desires in our heart, through faith. To try to hide transgression is foolish; we are called to confess them and forsake them (Prov. 28:13). If you do not uncover your sin, you rob yourself of the freedom, which mercy offers you; you block the life of Christ from effectually working in your life.

✞ **OPERATION OF GRACE:** (grace enables us to rid ourselves of unregenerate, evil practices)

"But now put away and rid yourselves [completely] of all these things: anger, rage, bad feeling toward others, curses and slander, and foulmouthed abuse and shameful utterances from your lips!

Do not lie to one another, for you have stripped off the old (unregenerate) self with its evil practices," (Colossians 3:8–9).

Note that it is we (both personally and corporately as the body of Christ) who are called to put away and get rid of unregenerate practices of the flesh. It is because of these things that the wrath of God is coming upon the sons of disobedience — those who opposed the will and purpose of God. It is these things that we ourselves once habitually walked and lived in (Eph. 2:2; 4:22). Grace calls us to put evil practices away from us and rid ourselves completely from the wickedness of the world.

Beloved, to utterly put off from one's self, and to separate ourselves from such things, requires the operation of the grace of God in our life. We cannot despoil or disarm our old nature by the power of man. It requires the Divine's intervention, as His grace teaches, instructs, and enables us to deny ungodliness to have power over our life. It is in fellowship that we tap into this working of the Spirit, and find the encouragement and power required to be overcomers, as He moves amongst His people.

The enablement is of God; but the choice is ours, and the time is now. Our life is not to be an instrument of falsity; it is to be an instrument of truth — perfection in Christ's righteousness. Polluted springs of water are never a testimony of truth; falsehood is natural to the father of lies and all that is false (Prov. 5:21–23; 25:26; John 8:44). Disciples of grace hear their Master's voice and follow Him; disciples of deception do not hear the truth when it is spoken (John 8:43–45). By the grace of God we have been translated from the kingdom of falsehood, and placed into the kingdom of Truth.

✞ **POSITION / OPERATION OF GRACE:** (grace clothes us and continually remoulds us into a more perfect knowledge of the Creator)

"And have clothed yourselves with the new [spiritual self], which is [ever in the process of being] renewed and remolded into [fuller and more perfect knowledge upon] knowledge after the image (the likeness) of Him Who created it" (Colossians 3:10).

The grace of God has clothed us with a new spiritual self, which continues to operate within us as we walk and live in the Spirit. We have put away the old, have been washed in the blood of the Lamb, and have clothed ourselves with a new kind of life which is opposed to the former corrupt state.

Grace has changed our position in the heavens; it now operates on our life here changing our character. Grace constantly conforms and moulds our character into the likeness of Him Who created it. It is only because of our position of grace in Christ that we are enabled to be changed into such divine likeness. Our position of grace is the foundation from which the eternal operation of the Creator works in our life.

✞ **POSITION / OPERATION OF GRACE:** (grace makes us represent God)

"Clothe yourselves therefore, as God's own chosen ones (His own picked representatives), [who are] purified and holy and well-beloved [by God Himself, by putting on behaviour marked by] tender-hearted pity and mercy, kind feeling, a lowly opinion of

yourselves, gentle ways, [and] patience [which is tireless and long-suffering, and has the power to endure whatever comes, with good temper]" (Colossians 3:12).

Because of the grace of God, we have been chosen as His representatives. As such, our life ought to portray the character of the Almighty in our daily doings, displaying His heart. Grace has placed us in the position of God's mercy and it is this same grace that enables us to manifest a heart in which mercy resides. A heart that truly understands mercy is a heart that shows mercy; a heart that truly shows grace is a heart that has truly received grace.

Forgiveness and love are the bricks and mortar, which form the path of grace (Eph. 4:32). It takes a soul founded on the forgiveness and love of God to offer these same divine qualities to those around it. Grace calls us to be humble, patient, and long-suffering with good temper. The more God-like we become, the more grace we reveal to a world that knows it not. The Gospel is God's plan for revealing His grace to the world, through us, His vessels.

Tireless, long-suffering, and with the power to find joy in whatever comes our way, is the calling of the saints of God. This should not be strange to us as we mirror our Master's life. We have been crucified with Christ; nevertheless, it is not we who live but Christ Who now lives in us as a result of our faith, a faith purchased at a great price, yet given to us so freely.

✞ **POSITION / OPERATION OF GRACE:** (grace gives us peace and it enables peace to operate in and rule over our life)

"And let the peace (soul harmony which comes) from Christ rule (act as umpire continually) in your hearts [deciding and settling with finality all questions that arise in your minds, in that peaceful state] to which as [members of Christ's] one body you were also called [to live]. And be thankful (appreciative), [giving praise to God always]" (Colossians 3:15).

To be at peace with God is to be at peace with life. To be at peace with life is to be at peace with Christ's one body. God's grace positions us in God's peace; it then operates and works this same peace into every fabric and corner of His body. Divine peace passes our understanding and brings tranquillity even in the midst of worldly chaos. God's grace is ever present to exempt us from the power and havoc of unbridled, worldly passions.

A soul assured of its salvation in Christ, needs to fear nothing; it can rest content with its earthly circumstances, no matter what they are (Prov. 28:14; Phil. 4:12; 1 Thess. 5:18). Grace has given us an eternal security and safety that cannot be over powered by affairs of the world — neither man's nor evil spirits'. Grace admonishes us not to allow anyone to defraud us of our position in grace by acting as an umpire over us, and declaring us unworthy of our salvation (Colossians 2:18). Beloved, no man gave us our salvation, and no man can declare that we have lost God's grace.

We should only permit the peace of Christ to umpire the affairs of our life. A soul, directed by the peace of God, is thankful, free, and rested in the will/authority of God. In Christ, we need not be anxious about anything because our all-knowing, ever-loving Father is ever-present with us. When God is for us, who can possibly be victorious over us (Rom. 8:31–35)? Peace is the natural calling and state of the body of Christ as its members bear and embody the life and praise of God under Christ's rule.

✞ **POSITION / OPERATION OF GRACE:** (grace promotes right doing in our life)

"For he who deals wrongfully will [reap the fruit of his folly and] be punished for his wrongdoing. And [with God] there is no partiality [no matter what a person's position may be, whether he is the slave or the master]" (Colossians 3:25).

The grace of God calls us to right relationship, and to right doing; this is only achievable in Christ Jesus. We are to do all things as unto the Lord and not as unto men. A man pleaser, in truth, actually fears man; but a God pleaser operates to please the Lord. He has a greater desire to please God than man; this is the essence of the fear of the

Lord — the hatred of evil (Ps. 97:10; Prov. 8:13; Amos 5:15).

Our grace in Christ is never a license to act unjustly or wickedly. Grace is never a calling to sin; it is always a calling to righteousness (right doing) in God (John 3:19–21). Our position in grace allows us to partake and operate in His grace. It teaches and trains us to deny ungodliness — allowing worldly passionate desires to have rule over us. We are called to be doers of the Word, not doers of wrongdoing. The fruit of wrong-doing never results in righteousness, but rather it will always result in personal loss — divinely ordained consequences (Prov. 8:36).

There is no one-sidedness with God. He corrects and chastises those whom He loves (Heb. 12:6; Rev. 3:19). Prejudice, bias, unfairness, and injustice are not methods of operating in God's kingdom. He is not impressed with any position or accomplishment of man; He is only moved by a humble and contrite heart that is actively seeking His will as its vital necessity (Phil. 1:10).

Grace is enjoyed only by resting in Christ. A life that knows and rests in the grace of God will display and dispenses the character of God. Every time Satan pitches a fiery fast ball and we swing and miss, we as saintly batters only hear our Beloved Umpire call out, "Peace!" He never calls us, "Out," even if we miss seven times seventy times (John 14:27; Matt. 18:21–22).

1 Thessalonians

✞ **POSITION OF GRACE:** (grace has drawn us from the wrath of God and placed us in the life of Christ)

"And [how you] look forward to and await the coming of His Son from heaven, Whom He raised from the dead — Jesus, Who personally rescues and delivers us out of and from the wrath [bringing punishment] which is coming [upon the impenitent] and draws us to Himself [investing us with all the privileges and rewards of the new life in Christ, the Messiah]" (1 Thessalonians 1:10).

Grace has delivered us from the eternal wrath of God. It draws us close to Him and bestows upon us all the privileges, blessings, and rewards given to us in our new life in Christ Jesus. To wait on God requires patience — *His* eternal trust and patience working in our souls, by His grace while we look toward His coming.

Just as Christ was raised from the dead, we are raised to works of eternal life in Him. Christ has raised us from the sleep of death and delivered us from the impending wrath of God; we have been raised to be revealed as a work of God. Grace presents us to the world as awakened to new life, re-born — constructed and empowered by God Himself.

We have been extracted from the world and grafted into the life of God with all of His blessings and benefits freely given to us. These promises and designs of God enable us to live a life, which is useful and fruitful in Christ (2 Peter 1:4). We have been drawn into Life itself, rescued from the death that our trespasses and sins so justly deserved. Beloved, there is no greater position or privilege than knowing Christ!

Any investment that God makes is never made in vain; we are the beneficiaries of His eternal investment. Grace heals us from blindness and short-sightedness; it purifies us from our former sins (2 Peter 1:9). Such purification is neither recognized nor loved by the world, which is doomed to God's impending wrath (Rom. 1:18; Eph. 2:3; Rev. 14:9–12; 20:12–15).

✞ **POSITION / OPERATION OF GRACE:** (grace charges us to live lives worthy of Christ)

"For you know how, as a father [dealing with] his children, we used to exhort each of you personally, stimulating and encouraging and charging you

To live lives worthy of God, Who calls you into His own kingdom and the glorious blessedness [into which true believers will enter after Christ's return]" (1 Thessalonians 2:11–12).

Grace exhorts us to live lives worthy of Christ and His kingdom. This is not something we can attain by our own effort. It takes the grace of God constantly working in our life teaching and training us to deny ungodliness and to live godly lives. Grace is not an invention/work of man; it is an enablement of God that stimulates, encourages, and charges us to live righteously. We need to constantly remind ourselves that it is not our actions, which make us worthy before God; yet we are called to live in a manner worthy of God.

Grace calls us to a life of honourable testimony, a life manifesting God's glory and blessedness. Note that God's grace exhorts every individual believer to live for Christ, just as Christ died for each and every one of us — grace is personal. Our life has been called into the kingdom of the Almighty's magnificence, the Eternal's excellence, the Creator's pre-eminence and dignity — God's gracious blessedness. We are not able to add anything to God's stature (Job 38:1–3; 40:1–2; 42:1–6).

Just as an earthly father corrects and encourages his children, the grace of God works through His body in fellowship. It is the place where the saints are perfected (matured) and fine-tuned. Grace works within us personally as we fellowship with one another; maturing in Christ is not a mass operation accomplished by sitting and listening to sermons being preached (Heb. 12:5–11).

✞ **OPERATION OF GRACE:** (grace works effectually in us)

"And we also [especially] thank God continually for this, that when you received the message of God [which you heard] from us, you welcomed it not as the word of [mere] men, but as it truly is,

the Word of God, which is effectually at work in you who believe [exercising its superhuman power in those who adhere to and trust in and rely on it]" (1 Thessalonians 2:13).

The Word of God works the grace of God into a believing soul. Grace acts like a purifier; it filters out the word and work of man, and enables us to fix our eyes and attention on the Word of God and His work. Grace allows us to see the divine plan which orchestrates the universe; it enables us to respond by allowing His Word to reproduce His work in our life.

Flesh follows and glorifies man; grace follows and glorifies God. A message of God will transform and work effectually in any soul that believes (hears, receives, loves, and obeys) with a heart of grace. God's word does not work outside of God's grace. Its superhuman capability is triggered only by faith and belief; it responds to our acknowledgement and reliance upon it. A soul that encounters the grace of God in such a way will be eternally affected. Only when we see the ways of God as vital, do we allow His virtue to work in us (Phil. 1:10).

✞ **OPERATION OF GRACE:** (grace does not prevent us from being hindered by Satan)

"Because it was our will to come to you. [I mean that] I, Paul, again and again [wanted to come], but Satan hindered and impeded us" (1 Thessalonians 2:18).

The grace of God has disarmed all principalities and powers that can possibly stand against us; it has triumphed over them on the cross of Christ (Col. 2:15). But grace does not make us immune to Satan's devices. He can still interfere with our plans and desires. However, God never abandons us; He is ever present to help us overcome. There are times when we may be impeded or hindered; but we are never conquered or left hopeless in Christ. Satan can hamper us, but he cannot stop us.

Eyes fixed on God's grace will take us through all things and keep us in the Almighty's will. God's grace does not place us in a position where we can never be tempted and lured by Satan; it make us over-comers, and it places us in a position of victory in all things, through Christ Jesus our Lord, regardless of the circumstances (Rom. 8:37).

The Lord's will, carried out in His timing, cannot be defeated or overcome by any power of darkness. "*...For this purpose the Son of God was manifested, that he might destroy the works of the devil"* (1 John 3:8c KJV). We have the priceless privilege of being God's vessels and instruments to display the authority of God. Success in God can be attained only by finishing where God wants us to be, not where our flesh desires us to be (Matt. 26:36–46). Beloved, Stephen was successful; he was not overcome by evil; he overcame evil with good, as he lived out the life of Christ (Acts 7:55–60).

✞ **POSITION OF GRACE:** (grace guarantees that we will be blameless at the coming of our Lord Jesus Christ)

"And may the Lord make you to increase and excel and overflow in love for one another and for all people, just as we also do for you,

So that He may strengthen and confirm and establish your hearts faultlessly pure and unblameable in holiness in the sight of our God and Father, at the coming of our Lord Jesus Christ (the Messiah) with all His saints (the holy and glorified people of God)! Amen, (so be it)" (1 Thessalonians 3:12–13)!

By God's grace, love is provoked to abound through us and towards one another, establishing our hearts in holiness. It is by His grace that we are caused to increase and abound in His love. This same grace declares us free from all blame, and makes us faultlessly pure in the sight of our Father at the coming of our Lord and Saviour, Jesus Christ.

At very best, the human heart is unstable and inconsistent in the exercise of grace. Holiness is not naturally found in the human heart (Jer. 17:9). The human heart empowered by the human will is at best only a fleshy demonstration of human goodness. It takes the grace of God working within a heart to introduce it to God's holiness. Grace keeps our heart in Christ, and it will present it eternally innocent before the Father.

It is God's grace that strengthens us; it is God's grace that confirms us, and it is God's grace that establishes us as holy in the sight of the Father, conferring upon us the sanction of sainthood. A heart touched by the hand of grace becomes blameless, deserving of no censure, and free from fault and defect in the presence of the Almighty (2 Tim. 2:25; Titus 2:8; 1 Peter 4:14).

✞ **OPERATION OF GRACE:** (grace teaches us to attain to greater perfection by living out the Christian faith)

"Furthermore, brethren, we beg and admonish you in [virtue of our union with] the Lord Jesus, that [you follow the instructions which] you learned from us about how you ought to walk so as to please and gratify God, as indeed you are doing, [and] that you do so even more and more abundantly [attaining yet greater perfection in living this life]" (1 Thessalonians 4:1).

The grace of God begs and admonishes us to walk in a way that is pleasing to God. This automatically implies that it is possible to walk in a way that is not pleasing to God. Our position of grace gives us assurance that our salvation is never at stake with regards to our walk in God — it is never our walk that places us in right standing with God. Our walk of righteousness is an operation of the grace of God instructing us in godly attitude and living, until the perfection of Christ comes again to take us home to be with the Father (Luke 23:43).

God's grace draws us closer and closer to His perfection in our life as we sojourn here in this world (Phil. 3:12). Grace joins us to God, and it is this divine association, which renews us daily and causes our mind, our will, and our emotions to become agreeable to the will of God (1 Cor. 15:31). Our union to Christ is by grace, our association with Christ is by grace, and it is this same grace, which keeps us blameless until His coming. We are not destined to become independent of the grace of God. True success is found only in the grace of God (Prov. 16:3).

✞ **OPERATION OF GRACE:** (grace commands a consecrated holy life)

"For you know what charges and precepts we gave you [on the authority and by the inspiration of] the Lord Jesus.

For this is the will of God, that you should be consecrated (separated and set apart for pure and holy living); that you should abstain and shrink from all sexual vice," (1 Thessalonians 4:2–3).

The grace of God commands us to abstain from sexual vice. The word of God charges us to be holy — to be separate and set apart for God, distanced from ungodly living. God's grace never ceases to operate in our life; it continually teaches us to deny ungodly living habits.

Sexual vice is a sin. The will of God is clearly stated here for God's people. Illicit sexual intercourse (adultery, fornication, homosexuality, lesbianism, intercourse with close relatives, intercourse with animals, etc.) is not to be indulged in. This is the will of God, and it is a commandment of the Lord Jesus Christ for His people. Grace does not redefined, condone, or excuse sin (Rom. 6:1–2).

It is on the authority of the Lord Jesus that we are called to live a life worthy of our heavenly calling. As we submit to His grace and His desire to have His way in our life, the authority of God works mightily both within and through us. Regardless of whether we have a complete revelation of how God is working in our life, we can still receive and walk in His authority. Many times we do not recognize God's gift of grace until after it has finished its work (John 19:30; Acts 3:5; 10:34; 11:2–3).

✞ **OPERATION OF GRACE:** (grace incites us to possess our body in knowledge and honour, not in ignorance)

"That each one of you should know how to possess (control, manage) his own body in consecration (purity, separated from things profane) and honour,

Not [to be used] in the passion of lust like the heathen, who are ignorant of the true God, and have no knowledge of His will," (1 Thessalonians 4:4–5).

The grace of God calls us to consecration — a separation from things profane. When we come under the grace of God, our body is no longer our own; it belongs to the Most High. If a brother under grace continues living a life of licentiousness, he has not learned how to possess his own body in consecration and honour (1 Cor. 5:11).

Lust is an affliction of the flesh, springing from a delusion of the mind. It is not founded on reality, truth, or divine love. Lust is never satisfied; it burns, consumes, and wastes the soul, never fulfilling it. Lust will degenerate a soul; God's love regenerates a soul.

Grace, operating in a saint's life will reveal and manifest a love unlike that of the heathen world around it. The world cannot understand God's love because it is ignorant of the true God (John 15:18–19; 1 John 3:13). Our soul is not to be found indulging in passions outside of God's will (Eph. 2:2).

To know God's will is to rightly discern what must be done in every situation; it is only by grace that God's power can bring meaning and purpose to our life. We are possessed by God, acquired and procured for Him alone — we are married to the Beloved. The world does not know, neither can it know the love and passion of God (1 John 2:15–17).

It makes me weep to think that before I knew Christ, I was actually choosing to live and die in this position.

✞ **OPERATION OF GRACE:** (grace plainly warns us not to defraud our brothers, lest we incur punishment from the Lord)

"That no man transgress and overreach his brother and defraud him in this matter or defraud his brother in business. For the Lord is an avenger in all these things, as we have already warned you solemnly and told you plainly" (1 Thessalonians 4:6).

The grace of God earnestly and religiously charges us not to overstep, trespass, or do wrong to our brother. In such actions, God has full licence to exact a penalty from the perpetrator, whether he is Christian or not.

Grace solemnly and plainly warns us of the Lord's action against those who defraud their brother in Christ. There is punishment from the gracious hand of God and a penalty to be paid, for works of deception. All such things are motivated by selfishness, and are found outside of the will of God. Transgression against a brother can bring punishment from God, because to sin against a brother is to sin against God. God does not call for us to get even; we are called to wait upon Him to handle our matters.

Note, salvation is not the issue here, consecration is the issue. Our bodies have been ordained by God to be vessels of blessing, so that the glory may be of God and not of man. Godly punishment is a result of godly love (Heb. 12:5–11; Rev. 3:19). Godly correction helps us to learn how to possess our own bodies in consecration and honour.

✞ **OPERATION OF GRACE:** (grace invites us to a life of purity in action and attitude)

"For God has not called us to impurity but to consecration [to dedicate ourselves to the most thorough purity].

Therefore whoever disregards (sets aside and rejects this) disregards not man but God, Whose [very] Spirit [Whom] He gives to you is holy (chaste, pure)" (1 Thessalonians 4:7–8).

The grace of God warns people to whom He has given His Spirit, not to disregard God. Grace never invites us to indulge in iniquity. Grace calls us to purity, not profanity. Grace does not empower us to act irreverently; it teaches us to deny ungodliness and its authority over our life's affairs. Lustful, profligate living and impure motives are a work of the flesh. We need God's grace to help and enable us to refrain and remove ourselves from impurity.

Whosoever disregards or sets aside the call to a consecrated holy life, disregards God. Beloved, the call of grace is divinely designed to release the effectiveness of godliness in our life. To refuse or to slight righteous enablement in our life is to reject and slight God (2 Peter 1:8–9).

The grace of God has positioned us in holiness in Christ. This same grace operates within our life enabling us to hear, receive, love, and obey righteous commands — accepting and responding to the holy and godly unction inspired by the Holy Spirit (1 John 2:27). Holy actions are the outcome of the Holy Spirit working and living within us; transgressions are a work of the flesh prompted by the prince of the power of the air who is now working in the sons of disobedience.

✞ **POSITION OF GRACE:** (grace appoints us to salvation, not wrath)

"For God has not appointed us to [incur His] wrath [He did not select us to condemn us], but [that we might] obtain [His] salvation through our Lord Jesus Christ (the Messiah)" (1 Thessalonians 5:9).

Beloved, since we are children of the day, we are called to be sober, to put on the breastplate of faith and love, and to don the hope of salvation for a helmet (Rom. 13:12–13; 1 Thess. 5:5, 8; Is. 59:17; Eph. 6:17; 1 John 4:17). God has not destined us for wrath, but to salvation (deliverance) through Jesus Christ, our Lord (John 3:36; Rom. 1:18; 5:9; Eph. 2:5). Our position of eternal life is forever sealed by the Faithful One.

Although the grace of God has delivered us from His wrath, it is by this same grace that our Father punishes and corrects us lovingly (Rev. 3:19; Heb. 12:7). We never need to fear loss of salvation, or being separated from the love of Christ Jesus our Lord, for it is this same love that reproves and disciplines us.

✞ **OPERATION OF GRACE:** (grace seriously advises and warns us to not be disorderly and unruly; but rather to be supportive and helpful to the fainthearted and weak)

"And we earnestly beseech you, brethren, admonish (warn and seriously advise) those who are out of line [the loafers, the disorderly, and the unruly]; encourage the timid and faint-hearted, help and give your support to the weak souls, [and] be very patient with everybody [always keeping your temper]" (1 Thessalonians 5:14).

The grace of God seriously admonishes and rebukes brethren who live disorderly, unruly, and outside of godly attitudes. Grace changes unregenerate attitudes into generous, helpful attitudes, which encourage and bear the fruit of the Holy Spirit with patience (Gal 5:22; Col. 1:11; Heb. 6:12). Grace is supportive and helpful to weak and fainthearted souls. The grace that we have been comforted with is the same grace that so readily flows to those in need around us (2 Cor. 1:4–6).

Grace, tempered by God, is able to keep its temper. We are not to be controlled by the flesh, but rather, controlled by the Spirit, which bears the fruit of patience and long-suffering. To be out of line with the purposes of God is not a good place to be. Beloved, there is not one Christian who is not out of line in some area of their life (Gal. 2:11; Phi. 3:11–15). We need to seek God, repent, and take this admonition seriously, so that we might be an example to the timid and faint-hearted, and be a source of encouragement to the weak.

✞ **POSITION / OPERATION OF GRACE:** (grace calls us to abstain from evil in whatever form or kind it may be)

"Abstain from evil [shrink from it and keep aloof from it] in whatever form or whatever kind it may be.

And may the God of peace Himself sanctify you through and through [separate you from profane things, make you pure and wholly consecrated to God]; and may your spirit and soul and body be preserved sound and complete [and found] blameless at the coming of our Lord Jesus Christ (the Messiah)" (1 Thessalonians 5:22–23).

The grace of God commands us to refrain from evil. We are admonished to keep aloof and shrink from evil's grasp, in whatever form it may come. God warns us here not to be misled (Rom. 16:17; 1 Tim. 6:5; 1 John 2:26; 2 Peter 2:1–2). Beloved, it is possible for Christians to be involved in activities that God defines as evil. Grace calls us to test everything, and to hold fast to that which is good — that which is from God (Jas. 1:17). Our position of grace guarantees us access to God's mercy and goodness, and the operation of grace teaches us to discern and abstain from all the forms of ungodliness, which come our way.

Our sanctification comes from the God of peace; it is not a human struggle that sanctifies us. As we live in the gracious position of eternal justification, we experience the work of grace within us as God works His will into the very fabric of our being, building completeness in our spirit, soul, and body. Beloved, separation from profane things and becoming pure and wholly consecrated to God is not just a 'spiritual matter'. It will manifest itself outwardly through our bodies as we dedicate them to God.

Consecration is not accomplished by the efforts of the flesh; it is accomplished by the grace of God, daily drawing us toward the perfection and completeness of our Lord and Saviour, Jesus Christ. Our salvation is a work of God which manifests itself through all the works of our spirit, soul, and body, reflecting the gracious work of our Father (John 5:19, 30).

✞ **<u>POSITION OF GRACE</u>:** (grace is eternally at work in us)

"<u>Faithful</u> is He Who is <u>calling</u> you [to Himself] and utterly trustworthy, and He will also do it [fulfil His call by hallowing and keeping you]" (1 Thessalonians 5:24).

It is God Who makes us holy, and it is God who preserves us. Divinely imputed holiness can neither be earned nor gained by the work of mere mortal flesh; it is only freely and graciously given to all who believe and have faith in the work of Jesus Christ, the Lord. The fact that our spirit, soul, and body will be kept sound and blameless until the coming of our Lord Jesus Christ is true because of God's faithfulness, not our own. It is His faithfulness, which guarantees the completion of the good work He has initiated. He who has begun a good work in us will bring it to completion at the day of Jesus Christ, developing and perfecting us as we are transformed into His image.

Beloved, *only* God knows what His perfect work in us will look like, therefore, *only* God is able to complete it. Anything that we could possibly add by our efforts would only pervert it. We have been invited to bear the name of Him who calls us and keeps us — we are Christians, by the grace of God (Acts 4:10–12; Rom. 10:9, 13).

2 Thessalonians

✝ **POSITION / OPERATION OF GRACE:** (grace is a sanctifying work, which causes thankfulness in our soul as we believe and rely on the Truth)

"But we, brethren beloved by the Lord, ought and are obligated [as those who are in debt] to give thanks always to God for you, because God chose you from the beginning as His first fruits (first converts) for salvation through the sanctifying work of the [Holy] Spirit and [your] belief in (adherence to, trust in, and reliance on) the Truth" (2 Thessalonians 2:13).

The grace of God only becomes revelation through belief *in* and reliance *upon* the Truth (John 6:14; 8:32). Any encounter with the Truth births within us thankfulness towards God for His gracious work of salvation and the sanctifying work of the Holy Spirit. With the knowledge of having judgment lifted from our soul, we no longer find any true pleasure in unrighteousness. The effect of grace on our life has truly given us cause to be grateful, and this joy can only be experienced by being born-again (1 Peter 1:22–23).

God chose us from the beginning of time to be the first fruits of His grace. The Holy Spirit has separated us from profane things; it has made us objects of holiness dedicated to God. It has purified us internally through the renewing of our soul — our mind, our will, and our emotions. Truth is the unchanging foundation upon which grace comes to us, and it is this same everlasting grace that determinedly teaches and trains us to deny ungodliness any place in our lives. It calls us to live according to the Way, the Truth, and the Life, and we are called to follow in His steps (1 Peter 2:21). We are not called to be polluted streams (Prov. 25:26).

✝ **POSITION OF GRACE:** (grace is the source of all hope, encouragement and comfort)

"Now may our Lord Jesus Christ Himself and God our Father, Who loved us and gave us everlasting consolation and encouragement and well-founded hope through [His] grace (unmerited favour)," (2 Thessalonians 2:16).

The grace of God places us in a position of ceaseless support and comfort. Righteous refreshment is the fruit of grace — eternally bestowed upon all believers. Just as grace is not attainable through human effort, true comfort, encouragement, and hope are also not truly obtainable outside of the grace of God (1 Peter 1:3). Grace is the channel of God's righteousness; it is a river of reassurance, an ocean of comfort, and an eternal rest given by God.

✝ **OPERATION OF GRACE:** (the work of grace brings comfort, encouragement and strength to those around it)

"Comfort and encourage your hearts and strengthen them [make them steadfast and keep them unswerving] in every good work and word" (2 Thessalonians 2:17).

The heart of God has been made accessible to man by the grace of God. Grace enables our heart to experience and share God's heart. When grace operates within us, our heart is strengthened and fixed in a divine direction; it gives eternal significance and security (Prov. 4:23; 23:26). Oh the blessedness of being apprehended by the grace of God! Only such a seizing work of grace can bring comfort and reinforcement to all who lie in its path, producing a life of word and deed that personifies and reflects that same grace.

As surely as God is unswerving, His imputed grace is unswerving and never-ending. A soul strengthened by the grace of God is a soul that displays the strength of the love of the Almighty God, hanging on the cross, and paying the price for the misguided words and deeds of the world. God's grace was given as a display of his love for the world (John 3:16–17).

✝ **OPERATION OF GRACE:** (grace gives us the authority to withdraw from fellow believers who are idle and lazy)

"Now we charge you, brethren, in the name and on the authority of our Lord Jesus Christ (the Messiah) that you withdraw and keep away from every brother (fellow believer) who is slack in

performance of duty and is disorderly, living as a shirker and not walking in accord with the traditions and instruction that you have received from us" (2 Thessalonians 3:6).

Obviously there are those who are idle and do not follow the tradition of hard work. They are lazy and become a burden, meddling in other people's business. It is the grace of God that commands us to withdraw from fellow believers who practice such laziness. Grace never trains us to indulge in unrighteousness; it trains us to discern and withdraw from the presence of anyone who calls himself a brother, and yet lives a life deviating from the prescribed way of God. Grace invites us towards godliness and doing right; it never entices us towards ungodliness and laziness.

The same grace that forgives us is the same grace that corrects us. The name of Christ is the name of grace; it is not a name representing wantonness. Grace brings the revelation of God's order to our life, not blind disorder or worldly order. Such spiritual withdrawal from worldly order is an act of grace, not an act of pride or up-man-ship. Grace never makes us better than someone else (Acts 3:11–12; 14:11–15).

The gracious charge of withdrawal from worldly love or receiving adoration from the world is not a negative thing, it is a divine calling (John 15:19; 1 John 2:15). It is not a demonstration of seeing one's self as being better than another; it is the Holy Spirit's endeavour to bring self-discipline into a soul, which has experienced restoration with God (Acts 24:25; 2 Tim. 1:7).

✞ **OPERATION OF GRACE:** (grace distinguishes between right and wrong and draws us to obedience)

"But if anyone [in the church] refuses to obey what we say in this letter, take note of that person and do not associate with him, so that he may be ashamed" (2 Thessalonians 3:14).

Grace distinguishes; it takes note of disobedience to truth. Note that even though grace is used to bring shame to ungodly actions habitually performed by God's people, the motivation and purpose of grace remains the same — reconciliation. A work of grace brings life to any soul floundering in a spiritual state of death; it always reflects obedience to the righteous will of God. Godly, gracious correction will always result in reverence towards God; it is never an act of wickedness motivated by arrogant pride (3 John 1:9–13).

We are commanded by grace not to keep company with or be intimate with any believer who habitually walks contrary to the path of the heritage we have so freely received (1 Cor. 5:11). A work of grace will establish righteousness and godliness in its recipient. Shame produced by any work of grace is healing; it is never disgracing, and it will accomplish what God desires — reconciliation.

✞ **OPERATION OF GRACE:** (grace warns and admonishes believers to love and good works)

"Do not regard him as an enemy, but simply admonish and warn him as [being still] a brother" (2 Thessalonians 3:15).

The grace of God surrounds our ungodly disobedience, and like a father's loving arms surround a child heading in the wrong direction, grace protects and pulls us back to safety. A brother in Christ is never an enemy. Since it is God Who has made him a brother, it is God who keeps him as such. The grace of God never authorizes us to consider or deem any brother in Christ as an enemy. God never authorizes anyone to put any member of the body of Christ out of the church; out of fellowship yes, but never out of the church. We have control of who we fellowship with; we do not have control over who is in the body of Christ.

The body of Christ is created by the hand of God. His unchangeable arms of justice spread themselves; His hands of righteousness opened themselves to willingly receive the piercing nails of injustice and hatred. He poured forth the blood of grace and truth as an offering to the world. Only God can place people into the church (the body of Christ); no one should possibly think that they can cast anyone out as an enemy. It is arrogant, presumptuous pride that condemns a vessel as unclean, what God has declared clean (3 John 1:10).

The breaking of fellowship never removes anyone from the church; it is designed to produce a godly reverence that will cause a wayward soul to turn towards holiness — repentance and reconciliation (1 Cor. 5:1–5; 2 Cor. 2:1–11). It is designed to admonish, warn and exhort the recipient to bear the fruit of love and good works. A work of grace never disposes of a soul as an undesired piece of rubbish.

It takes a soul moved by grace to convey such grace towards others. The fruit of gracious discipline is peace, and the motivation of gracious discipline is godliness, restoration, and reconciliation.

1 Timothy

✞ **POSITION / OPERATION OF GRACE:** (grace teaches us to identify unwholesome and unsound living practices defined by the Law)

"Knowing and understanding this: that the Law is not enacted for the righteous (the upright and just, who are in right standing with God), but for the lawless and unruly, for the ungodly and sinful, for the irreverent and profane, for those who strike and beat and [even] murder fathers and strike and beat and [even] murder mothers, for manslayers,

[For] impure and immoral persons, those who abuse themselves with men, kidnappers, liars, perjurers — and whatever else is opposed to wholesome teaching and sound doctrine" (1 Timothy 1:9–10).

The Law is not enacted for the righteous, but for the lawless and disobedient. We have been declared approved and acceptable to God by His grace; He has cancelled the certificate of debt the Law held against us (Col. 2:13–15). He took us out from under the condemnation of the Law and placed His eternal 'paid-in-full' seal upon us, giving us the Holy Spirit as our guarantee of this transaction (2 Cor. 1:22; 5:5). God's grace continually keeps our lives in right standing before the Eternal.

Our deeds and actions can never justify us before God. Our salvation never depends upon our obedience to the law of God; we are justified *only* by our faith in the blood of the Lamb.

When anyone departs from or violates the law, they are called lawless. Outside of Christ, everyone is condemned by their lawlessness — their sin (John 3:18; 1 John 3:4). In Christ, when a righteous person commits a lawless act, he is not eternally condemned like those outside of Christ. Albeit, if we as Christians act with disobedience and rebellion, the Holy Spirit who has written the Law on our heart will convict us of sin — the violation of God's law.

The unwholesome and unsound living practices mentioned in this scripture are invariably identified by the Law. The Law is enacted to point out lawlessness — sin (Rom. 3:20; 7:7; 1 John 3:4). It is the grace of God that saves us from the condemnation of eternal death and hell; and it is this same grace of God that continually trains and teaches us to reject all ungodliness in our life. Grace does not call us to become slaves of sin (Rom. 6:12–18).

The Law is a very useful tool for knowing the will of God. All things contrary to sound teaching and precepts are pointed out and identified by the Law. The law was given to distinguish right from wrong; grace gives us eternal life and teaches us to live uprightly. The purpose of the righteous law of God is to define unwholesome and unsound practices that can enslave us and make us unfruitful in the kingdom of God (2 Peter 1:8).

Grace does not turn a blind eye to licentious living (Prov. 5:21; 15:3). When we find ourselves in sin, our only recourse is to acknowledge it, forsake it, and turn to God (repentance) (Prov. 28:13). As we continue to submit to the Spirit of grace, it will teach and train us by drawing us toward good and righteous living habits — a humble, repentant lifestyle working godly sorrow into our life and keeping us free from the power of sin (1 John 1:7–9).

✞ **OPERATION OF GRACE:** (grace can even use Satan to chastise us)

"Holding fast to faith (that leaning of the entire human personality on God in absolute trust and confidence) and having a good (clear) conscience. By rejecting and thrusting from them [their conscience], some individuals have made shipwreck of their faith.

Among them are Hymanaeus and Alexander, whom I have delivered to Satan in order that they may be disciplined [by punishment and learn] not to blaspheme" (1 Timothy 1:19–20).

Grace calls us to keep a firm grasp on our faith; it is a vital necessity for the Christian life. Our entire being is permeated by our faith; there is nothing in our life that is not touched by our faith. What we believe will determine what we see, and hence what we do (John 9:26–34). It is imperative for a believer to establish his faith in truth. When we believe a lie (John 8:43–45), we actually end up shunning truth, and in essence become a scoffer (Prov. 15:12). The exercising of our faith causes an unswerving confidence to grow and mature in our life in Christ (Heb. 5:12–14). Godly confidence comes from a clean conscience, not a dead, seared, or calloused one.

Our conscience is what makes us knowledgeable of all the affairs of our soul — the actions of our mind, our will, and our emotions (Prov. 20:27). It causes us to be mindful, willful, and able to distinguish between what is morally good and bad; it prompts us to overcome evil with good. Our conscience should be founded on God's truth, not on belief systems or lies that Satan has fed us (John 8:42–44).

The entrance of grace into our life does not rid us of our conscience; it trains and brings godly regulation to it. If we ignore conscious warnings of impending spiritual storms, we will find ourselves clinging to the debris of a shipwrecked life. A clear conscience has been trained by the grace of God to discern between good and bad morals. Grace commends; it does not condemn (John 8:11).

It was by the grace of God that Hymanaeus and Alexander were turned over to Satan. Note that being turned over to Satan did not mean that they had lost their eternal life in Christ. The purpose and objective — the spiritual motivation — of such disciplinary action was to chasten them, bringing them to a place of restoration. The objective was to punish, with the intention of sanctification — to make them more restrained, humbled, and subdued to the grace of God. To be restrained by the grace of God is to be set free indeed (John 8:34–36).

Just as Job was chastened by God, our omniscient Lord can even use Satan to train and cause us to learn a life lesson. The lesson that Hymanaeus and Alexander needed to learn was not to blaspheme — to speak evil of, or be slanderous, reproachful, railing, or abusive towards truth. Truth is always just, right, and good, in God's sight; it is never good for us to judge God's ways. Grace calls us to follow the plans and purposes of God.

Beloved, only God can throw a soul into hell. There is no man on earth who has the authority and power to 'save' a soul, or even to declare a soul saved. There is no man on earth who has the authority to 'un-save' a soul or even declare another soul to be unsaved. Such claims come from an arrogant, proud spirit motivated by the fleshy desire for control. Such pompous proclamations within the body of Christ are not perpetrated by the grace of God. Beloved our eternal destination is fixed by God, not formed by man. Heavenly discipline is always for our good, so that we may become partakers of His holiness (Heb. 12:10).

When we first believed, we received our salvation. Faith was birthed in us, but we need to be cautious so as not to shipwreck our faith. Our faith is our living link to God and hence it becomes the main target of the enemy as he tries to pervert and mislead us. Faith comes through hearing the living word of God, and it calls our life to be in submission to the Living Word (Rom. 10:17). It is necessary for Christians to be able to discern the living word of God, and hence to recognize and reject all things that are untrue (Gal. 2:5).

✝ **POSITION OF GRACE:** (grace positions us in precise and correct relation to divine Truth)

"For such [praying] is good and right, and [it is] pleasing and acceptable to God our Saviour,

Who wishes all men to be saved [increasingly] to perceive and recognize and discern and know precisely and correctly the [divine] Truth" (1 Timothy 2:3–4).

Prayer is one of the highest duties to enjoy in a Christian life. Whether for governing authorities or for all men, we are to plead for God's mercy upon them and give thanks. This is good and pleasing to God our Saviour who desires to have all men saved by His grace. God's pre-determined plan is the salvation of all mankind; He desires that mankind come to a correct knowledge of things divine. The complete fulfilment of His desire can only be thwarted by something that has been ordained and created in His own image — mankind's will.

Our will was created in the image of God and hence it has a strong ability to decide and choose its own way. Our free will gives us the power and right to make wrong choices and to choose a way contrary to God's will. He gives us authority over our will.

The word 'authority' in the Greek language, means 'freedom of choice'. Adam and Eve followed the wrong authority, which caused the fall of man. Jesus, the second Adam, has given us access to God's authority again and commissions us to make choices in agreement with His will (1 Cor. 15:21–22). This brings with it the eternal encouragement that He is always with us (Matt. 28:18–20).

Mankind's fallen will needs the grace of God to enable and empower it to choose God's will. Nevertheless, God has still given mankind the right to choose contrary to His will and remain outside of God's grace even for all eternity, if they so choose. How sad this would be. A will that chooses to love God is more precious than a love that comes out of obligation; this is why God respects our freedom of choice. He does not go against our will. He teaches us to understand that His love is greater than even life itself (Ps. 63:3).

Our only entrance into the realm of truth is through the door of grace (John 10:7; 14:6). Truth is part of God's character and He desires that we come to know Him — the Truth. We can only respect God and the operation of His purposes, through a relationship with the Truth — He is the standard set by God. Truth is unchangeable and established forever with regards to the duty of mankind. It opposes superstitions, inventions of corrupt minds, and false teachings (Col. 2:8; 1 Tim. 1:4; Titus 3:9; 2 Peter 3:16; 1 John 2:26). Grace positions us in Truth, and then works that truth into our life. This is the renewing of our soul.

Truly with all this in mind, prayer is a full time job; it is good and pleasing to God, and hence to the body of Christ.

✞ **OPERATION OF GRACE:** (grace works a good reputation into our life and portrays it before men)

"Furthermore, he must have a good reputation and be well thought of by those outside [the church], lest he become involved in slander and incur reproach and fall into the devil's trap" (1 Timothy 3:7).

Since godly leadership is executed by example and not coercion, a good reputation is an essential quality for a godly leader to have. Note, that just because we are under God's grace does not mean that a righteous person cannot be trapped by the devil (Acts 26:11; 1 Tim. 1:20; James 2:7). It is particularly important for leaders not to fall for the devil's cunning devices, thus fulfilling the proverb 'the blind leading the blind' (2 Cor. 5:12).

As believers, we should never allow evil works to taint us with a bad reputation. Any reproach we ever incur should always be for righteousness, never unrighteousness (1 Peter 3:17).

✞ **POSITION / OPERATION OF GRACE:** (grace teaches us proper conduct in the body of Christ — the house of God)

"If I am detained, you may know how people ought to conduct themselves in the household of God, which is the church of the living God, the pillar and stay (the prop and support) of the Truth" (1 Timothy 3:15).

Grace is constantly building the pillar and stay of Truth — the church. Proper conduct in the body of Christ — the household of God — is the outcome of the operation of grace in our life. A life founded on truth is not a life that displays debauchery, but rather it is a life that conducts itself according to the revelation of truth (2 John 1:4; 3 John 1:4). Grace acts upon our life enabling us to say, *"I can do nothing against the Truth, I cannot serve any particular party or personal interest, but only serve the Truth, which is the Gospel"* (2 Corinthians 13:8). It needs to be noted here that to serve factions of the church or to serve personal interest is not a representation of the Gospel (Gal. 2:4–5).

Although God is building His church with living stones that are not yet perfected, it is not correct to conclude that God builds His house contrary to His holy principles (1 Peter 2:5). God's house of grace constrains and trains us to proper conduct; it declares that we should know how to walk uprightly in grace. A house built on truth is a house built upon the eternal principles of God (Prov. 24:3–4); it is founded upon the Rock (Matt. 7:24–27). To divide or faction the church is like dividing a rock into pieces (sand) — a very unstable and foolish place to build.

✞ **POSITION / OPERATION OF GRACE:** (grace warns us not to be misled by seducing spirits)

"But the [Holy] Spirit distinctly and expressly declares that in latter times some will turn away from the faith, giving attention to deluding and seducing spirits and doctrines that demons teach," (1 Timothy 4:1).

The grace of God warns us not to turn away from the faith and give heed to demonic teachings. Demonic distortion of truth is constantly presented to us by the enemy of our souls. Our position of being saved by faith and our assurance of salvation is a common target for the enemy. Whenever we believe and hence follow after any error, the word of God is made of no effect in that particular area of our life (2 Peter 1:8–10). Christians are not immune to the wiles of the devil; we are called to be wise and alert, and to know the word and will of God (Eph. 4:14; 6:11).

To depart from truth is to withdraw from the power and authority of God and stand aloof from His promises. God's life instructions do not change just because we come under His grace. "*What shall we say [to all this]? Are we to remain in sin in order that God's grace (favour and mercy) may multiply and overflow? Certainly not! How can we who died to sin live in it any longer*" (Romans 6:1–2)? What God defines as wrong before we knew Christ, it is still wrong when we are under His grace. The blood of Christ washes us forever clean but it does not give us licence to violate the life principles of God (1 John 1:7; 3:4).

The Spirit of Christ takes us from unclean to clean, while demonic seducing spirits try to take us from clean to unclean. Of what profit were the things that brought death to our life before we knew Christ, and what profit can they possibly be after we know Christ? Seducing spirits entice us towards wrong doing and ungodly living; they always adulterate the truth, which brings us into bondage. They try to shipwreck and pervert our position of faith and the working out of faith in our lives. Error often masquerades as truth; it slyly replaces truth with philosophical religious sounding words and logic (Gen. 3:1–6; Col. 2:8; 1 Tim. 1:4; Titus 3:9).

✞ **POSITION / OPERATION OF GRACE:** (grace holds promise both for now and forevermore)

"For physical training is of some value (useful for a little), but godliness (spiritual training) is useful and of value in everything and in every way, for it holds promise for the present life and also for the life which is to come" (1 Timothy 4:8).

The grace of God calls us to exercise godliness. Just as there is physical or natural training, there is spiritual training. The former is useful for a little, but the latter is of great value in everything, for all time. Grace holds promise for the life to come (position), and it also holds promise for the present life (operation). During our sojourn here on earth we are continually called to the training ground of God's grace; we are constantly being led towards godliness (2 Peter 1:8–11).

✞ **OPERATION OF GRACE:** (grace calls us from death to life)

"Whereas she who lives in pleasure and self-gratification [giving herself up to luxury and self-indulgence] is dead even while she [still] lives.

Charge [the people] thus, so that they may be without reproach and blameless" (1 Timothy 5:6–7).

The habitual indulgence in self-gratification and fleshy pleasures renders us dead even while living under grace (James 2:20, 26). This is not to say that eternal life is lost; it means that the person is producing the same fruit as the spiritually dead (Eph. 2:1–3).

Grace draws us from the path of selfishness and places us on the path of life — a path which enables us to check our indulgences and die to self. Grace calls us from the broad road of reproach, to the narrow highway of holiness in faith; it cleanses us from eternal blame and commands us to walk uprightly. Selfishness always brings reproach; selflessness opens the door to holiness through the continuous renewal of our soul.

When a person *demands*, it is usually for the purpose of control and the benefit of self; it is motivated by the spirit of the world. When a person *commands*, it is for the purpose of fulfilling the will of God; it is motivated and empowered by the Holy Spirit (Luke 22:31–32; John 18:19–23, 33–38; 19:8–11). A person without God's authority can demand; a person under God's authority can command (Matt. 8:5–13). Demanding our own way is not the same as commanding God's way. As Christians it is vital to discern when you are being demanded upon by man's authority or being commanded by God's authority. Demanding is an attempt to gain authority or control over something or someone else; commanding comes from God's authority and makes one a co-worker with God.

✞ **OPERATION OF GRACE:** (grace erases eternal condemnation and yet we can still be guilty of wrong doing)

"But refuse [to enrol on this list the] younger widows, for when they become restive and their natural desires grow strong, they withdraw themselves against Christ [and] wish to marry [again].

And so they incur condemnation for having set aside and slighted their previous pledge" (1 Timothy 5:11–12).

It is possible for a saint under the grace of God to withdraw their self against Christ, and incur condemnation for their actions. This is not the condemnation of eternal death, which Christ has forever removed us from; it is the guilt felt by a soul that withdraws itself against Christ and His holiness. Such conviction can be felt as grace teaches and trains a soul, renewing and drawing it towards the righteous and holy nature of Christ (Rev. 3:19). Conviction by the Spirit of God is a gracious part of our normal Christian walk — our grace-covenant life.

✞ **OPERATION OF GRACE:** (grace corrects elders/leaders to instil the fear of God in us)

"As for those who are guilty and persist in sin, rebuke and admonish them in the presence of all, so that the rest may be warned and stand in wholesome awe and fear" (1 Timothy 5:20).

Being under the grace of God does not mean that Christians are incapable of sinning. Here we see Christian leadership falling into and persisting in sin. The gracious response to such a situation is to rebuke and admonish them in the presence of all. This gracious action is designed to accomplish the will of God and bring about a wholesome, godly awe and fear in all (Gal. 2:14).

Mutual dependence upon one another automatically means mutual discipline towards one another. The church has been rendered ineffective in the area of discipline by the false doctrine that discipline must only come from leadership. The amount of gracious correction we show towards one another is directly related to the amount of love we show towards one another. A body void of self-discipline is a body void of love and grace; it is a body that lacks self-control and ends up in problems (Prov. 1:24–33; 5:21–23).

Leadership is never 'above' the body in respect to discipline; godly rendering of discipline is an act of the Holy Spirit, not the responsibility of a man in a position of leadership (Acts 5:4–5). If the same history of Ananias and Sapphira repeated itself today in *a church*, nobody would be in next week's church service. Members of that particular faction would either go to another church, or start another one of their own (Acts 20:28–31).

To not correct leadership when they are persisting in sin is to not love the body of Christ, and it is an example of not walking in grace. To 'not touch God's anointed' is often used as an excuse towards not correcting leadership (1 Chron. 16:22; Ps. 105:15). In the body of Christ, all of

God's people are 'the anointed'. Beloved, David 'did not touch God's anointed' by not killing Saul; but he definitely did rebuke and admonish him in the presence of all (1 Sam. 26:9–25). It is only arrogant pride that places itself above correction, and it is only arrogance not to receive correction from those supposedly *below* you.

Such arrogance is not of God and needs to be repented of; it is of the teaching of the Nicolaitans — the separating of the ministry from the laity, giving ministry power over the common people or laity (Rev. 2:6, 15).

Godly church leadership is only truly leading when it walks by example. It is hypocritical and ungodly when leaders do not submit to one another, or the body of Christ, while expecting others to submit to them. God is not impressed or enthralled with 'leadership'. He supports truth and righteousness, and He is represented by anyone who speaks truth by the Spirit of God. It is only the Holy Spirit that has the position of leading, not man (3 John 1:9–10).

The purpose of all correction and discipline is reconciliation and restoration, instilling a wholesome fear, dread, and awe into the whole body of Christ. A wholesome fear of the Lord is the godly outcome of divine correction, whether you are in leadership or not. Divine correction offends the flesh, but rejoices the spirit (John 9:1–41).

✞ **OPERATION OF GRACE:** (grace admonishes us to avoid being involved in another person's sin)

"Do not be in a hurry in the laying on of hands [giving the sanction of the church too hastily in reinstating expelled offenders or in ordination in questionable cases], nor share or participate in another man's sins; keep yourself pure," (1 Timothy 5:22).

Grace admonishes us not to be in too much of a hurry to sanction or ordain questionable behaviour. It also warns us not to be a partaker in another man's sins. We are to keep ourselves pure from every fault, reproach, and blame. Grace teaches us to not enter into fellowship with, or join ourselves to, or even associate as a partner, with others who practise impurity (1 Cor. 5:11).

Grace and carnality do not mix. Like oil and water, grace will always rise to the top covering the cost of carnality, but it never calls us to associate with it. Our position of grace in Christ has paid the price for our carnality (Col. 2:14). The operation of grace deals with our carnality on a day to day basis, changing our heart and attitudes as we become more Christ-like. Our position of grace guarantees our salvation, and the operation of grace continually works on these carnal vessels, purifying them and teaching them to deny ungodliness.

The hand of God is a symbol of might, activity and power as He upholds and preserves righteousness. In a parallel manner, hands of grace should never be quick to uphold unrighteousness. A hand of grace is not to be found employed in the work of iniquity. What do righteousness and wickedness have in common?

✞ **POSITION / OPERATION OF GRACE:** (our position of grace gives us boundless riches; the operation of grace teaches us to be content with what we have in the natural and to covet only after spiritual riches)

"But those who crave to be rich fall into temptation and a snare and into many foolish (useless, godless) and hurtful desires that plunge men into ruin and destruction and miserable perishing" (1 Timothy 6:9).

The gain we have in God is godliness, with contentment. We need to constantly remind ourselves that we brought nothing into this world; and that will we take nothing out of it (Job 1:21). Grace calls us to be content with all that the Almighty so graciously provides for our needs. Grace can neither be added to nor taken away from. Beloved, our contentment lies not in our possessions, but rather in our position in Christ; we ought to be found content at all times, having learned how to abase and how to abound (Phil 4:11–12).

Craving after more things when we already possess all things in Christ, is not a passion inspired by grace; it is a desiring inspired by carnality. There is nothing that we receive that does not come from the hand of God. How can we possibly give Him anything?

A desire to be rich is a snare, eventually bringing ruin and despair (1 Tim. 6:10). Satan tempted Jesus to become rich and powerful, and it is the same temptation that he presents to saints today (Matt. 4:8–10). Faith in the Lord's provision is far superior to all the riches of the world. A mind set on riches is a mind that has not yet discovered the riches of Christ (Mark 8:36).

Eyes set on riches and power, are eyes that know not the grace of God or His bountiful provision. Just as birds and beasts are caught unawares by a snare, saints with eyes set on riches fall into temptation and end up being allured into a position where the devil traps them into bondage.

All our desires, cravings, and longings should be towards what is holy, just and good; and to put mammon into this category is to err. The craving after riches will drown men in destruction causing them to perish miserably. To equate monetary riches with the grace of God is a foundational error that the saints of Laodicea fell into (Rev. 3:14–22). It is the carnal nature of man that causes him to desire to both have his cake and eat it too; it is the carnal nature of man that says, "If I just won the lottery, I could give more to God."

Our coveting should always be after spiritual riches, not carnal riches. Anything you can put a monetary value on is perishable and is not the kingdom of God. It is not money that is evil; it is the love of money that is evil. In like manner, it is not natural things that are evil; it is the love of them that entices one away from faithfulness in the kingdom of God.

✞ **POSITION / OPERATION OF GRACE:** (grace teaches us to avoid the grief of the love of money)

"For the love of money is a root of all evils; it is through this craving that some have been led astray and have wandered from the faith and pierced themselves through with many acute [mental] pangs" (1 Timothy 6:10).

Carnal desires and cravings lead one astray. The grace of God again reminds us not to be led astray by the desire for money and riches, or the yearning for power and prestige. Beloved, the kingdom of God is righteousness, peace, and joy in the Holy Spirit — these things are beyond all earthly value (Rom. 14:17; 2 Tim. 2:22). When we follow after fleshy, carnal desires, we wander from the realm of faith.

To use faith as a tool to become rich is evidence of true spiritual poverty. God has positioned us in a place of prosperity; we need not desire more. We only deceive ourselves when we think that we need more so that we can give more to God; for all things come from God (Mark 12:42–44). When you have given your all to God, how much more can you give? When you have all things given to you by God, how much more can you ask for (Matt. 7:11; 2 Peter 1:3)? The concept of tithing to God is self-righteous, religious logic; it is not a spiritual truth found in our new life as Christians. God's goal of grace is for us to be giving one hundred percent of ourselves to Him. I cannot imagine Jesus giving ten percent to the Father, thinking that He is fulfilling God's requirements (Luke 22:42).

As the root of any plant is the foundation of the plant's life and existence, note here that grace teaches us that the love of money and riches is the root of all kinds of evil. Beloved, the love of money may make one rich and prosperous in the eyes of the world, but never in the kingdom of God. Evil is always the progeny spawned by a heart mired in the love of money (Prov. 16:16).

✞ **POSITION / OPERATION OF GRACE:** (grace commands us to flee from the love of money and to develop godliness)

"But as for you, O man of God, flee from all these things; aim at and pursue righteousness (right standing with God and true goodness), godliness (which is the loving fear of God and being Christlike), faith, love, steadfastness (patience), and gentleness of heart" (1 Timothy 6:11).

The grace of God warns the man of God to flee from the temptation of riches, and to aim at and pursue righteousness, godliness, faith, love, patience, and gentleness of heart. These things are the true riches of God. Temporary things have temporary value; eternal things have eternal value. A desire to be rich comes from a heart that knows not of the riches of its position in Christ. The desire for more wealth is a chasing after the wind, and such chasing will always distract us from working in the kingdom of God (Prov. 22:16; 28:20). Grace calls us to aim at and pursue the true riches in God — righteousness and wisdom (Rev. 3:18). From our position of grace in Christ, we are righteous. By the operation of grace, we are inspired to apply righteousness to all areas of our life.

Being Christlike does not allow a foothold for ungodly actions and works. By God's grace we have both 'been made' and 'are being made' righteous. Grace births a gentleness and steadfastness into our life that demonstrates God's love to those around us. Faith without works is dead, and faith never works in an ungodly manner (Jas. 2:14–26).

✞ **POSITION / OPERATION OF GRACE:** (grace calls us to struggle towards righteousness)

"Fight the good fight of the faith; lay hold of the eternal life to which you were summoned and [for which] you confessed the good confession [of faith] before many witnesses" (1 Timothy 6:12).

The grace of God commands us to contend for and struggle after the things of faith. Sometimes things can bring great difficulty and danger to our body, but never our soul. We have been invited by God to lay hold of and partake in His righteousness. We have been called to eternal life through Christ Jesus; this calling was birthed by a confession of faith, and is carried out by His grace as we walk by faith. We have not been invited to iniquity; we have been rallied to righteousness. The choice is always ours (Josh. 24:15). Our calling is to godly warfare, rather than minding the things of the world, and battling against flesh and blood. We are to bring all our thoughts and imaginations captive and obedient to the Lord Jesus Christ (2 Cor. 10:5)

The world knows not of our battle because it sees not the kingdom of God. In fact, the things of God are seen as foolishness to the world (1 Cor. 1:23–29). Our life in Christ witnesses openly that righteousness rules, and can only be found in Jesus Christ our Lord. The world is not the source of eternal life, and therefore it cannot to be looked upon as a source of anything godly. The world is incapable of manifesting works of faith; it is only destined to witness such works (Mark 16:17–20).

✞ **POSITION / OPERATION OF GRACE:** (from our position of righteousness, we are called to walk in righteousness)

"To keep all His precepts unsullied and flawless, irreproachable, until the appearing of our Lord Jesus Christ (the Anointed One)" (1 Timothy 6:14).

Grace calls us to attend carefully and guard with all diligence, the precepts of God. It is only Christ, Who makes us flawless and irreproachable It is only His grace which keeps us and teaches us to walk in like manner, until the appearing of our Lord Jesus Christ. Grace calls us to be free from censure and vice. Freedom founded in the righteousness of Christ is freedom indeed; freedom founded in self-righteousness is deceptive. It ends in bondage (John 8:36). Freedom can only be found in Christ; it is never found by being a part of any religious organization. The Living God has never needed a religious organization to represent Him; He is building His church (Matt. 16:18).

✞ **OPERATION OF GRACE:** (grace calls us to turn away from godless activities and the thoughts that birth them)

"O Timothy, guard and keep the deposit entrusted [to you]! Turn away from the irreverent babble and godless chatter, with the vain and empty and worldly phrases, and the subtleties and the contradictions in what is falsely called knowledge and spiritual illumination" (1 Timothy 6:20).

The spirit of the world constantly bombards us with vain, empty worldly phrases and parables, falsely called knowledge and spiritual illumination: "The proof is in the pudding.", "The buck stops here.", "Only one can drive the bus.", "God helps those who help themselves.", "Don't touch God's anointed.", "If man can show this much compassion, surely God will show more.", etc. The list of half-truths and irreverent babble goes on and on.

Godless chatter is the foundation of harmful heresies. They are evidence of 'worldly wisdom' often falsely called 'godly knowledge'. They attempt to make God into man's image rather than submitting themselves unto God's image.

The church is often despoiled by godless, worldly wisdom. We are called to keep truth from being snatched away from us; we are called to preserve safe and unimpaired the pure unadulterated word of God (Prov. 23:23; Rev. 3:18). Worldly wisdom causes godly wisdom to be nullified and be made of no effect, resulting in the things of God being lost or perishing unawares before our very life (Matt. 15:2–6).

2 Timothy

✞ **POSITION OF GRACE:** (grace is a blessing, a greeting that brings life)

"To Timothy, [my] beloved child; Grace (favour and spiritual blessing), mercy and [heart] peace from God the Father and Christ Jesus our Lord" (2 Timothy 1:2)!

The grace of God, the mercy of God, and the peace of God are all things in which a fresh discovery is ever available and only beneficial. These free gifts of God are given to us without restraint, and we are privileged beyond measure to freely and lavishly bestow these same gifts upon others as a blessing and an increase. Oh Lord, help us catch the revelation that blessing others means benefit for all.

God the Father and our Lord Jesus Christ give from an eternal supply, and thus there is always an unending surplus available for us to give to others. A greeting from God is always a gracious greeting and a blessing, even if it comes with trials, tests, or persecutions (John 14:27; 16:13; 20:19–26). A more affectionate and active greeting cannot be found, as it imparts the very life of God into the heart of the recipient. Grace, mercy, and peace are our eternal inheritance, and no one can take away what God gives. What more do we need in our life than these blessed gifts (2 Peter 1:3, 8–9)?

Just as the Word of God is alive and active, any blessing prompted by the Holy Spirit and spoken from the mouth of a saint is alive, active, and able to impart life to those who listen. Oh, that we would greet one another with a blessing more often.

✞ **POSITION OF GRACE:** (grace spans generations and brings its blessing upon all)

"I am calling up memories of your sincere and unqualified faith (the leaning of your entire personality on God in Christ in absolute trust and confidence in His power, wisdom, and goodness), [a faith] that first lived permanently in [the heart of] your grandmother Lois and your mother Eunice and now, I am [fully] persuaded, [dwells] in you also" (2 Timothy 1:5).

The grace of God evidenced in the past is always an inspiration for the present. Grace comes to us as we lean on God, asserting our trust and confidence in our Saviour. Our life needs to express permanent faith, not temporary faith. Faith made permanent by God is not easily tossed to and fro, and not easily set aside. Absolute trust in God opens the eyes of our spirit to see the absoluteness of God's power, wisdom, and goodness so graciously given to us (Eph. 1:17–19). It shows and leads us in the ways of God.

Our heart is to be a tower of trust, and a castle of confidence founded on the ability of the Almighty. Oh, the joy of seeing God in our eternal inheritance, and knowing that God can and will continue to bestow this same inheritance upon future generations. No greater joy can be found than seeing our children walk in truth (3 John 1:4; 2 John 1:4). God wants an abiding faith, one that is permanently present and ever ready to give an answer to the hope that lies within (Col. 4:6; 2 Tim. 4:2). It is a living faith that testifies to future believers and builds a foundation for their own faith (Rom. 1:17).

✞ **POSITION OF GRACE:** (grace empowers us with love and well-balanced self-control)

"For God did not give us a spirit of timidity (of cowardice, of craven and cringing and fawning fear), but [He has given us a spirit] of power and of love and of calm and well-balanced mind and discipline and self-control" (2 Timothy 1:7).

The Spirit of grace is gentle and self-controlled; it is not one of timidity. It is full of peace and patience; it is not one that faints from fear. It is one that is kind and faithful; it is not one that is cowardly and spineless in its affairs.

It is by the grace of God that we receive access to the power and love of God. It brings with it divine discipline, self-control, and authority. A mind touched by the grace of God is a mind, which is well-balanced, stabilized, and tempered by God. Such godly attributes given so freely to us are to be exercised and allowed to increase in our life. Such exercise will keep us from being idle and unfruitful, and will bring about a diligent increase of the personal knowledge of our Lord Jesus Christ (2 Peter 1:8).

What problem can stand against a God fearing soul with a well-balanced mind, a calm and disciplined will, and self-controlled emotions? What problem can stand against a soul demonstrating the power, love, and authority of God? Timidity spawns self-doubt; it tenders trepidation, and it engenders insecurity. Such things do not reflect the grace of God (James 1:5–8). Beloved, whatever God imparts to us, will reflect the character and nature of God, and will bring the presence of God to every situation we find ourselves in.

Fear does not come from God. Fear of man, fear of the unknown, fear of the future, fear of failure, etc. are all birthed from a soul that is neither trusting, nor resting in God. God has not given us a spirit of fear, but of power, love, and a sound mind. These things dispel all fears in our life (1 John 4:18).

✞ **POSITION / OPERATION OF GRACE:** (grace makes us holy and calls us to holiness; grace is motivated by God's purposes, not human merits)

"[For it is He] Who delivered and saved us and called us with a calling in itself holy and leading to holiness [to a life of consecration, a vocation of holiness]; [He did it] not because of anything of merit that we have done, but because of and to further His own purpose and grace (unmerited favour) which was given us in Christ Jesus before the world began [eternal ages ago]" (2 Timothy 1:9).

The grace of God calls and places us 'in holiness', and then operates in our life, leading us 'to holiness'. This is not accomplished by any human effort whatsoever, but only by the effort of the Almighty. God is not motivated by our goodness or efforts; He works to further His own purpose. Grace is rooted in the eternities and was given to us in Christ Jesus before the world began.

Our calling and sainthood were provided for, eternal ages ago. They were established outside of time; they work their way through time, bringing us into the purposes of God and into eternity itself. Beloved, something that is established outside of time cannot be set aside or lost because of something we have done within the temporary realm of time.

Our life in Christ is seen as a vocation of holiness — a profession of righteousness. Our whole life is to be an example of holiness. We are made the property of a holy God, in Christ, and our God does not own junk. We have been set free from the power of sin, and are made pure and clean from our carnal faults; we are immaculate and clean before the all-seeing eye of the Almighty (Col. 2:13–15). We have received the very purpose and grace of God through Jesus Christ, and in Christ, our life is our ministry (Gal. 2:20).

✞ **POSITION / OPERATION OF GRACE:** (grace is made known through Christ Jesus, Who gives us eternal life)

"[It is that purpose and grace] which He now has made known and has fully disclosed and made real [to us] through the appearing of our Saviour Christ Jesus, Who annulled death and made it of no effect and brought life and immortality (immunity from eternal death) to light through the Gospel" (2 Timothy 1:10).

The grace of God brought us into the reality of God; it has bought us immunity from eternal death. Grace and truth have been made known to the world through Jesus Christ (John 1:14, 17). Grace annulled death and brought life; mortality has been swallowed up by immortality (1 Cor. 15:51–58). When the Gospel is received, a soul is given eternal life and forever released from eternal death. It took the power of God to annul death for us; no strength of man can ever reverse that process (Rev. 2:11; 20:6; 21:8).

The full disclosure of God's purposes and grace are revealed through the person of Jesus Christ. The realization of salvation is the most real and relevant thing a person can ever know. We have been transferred from the kingdom of darkness into the kingdom of Light (Col. 1:13).

✞ **OPERATION OF GRACE:** (grace empowers us to endure; it causes us to hear, receive, love and obey God, and hence reign with Him)

"If we endure, we shall also reign with Him. If we deny and disown and reject Him, He will also deny and disown and reject us" (2 Timothy 2:12).

The grace of God calls us to abide, not to draw back or flee. We are to persevere under misfortunes and trials holding fast to our faith in Christ, which contributes to the renewing of our soul. Truth bears witness to truth, it cannot deny itself. We as people of truth bear witness to the truth, placing our hope and faith in Him. He who is able to keep us cannot deny Himself (2 Tim. 2:13). He sees us through our unfaithfulness and calls us to change (Matt. 26:33–35, 74–75; 21:15–22; Acts 2:14).

Grace calls us to endure and abide in Christ; He becomes our very existence. To deny or reject Christ is to deny or reject life, and to reject life and truth is to live in darkness and death. Christ did not overcome death in order that we would continue to dwell in it (1 John 3:8). How could we ever desire to have the power of sin eternally master us? Thank you Father for Your revelation of the Lord Jesus Christ!

To have dominion over death is to reign in the government of God — a government established by Christ Jesus Himself. To deny the government of God is a fearful and foolish thing to do.

It is possible to deny Christ in words: to deny that Christ is come in the flesh, to deny that Jesus is the Messiah, to deny Jesus His true deity or His true humanity, to deny the divine virtue of His blood and sacrifice for our justification (John 5:16–18; 19:7; 1 John 4:2–3; 2 John 1:7).

It is possible to deny Christ in works: to profess to know Him yet in works deny Him, to have the form of godliness, but to deny the power of it (2 Timothy 3:5; Titus 1:16).

It is possible to have a secret and silent denial of Christ: when men do not confess Him and are ashamed of Him (Mark 8:38; John 9:18–23).

It is possible to have an open denial of Christ: when men set their mouth against the heavens, and revile and scoff at the power of spiritual beings (Jude 1:8).

It is possible to have a partial denial of Christ: to deny that you know Him even when you do know Him (Luke 22:61).

It is possible to totally deny Christ: those who have named the name of Christ and yet deny Him. He will deny them and set them at His left hand. He will declare that He knows them not and will banish them from his presence forever (Matt. 10:33; 25:31–46).

✞ **OPERATION OF GRACE:** (grace is not empty, useless, vain, nor idle)

"But avoid all empty (vain, useless, idle) talk, for it will lead people into more and more ungodliness" (2 Timothy 2:16).

The grace of God calls us to be attentive to the things of God. It calls us to turn ourselves about for the purpose of avoiding ungodliness. We are called to repentance and the renewing of our soul, and to shun senseless, useless talk — empty discussion of vain, useless matters. Note that participation in uselessness is not without effect. Such activity tends towards and increases ungodliness. Such activity is worthless and a waste of time. When vanity leads us, our godly destination soon becomes obscured and undermined (Phil. 1:15–17; 1 Tim. 1:18–20; 2 Tim. 4:14–15; Rev. 2:5; 3:16).

✞ **POSITION / OPERATION OF GRACE:** (grace calls us to cleanse ourselves making us fit for good works)

"But the firm foundation of (laid by) God stands, sure and unshaken, bearing this seal (inscription): The Lord knows those who are His, and, Let everyone who names [himself by] the name of the Lord give up all iniquity and stand aloof from it.

But in a great house there are not only vessels of gold and silver, but also [utensils] of wood and earthenware, and some for honourable and noble [use] and some for menial and ignoble [use].

So whoever cleanses himself [from what is ignoble and unclean, who separates himself from contact with contaminating and corrupting influences] will [then himself] be a vessel set apart and useful for honourable and noble purposes, consecrated and profitable to the Master, fit and ready for any good work" (2 Timothy 2:19–21).

The grace of God places us on the firm foundation of belonging to the Beloved. Such a position places us in the hands of the Almighty as He shapes and fits each of us for His good work and pleasure. His Spirit has been given to us as a guarantee, confirming, proving, and authenticating His stewardship over our lives. We, as possessions of God, are called to depart from and stand aloof from all unrighteousness in our heart and life.

It is in the potter's hands that a vessel is formed and called to use. It is the call of grace to cleanse ourselves from unclean activities and to separate ourselves from corrupt influences, sealing ourselves as consecrated vessels, profitable to God, and ready for good works. Our position of grace places us on His path; the operation of grace purges us and purposes us to honourable and noble deeds.

Only a fool thinks that he can ignore or pervert the word of God and get away with it. Our significance must be in Christ and Christ alone (John 5:44). It is pure carnality and the love of the praise of man, which makes leadership in the church ignore scriptures and think that they are furthering their ministry (1 Tim. 3:1–10; Titus 1:6–9). Jesus calls us to a life of truth, not a ministry of self-justification (Phil. 1:17; Acts 20:30; 1 Tim. 6:5).

✞ **OPERATION OF GRACE:** (grace calls us to flee lusts and pursue righteousness)

"Shun youthful lusts and flee from them, and aim at and pursue righteousness (all that is virtuous and good, right living, conformity to the will of God in thought, word, and deed); [and aim at and pursue] faith, love, [and] peace (harmony and concord with others) in fellowship with all [Christians], who call upon the Lord out of a pure heart" (2 Timothy 2:22).

The grace of God calls us to disdain pubescent passions and to set our resolve on the road of righteousness, faith, love, and peace (Matt. 5:6, 9). We are called to eagerly and earnestly endeavour to acquire virtue and purity of life in the context of fellowship with *all* Christians. The purpose of fellowship with all Christians is not to get them to 'join your church', it is to be truly joined to Christ and bring life to one another. False leadership and denominationalism deter fellowship; they dissuade Christians from truly loving one another (John 13:35).

The goal of grace is to allow the love coming from God to be extended towards His people. Pursuing pureness of heart in love will engage a man to bear up under anything, to hope in all things, and to believe the best in every person (Matt. 5:8; 1 Cor. 13:7). Pursuing pureness of heart without exercising love, makes all gifts and works of no account — a gain of nothing (1 Cor. 13:1–3).

Fellowship, which is a distinguishing mark of Christians, is a grace of God designed to cleanse God's people from all sin and all its manifestations (1 John 1:7). It equips us with God's purpose and power to live as His children. It recreates us into His will in thought, word, and deed. Our sights should be set on faith, love, and peace in fellowship with *all* believers. This is the work of grace in our life.

✞ **OPERATION OF GRACE:** (grace calls us to not be contentious; and to willingly suffer wrongs)

"But refuse (shut your mind against, have nothing to do with) trifling (ill-informed, unedifying, stupid) controversies over ignorant questionings, for you know that they foster strife and breed quarrels.

And the servant of the Lord must not be quarrelsome (fighting and contending). Instead, he must be kindly to everyone and mild-tempered [preserving the bond of peace]; he must be a skilled and suitable teacher, patient and forbearing and willing to suffer wrong" (2 Timothy 2:23–24).

Grace guards our mind from useless reasoning and quarrelsome questions. A servant of the Lord should be quick to refuse and decline ignorant controversies. It is required that he be found faithful to the ways of the Lord, being a preserver of peace, a skilled and truthful teacher, and willing to suffer wrongly. The operative word here is, 'willing' (1 Cor. 13:7; Gal. 6:1–2; 1 Peter 4:12–16).

The will of the God of grace becomes the will of the servant of grace. The work of righteousness will be peace, and the effect of righteousness will be willingness to suffer wrongs patiently (John 18:19–23; Acts 7:55–60; 23:1–5). It is slow to anger, slow to speak, quickly to forgive, and always ready to forbear one another's faults (Jas. 1:19–20).

A skilled teacher is not one who has credentials; it is one who speaks by the Spirit of God (John 9:34). It is one who has no need to put others down or harbour an elevated opinion of oneself. A skilled teacher can rightly divide the Word of truth and hold it out to others, so that they may embrace the authority that comes with it (2 Tim. 2:15). God is not interested in us airing our opinions about His word; He desires His vessels to receive His revelation and speak it, enabling others to learn from that same anointing that dwells in them (2 Cor. 1:2–9; 2 Peter 3:15–18; 1 John 2:27).

✝ **OPERATION OF GRACE:** (grace enables us to call people to their senses)

"He must correct his opponents with courtesy and gentleness, in the hope that God may grant that they will repent and come to know the Truth [that they will perceive and recognize and become accurately acquainted with and acknowledge it].

And that they may come to their senses [and] escape out of the snare of the devil, having been held captive by him, [henceforth] to do His [God's] will" (2 Timothy 2:25–26).

Through fellowship, the grace of God equips us to courteously correct and instruct one another. As servants of God we are teachers of divine learning. Grace calls us to correct opponents of the faith with all gentleness so that they may perhaps repent, come to their senses, and come to the knowledge of truth.

Any diversion from divine truth is a snare set by the devil, and is designed to cause its captor to bow its knee to the ungodliness of religious half-truths. We cannot perform God's will *for* others; we are called to perform God's will for ourselves. The grace of God will never authorize anyone to determine the will of God for others (Acts 19:21; 20:22–25; 21:10–14).

The act of repentance is personal; it is not something we can do for others. Hence, we are servants of spiritual persuasion, not natural persuasion. The renewing of the soul — our mind, will, and emotions — is a spiritual operation, not a natural one. To turn your will over to anyone but the Holy Spirit never results in fruitful direction in the kingdom of God; it only results in control by ungodly authority (Dan. 3:1–30; Gal. 2:11–14).

✝ **OPERATION OF GRACE:** (grace operates as the Word of God breathes upon us)

"Every Scripture is God breathed (given by His inspiration) and profitable for instruction, for correction of error and discipline in obedience, [and] for training in righteousness (in holy living, in conformity to God's will in thought, purpose, and action),

So that the man of God may be complete and proficient, well fitted and thoroughly equipped for every good work" (2 Timothy 3:16–17).

When the grace of God breathes upon a soul, it is profitable. Grace brings with it the odour of peace and completeness — the essence of the new covenant. Only wholeness and completeness can bring life to a weary soul.

There is much to be gained in being corrected and disciplined in obedience to God. There is much to lose by not. It is profitable to be trained by the grace of God in righteousness. A life that is conformed to the will, thought, and purpose of God, is a life fitted for godly work — equipped for its intended task. When the Word of God breathes on us, it gives us divine authority and life, which enables us to do all things through Christ Jesus (Heb. 4:9–12).

Christian fellowship should be a day to day lifestyle for a man of God. You cannot hide for long in fellowship when the body of Christ is instructing, equipping, correcting, disciplining, and training itself by the Spirit of God. Equipping always carries with it a purpose of employing action in the kingdom of God. The receiving of the word of God is always for the purpose of doing the Word.

Revelation from God's Word transcends all human understanding as it speaks from the past, operates in the present, and brings hope to the future. It is powered by the eternal nature of God. Our completeness and proficiency is found by the grace of God operating, as the Word of God breathes upon us (Rev. 22:17).

Titus

✞ **POSITION / OPERATION OF GRACE:** (grace has converted us into bond servants of Truth)

"Paul, a bond servant of God and an apostle (a special messenger) of Jesus Christ (the Messiah) to stimulate and promote the faith of God's chosen ones and to lead them on to accurate discernment and recognition of and acquaintance with the Truth which belongs to and harmonizes with and tends to godliness,

[Resting] in the hope of eternal life, [life] which the ever truthful God Who cannot deceive promised before the world or the ages of time began" (Titus 1:1–2).

Our position of grace guaranteed to us by the Almighty, was promised even before the ages of time began. The grace of God working through Paul incited Titus to prompt and promote the faith of the saints — God's chosen ones. As bond servants of Christ, grace operates within us, leading us into an accurate understanding and recognition of the Truth. It urges us on towards godliness, and enables our life to harmonize with it.

A soul rested in grace finds its respite in the hope of eternal life. Grace is truthful; it cannot lie or deceive (1 John 2:26–27). Operating within us, grace causes us to see our position as servants. There is no higher calling or position that can be attained or aspired to than being a bond servant of the Lord Jesus Christ. It is only by the grace of God that we become such. God is not impressed with the positions that men hold. He recognizes no external distinctions; grace does not call us to indulge in respect of persons. To hold men of repute as higher than you, or to bow down to men who like to take the lead among God's people is a work of the flesh, not the Spirit (Gal. 2:6; 3 John 1:9).

Christians often believe that other believers can do greater things than they can. Whether it is church leaders or our brothers and sisters in Christ, we often look at them with the natural eye and feel that they have something greater than we do; when in truth, everything we have comes from God and He looks at us all with the same eye. Comparing ourselves with others is foolish (2 Cor. 10:12); the root of this type of attitude is jealousy (Prov. 12:12). In truth, we should be thankful for what God has made us to be — servants of the Most High God — and to joyfully bear our own fruit (Rev. 1:5–7).

As Christians we are called to stimulate and promote the faith of Christ in one another and to walk in the fullness of what God has given us to do (John 21:21; Heb. 10:24–25). To do this we must recognize for ourselves and be acquainted with the Truth, which always draws us into harmony with godliness and hence with each other (1 John 1:7).

✞ **OPERATION OF GRACE:** (grace produces godliness and Christian order)

"[These elders should be] men who are of unquestionable integrity and are irreproachable, the husband of [but] one wife, whose children are [well trained and are] believers, not open to the accusation of being loose in morals and conduct or unruly and disorderly" (Titus 1:6).

The grace of God promotes within us, life of undeniable, righteous character — a character that is irreproachable. As husbands and fathers, the elders of the church are to be examples and teachers of the faith, principles, doctrines, and the ways of Christ.

The families of church leadership should be an example of training in the nurture and admonition of the Lord, and not guilty of disobedience, rebellion, or open immorality. When a church leader tolerates immorality in the midst of his family, he is only deceiving himself to think that he is leading God's people towards godliness, no matter how pious his excuses sound (1 Sam. 3:12–14).

In all the Scriptures in the New Testament on church leadership, there is no mention of a man called 'the Pastor' being the leader of any church. Leadership in the church is always mentioned within the context of a plurality of elders (Acts 11:30; 14:23; 15:2, 4, 6, 22, 23; 16:4; 20:17; 21:18; 1 Tim. 4:14; 5:17; Titus 1:5; Jas. 5:14; 1 Peter 5:1,

5). The church position of 'the Senior Pastor' is never mentioned anywhere in Scripture.

The church has an obligation to distinguish between God's authority and worldly hierarchal authority (1 Cor. 3:1–4). To turn the responsibility of your spiritual growth over to any authority other than the Lord Jesus Christ, is foolish and will prove unfruitful in the maturing of the body.

✞ **POSITION OF GRACE:** (grace defines for us what is pure)

"To the pure [in heart and conscience] all things are pure, but to the defiled and corrupt and unbelieving nothing is pure; their very minds and consciences are defiled and polluted" (Titus 1:15).

A soul soiled with sin can only be cleansed by the grace of God. The pureness of the blood of Christ transforms a heart contaminated with the colour of corruption, and redeems it into the hue of the kingdom of the Son of His love. Our position of grace has brought us from defilement into holiness, from pollution into purity, from contamination into consecration, as it turns a sin soiled soul into a saint.

Grace draws us into a position where we are free from the command of corrupt desires, from the power of sin and guilt, and from everything that is false. Our mind and conscience are divinely reconciled to God, and genuinely sealed by His Holy Spirit. It is only a heart positioned in the grace of God that is blameless and innocent, and is able to recognize purity (Heb. 5:11–14).

✞ **OPERATION OF GRACE:** (grace models godliness and promotes instruction in righteousness)

"And show your own self in all respects to be a pattern and a model of good deeds and works, teaching what is unadulterated, showing gravity [having the strictest regard for truth and purity of motive], with dignity and seriousness.

And let your instruction be sound and fit and wise and wholesome, vigorous and irrefutable and above censure, so that the opponent may be put to shame, finding nothing discrediting or evil to say about us" (Titus 2:7–8).

There is no aspect of our life that grace leaves untouched. Grace forms and fashions us until we resemble the character of the Potter. Godly character produces soundness, integrity of mind, and a reverent regard for truth. Only actions motivated by grace cannot be censored. When we oppose grace, we stand in the field of disgrace and shame. Grace imparts a reverence and a high respect towards righteous living. It transforms us into models and instructors of righteousness.

There is a saying, 'preach the Gospel and use words if necessary'. What this saying implies, is that we should be doers of the word and not hearers only. Hypocrisy is a life that preaches one thing, and then does another. Our life is to be a model of good deeds and works, which reflect our faith and the fruit of our mouth. Both our words and deeds should reflect truth (Jas. 2:17, 26).

Our life speaks of the truth, which is hidden within our heart (Matt. 12:34). When we give the Lord our heart, our eyes observe and delight in His ways of wisdom, and we end up living the truth that is hidden within us. Beloved, our life is our ministry, not our mouth. Our life should declare, "Follow me as I follow Christ." When a saint's life is living the truth and word of God, his life becomes an irrefutable teaching. We are called to be examples for others in the body of Christ and to the world around us (Phil. 4:9).

✞ **OPERATION OF GRACE:** (grace is the free gift of God; it is worn as an ornament as we ourselves become ornaments of grace)

"Nor to steal by taking things of small value, but to prove themselves truly loyal and entirely reliable and faithful throughout, so that in everything they may be an ornament and do credit to the teaching [which is] from and about God our Saviour" (Titus 2:10).

The grace of God will always recognize the commandments of God. It calls us to prove our faithfulness by not taking unfaithfulness into our hands. We are not called to embezzle and appropriate the things of others to our own use — no matter how small and insignificant they may seem. We are called to appropriate only that which has appropriated us — Christ Jesus — the Way. Our life is a living epistle — an ornament displaying the grace and provision of Christ (Phil. 3:8–12). Grace is an adornment that reflects the Gospel of God. In fact, this Scripture proclaims that we ourselves are the very ornament that God has chosen to display His grace and truth (John 1:17).

Our beauty is not of ourselves; it is not a charm of carnality or a vessel of vain beauty that passes with time. Grace has given us an eternal beauty of godly virtue and nobility. Godly character is not fleeting; it is eternal. It never gets old or passes away (Prov. 31:30).

✝ **POSITION OF GRACE:** (grace positions us in eternal salvation)

"For the grace of God (His unmerited favour and blessing) has come forward (appeared) for the deliverance from sin and the eternal salvation for all mankind" (Titus 2:11).

The grace of God has brought evidence of the Light that brings salvation to all mankind. As vessels of grace, we have been commissioned by God to go into the entire world to proclaim that all men may receive grace by faith. Faith comes by hearing the word of God and by placing one's trust and conviction in the truth (Luke 8:15; Rom. 10:17; Jas. 1:22–25).

Our position of grace is kept secure by the power of God, through faith. Faith without works is dead. God's grace is perfect; it is only our lack of reception, which causes us to neglect it, shipwreck it, or fall away from it (Jas. 2:17; 1 Tim. 1:19; Gal. 5:4).

"For by grace ye are saved through faith; and that not of yourselves: it is the gift of God" (Eph. 2:8 KJV). When we believe, we receive by faith; hence, even faith is a gift of God. There is no work on man's part, which brings him to salvation — deliverance from sin. Faith is a grace/work of God, waiting to be received by needy vessels (John 9:40).

✝ **OPERATION OF GRACE:** (grace operates in our life, training us to reject ungodliness)

"It has trained us to reject and renounce all ungodliness (irreligion) and worldly (passionate) desires, to live discreet (temperate, self-controlled), upright, devout (spiritually whole) lives in this present world," (Titus 2:12).

The grace of God is a trainer, correcting the character of its recipient. It teaches and trains us to renounce ungodliness, to deny worldly desires and to live soberly in this present world. Only the operation of grace can bring about spiritual wholeness. Our passion should be for the things of God, not the things of this world.

A person without self-control is like a city with its walls broken down, open to all kinds of evil (Prov. 25:28). When you live in a city with broken walls, you do not perceive the brokenness and the vulnerability of your position (Rev. 3:17). It takes the balm of grace to reveal a soul's need to be renewed. This same grace will heal spiritual blindness and bring wholeness. When you have been born into, and raised with brokenness all around you, you see it as normal, and do not recognize it as a hindrance to life. Beloved, when you are born in a barn, you cannot smell it (Prov. 4:19).

Only by coming to know the grace of God does the human heart start the journey on its eternal path. You must be born-again to see the kingdom of God, and to refuse re-birth is blind foolishness.

Religion tries to re-make man; Jesus Christ recreates man, bringing newness of life — a new creation. It is only in Christ that we can attain to a life of godliness — a life directed by His Spirit (2 Cor. 5:17).

All religion outside of Christ is antichrist; it applies man's powers, wisdom, and efforts to attempt to reach a state of godliness. All such efforts are futile because they can never change the heart of man. To lack the true knowledge of our Lord Jesus Christ makes one lack the qualities of Christ; it makes one blind and short-sighted (2 Peter 1:9).

✞ **POSITION OF GRACE:** (grace makes hope a reality)

"Awaiting and looking for the [fulfilment, the realization of our] blessed hope, even the glorious appearing of our great God and Saviour Christ Jesus (the Messiah, the Anointed One)," (Titus 2:13).

Grace gives our hope a reality that the world knows nothing of. A hope in the world is usually a hope for some temporary material gain or relief from experiencing the fruit of sin; it is not founded in the eternities. A soul touched by the eternal grace of God is expectant; it accepts and receives as a steadfast companion the blessed hope of the coming of our great God and Saviour, Christ Jesus.

Grace introduces us to the divine reality of Jesus positioning us in Him, and then operating in our lives, bringing a glorious reality and meaning to His second coming. The hope we receive from Jesus is a hope that lasts infinitely longer than any hope found in the world. The world and all its hopes and possessions will pass away, but the Word of the Lord remains forever (Matt. 24:35; Mark 13:31; Luke 21:33; 1 Peter 1:25).

✞ **POSITION / OPERATION OF GRACE:** (grace both redeems us and rebukes us with full authority)

"Who gave Himself on our behalf that He might redeem us (purchase our freedom) from all iniquity and purify for Himself a people [to be peculiarly His own, people who are] eager and enthusiastic about [living a life that is good and filled with] beneficial deeds.

Tell [them all] these things. Urge (advise, encourage, warn) and rebuke with full authority. Let no one despise or disregard or think little of you [conduct yourself and your teaching so as to command respect]" (Titus 2:14–15).

The grace of God has made us His people. Grace has released us from lawful obligation with regards to obtaining righteousness. It has liberated us from licentious action and delivered us from demonic dominion of every kind — internal and external. The divine operation of grace within us makes us eager and enthusiastic to be a blessing towards others, especially to the household of God. We become a purified people, peculiarly His own, fit and equipped to do good works, eagerly desirous to show excellence in nature and motive, and well adapted to all that we undertake to do.

Grace encourages, advises, warns, and rebukes with full authority. It is not the authority of man, which powers grace. Grace operating in a life, commands respect, because it is God doing the work. Religious authority derived by man at best can only give lip service to God's authority. It can only impersonate it or demand obedience; it cannot command it (Acts 19:13–16). God's authority is manifest when any believer operates by the Spirit of God. Authority from God is not a position found in the church; it only operates when a believer is positioned in God's Spirit. It is only accessible by the working of God's grace. It is never accessible simply because one holds a 'position of authority' in the church. Such belief is a worldly corporate concept, not a kingdom principle. When you walk in the Spirit you speak as one who is authority, not as one who claims to have authority (Matt. 7:29; John 7:46).

Grace places everyone on equal footing; it does not tolerate anybody despising or disregarding another (Gal. 2:6). Being positioned in the grace of God is the safest, most loving place to be; being operated on by the grace of God is the most harmless, loving way to be trained.

Who can harm you if you are a follower of what is good? Beloved, the grace of the Lord has plans for us — plans for our peaceful welfare and not for evil, plans to give us a future and a hope (Jer. 29:11). Let us strive to enter into this gracious rest; let us apprehend that which has apprehended us. True authority is this: to be mandated by God to carry out His plans and purposes in our life. This is true freedom in Christ, and is never irksome (Mark 9:40; Rom. 8:31).

✞ **POSITION OF GRACE:** (we are saved by grace, not by works)

"But when the goodness and loving-kindness of God our Saviour to man [as man] appeared,

He saved us, not because of any works of righteousness that we had done, but because of His own pity and mercy, by [the] cleansing [bath] of the new birth (regeneration) and renewing of the Holy Spirit,

Which He poured out [so] richly upon us through Jesus Christ our Saviour" (Titus 3:4–6).

The goodness and loving-kindness of God towards man has appeared for the redemption of man, richly provided for us by Christ Jesus our Saviour. This results in our birth from above, and the renewing of our soul. It is not the accomplishment of man, which makes grace become effective in our life; grace, powered by God's pity and mercy, births us, bathes us, and blesses us with renewed life in the Holy Spirit. When God pours the life of Jesus Christ into us, it is a richness that results in abundant life (John 10:10; Rom. 9:15–18).

✝ **POSITION OF GRACE:** (grace justifies us, conforms us into the divine will, making us heirs of eternal life)

"[And He did it in order] that we might be justified by His grace (by His favour, wholly undeservedly), [that we might be acknowledged and counted as conformed to the divine will in purpose, thought, and action], and that we might become heirs of eternal life according to [our] hope" (Titus 3:7).

God justifies all that receive Him. As children of God, we become heirs of eternal life. Grace is absolutely undeserved. Its reception results in the birthing of a hope, which identifies us as eternal heirs with a joyful and confident expectation of receiving our allotted possession by right-of-son-ship. Grace acknowledges us, and counts us as conformed to God's will in thought, purpose, and action.

It is only God's grace that gives us purpose; it gives us thoughts and actions that are sourced in His divine will (Prov. 1:1–6). Better to be an inheritor of God's divine grace than to gain the whole world and lose your soul.

✝ **POSITION OF GRACE:** (grace is a trustworthy message insisting on good works which are profitable)

"This message is most trustworthy, and concerning these things I want you to insist steadfastly, so that those who have believed in (trusted in, relied on) God may be careful to apply themselves to honourable occupations and to doing good, for such things are [not only]

excellent and right [in themselves], but [they are] good and profitable for the people" (Titus 3:8).

Grace is a most trustworthy message. It calls believers to be careful and do good, excellent and right works. The message of grace can be relied upon — even as God can be relied upon. It is a message, which we are to model and assert strongly, confidently, and constantly before God and man. The message of grace is both a benefit and an advantage for the individual believer as well as those around him.

Christianity is the only belief system birthed by God's grace, and it is the only keeper of truth that exists. This is not an arrogant statement; it is a true statement of faith spoken in humility by the grace of God.

Philemon

✞ **POSITION / OPERATION OF GRACE:** (grace calls us to be soldiers of peace in our warfare in the world)

"Paul, a prisoner [for the sake] of Christ Jesus (the Messiah), and our brother Timothy, to Philemon our dearly beloved sharer with us in our work,

And to Apphia our sister and Archippus our fellow soldier [in the Christian warfare], and to the church [assembly that meets] in your house:

Grace (spiritual blessing and favour) be to all of you and heart peace from God our Father and the Lord Jesus Christ (the Messiah)" (Philemon 1:1–3).

Even as the moving of the shadow of a tree reveals the path of the sun across the sky, the grace of God working in our lives reveals the image of the Lord Jesus Christ. As Christians dwelling in the world, we cast the shadow of His grace when we manifest His light and spiritual favour through our lives.

Grace has apprehended us; it has made us prisoners and bond slaves of righteousness. Grace takes two 'strangers' — God and mankind — and births them into 'brotherhood' in one body, the church — a divine, family fellowship. Grace calls us to be co-workers with Christ; we are fellow servicemen with Christ, bringing freedom to spiritual prisoners.

Grace has made us objects of God's love and bestows upon us a calling of companionship with Him in His work; it associates in the labour and conflict, which we encounter for the cause of Christ (John 3:16). We are engaged in a war, which has been *eternally* won because of our position of grace, and *daily* won by the operation of grace. Grace has made us fruitful fellow soldiers whereby we rest in the Beloved.

A soldier of grace is carried through the rage and havoc of the war in the world, which comes to kill, steal, and destroy (John 10:10). Though we are *in* the world, we are no longer *of* the world. It is only through the merciful kindness of God that grace operates in us, exerting His holy influence upon our souls. Grace keeps us, strengthens us, and increases our faith, causing us to burn with godly affection, and kindling our lives unto the exercise of Christian virtue.

"This is what I command you: that you love one another.

If the world hates you, know that it hated Me before it hated you.

If you belonged to the world, the world would treat you with affection and would love you as its own. But because you are not of the world [no longer one with it], but I have chosen (selected) you out of the world, the world hates (detests) you.

Remember that I told you, A servant is not greater than his master [is not superior to him]. If they persecuted Me, they will also persecute you; if they kept My word and obeyed My teachings, they would also obey and keep yours.

But they will do all this to you [inflict all this suffering on you] because of [your bearing] My name and on My account, for they do not know or understand the One Who sent Me.

If I had not come and spoken to them, they would not be guilty of sin [would be blameless]; but now they have no excuse for their sin.

Whoever hates Me also hates My Father" (John 15:17–23).

The Author of the Christian faith is alive; hence our faith is also alive. He rose from the dead; no other religious leader has ever done this. The Christian's warfare is not against flesh and blood (2 Cor. 10:3–4). Grace never calls us to natural warfare like suicide bombings, mercy or righteous killings, the stoning or beating of people, etc. Our warfare is not a natural/carnal one (John 7:5–8; 1 John 3:10–14).

Our kingdom is not of this world (John 18:36); hence, true Christianity never needs to defend itself (Matt. 26:50–57). Jesus came into the world and won the battle against sin and death — the works of the evil one (1 John 3:8). He won this battle by taking on our sins and dying on the cross. This indisputable truth does not need to be defended, either by God, or His children. The only way Christians defend their faith is to die to their selves, and live by the Spirit (Acts 7:55–60; 2 Cor. 11:23–27; Heb. 11:33–40).

The spirit of the world accuses the Christian faith for past killings such as the Crusades, or even 'religious' wars of today (Roman Catholic/ Protestant conflict in Ireland). In truth, none of the aforementioned have never been commanded by Jesus (1 John 2:18–25).

When we become a prisoner of God's grace, our soul is placed in a tranquil state of heart peace and in the assurance of salvation through Christ. Under grace a soul need fear nothing from God and can rest content with its heavenly calling — hidden under the shadow of the Almighty (Psalm 17:8; 36:7; 57:1; 63:7).

From our position of grace, as soldiers and prisoners, we have authority to pronounce spiritual blessing, favour, and peace upon one another, and preach the Gospel of peace to the world around us. The peace we give to others is the peace that comes from God our Father and the Lord Jesus Christ (John 14:27).

"I have told you these things, so that in Me you may have [perfect] peace and confidence. In the world you have tribulation and trials and distress and frustration; but be of good cheer [take courage; be confident, certain, undaunted]! For I have overcome the world. [I have deprived it of power to harm you and have conquered it for you.]" (John 16:33).

✝ **POSITION / OPERATION OF GRACE:** (grace takes the unprofitable and makes it profitable)

"I appeal to you for my [own spiritual] child, Onesimus [meaning profitable], whom I have begotten [in the faith] while a captive in these chains.

Once he was unprofitable to you, but now he is indeed profitable to you as well as to me" (Philemon 1:10–11).

Grace converts the unprofitable to the profitable. It takes the useless and turns it into something, which is full of use — even abundantly overflowing. As the work of grace abounds more and more in a vessel, it causes its usefulness to abound and to be a blessing in deed for all.

After Paul led Onesimus to the Lord, he was a blessing to Paul even while in prison. Grace makes us profitable to one another wherever we are. God uses us to encourage our brothers and sisters whether we are free or in such bondage. A work of grace can only be orchestrated by God Himself (John 8:33–36; Gal. 2:4; 4:8; Heb. 2:15). When you are free from spiritual bondage, physical bondage is utterly irrelevant (Acts 16:20–34).

✝ **POSITION / OPERATION OF GRACE:** (grace takes that which is lost and recreates it into a more precious possession)

"Perhaps it was for this reason that he was separated [from you] for a while, that you might have him back as yours forever,

Not as a slave any longer but as [something] more than a slave, as a brother [Christian], especially dear to me but now much more to you, both in the flesh [as a servant] and in the Lord [as a fellow believer]" (Philemon 1:15–16).

Grace takes lost, useless vessels and turns them into useful, priceless possessions. Grace makes new creations, and what we were becomes faded past history. It takes us beyond the limits of the flesh — things temporary, and makes us abound exceedingly in things of the Spirit — things eternal. Christ has made us one another's eternal possession (Rom. 7:4; Heb. 10:34).

In truth, each member of the whole body of Christ was at one time a slave to the world, habitually obedient to the prince of the power of the air (Eph. 2:2). However, grace supersedes slavery. It takes a slave in the world and frees it to be a prisoner for Christ, recreating slavery into brotherhood. Everybody is born as a slave and a debtor to sin; it is only by the grace of God that one is re-born and drawn from this eternal position of doom, and placed lovingly into the kingdom of God (Col. 1:13).

Onesimus was dear to Paul, and now in Christ he is even more so to Philemon. Paul begins his appeal to Philemon by proclaiming that Onesimus was not only a blessing but was very dear to his heart. In truth, as Onesimus returns to Philemon he returns not just as a slave but more than a slave — a brother in Christ. This makes him even dearer to Philemon than to Paul.

Sometimes we have to let loved ones go from our presence to allow God to do a work in both their hearts and ours. We need to rejoice as we see that God has done this work, and truly we can say that our loved one is now even dearer to us. *"But it was fitting to make merry, to revel and feast and rejoice, for this brother of yours was dead and is alive again! He was lost and is found"* (Luke 15:32)!

✞ **POSITION / OPERATION OF GRACE:** (grace makes us comrades in fellowship)

"If then you consider me a partner and a comrade in fellowship, welcome and receive him as you would [welcome and receive] me.

And if he has done you any wrong in any way or owes anything [to you], charge that to my account" (Philemon 1:17–18).

Grace, positioned from eternal love, commands the operation of forgiveness to be evident in our daily life. In fellowship, we are partners together and companions in the grace of God. As the body of Christ, we are to share and partake in the divine blessings and character of God with one another. Beloved, a little leaven leavens the whole lump, and unforgiveness is a cancerous leaven, which thwarts the purpose of grace. Unforgiveness treats the gift of God as something of minor importance, setting it aside and defeating its very purpose. Grace did not set aside and nullify us, and it does not call us to set aside and nullify others (Rom. 3:3). Gracious discipline does not look down upon others; it presents truth and passionately endeavours to reach reconciliation (1 Cor. 5:4–8; 2 Cor. 2:4–11).

Just as Christ took upon himself the penalty so rightly due us, grace, operating in our life takes upon itself the penalty so rightly due others (Acts 7:54–60). Beloved, we cannot afford to nurture offense. The gracious, loving response to any offense is, *"If anyone has done anybody any wrong in any way or owes anything, charge it to my account."*

True fellowship does not exist outside of this attitude of godly love towards one another (John 13:35). Paul was a partner and comrade in fellowship with Philemon and even today, by the Spirit, we can sense this same like-mindedness in the Spirit, as we live in the Word, and fellowship with one another. The kingdom of God does not come in word only; it must be manifested in deed also (Luke 24:19; Rom. 15:18; Col. 3:17; 1 John 3:18).

✞ **POSITION / OPERATION OF GRACE:** (grace is a spiritual blessing and favour to be declared upon one another)

"The grace (blessing and favour) of the Lord Jesus Christ (the Messiah) be with your spirit. Amen (so be it)" (Philemon 1:25).

Our spiritual position in grace allows us to manifest the power of God in reality. Grace is the blessed and evident favour of God that operates in our life. It is to be declared and pronounced upon the lives of others, especially those in the body of Christ — the church.

Hebrews

✞ **POSITION OF GRACE:** (grace cleanses us from sin; it works within us as a demonstration of the word of God's power)

"He is the sole expression of the glory of God [the light-being, the out-raying or radiance of the divine], and He is the perfect imprint and very image of [God's] nature, upholding and maintaining and guiding and propelling the universe by His mighty word of power. When He had by offering Himself accomplished our cleansing of sins and riddance of guilt, He sat down at the right hand of the divine Majesty on high," (Hebrews 1:3).

By the grace of God we have been cleansed from the guilt of sin through the blood of Jesus Christ. Grace operates through the word of His power. Note that it does not say here, 'the power of His word'; but rather, 'the word of His power'. Such word is a *living* word and is the result of God desiring His power to be manifested in our life (Phil. 2:6–7). God's power is revealed by His word; it defines how the kingdom of God works, and brings it into reality. The living Word is the instrument of the Almighty. By the Spirit, the power of God uses His word to manifest His purposes, making them a practical reality in our life (Heb. 4:12).

As people of grace, we have been positioned into membership in the body of Christ — the Word of God made flesh. This grace working in our lives has been divinely purposed to illuminate the mighty power of God. Grace is not for us to use as *we* desire; but rather its workings manifest the desire of God. Our lives as living epistles become evidence of the grace of His power — a *living* grace, which is the result of God's power becoming our life. It is we who serve the living God, not God who serves our worldly whims.

God's incredible grace is positioned at His right hand, and it is actively working within our hearts, equipping us with God's power in the midst of worldly unrighteousness. Oh, the grace of God's power, humbly standing to receive Stephen as he was brutally murdered by man, yet honoured by the God of grace (Acts 7:55–56).

✞ **POSITION / OPERATION OF GRACE:** (grace experienced the humiliation of undeserved death; grace is the divine nature)

"But we are able to see Jesus, Who was ranked lower than the angels for a little while, crowned with glory and honour because of His having suffered death, in order that by the grace (unmerited favour) of God [to us sinners] He might experience death for every individual person.

For it was an act worthy [of God] and fitting [to the divine nature] that He, for Whose sake and by Whom all things have their existence, in bringing many sons into glory, should make the Pioneer of their salvation perfect [should bring to maturity the human experience necessary to be perfectly equipped for His office as High Priest] through suffering" (Hebrews 2:9–10).

By the grace of God, Jesus experienced death for every individual person. The grace that we received for our salvation is the same grace that we walk and live in as the body of Christ. Grace allows us to see Jesus. It illuminates the Pioneer of our salvation first to us as a member of the body of Christ, then to the world around us as grace perfects and equips us for our office — ministers of reconciliation (2 Cor. 5:18).

Even as Jesus was equipped for His office of High Priest through His suffering, it is through suffering that we are equipped for our office as priests to bring grace to those around us. The Gospel is the only message that presents eternal life to every individual person as an act of grace. Grace positions us as worthy before God, and then it operates in our life conforming us into the divine nature according to His plans and purposes.

Grace guides us through the valley of suffering, trains us, and brings us to a maturity, which reflects the nature of God. Just as a wine is never totally mature, we too, never arrive, but one thing we do is to forget the things of the past and press on towards the mark of the high calling in Christ.

We fix our eyes on Jesus, the Author and Refiner of our faith (Heb. 12:2).

The Gospel is offensive to the world because it is free; it requires a humble heart to receive it. It requires its recipients to approach the Truth personally, and receive it as their own, accepting the fact that they can do nothing what-so-ever to merit it. One must seize the Gospel; we must not refuse or reject grace. Grace is offensive to the world because it requires a humble agreement with the Truth in order to receive it.

With the heart one believes, and with the mouth confession is made unto salvation. To receive grace one needs to choose it, to confess it, and possess it as one's own (Rom. 10:9–10). Spiritual blindness is a condition whereby one does not see the truth because he does not believe it; hence, he does not receive life from it — without faith it is impossible to please God (Heb. 11:6).

✞ **POSITION OF GRACE:** (grace makes us brethren)

"For both He Who sanctifies [making men holy] and those who are sanctified all have one [Father]. For this reason He is not ashamed to call them brethren;

For He says, I will declare your [the Father's] name to My brethren; in the midst of the [worshipping] congregation I will sing hymns of praise to You" (Hebrews 2:11–12).

The Grace of God is not ashamed to call us brothers; it has made us blood-brothers, by Jesus' blood. We are fellow believers united to one another in the bond of love, and this is how the world shall know that we are brothers — by our love one for another (John 13:35; 1 John 4:7). Grace has positioned us into the family of God and bestowed its kinship upon us. As the body of Christ, we praise the Father and openly proclaim His name to those around us. Grace declares the personage of God to the world, through the whole body of Christians living throughout the earth — the body of Christ.

✞ **POSITION OF GRACE:** (grace makes us God's children)

"And again He says, My trust and assured reliance and confident hope shall be fixed in Him. And yet again, Here I am, I and the children whom God has given Me.

Since therefore, [these His] children share in flesh and blood [in the physical nature of human beings], He [Himself] in a similar manner partook of the same [nature], that by [going through] death He might bring to naught and make of no effect him who had the power of death — that is, the devil" (Hebrews 2:13–14).

The grace of God has discharged and loosed us from the grasp and power of the devil. Death has lost its sting, and is made inoperative over our new life in Christ. We have been freed from our habit of following the prince of the power of the air — that demon spirit that works in the disobedient and rebellious. We have been severed from the power of obedience to sin (Eph. 2:1–7; Col. 2:13–15).

Grace declares us to be the children of God with a confident hope and a rested reliance in God — a trust fashioned and fixed by our Father Himself. The Grace of God became flesh and dwelt amongst us; to all who receive Him — to all who believe in His name — He gives them authority to be His children. We become born-again, born not of the flesh, but by the Spirit of God from above. Grace became flesh and dwelt among us, so that we might become children of grace and truth (John 1:14, 17).

Grace has established us as members of the body of Christ, and in Him we have overcome the world. We are born into the kingdom of Christ and are members of His body. As His grace operates in our life, it continuously gives us victory over the devil and our carnal tendencies. Our confidence in life is now founded on the hope that has been birthed within us by God (John 16:33).

✞ **POSITION / OPERATION OF GRACE:** (Grace experienced humanity and hence we can identify with it)

"So it is evident that it was essential that He be made like His brethren in every respect, in order that He might become a merciful (sympathetic) and faithful High Priest in the things related to

God, to make atonement and propitiation for the people's sins.

For because He Himself [in His humanity] has suffered in being tempted (tested and tried), He is able [immediately] to run to the cry of (assist, relieve) those who are being tempted and tested and tried [and who therefore are being exposed to suffering]" (Hebrews 2:17–18).

The grace of God is often coupled with suffering. Grace is acquainted with trials and tests — suffering often is a prerequisite for the seed of grace to take root in a heart (Acts 9:16; 1 Peter 4:16). It was essential that Grace be made like us that we could be conformed into the image of Grace. We are called to be participants of God's grace, allowing its enablement to assist us in our time of need.

If Christ had not taken on the form of man and suffered even unto death, the love of God would not have been made available to us. It took the love of God for Jesus to hang on the cross in order to bring His grace and love to us. It is this same love and grace, which we are privileged to partake in as we walk out our life of faith here on earth (James 1:2–4).

There is never a time when God does not understand or empathize with us in our trials. He knows and is intimate with any and all temptations that we encounter in our life. We can know with assurance that His presence is there to support us in all our trials. He even knows what it is to be forsaken (Mk. 15:34). The grace of God gives us access to His character and enables us to live out *His* life in *our* life.

✝ **POSITION OF GRACE:** (grace confesses Jesus)

"So then, brethren, consecrated and set apart for God, who share in the heavenly calling, [thoughtfully and attentively] consider Jesus, the Apostle and High Priest Whom we confessed [as ours when we embraced the Christian faith]" (Hebrews 3:1).

Embracing the Christian faith sets us apart for the works of God. We are called to fix our eyes and minds upon the Author and High Priest of our faith. It is only through determined, purposeful looking that we perceive our heavenly calling and the wisdom that comes with it. We are to make our ears attentive to His wisdom and we must incline our hearts towards it. We are to seek it as we would search for hidden treasures, applying all our powers in the quest for it (Prov. 2:1–5).

Grace gives us an unlimited guarantee and share in the economy of heaven. When we consider Jesus, we uncover the wealth of grace as we enter into the rest found in the Holy of Holies through the blood and cross of Christ. Godly treasures are only acquired by faith that is exercised; faith that is inactive will never bring about God's purpose and place for these treasures in our life.

✝ **OPERATION OF GRACE:** (grace reveals the stratagem of sin)

"[Therefore beware] brethren, take care, lest there be in any one of you a wicked, unbelieving heart [which refuses to cleave to, trust in, and rely on Him], leading you to turn away and desert or stand aloof from the living God.

But instead warn (admonish, urge, and encourage) one another every day, as long as it is called Today, that none of you may be hardened [into settled rebellion] by the deceitfulness of sin [by fraudulence, the stratagem, the trickery which the delusive glamour of his sin may play on him]" (Hebrews 3:12–13).

The grace of God calls us to stand in Christ — the only safe position that exists. Grace warns us to beware and take precaution against unbelief. Unbelief leads us into tolerance towards sin and compromise of integrity, where we end up living aloof from the plans and purposes of God. Blessed is the man who does not walk, stand, or sit in the counsel of the ungodly (Ps. 1:1–3). By the grace of God we daily admonish, urge, and encourage one another to remain aloof from the delusive deceitfulness of sin — the deceptive glamour of ungodliness. It is only by the operation of grace in our life that unrighteousness can be despised.

Grace has freed us from the bondage of sin and translated us into the freedom found only in the kingdom of God. Grace operates through the body of Christ. Fellowship is the distinguishing mark of

Christians, and it is in fellowship that the glamour of sin is revealed and can be broken in our life (1 John 1: 5–7).

Just as belief in the grace of God leads us into the work of God, unbelief will lead us away from the purposes of God, and will cause us to live aloof from the works of His kingdom. It is by the grace of God that we love one another — warn, admonish, exhort, and counsel one another, daily.

Spiritual hardness comes from being settled in things that are not of God. It is the result of being deceived into calling bad, good and good, bad. Sin tricks its victims and defrauds them of the life available in Christ. It can portray a delusive glamour, which comes in the guise of Christ, but in truth is really anti-Christ. Beloved, a little leaven leavens the whole lump. Spiritual hardness/blindness is never easily seen or broken, therefore we should be ever ready to pray for God to expose the areas of deception in our life that are causing us to reject truth (John 8:38–45).

✞ **POSITION OF GRACE:** (grace makes us fellow heirs with Christ)

"For we have become fellows with Christ (the Messiah) and share in all He has for us, if only we hold our first new-born confidence and original assured expectation [in virtue of which we are believers] firm and unshaken to the end" (Hebrews 3:14).

The grace of God gives us a commissioned confidence, which has been birthed by God. It furnishes us with a secure expectation of the eternal work of God operating in our life. Grace has made us partners with Christ as we hold fast and stand firm in our assurance of the work accomplished in His death and resurrection. We have been placed in partnership with Christ and birthed into union with all that He has, where we now cling to and nurture our new-born confidence. There is only one foundation on which to build and that foundation is Christ Jesus (1 Cor. 3:11; 2 Tim. 2:19).

Grace has made us fellows with Christ; a fellow is a companion. A fellow is a colleague, an associate, a partner, a co-worker, and an equal. This is how God views us in Christ. When we walk in the Spirit, we are the very representatives of God here and now (2 Cor. 5:20). It is sweet to believe and receive this grace, and see it living in our heart. His grace has introduced us to Christ's spiritual riches, and has drawn us out of the allurement of the world and its wages of death (Rom. 5:17; 6:23).

✞ **POSITION OF GRACE:** (grace places us in a position of rest)

"For we who have believed (adhered to and trusted in and relied on God) do enter that rest, in accordance with His declaration that those [who did not believe] should not enter when He said, As I swore in My wrath, They shall not enter My rest; and this He said although [His] works had been completed and prepared [and waiting for all who would believe] from the foundation of the world" (Hebrews 4:3).

To know the grace of God is to know the rest of God, to be in His grace is to be in His rest — His Sabbath. When we believe, we acknowledge God's grace, and we actively entrust and place our confidence in the work of God. Because of His work, we can now enter His rest, which is accessible *only* through His grace. Our belief in the work of God has brought us into our position of rest, declared and defined by God, not accomplished by the work of man.

To enter the rest of God one must believe that Jesus entered the Holy of Holies by the sacrifice of His own blood. We now have free, bold access to that same Holy of Holies. Beloved, this is an eternal entrance, done once and for all time. Those who enter find the eternal rest of God; those who are busy working to please God, hoping to get into His grace by doing good things, do not enter His rest. They shall not (Matt. 11:27–30).

✞ **OPERATION OF GRACE:** (grace calls us to strive to enter into His rest)

"Let us therefore be zealous and exert ourselves and strive diligently to enter that rest [of God, to know and experience it for ourselves], that no one may fall or perish by the same kind of unbelief and

disobedience [into which those in the wilderness fell]" (Hebrews 4:11).

The grace of God calls us to exert all our powers to the quest for our rest in God. It warns us to guard ourselves from falling away and perishing through unbelief and disobedience. The 'rest' spoken of here is meant to be entered into now — today. Through belief, not works, we enjoy God's rest and avoid the inevitable corruptions of the heart and the temptations of Satan, which work through our flesh. Grace is designed to quicken and awaken a godly jealousy within us as we love the Lord God with all our heart, and love one another just as He loves us (2 Cor. 11:2).

There is a rest to be found in the wilderness — a rest that brings us into the knowledge of God as we experience the presence of the Lord (Ps. 68:7; 78:15, 19; 136:16). When we long for fellowship with a brother, it is the jealousy of God operating within our heart, yearning after God breathed communion. To replace this life of Christ with liturgy is both foolish and unproductive.

✝ **OPERATION OF GRACE:** (the throne of grace ministers mercy; grace helps us in time of need)

"For we do not have a High Priest Who is unable to understand and sympathize and have a shared feeling with our weaknesses and infirmities and liability to the assaults of temptation, but One Who has been tempted in every respect as we are, yet without sinning.

Let us then fearlessly and confidently and boldly draw near to the throne of grace (the throne of God's unmerited favour to us sinners), that we may receive mercy [for our failures] and find grace to help in good time for every need [appropriate help and well-timed help, coming just when we need it]" (Hebrews 4:15–16).

The throne of grace draws believers onwards and upwards, into the presence and rest of God; it is a throne, which is unseen by unbelievers (2 Cor. 4:3–4). The evil one assaults us with temptations and tests, craftily designed to strike at our weaknesses and infirmities founded in our flesh. The demonic realm constantly attempts to lure us into the grip of sin (James 1:14; 1 Peter 5:8).

Grace gives us mercy for our failures and practical help in our time of need; it produces a fearless confidence to boldly draw near to the very throne of God — the throne of grace. When such a grace is operating in our life, it produces a godly empathy towards weakness and infirmity in others. Grace looks not at the vessel, but rather, at the precious gift dwelling within it (Gal. 6:1–5).

✝ **OPERATION OF GRACE:** (grace trains us to discern between good and evil — maturity)

"For everyone who continues to feed on milk is obviously inexperienced and unskilled in the doctrine of righteousness (of conformity to the divine will in purpose, thought, and action), for he is a mere infant [not able to talk yet]!

But solid food is for full-grown men, for those whose senses and mental faculties are trained by practice to discriminate and distinguish between what is morally good and noble and what is evil and contrary either to divine or human law" (Hebrews 5:13–14).

Grace births us into the family of God; it nurtures us and causes us to grow in the purposes of God. The mark of maturity is the ability to distinguish between what is morally good and honourable, and what is contrary to divine law. Maturity is brought about when we *do* what the word says to do. Grace trains us to deny lawlessness; we grow as we become experienced and skilled in the precepts of righteousness — conformity to the divine will in motive, thought, and action. A mature Christian is one who is busy doing the will of the Father.

As we are trained by the operation of God's grace in our life, we become full-grown men whose senses and mental faculties have been mentored by godly discipline. A life conformed to the divine will in purpose, thought, and action will have no other gods before or besides the Lord God (Ex. 20:3; Is. 57:7–8; 1 John 5:21).

All the words that come from a mouth of maturity will portray truth, for to speak untruth is loathsome. As words of truth are being spoken to a teachable heart, they will be plainly received and understood (Prov. 8:7–9).

The words: 'Not able to talk yet' are a sign of immaturity and being under the control of worldly and carnal ideals (1 Cor. 3:1). An abundance of words is not a sign of maturity; it is quite often a sign of a spirit of control (Prov. 10:9; 17:27–28; 18:2; 29:20)

The grace of God never leads us in a direction contrary to divine Law. The only time grace leads us to resist a human law is when that particular human law asks us to disobey God's law, causing us to violate our conscience towards God (Dan. 3:18; 6:10; Acts 4:19; 5:29). The world persecutes truth; the Gospel of grace is at variance to the spirit of the world (John 15:17–21; 1 Cor. 2:14).

Lawlessness and God's grace are never partnered together; for what alliance has righteousness with iniquity? Or what companionship has light with darkness? *"But if we [really] are living and walking in the Light, as He [Himself] is in the Light, we have [true, unbroken] fellowship with one another, and the blood of Jesus Christ His Son cleanses (removes) us from all sin and guilt [keeps us cleansed from sin in all its forms and manifestations]"* (1 John 1:7).

✞ **POSITION OF GRACE:** (grace, guaranteed by the oath of God, gives us an indwelling strength and hope)

"Accordingly God also in His desire to show more convincingly and beyond doubt to those who were to inherit the promise the unchangeableness of His purpose and plan, intervened (mediated) with an oath.

This was so that, by two unchangeable things [His promise and His oath] in which it is impossible for God ever to prove false or deceive us, we who have fled [to Him] for refuge might have mighty indwelling strength and strong encouragement to grasp and hold fast the hope appointed for us and set before [us]" (Hebrews 6:17–18).

The grace of God is as omnipotent as the oath/word of God. His promise is sufficient guarantee that our inheritance is unshakable and unchangeable. Grace has caused us to flee to Him for refuge; it is there that we find mighty indwelling strength and encouragement to hold fast to the hope appointed and set before us. It is God's desire for us to inescapably know that we are saved, and that He is able to keep us.

The enemy continually tempts us to doubt God's word, and to not trust the keeping ability of His grace (Gen. 3:1; Matt. 4:1–10). The operation of grace in our life will cause us to strengthen and encourage one another in the hope of our calling in Christ Jesus (1 Thess. 5:11; Heb. 3:13).

✞ **POSITION OF GRACE:** (grace will not slip or break down; it places us in the presence of God)

"[Now] we have this [hope] as a sure and steadfast anchor of the soul [it cannot slip and it cannot break down under whoever steps out upon it — a hope] that reaches farther and enters into [the very certainty of the Presence] within the veil,

Where Jesus has entered in for us [in advance], a Forerunner having become a High Priest forever after the order (with the rank) of Melchizedek" (Hebrews 6:19–20).

The grace of God has entered into the presence of God in advance for us. It is a sure and steady anchor for our soul. Grace will never slip or break down under anyone who puts their trust in it. Grace takes us into the very presence of God, within the Holy of Holies. We can also be assured that in the trials of our day to day walk, our Forerunner (Jesus) has walked before us and knows the way (1 Peter 2:21). His grace is sufficient. The more we are certain of God's grace, the more our lives portray this certainty.

The Almighty has carried the anchor of our hope into the Holy of Holies, and firmly fixed it in place there forever. We are eternally attached to that steadfast anchor; and we can continually draw His strength from it, knowing that it cannot slip or break down. The anchor of our soul is held by God Himself; we need not fear that He will ever let us go (John 6:37; Heb. 13:5–6).

✞ **POSITION / OPERATION OF GRACE:** (grace's High Priest is of the order of Melchizedek)

"Now if perfection (a perfect fellowship between God and the worshipper) had been attainable by the Levitical priesthood — for under it the people were given the Law — why was it further necessary that there should arise another and different kind of Priest, one after the order of Melchizedek, rather than one appointed after the order and rank of Aaron" (Hebrews 7:11)?

The grace of God existed before the law was given to Moses. Under the Law there was an order of priesthood given to the family of Levi. Just as the law of God did not nullify the promise given to Abraham, the Levitical priesthood did not nullify the priesthood of Melchizedek. Christ was not of the Levitical priesthood, He was made priest not by physical ancestry, but on the basis of the power of endless and indestructible life. Melchizedek, king of Salem and priest of the Most High God, knew neither beginning of days nor ending of life but was a priest without interruption and without successor.

When Jesus went into the Holy of Holies as our High Priest, the law's requirement of sacrifices for sin was fulfilled, once and for all time. Jesus, after the order of Melchizedek, became the perfect Sacrifice fulfilling the requirements of the Law forever (Heb. 7:25; 10:12; John 19:30). We no longer need the old order of the law because Jesus has completely and forever fulfilled the Law by the sacrifice of His blood. The perfect Sacrifice has been made and no more sacrifices need to be made. The Law's requirements have been fulfilled for us in Christ Jesus. He has balanced our account and absolved us from all guilt and condemnation before God.

The law was given through Moses but Jesus, brought grace and truth to us (John 1:14, 17). The Word of God, full of grace and truth, became flesh and dwelt among us, and now through Christ we behold the glory of God. It is only through recognition of the body of Christ that perfect fellowship between God and the worshipper is realized. A soul is perfected within the context of fellowship with Christ on a personal level. Fellowship within His body builds the body up in love.

Because there is a change in the priesthood, this automatically means that there is a change in the law regarding the priesthood as well. In Christ, we have been made kings and priests and we present ourselves as living sacrifices, well pleasing to God. It is our reasonable and spiritual worship (Rom. 12:1; James 1:26–27; Rev. 1:6; 5:10).

✞ **POSITION OF GRACE:** (grace is a more excellent and advantageous covenant)

"In keeping with [the oath's greater strength and force], Jesus has become the Guarantee of a better (stronger) agreement [a more excellent and more advantageous covenant]" (Hebrews 7:22).

The grace of God has given us a covenant more excellent and more advantageous than that of, priests who were themselves, subject to sin and death. Our grace is guaranteed to us by the oath of God. Our new covenant is a covenant that has been perfected and presented by God; it does not require maintenance by man. Works of improvement are not required when one is dwelling in the Holy of Holies.

✞ **OPERATION OF GRACE:** (grace imprints God's Law upon our hearts)

"For this is the covenant that I will make with the house of Israel after those days, says the Lord: I will imprint My laws upon their minds, even upon their innermost thoughts and understanding, and engrave them upon their hearts; and I will be their God, and they shall be My people" (Hebrews 8:10).

The grace of God imprints God's laws on our minds and engraves them upon our hearts. Grace makes us the people of God, and grace makes Him, the God of His people. Grace has made covenant with us; we are a people of the Covenant of Grace — a covenant that has fulfilled the law for us. It is finished, and we need do no works to obtain it, or maintain it — else grace would not be grace (Rom. 11:6).

Grace trains us to deny ungodliness and does not allow iniquity to have a foothold in our life. It trains us to be obedient to the law of God by the Spirit, not by the letter. Grace has placed the will of God as a treasure deep within the heart of every believer. Our teacher is now the Holy Spirit helping us to combine spiritual truths with spiritual language (1 Cor. 2:12–13). The mind of Christ is found within the members of the body of Christ where the thoughts, feelings, and purposes of God are hidden (1 Cor. 2:16). God's grace is a living gift, waiting to be revealed and employed as we commune with one another in Christ. Beloved, such revelation of His glorious plan by which we are built and nurtured together in Christ can only cause the knee of our soul to bow to the Father of our Lord Jesus Christ (Eph. 3:14).

✝ **POSITION OF GRACE:** (grace erases our unrighteousness)

"For I will be merciful and gracious toward their sins and I will remember their deeds of unrighteousness no more" (Hebrews 8:12).

God's grace has placed us in a position where He is no longer condemningly mindful of our unrighteous deeds. Mercy and grace is the way that God has dealt with and continues to deal with our sins. To receive God's mercy and grace is to receive God's precious gift of eternal life, realizing that it is also there to empower us in our everyday walk with Him.

Because we as the people of God are vessels, which have received His mercy and grace, we become reflections of this same nature. A vessel that carries mercy and grace is not a perfect vessel; it is merely a vessel of clay carrying a perfect message (2 Cor. 4:7; Phil. 3:12). Although God's grace is in the process of renewing our souls, we have not arrived, and His grace is forever sufficient. Oh, the mystery of the Gospel of how God can place such perfection — mercy and grace — in such unworthy vessels. Beloved, to be a vessel of mercy and grace is sufficient. A vessel that finds its source of life in the grace of God is a godly vessel indeed.

✝ **POSITION OF GRACE:** (grace is the new covenant)

"When God speaks of a new [covenant or agreement], He makes the first one obsolete (out of use). And what is obsolete (out of use and annulled because of age) is ripe for disappearance and to be dispensed with altogether" (Hebrews 8:13).

The God of grace has cancelled the old covenant. We have entered the new covenant — a covenant of perfection by position through faith, not by works. The covenant of grace does not negate our need to be obedient to God, but rather, it fulfils it. The old is declared to be obsolete; the new is eternal and accessible only by the grace of God — faith in the Lord Jesus Christ. The New Covenant places the Holy of Holies within our heart where we need only rest in the work already finished by Jesus. We no longer need to work up sacrifices for our heavenly Father — for he who has entered into the rest of God has ceased from his own labours.

The Holy Spirit expressly teaches us that the way into the true Holy of Holies is not thrown open for those who remain in the outer portion of the tabernacle, those who recognize it as a standing institution (Heb. 9:7–12). Grace has secured a complete redemption and an everlasting release for us — there is no longer any offering to be made to atone for our sin. The final offering (the Son of God) is complete and its perfection has made the requirements of the law stand fulfilled and finished, for all time for all believers. We no longer serve God in obedience to a written code unable to deliver us; we now serve God as new creations, by the Spirit which works within us (Rom. 7:6; 2 Cor. 3:6). God has done what the Law could not do, its power being weakened by the flesh. Christ has deprived sin of its power (Rom. 8:1–4).

✝ **POSITION / OPERATION OF GRACE:** (grace purifies our consciences)

"How much more surely shall the blood of Christ, Who by virtue of [His] eternal Spirit [His own preexistent divine personality] has offered Himself as an unblemished sacrifice to God, purify our consciences from dead works and lifeless observances to serve the [ever] living God" (Hebrews 9:14)?

The grace of God purifies our conscience from dead works, reveals what is right and wrong, and calls it to serve the living God. We have been freed from the defilement and guilt of sin along with its faults and eternal consequences (Col. 2:13–14). We have been purified and pronounced clean by the grace of God and are now free to perform sacred works of service for Him in our everyday lives. Our life now becomes a life of worship, ministering to God and to one another (Rom. 12:1).

We are now free from the condemnation of the Law; we serve not by the letter of the Law, but rather by the Spirit, bringing God's mercy and grace to those around us. A heart working to observe the Law is lifeless, and will produce only dead works. A heart with the Law graciously engraved on it, abundantly overflows with life, and will also reproduce life.

It is important to note that grace has written the Law of God on our heart; it is not the Law of God, which wrote grace on our heart. Grace has super abounded (Rom. 5:20). A heart outside of the grace of God cannot reproduce life in God; it can mimic or imitate it at best. To reproduce God's purpose in our life, it takes a heart founded in grace birthing the will and life of God in us by the Spirit of God.

✝ **POSITION OF GRACE:** (faith erases guilt)

"For since the Law has merely a rude outline (foreshadowing) of the good things to come — instead of fully expressing those things — it can never by offering the same sacrifices continually year after year make perfect those who approach [its altars].

For if it were otherwise, would [these sacrifices] not have stopped being offered? Since the worshippers had once for all been cleansed, they would no longer have any guilt or consciousness of sin" (Hebrews 10:1–2).

Grace removes the condemnation of sin from our life. It has positioned us, once-and-for-all-time, into a place of perfection. We no longer require sacrifices to maintain it, nor to keep possession of it (Rom. 7:4; Gal. 2:19). The sacrifice of tithing does not perfect us. The Law cast a shadow because it stood between God (the Light) and man. Man could not come into the presence of God as long as the Law was the intermediary — the Law cannot make mankind eternally perfect. The Lord Jesus Christ becomes our Advocate, and as we place our faith in Him, He re-creates us into His purpose, thought, and action — the kingdom of God in us.

In Christ, the shadow and darkness of the law with its condemnation has been removed. Grace has written the law on our hearts so that we can now operate without condemnation, giving the Light of God full expression through us. The veil has been removed. The Law is holy, just, and good; that is why without grace the law kills us. And that is why a heart without grace, working in obedience to the Law, cannot reproduce life; it can only reproduce death (Rom. 7:24). It is not obedience that brings life; it is Life that brings obedience. A heart motivated by grace reproduces life; a heart motivated by works keeps you busy — like rocking chair races — but does not produce any kingdom fruit (John 6:63; Rom. 8:10; 2 Cor. 3:6).

✝ **POSITION OF GRACE:** (grace has made us holy)

"And in accordance with this will [of God], we have been made holy (consecrated and sanctified) through the offering made once for all of the body of Jesus Christ (the Anointed One)" (Hebrews 10:10).

Jesus, the grace of God, obeyed the will of the Father (Matt. 26:39). This perfect Sacrifice has made us holy, and because it is perfect, it need not be offered again. It is finished once for all time. Just as Christ's obedience to His Father's will was manifested through His body, our obedience to our Father will also be manifested through our body — by what we do. Grace manifests the will of God. As the body of Christ, we reveal the will of the Father to the world. Christ is still active and alive in the world today; He communicates, moves, and manifests the Father's will through His body — the church (Phil. 2:12–16).

As we speak the truth in love to one another, we will grow up in every way and in all things. Because of Him, the whole body is joined together with every part functioning as He directs, resulting in the body building itself up and maturing in the love of God (Eph. 4:15–16).

Beloved, grace has come to us because of the work accomplished by that one perfect Sacrifice; we are eternally justified before God, and our obedience to the law is forever accomplished in Christ. When Jesus said that 'it is finished', it was a declaration of the eternal victory of grace over sin — the fulfilling of the law (Heb. 10:12).

✞ **POSITION OF GRACE:** (grace has once and for all, consecrated and perfected us)

"For by a single offering He has forever completely cleansed and perfected those who are consecrated and made holy" (Hebrews 10:14).

This single offering of God on the cross of Christ is sufficient to have spawned the innumerable acts of grace, which we have ever known or will ever know (Heb. 13:8). Oh, the joy a soul experiences when it receives the grace of God's power expressed in the greatest single act of love the world has ever known! The perfect Offering has made us perfect. The holy Offering has made us holy. There need no longer be any offering made to atone for sin. It is finished (John 19:30).

✞ **OPERATION OF GRACE:** (the Holy Spirit confirms that we are cleansed and perfected; He has written His laws on our heart)

"And also the Holy Spirit adds His testimony to us [in confirmation of this]. For having said,

This is the agreement (testament, covenant) that I will set up and conclude with them after those days, says the Lord: I will imprint My laws upon their hearts, and I will inscribe them on their minds (on their inmost thoughts and understanding)," (Hebrews 10:15–16).

The grace of God is sealed in us by the Holy Spirit, confirming the testimony of God that we are eternally justified in His presence (2 Cor. 1:22; Eph. 1:14). Grace engraves and imprints the will of God on the human heart and mind. It is by knowing God in the Spirit that we come to understand Him. To try to understand Him before you know Him is foolish, worldly wisdom. Knowing comes before understanding.

With God's law written on our heart, we need only listen to the promptings of the Spirit as it guides us in the ways of God. We obey God because He was obedient to the cross, and we have been touched by his grace. We do works of righteousness because we are righteous; we walk in the ways of justice because we are justified; we love because we are loved; we show acts of grace because we have received it — we are the people of grace.

✞ **POSITION OF GRACE:** (grace opens the door to the Holy of Holies for us)

"He then goes on to say, And their sins and their law-breaking I will remember no more.

Now where there is absolute remission (forgiveness and cancellation of the penalty) of these [sins and law-breaking], there is no longer any offering made to atone for sin.

Therefore, brethren, since we have full freedom and confidence to enter into the [Holy of] Holies [by the power and virtue] in the blood of Jesus," (Hebrews 10:17–19).

The grace of God places us in a position of full freedom and confidence to enter into the very presence of God. The blood of God's grace has been shed for us; it is our covering, imparting to us His authority. Our covering is the grace of God. Man's covering — the church system's covering — will only take away from our covering of God's grace. Grace is an eternal expression of God's power, love, and virtue, and the operation of this grace in our life will manifest and reproduce an expression of our Lord as it works in and through our daily lives (2 Cor. 5:20; Eph. 6:19–20).

Our sins and lawless deeds are no longer remembered by our blessed Saviour. God did not atone for all our sin just so that He could now hold it against us again. Love has forever cleansed and consecrated us — made us fit for the Lord's work. God is not a God of coercion; He is the God of love. He is the God of grace. Grace does not dredge up the past to bear it against us; it does not summon up the sentence of condemnation again. Our knowledge of being free from condemnation gives us confidence to truly enter the Holy of Holies.

To say that God does not remember our sins anymore is not to say that God is blinded to our acts of disobedience to Him, now that we are justified before Him by faith. To say that God cannot see our sins is untrue and makes Him less than omniscient (Prov. 5:21; 15:3). When a Christian sins and denies such, he is denying the truth (1 John 1:8–10). God wants us to acknowledge our sin, to renounce it, and not continue to live in it (Prov. 28:13; Jas. 5:16; 1 John 1:9; 3:7–10).

✞ **POSITION OF GRACE:** (grace gives us absolute, unqualified assurance that we are right with God)

"Let us all come forward and draw near with true (honest and sincere) hearts in unqualified assurance and absolute conviction engendered by faith (by that leaning of the entire human personality on God in absolute trust and confidence in His power, wisdom and goodness), having our hearts sprinkled and purified from a guilty (evil) conscience and our bodies cleansed with pure water" (Hebrews 10:22).

The grace of God is received by faith, without which it is impossible to please God. We exercise faith by leaning our entire confidence and trust in His power, His wisdom, and His goodness. Grace places its charge on the foundation of God's work, rather than man's abilities and works — his pride. In Christ, we are able to draw near to God in absolute confidence and assurance of receiving His love, knowing that all of God's resources are positioned for our good, not our harm (Jer. 29:11; Rom. 2:4; 11:22).

Grace calls out to the souls of man, *"Come to Me, all you who labour and are over-burdened, and I will cause you to rest. [I will ease and relieve and refresh your souls.]"* (Matthew 11:28). What a precious calling of grace to be able to say to one another, "Come, and in Christ together we will find living water to refresh our souls (John 4:10)." What a precious privilege of grace to bring God's relief and refreshment to one another in the body of Christ.

✞ **POSITION / OPERATION OF GRACE:** (grace keeps us from opposing and mocking God)

"For if we go on deliberately and willingly sinning after once acquiring the knowledge of the Truth, there is no longer any sacrifice left to atone for [our] sins [no further offering to which to look forward].

[There is nothing left for us then] but a kind of awful and fearful prospect and expectation of divine judgement and the fury of burning wrath and indignation which will consume those who put themselves in opposition [to God]" (Hebrews 10:26–27).

The grace of God is never found to be in opposition to God and His ways. To go back to a life of deliberate and willful sin, would be to position yourself outside of the Holy of Holies, where you would try again to offer sacrifices to atone for these sins. Beloved, the perfect Sacrifice has already been made, so where else can you now turn (1 Sam. 2:25; John 6:68)?

There need be no more sacrifice for sin, no other Saviour, no other salvation to be found in any other way (Acts 4:12; Phil. 2:10). There is no help or hope outside of Jesus Christ, and for one to put confidence in anything other than Jesus, is to close the way to deliverance.

The way into the true Holy of Holies is not accessible as long as the outer portion of the tabernacle remains a recognized institution and is still standing. It is foolish to take the perfect work of God and attempt to add to it by demanding voluntary submission to rules and regulations, or to mock it (Acts 15:1, 22–29; Gal. 2:1–21; 6:7; Col. 2:8, 16–18, 20–23).

Jesus has brought to the world the *only* salvation God has offered, or ever will offer. A person can *only* truly come to know God through faith in the work that Jesus Christ accomplished on the cross over two thousand years ago. There is no salvation or knowledge of God outside of this: Jesus died for His church — His body. This is the church, which we belong to, the church that Jesus died for, and the church for which He is coming for again. This is the church that we are members of. God does not call us to belong to some church system that started decades ago, and we should not place significance in such an organization. God is not impressed with any institutions, which man has come up with. We count all such things as refuse compared to the gaining of the knowledge of the Lord Jesus Christ, and the work He completed on the cross.

To make any organization attempt to represent our living Lord Jesus Christ is to lose the significance of Christ's death on the cross and His subsequent resurrection. Much of the power of the resurrection gets nullified and made of no effect by institutional denominationalism. In truth, we end up in opposition to the ways and purposes of God, the work of Christ through His body (Acts 5:39).

✞ **POSITION / OPERATION OF GRACE:** (grace warns us of judgement)

"Any person who has violated and [thus] rejected and set at naught the Law of Moses is put to death without pity or mercy on the evidence of two or three witnesses.

How much worse (sterner and heavier) punishment do you suppose he will be judged to deserve who has spurned and [thus] trampled underfoot the Son of God, and who has considered the covenant blood by which he was consecrated common and unhallowed, thus profaning it and insulting and outraging the [Holy] Spirit [Who imparts] grace (the unmerited favour and blessing of God)" (Hebrews 10:28–29).

The grace of God imparted unto us by the Holy Spirit is not to be spurned or treated with insulting neglect or rudeness. The more the grace of God is revealed to us, the more we are unable to reject, it or set it aside. The more we grow in it, the more we recognize its incredible beauty and protective power (2 Peter 3:14–18).

The covenant blood of grace is holy. Grace will never lead us in the direction of either purposefully disrespecting or desecrating it. Such action would be blasphemous and would outrage the Holy Spirit, who is the seal of His divine grace imparted unto us (Eph. 1:13; 2 Tim. 2:19). The fear of God draws us closer to Him; it does not cause us to depart from Him.

✞ **POSITION / OPERATION OF GRACE:** (grace judges us)

"For we know Him Who said, Vengeance is Mine [retribution and the meting out of full justice rest with Me]; I will repay [I will exact the compensation], says the Lord. And again, The Lord will judge and determine and solve and settle the cause and the cases of His people.

It is a fearful (formidable and terrible) thing to incur the divine penalties and be cast into the hands of the living God" (Hebrews 10:30–31).

The grace of God has perfectly paid the required penalty due us because of our sin. It has totally fulfilled God's demand for justice. The Word of God, made flesh, has completely acquitted us and carried out the vindication of God for us, on the cross. We stand justified before God because of Jesus Christ dying on the cross, paying the full price for our sins.

The Passover defined when God's judgement passed over His people; judgement was set aside (Ex. 12:12–13). On the cross, however, judgement is not just *passed over* it is *fulfilled* for us (John 19:30). By grace, we now have faith in Him who died for our judgement, and has resurrected, making us His body — the body of the living Christ.

In Christ, our judgement has been completed, and by His grace, we have been pronounced eternally cleansed. All our causes have been placed into the hands of Him Who says, "Vengeance is Mine." We live and breathe entirely by the mercy and grace of God. This births within us the knowledge of God which is eternally significant. Grace contains a force and an enablement that we are called to pay attention to.

When we understand that vengeance is the Lord's, it is easier to let any negative situation in our life rest in His hands. In truth, and as a perfect understatement, we can say that God is much better equipped, and a whole lot wiser than us in solving any of our life's trying circumstances. Self-retribution is very arrogant on our part; it comes from us thinking we can define godly justice (Jas. 4:11). Beloved, we need to rest in the Lord, not wrestle against flesh and blood. Any solution not activated by the Holy Spirit is a work of the flesh; it is founded in wickedness, and will bear the same fruit (Eph. 6:10–13).

Whoever has been forgiven much, loves much. Even a brief understanding of what we have been forgiven of, is sufficient to make us bow our knee and allow God's grace to have its way in our life (Eph. 3:14). Beloved, our destiny is in His hands only when we allow Him to be the Lord of our life. We need to accept the fact that His solutions to life's trials are far superior to anything we can conger up. In truth, there are many plans that are birthed in a man's mind, which seem right, but they inevitably end in death, and we miss God's desired and blessed outcome (Prov. 14:12; 19:3, 21; 21:2).

✞ **POSITION / OPERATION OF GRACE:** (the God of grace is not ashamed to be called by our name)

"But the truth is that they were yearning for and aspiring to a better and more desirable country, that is, a heavenly [one]. For that reason God is not ashamed to be called their God [even to be surnamed their God — the God of Abraham, Isaac, and Jacob], for He has prepared a city for them" (Hebrews 11:16).

Grace causes our eyes to be fixed upon the Author and Finisher of our faith (Heb. 12:2). Eyes glued to the grace of God are not searching for earthly, material benefits; they are set on a country — a heavenly one — and a city that is built by God Himself. Eyes that scan for worldly benefits and positions have been blinded and seduced by the prince of the power of the air; their direction is set by the spirit that works in the sons of disobedience.

But to those who have called upon His name, He is not ashamed to be called their God. How incredibly humbling it is to have the God of all grace introduce Himself as the God of Abraham, the God of Isaac, the God of Jacob, the God of (*put your name in these brackets*). Even in the New Testament some tried to use Jesus' name, in the name of Paul, and they were thoroughly rebuked with the devil's response of "*...Jesus I know, and Paul I know about, but who are you* (Acts 19:15)?" As people of God, we have full authority to operate in His name; we do not need to be qualified through any human authority or institution (Acts 4:13; Eph. 2:2).

The truth is that we should be yearning for and aspiring to a better and more desirable country (city/home), our heavenly one. We should be seeking first the kingdom of God and His righteousness, and not fixing our desires upon the things He so graciously provides for us (Matt. 6:33; 16:26).

✞ **POSITION / OPERATION OF GRACE:** (by grace we run the race set before us towards the throne of God)

"Therefore then, since we are surrounded by so great a cloud of witnesses [who have born testimony to the Truth], let us strip off and throw aside every encumbrance (unnecessary weight) and that sin which so readily (deftly and cleverly) clings to and entangles us, and let us run with patient endurance and steady and active persistence the appointed course of the race that is set before us,

Looking away [from all that will distract] to Jesus, Who is the Leader and the Source of our faith [giving the first incentive for our belief] and is also its Finisher [bringing it to maturity and perfection]. He, for the joy [of obtaining the prize] that was set before Him, endured the cross, despising and ignoring the shame, and is now seated at the right hand of the throne of God" (Hebrews 12:1–2).

The grace of God has placed a great multitude of witnesses about us — people who have passed on before us and have lived as a testimony to the truth. These people are still a vital part of the body of Christ. Even though they are not with us in the flesh, their spiritual testimony still speaks to us today (Gal. 3:28–29; Heb. 11:4, 39–40; 12:13, 23).

Grace calls us to put off and cast aside every encumbrance and sin that would make us disobedient to God. From our position of righteousness in Christ, grace calls us to operate in righteousness. It trains us not to miss the will of God and wander from the path of uprightness (Heb. 10:36). When we sin, we wander from the law of God and we violate the way of God. All that is done wrong in thought or action is an offence and violation to divine will. Grace, by the blood of the Lamb of God, has taken our wanderings and paid the penalty for us. Before we knew Christ we did not share in His nature, but now in Christ we both partake in and manifest His divine will in purpose, thought, and action (2 Peter 1:4).

Within the body of Christ, we as sanctified earthen vessels have hidden within us heavenly blessings, gifts, and promises. It is in fellowship within the body that we encourage one another to partake in the will of God and these heavenly treasures. We then take these promises into our life, where we can manifest the glory of God and His grace, and live in such a way that the world may know we are His disciples (John 14:9; Acts 4:13).

Sin subtly and skilfully surrounds its victim, and deftly deceives it into carrying an unnecessary weight — the bondage of sin. Entanglement with sin ensnares and hinders an upright walk (Prov. 22:25; 29:6). Once entangled, it is easy to be led by that same sin over and over again (Ps. 1:1). The spirit of disobedience skilfully surrounds its victims, often using even religious traditions to nullify the work and word of God (Mark 7:13).

Grace calls us to disregard all that distracts from Jesus, and to fix our eyes on the Finisher of our faith. Faith has positioned us into the presence of perfection, and will lead us fearlessly into all things, which are upright and of noble purpose, enabling us to manifest His works of grace. As we exercise grace, it builds maturity into our lives (Heb. 5:14).

Grace came to us because of our sin. The Just One died unjustly for us, and hence, He now justifies the unjust. This same grace now works within us to manifest the character of Jesus. We are seated together with Him in heavenly places, and from there we manifest mercy and grace to those around us (Eph. 2:6).

It is with joy that we endure the pressure of trials and temptations, turning our eyes away from the cares of the world, and fixing them upon the God of grace (Phil. 3:13–14). Our faith has placed us into Christ where we are ashamed of nothing and unaffected by all condemnation and worldly criticism, which comes our way.

✝ **OPERATION OF GRACE:** (grace covers us and carries us through all grievous opposition and bitter hostility)

"Just think of Him Who endured from sinners such grievous opposition and bitter hostility against Himself [reckon up and consider it all in comparison with your trials], so that you may not grow weary or exhausted, losing heart and relaxing and fainting in your minds.

You have not yet struggled and fought agonizingly against sin, nor have you yet resisted and withstood to the point of pouring out your [own] blood" (Hebrews 12:3–4).

We are called to ponder our position of grace, and as we do, we are empowered to endure grievous opposition and bitter hostility, neither fainting nor losing heart in the face of ungodliness. Our spiritual consideration of the grace of God enables us to withstand and overcome malevolence and animosity, with joy (Col. 3:12–14).

It was the obedient pouring out of the sacrificial blood of the Lamb, which is the very source of our enablement to walk in His steps. Grace agonizes against sin. It resists it; it does not participate in it, and it has no share in it, because sin has no part or share in the grace of God. Sin is not at home in a Christian.

A heart empowered by grace is a heart destined to encounter grievous opposition and bitter hostility from the world. Yet, it is because of these very things that the grace of God is destined to be manifested, and it is our grace-response, which causes the world consternation as to how we can possibly find joy in the midst of our trials and persecutions (1 Peter 4:4).

✝ **OPERATION OF GRACE:** (grace disciplines us as sons of God)

"And have you [completely] forgotten the divine word of appeal and encouragement in which you are reasoned with and addressed as sons? My son, do not think lightly or scorn to submit to the correction

and discipline of the Lord, nor lose courage and give up and faint when you are reproved or corrected by Him;

For the Lord corrects and disciplines everyone whom He loves, and He punishes, even scourges, every son whom He accepts and welcomes to His heart and cherishes" (Hebrews 12:5–6).

The grace of God loves and corrects us. We are not to despise or shrink from divine discipline. Discipline is the way of life for a Christian (Prov. 6:23). Maturity comes through holy correction and endurance under the task master of sufferings and trials. A change within a soul will always manifest a change without. Happy is the soul that feels the hand of skilful and godly discipline shaping it. Such workings bring an understanding of the Word of life, which in turn enables the recipient to hold it out for the benefit of others, not as an arrogant ministry, but as a humble truth (Phil. 2:16, 21; 2 Peter 3:15–16).

To be called a son of God is not a light or insignificant thing; it is a divine appeal. A soul that has recognized God's grace is a soul that manifests the grace of God. Conviction and chastisement by grace are a blessing — a demonstration by God that we are not rejected, but rather acknowledged as His own. Grace warns us not to quickly forget the divine reasoning and appeal of God in our life. Divine discipline not only acts as a deterrent, it also has the effect of purifying the heart. It is the way of life, and the way to life (Prov. 6:23).

It is vital for Christians to be able to discern when the Spirit of God is correcting you or when the spirit of man (the world) is attempting to control (correct) you. False discipline occurs when man assumes authority that God has not given him. Authority is not a position that man holds. God's authority only operates when man is under the control of the Spirit of God. False discipline is designed to distract us from the race we are running in Christ; it occurs when we correct someone outside of the will of God (Gal. 2:4–5, 11–14; 3 John 1:9).

As members of the body of Christ, we need to make sure that we are not operating in the spirit of the world — neither giving false discipline, nor receiving it as if it were from God. False discipline most often has a selfish, worldly motive, and only perverts the will of God for our life. It will always result in bondage (worldly control). In Christ, we need to make sure that we are always giving and receiving counsel and correction within the Spirit of God — submitting to one another in the fear of the Lord. This is what causes the body of Christ to grow and mature (John 9:1–41; Acts 9:31; 1 Cor. 3:1–4).

It is vital for a disciple to discern between the Spirit of God and the spirit of man. When you know what is true, you can hear when something is false; when you believe what is false, you cannot hear what is true. *"Whoever is of God listens to God. [Those who belong to God hear the words of God.] This is the reason that you do not listen [to those words, to Me]; because you do not belong to God and are not of God or in harmony with Him"* (John 8:47).

✝ **OPERATION OF GRACE:** (grace disciplines us as sons)

"You must submit to and endure [correction] for discipline; God is dealing with you as with sons. For what son is there whom his father does not [thus] train and correct and discipline?

Now if you are exempt from correction and left without discipline in which all [of God's children] share, then you are illegitimate offspring and not true sons [at all]" (Hebrews 12:7–8).

The grace of God has made me a legitimate offspring of God, and as such, I need to submit to and endure His hand of grace operating in my life. In fact, I should let it be an opportunity for joy (Jas. 1:2). To be exempt from the correction of God and left without discipline is to be identified as a bastard — an illegitimate child. Grace has legally made me a child of God, which bestows upon me the priceless privilege of divine discipline (Prov. 3:11–12). We are to bravely bear up under godly discipline, and are not to recede nor flee from such a gracious handling by God. Grace places us in the position of and under the operation of the eternal love and care of God.

In truth, we know that God has only our best in mind, so why spurn the very thing that is going to make us better? Every circumstance we encounter in our life gives us opportunity to become either bitter, or better, and it is our choice (Joshua 24:15; Prov. 1:22–33).

✞ **OPERATION OF GRACE:** (grace brings us into the Father's discipline)

"Moreover, we have had earthly fathers who disciplined us and we yielded [to them] and respected [them for training us]. Shall we not much more cheerfully submit to the Father of spirits and so [truly] live?

For [our earthly fathers] disciplined us for only a short period of time and chastised us as seemed proper and good to them; but He disciplines us for our certain good, that we may become sharers in His own holiness" (Hebrews 12:9–10).

The motivation of God's discipline is always for our certain good as well as those around us. Gracious discipline is not a rejection of us as God's children. It comes upon us as we accept God's ways, and it is a reflection of the love and holiness of God (Gen. 4:7; 2 Cor. 5:9–11; Eph. 1:6). A righteous reprimand works on a wise soul as it brings instruction and holiness; a righteous reproof to a scorner is wasted (Prov. 9:7–9; 10:17; 23:23). To be a sharer in His holiness does not make us better than anyone else; it makes us better than our old self. Godly discipline is never a vengeful punishment; it is always exposes the loving character of Christ.

✞ **OPERATION OF GRACE:** (grace trains us unto righteousness)

"For the time being no discipline brings joy, but seems grievous and painful; but afterwards it yields a peaceable fruit of righteousness to those who have been trained by it [a harvest of fruit which consists in righteousness — in conformity to God's will in purpose, thought, and action, resulting in right living and right standing with God]" (Hebrews 12:11).

The grace of God does not always make our flesh feel joyous. Gracious discipline may seem grievous and painful for a season; however it works the blessed fruit of righteousness into our life as we endure the cross for the joy that is set before us. Discipline cultivates the soil of our soul by correcting our mistakes, and curbing our passions. It trains us and plants godly instruction into our heart, which results in an increase of virtuous fruit and the character of God in our life (1 Cor. 4:6; 1 Tim 1:20; 2 Peter 1:8).

The renewing of our mind and morals is the goal of grace; it will always result in conformity to God's will in thought, purpose, and action. Our right standing in God will always manifest itself as it trains us in right living before God and man (Acts 14:15; Jas. 5:16–20).

✞ **OPERATION OF GRACE:** (grace is sufficient in our weakness)

"So then, brace up and reinvigorate and set right your slackened and weakened and drooping hands and strengthen your feeble and palsied and tottering knees,

And cut through and make firm and plain and smooth, straight paths for your feet [yes, make them safe and upright and happy paths that go in the right direction], so that the lame and halting [limbs] may not be put out of joint, but rather may be cured" (Hebrews 12:12–13).

Grace calls us to fortify, refresh, and set right the slackened and weakened areas of our life. The path of God is often concealed from us by our unbelief, but we are called to find the way of God by faith. Like land-mines, the path of God can be imbedded with unbelief, with rocks of affliction and persecution, or with worldly cares (Matt. 13:19–22). These things can cause the path of God to be covered over, clouded, and hidden from us, but we are called to make smooth straight paths before our feet. As the Spirit leads, we need to remove the rocks, thorns, and thistles to reveal a clean tilled path of righteousness before us — a safe, upright, and happy path.

The grace of God operating in our life is sufficient to set aright areas of weakness that can so easily beset us and cause us to stumble and put our life out of joint. We become dislocated from the path and way of God. Grace will locate the path of God before us and guide our way through, making our way firm and straight before our feet. A path bordered by grace is a happy path that progresses in the right direction, curing lame, halting limbs and healing that which is disjointed from God's will and purpose (Gal. 5:4). It is only on the pathway of grace where we are safe and secure. It is there that God changes our worldly dysfunction into godly function (1 Tim. 1:20; 2 Tim. 4:14).

✞ **POSITION OF GRACE:** (grace causes us to strive after peace; it causes us to exercise foresight in watching over one another)

"Strive to live in peace with everybody and pursue that consecration and holiness without which no one will [ever] see the Lord.

Exercise foresight and be on the watch to look [after one another], to see that no one falls back from and fails to secure God's grace (His unmerited favour and spiritual blessing), in order that no root of resentment (rancour, bitterness, or hatred) shoots forth and causes trouble and bitter torment, and the many become contaminated and defiled by it —" (Hebrews 12:14–15).

The grace of God cleanses and secures us from the contamination of sin. It calls us to eagerly seek and swiftly pursue peace and harmony with others. As this becomes our focus, the divine attributes of consecration and holiness will surely follow. This is an active calling. Grace positions us in holiness, and then grace works holiness into our life.

We are to look carefully and diligently after one another to make sure that no one fails to secure God's blessings. The absence of grace is fertile soil for bitterness and hatred. The presence of grace dispels that which contaminates, pollutes, and defiles; it brings healing to a soul. Grace does not eliminate hurt; it enables us to let hurt positively shape the character of our life (2 Cor. 1:3–4; 2:7; 7:13).

When the body of Christ is not watchful over itself, troubling roots of bitterness, animosity, and jealousy will defile it. When the responsibility for the spiritual welfare of believers is handed over into the hands of a professional hireling, the body begins sliding down the path of apostasy (Jer. 5:30–31; Rev. 2:6, 15).

When grace operates in the body of Christ, all of the parts of the body become closely joined and firmly knit together for the edifying of itself in love. Divisions and factions in the church are a sign of carnality and worldliness, ruling in Christ's body; they are not a sign of the operation of grace (1 Cor. 3:1–4).

All the members of the body of Christ are divinely called to look upon, oversee, and care for one another. This is God's plan and He will not tolerate any religious system to replace it. Such gracious care of the church rests upon every believer and is to be carefully observed if the body of Christ is to mature. This is what overseers (elders) in the church today should be exemplifying and equipping the body to do (Eph. 4:11–16).

When the responsibility of watching over one another is relinquished to a religious system, the result will be resentment, bitterness, hatred, and lack of submission towards one another — factions. Religious systems cannot do what the saints are divinely called to do. Love cannot be institutionalized.

Dealing with a religious society (organisation) is similar to dealing with civil government. Government does not and cannot love you. It is only saints who are vessels of God's love, and only saints are called to give and receive love. Institutional system mentality equates unfaithfulness to the system as unfaithfulness to Christ; when in truth, unfaithfulness to Christ breeds faithfulness to a system (Acts 20:30; 3 John 1:9).

To love institutions is an idolatrous love, which shows affection, significance, and loyalty toward an object made by the work of man's hands. The lack of love towards one another within the body of Christ today is a direct result of this idolatrous love for institutions. Many believers are defiled by this type of love, and they are left feeling insecure if they do not support it. Our security should be in Christ alone, not in an institution.

God never called His body to turn over its responsibility of loving one another to an organization, no matter how pious it may appear. Institutionalism will cause you to fail to secure God's gracious spiritual blessings in your life; it will keep you as infants in Christ, unable to spiritually talk yet (1 Cor. 3:1; Heb. 5:13). Institutions are full of Christians who have known the Lord for many years and yet are not actively walking in the Spirit — not leading people to their Saviour, never baptizing new disciples, and rarely teaching anyone what God has shown them (Matt. 28:18–20).

Our daily walk with the Lord is a continuous seeking and following after Him. We *are* the church; hence, we are *in* church '24/7'. Church is not something we go to on Sunday (or Saturday) mornings, while living in a less spiritual state for the rest of the week.

✝ **OPERATION OF GRACE:** (grace is a precious inheritance)

"That no one may become guilty of sexual vice, or become a profane (godless and sacrilegious) person as Esau did who sold his own birthright for a single meal.

For you understand that later on, when he wanted [to regain title to] his inheritance of the blessing, he was rejected (disqualified and set aside), for he could find no opportunity to repair by repentance [what he had done, no chance to recall the choice he had made], although he sought for it carefully with [bitter] tears" (Hebrews 12:16–17).

The grace of God does not call us to violate our rightful heritage in God (Gen. 25:34; Mal. 1:3). As Christians, we should never disrespect or treat lightly the gift of God with an ungodly attitude, nor should we ever profane the things of God or become guilty of sexual vice. To do so is to reject your birth-right.

Esau had no true repentance toward the sin of giving up his birthright, even though he was very eager for the blessing, and shed many tears to obtain it. He could not even prevail upon his father to change his mind — to nullify the blessing he had bestowed on Jacob, and confer it on him. Beloved, illegitimate pregnancy cannot be undone by crying endless tears of repentance (Gen. 27:30–34).

Tears are not an infallible sign of repentance, as men may be more concerned about personal loss, than hating their evil actions. Artificial repentance comes from the love of self; true repentance comes from the love of God and a hatred of evil (Prov. 1:7; 8:13; 9:10; 14:27; 16:6). False repentance hates the symptoms of sin; true repentance hates the sin that causes the symptoms. When a Christian argues for and justifies his sin, it is neither a picture of righteousness nor an act of grace (Gen. 4:13–14). Godly sorrow procures life; worldly sorrow produces death (2 Cor. 7:10).

✝ **POSITION OF GRACE:** (grace has brought us to the church as members of the Firstborn — heavenly citizens, made perfect and to Jesus our Mediator)

"But rather, you have come to Mount Zion, even to the city of the living God, the heavenly Jerusalem, and to countless multitudes of angels in festal gathering,

And to the church (assembly) of the Firstborn who are registered [as citizens] in heaven, and to the God Who is Judge of all, and to the spirits of the righteous (the redeemed in heaven) who have been made perfect,

And to Jesus, the Mediator (Go-between, Agent) of a new covenant, and to the sprinkled blood which speaks [of mercy], a better and nobler and more gracious message than the blood of Abel [which cried out for vengeance]" (Hebrews 12:22–24).

The grace of God has taken us from a position of death and disaster to one of bold entrance into the very presence of God, making our heart the Holy of Holies. Although the operation of working out our salvation is to be done in fear and trembling, the position of grace in Christ is forever set, and we are allowed to boldly live in the presence of God — a fearless, festal gathering of God, angels, and saints — His church, not 'my' church (1 Cor. 2:3; Phil. 2:12).

By grace we can shamelessly approach God, and we now have authority to approach life by this same grace and truth. This is the reality of God's kingdom here on earth. To approach God outside of grace (by works) is certain death. In grace, the presence of God is an aroma of life; outside of grace, the presence of God is the aroma of death (2 Cor. 2:14–16).

When our life is crucified with Christ, the resurrected life of Jesus is manifest in our mortal flesh (Rom. 8:11). Only the atoning blood of Christ shed for us speaks of mercy. All other shed blood speaks of vengeance.

When sin entered into the world, righteousness and mercy were aborted. It took the gracious blood of God's perfect Sacrifice to seek out man in his fallen state, and re-introduce him to God's righteousness and mercy (Is. 62:12). The blood of Able cried out for vengeance; the blood of Christ cries out, "Mercy!" (Gen 4:6–11).

✞ **OPERATION OF GRACE:** (grace cautions and admonishes us not to reject Him and His word)

"So see to it that you do not reject Him or refuse to listen to and heed Him Who is speaking [to you now]. For if they [the Israelites] did not escape when they refused to listen and heed Him Who warned and divinely instructed them [here] on earth [revealing with heavenly warnings His will], how much less shall we escape if we reject and turn our backs on Him Who cautions and admonishes [us] from heaven" (Hebrews 12:25)?

The grace of God forewarns everyone to accept the invitation to the wedding feast. If we turn our backs on Him Who cautions us from heaven and if we refuse His admonition, we are foolish. The preaching of the Gospel carries with it a message of paramount (eternal) importance — to reject the Gospel is to reject Life. Grace calls us to listen to and heed the word of God; it empowers us to be doers of the word and not hearers only (Jas. 1:21–25).

God reveals His will to us individually; He never holds back from a heart that truly seeks Him. Grace cautions us to keep our eyes fixed on Jesus — hearing, receiving, loving, and obeying Him (Heb. 12:2). He who spurns correction from the Lord does hurt to his own soul (Prov. 1:32; 5:22; 8:36).

✞ **POSITION / OPERATION OF GRACE:** (grace calls love to be a fixed practice in our life)

"Let love for your fellow believers continue and be a fixed practice with you [never let it fail]" (Hebrews 13:1).

The grace of God commands love to be a fixed Christian practice towards all believers. The world may fall in and out of love, but Christians are commanded to live in love. We are to continually cherish each other as brethren — of the same family in faith. As we abide in love, we manifest the love of God towards those around us. Contentment in Christ is tangible and meant to be experienced. Adam was in paradise, yet not content. Many of the angels in heaven were not content (Luke 10:18; 2 Peter 2:4). But Christians, though abased and humbled, are taught by grace to rest content in whatever state or circumstances they find themselves (Phil. 4:11–13).

We have an eternal, living reason to be satisfied with our present circumstances and it is found in the promise, "*... I will not in any way fail you nor give you up nor leave you without support. [I will] not, [I will] not, [I will] not in any degree leave you helpless nor forsake nor let [you] down (relax My hold on you)! [Assuredly not!]*" (Hebrews 13:5c).

Every believer has the gracious presence of God within him — in life, in death, and forever. We rest content that man can never prevail against God, and that God's grace is sufficient to make all things work together for good to them who love the Lord, and walk according to His purposes. It is the goodness and the love of God that draws all men unto repentance (Rom. 2:4; 2 Peter 3:9). Love is to be a permanent and ongoing practice of every Christian (Rom. 12:5, 16; 13:8).

As the body of Christ, we are to love and care for one another — we belong to one another (1 Thess. 3:12; 4:9). By the grace of God we say to one another, "I will never, no, never leave you; no, never forsake you." Beloved, this Christ-like attitude is sadly lacking in much of the church today.

✞ **OPERATION OF GRACE:** (grace honours marriage)

"Let marriage be held in honour (esteemed worthy, precious, of great price, and especially dear) in all things. And thus let the marriage bed be undefiled (kept undishonoured); for God will judge and punish the unchaste [all guilty of sexual vice] and adulterous" (Hebrews 13:4).

Because marriage has been instituted by God, it is to be held in honour — kept undishonoured. Marriage is a spiritual union, and hence to defile marriage is to spiritually defile one's self. The prince of the power of the air is constantly attacking the institution of marriage and family because it is divinely designed by God to be the foundation for society and all the workings found within that society (Eph. 6:1–4; Col. 3:16–21).

All things ordained of God are precious and of great price. It takes a heart, aroused by grace, to hold dear the things of God. Grace calls us to humbly walk a life honourable before God. Husbands are to love their wives as Christ loves the church — what more needs to be said about keeping marriage undefiled (Eph. 5:25)? A heart that respects honour reflects honour.

✞ **POSITION OF GRACE:** (grace calls us to praise)

"Through Him, therefore, let us constantly and at all times offer up to God a sacrifice of praise, which is the fruit of lips that thankfully acknowledge and confess and glorify His name" (Hebrews 13:15).

Grace calls us to constantly offer praise and glory to the name of God. Only from the position of grace can the fruit of our lips bring praise to Him. Whether we are actually singing songs or offering our life as a sacrifice of praise, our words are to be seasoned with grace (Acts 16:25; Eph. 5:19; Col. 3:16; 4:6).

Our lips become holy instruments as they warn, encourage, call to repentance, and proclaim the very purposes and plans of God. As we offer a sacrifice of praise to God, our lips are thankfully acknowledging, confessing, and glorifying His name. When we speak the living words of God to one another either in instruction, encouragement, or correction, we glorify His name (Rom. 14:19; 1 Cor. 5:8; 13:6; 2 Cor. 4:2; 13:8; Gal. 2:14; Eph. 4:15).

✞ **OPERATION OF GRACE:** (leadership gives and receives grace as a spiritual operation; it guides the rule of the Spirit over the body of Christ)

"Obey your spiritual leaders and submit to them [continually recognizing their authority over you], for they are constantly keeping watch over your souls and guarding your spiritual welfare, as men who will have to render an account [of their trust]. [Do your part to] let them do this with gladness and not with sighing and groaning, for this would not be profitable to you [either]" (Hebrews 13:17).

Leadership is to exemplify authority that flows from the Spirit of God. It is not something, which we possess, but rather it possesses us that we might accomplish an act of God. We are called to submit to the Spirit's leadership found resident within the church (Gal. 1:4–5, 11–14).

True spiritual leadership is a work of the Holy Spirit guiding His rule of authority over and within the body of Christ, that it might build itself up in love (Eph. 4:11–13). Christ's authority is only effective when His people recognize the guide and rule of the Holy Spirit.

One who leads but demands submission and compliance is one who believes that he is above or has authority over God's people. He is one who likes to put himself first (3 John 1:9). This type of leadership likes to rule and have authority over others; their guide is the spirit of the world, not the Holy Spirit.

Saints are never called to follow man; they are called to follow the Holy Spirit (Acts 20:30–31). All saints (leaders included) have the responsibility of watching over and guarding the spiritual welfare of each other. Leaders are to lead by example, with *all* saints following the Spirit (Acts 20:27–28), and give an account to God (1 Cor. 5:10). We are never called to be accountable to a man or an organization — accountability is always to God.

Factions (denominations) in the church are the fruit of not recognizing godly authority and godly submission, resulting in an attitude of division. *"For who separates you from the others [as a faction leader]? [Who makes you superior and sets you apart from another, giving you the preeminence?....]"* (1 Corinthians 4:7a).

True and effective leadership equips and provides others to be the best they can be in Christ. When others are doing what God has called them to, it will bring joy and will be profitable to all. True leadership promotes experience through Christ (1 Peter 5:1–4). True leadership does not divide the body of Christ.

✝ **POSITION OF GRACE:** (the Prince of Peace has sealed and ratified an everlasting covenant)

"Now may the God of peace [Who is the Author and the Giver of peace], Who brought again from among the dead our Lord Jesus, that great Shepherd of the sheep, by the blood [that sealed, ratified] the everlasting agreement (covenant, testament)," (Hebrews 13:20).

The God of peace has positioned us in perpetual peace — the tranquil state of a soul assured of its salvation through Christ Jesus. Because of our position, we need not fear any harm coming our way; we can contentedly rest in any earthly circumstance that comes our way (Phil. 4:12–13). God is the Author and the Giver of peace; hence He is the Source of peace. It is through Christ Jesus — the Prince of Peace and the Great Shepherd of the sheep — that everlasting peace has become not only our future inheritance but also operates in our life here and now (Is. 9:6; John 14:27; 16:33; Acts 10:36).

The blood of Peace has brought us into covenant with God. The blood shed by animal sacrifices was only a temporary covering for sin (Heb. 9:12–14). The blood shed by His sacrifice has eternally sealed, sanctioned, and positioned us as the righteous of God in Christ (2 Cor. 5:21). God's peace carries with it the fragrance of everlasting reconciliation (Eph. 2:16; Col. 1:20). Worldly peace is temporary and begets death.

✝ **OPERATION OF GRACE:** (grace strengthens and equips us to carry out His will)

"Strengthen (complete, perfect) and make you what you ought to be and equip you with everything good that you may carry out His will; [while He Himself] works in you and accomplishes that which is pleasing in His sight, through Jesus Christ (the Messiah); to Whom be the glory forever and ever (to the ages of the ages). Amen (so be it)" (Hebrews 13:21).

The God of peace strengthens and perfects us as He works in our life. He makes us what we ought to be and equips us with everything good to carry out His will, bringing to fruition glory-revealing works pleasing to God. Grace makes us what we ought to be, putting in order, arranging, and adjusting our life, until we become a reflection of the grace and character of God (Matt. 5:48; 2 Cor. 3:18).

The body of Grace (the church) is God's instrument used to strengthen, complete, and perfect itself. Christ's body is designed to equip and build itself up through the anointing that resides within each member (Eph. 4:16). The gift we received is the Holy Spirit, and it is up to Him to decide how He will manifest Himself through us. When you have the Holy Spirit living within you, no greater gifting is required (Acts 2:38; 8:20; 10:45; 11:17).

The body of Christ is divinely equipped to carry out His will. It is within the framework of fellowship where equipping and maturing is carried out. As the Spirit of God moves within the body of Christ, He is able to accomplish His work through us, and thus bring glory to Him. It is His anointing within us that teaches us, not someone else's anointing. For this reason we ought to pay close attention to Him (John 10:3–5, 27; 16:13; 1 John 2:27).

✝ **OPERATION OF GRACE:** (grace as a blessing)

"Grace (God's favour and spiritual blessing) be with you all. Amen (so be it)" (Hebrews 13:25).

One of the most authoritative and loving things we can ever say to one another is, "May the grace of God be with you." It reminds us that grace is always with us. It surrounds us, and it keeps us, permeating, impregnating, and inspiring the life of every Christian soul to be filled with Christ. Amen.

James

✞ **POSITION / OPERATION OF GRACE:** (grace makes trials joyous)

"Consider it wholly joyful, my brethren, whenever you are enveloped in or encounter trials of any sort or fall into various temptations" (James 1:2).

The grace of God has called us to suffer under various circumstances — wrongful criticism from brethren who mean well, confiscation of goods, imprisonment of body, banishment, scourging, persecution, and even death. These come to us not by chance, or altogether unexpectedly, but through the wickedness of the fallen world and the malice of mankind. There is no glory when we bring trials upon ourselves through our own faults and wrong doings (1 Peter 2:20; 3:17), but even these afflictions and trials can bring us into the presence and working of grace — they always work towards our good.

Many times God allows trials to come upon us that cannot be understood. At times like this we must convert our, "Why?" into a, "How do I get through this, Lord?" Trials are times of patient, perseverant trust in Him (Job 1:6–12; 2:1–6). Trials do not bring joy in themselves, but rather our joy is the fruit of the Spirit of grace working within us in the midst of these afflictions. Tribulations produce the eternal, peaceable fruit of righteousness, attended with the presence of the Spirit of grace and glory. A spirit that graciously rejoices in afflictions is a spirit that manifests the Gospel to the world. The choice is ours to rejoice, or to become bitter in affliction, which is not a godly testimony to the world. The grace of God enables us to endure the trial of the cross for the joy set before us (Heb. 12:2).

The peace that passes our understanding covers us when we rest in His grace (Phil. 4:7). Even in the middle of seemingly impossible loss, grace sustains and holds us in the company and communion of God. Such peace the world can neither know nor comprehend. Joy conceived in eternity cannot be experienced by a temporal attitude. The carnal man simply cannot receive the things of God (1 Cor. 2:12–14).

✞ **OPERATION OF GRACE:** (grace works through patience)

"Be assured and understand that the trial and proving of your faith bring out endurance and steadfastness and patience.

But let endurance and steadfastness and patience have full play and do a thorough work, so that you may be [people] perfectly and fully developed [with no defects], lacking in nothing" (James 1:3–4).

The grace of God produces perseverance and patience in our life. We discover the character of God at work during our times of trials and need. Like a little butterfly pressing its way out of its cocoon, we require persistence and patience in letting the character of God work His way into our new life in Christ. We need to submit to His way if we desire to develop mature fruit. Training by trials is necessary if we want to be established in Christ. Wisdom is learned by actual and costly experience; it purchases the truth that we need to live a mature Christian life (Prov. 5:1; 23:23). It is necessary to have our spiritual senses exercised in order for growth and maturity to come to ripe fruition (Heb. 5:14).

Trials are crossroads to maturity. Our choice is what makes our life either bitter or better. Under the gracious hand of God, trials are never designed to destroy us; they are purposed to perfect us and bring us into a closer companionship with Him. Intimacy with God changes our perspective of trials *automatically*; relationship with God discloses dross in our life.

Grace is the power of God's favour working in and through us; it *never* turns us into its victim. Neither should we abuse grace to victimize others (Rom. 6:1–2; Gal 2:14; Phil. 1:15–17). To love the Lord God with all our heart and to love our neighbour as ourselves is the purpose of a life driven by the grace of God. Trials either make us *bitter* or *better*; the choice is ours, and is easier to make when we realize that nothing can separate us from the love of God in Christ Jesus (Rom. 8:35–39).

Trials prove our faith even as fire proves a metal's worth, whether it be of silver and gold, or wood, hay, and stubble (1 Cor. 3:10–15).

✟ **OPERATION OF GRACE:** (grace works with wisdom to the unwavering)

"If any of you is deficient in wisdom, let him ask of the giving God [Who gives] to everyone liberally and ungrudgingly, without reproaching or fault-finding, and it will be given him.

Only it must be in faith that he asks with no wavering (no hesitating, no doubting). For the one who wavers (hesitates, doubts) is like the billowing surge out at sea that is blown hither and thither and tossed by the wind" (James 1:5–6).

The grace of God does not reproach or find fault with us and as we walk in grace, we should approach others with this similar attitude. Wisdom lies in wait for the asking; God desires to give it, not withhold it. When God is working on our character in the midst of various trials, we need to call out for wisdom. Grace does not prevent us from hanging on the cross; it is given to us liberally so that we may not just endure, but learn to love our precious cross (Gal. 6:14; Heb. 12:2; 1 Peter 2:21–25).

Wisdom is not given to us to make us great. It is given to us to reveal and manifest His great wisdom through us (Rom. 16:27; 1 Tim 1:17; Jude 1:25). There is no such thing as 'great men of God'; there are only 'men who know a great God'. His confidential communion is ever waiting to encourage us and to keep us within the bounds of His purpose in our thoughts and actions.

Oh how graciously God says, "If any of you lack wisdom." Wisdom is the principal thing. We are called to *get* it, and along with wisdom we need understanding. Wisdom is most often acquired by the trials of life, and when it is attained in such a way it is not easily slighted or laid aside. Oh how much better it is to get wisdom than gold, and to get understanding rather than silver! The acquiring of wisdom has only one prerequisite; it must be desired by its recipient. The fool has no heart for it because his very attitude blinds and deafens him to it (Prov. 1:7; 4:7; 8:11).

Grace invites us to get wisdom, to get understanding, and not to forget it. Wisdom obtained through trials cause us to count it all joy during our acquisition of it. Life has been divinely designed to require wisdom, so to reject God's wisdom is to be at variance not only with God, but also with one's self. The training ground of grace teaches us to learn by divinely inspired discernment — to spiritually separate the things of the world from the things of God, by the knowledge of His Word, and the leading of His Spirit. We need to appraise what is of real value according to the divine principles found in His Word, and to prefer God's ways over our own (Prov. 1:1–5; Phil. 1:8–11).

We are not called to be like a wave of the sea, tossed by every spirit and attitude that comes our way — separated from divine direction and self-set in a hostile world. To oppose God (to strive and contend with His ways) is not the path of true joy. We are to be firmly and faithfully attached to the Rock; we are not to be habitually driven by every fancy of man. Grace calls us to be unmoved and unwavering as life's storms blow upon us (Luke 6:46–49). Life's waves of trial are designed by God to make us more deeply rooted in Him, not to make our faith flounder and waver.

Faith is the assurance of things hoped for, the conviction and evidence of things not yet seen. Christians are never left hopeless and forsaken; we are called to patiently wait for things, which are not yet seen. We are known and loved by the God of all creation, the God who holds the keys of hell and death (Heb. 11:1, 13, 32–40).

Beloved, our confidence in the Lord is to be exercised whether things are going well or proceeding contrary to our desires. When we feel indecisive as to whether Jesus is Lord, or feel fickle in our faith, this is the time to cry out to God from a sincere heart for the wisdom that we need, "Lord, I believe, help my unbelief!" Beloved, faith is the evidence — the reality — of things not seen (2 Kings 6:14–23; Mk. 9:20–27).

✞ **OPERATION OF GRACE:** (grace calls us to single-mindedness)

"For truly, let not such a person imagine that he will receive anything [he asks for] from the Lord,

[For being as he is] a man of two minds (hesitating, dubious, irresolute), [he is] unstable and unreliable and uncertain about everything [he thinks, feels, decides]" (James 1:7–8).

The grace of God patiently awaits to be received (Matt. 10:14; 11:14). A soul led by grace does not waver, but rather, it absorbs the beatings of the storms of life as it goes from strength to strength (2 Cor. 1:8–10; 12:9). A renewed soul finds its significance and its source of strength in the work of Christ. When our interest is divided between the world and God, our thoughts and actions become wavering and uncertain. We need grace to pursue the purposes of God. It is only from our position of grace that we find certain and reliable focus. A soul wavering in faith has no good soil on which to plant the Word of God (Matt. 13:18–23).

Seeds sown by the wayside do not even taste faith. When the evil one steals away anything that could be received, it is never allowed to come to life. Seeds sown on the rocky soil are received, but to a wavering heart, which only sees temporary value. There may be joy upon its reception, but time tests faithfulness. As affliction comes, the seed having no significant root, causes the person to fall away from the Word of life — the very thing they ought to trust and obey. As for the seed that is sown among the thorns, it is received and takes root, but it grows only for a short time. Growth is stunted, and fruitfulness is choked out by the cares and the deceitfulness of the riches rooted in the world. It is alive, albeit fruitless (Jer. 5:3; John 14:7; Rev. 3:1).

Since it requires faith to receive anything from God, we need to let God prepare the soil of our heart and repent of any interference that may hinder His work. It is by faith that we receive the Lord Jesus Christ as Saviour, and it is by faith that we continue to receive the righteous, gracious gifts of life from God. A hand held out in faith places its trust in the Giver, and waits for His desires. When we let go of our self, God can get a better grip on us. Our faith must rest in the power of God, not in the wisdom of man. Our worth or significance must be found in God, and our life can be successful only when ruled by His grace (Heb. 10:23; 11:6; Jas. 2:26).

A man of divided soul is a man of divided mind, divided will, and divided emotions, each one pulling and dragging in opposing directions. The natural, non-spiritual man is incapable of recognizing and becoming acquainted with the gifts and revelations of the Spirit of God (1 Cor. 2:14). There is no rest to be found in a heart that is not spiritually upright in its request — it asks for one thing and yet desires another (Jas. 4:1–3). The carnal man may find himself asking God for help, but in truth he just wants the circumstances to change; he is not interested in having his own heart changed. Repentance is a foreign concept to the carnal man destitute of truth (Mk. 14:65). Carnality hates repentance.

✞ **POSITION / OPERATION OF GRACE:** (grace turns temptation into a blessing; grace does not tempt with evil)

"Blessed (happy, to be envied) is the man who is patient under trial and stands up under temptation, for when he has stood the test and been approved, he will receive [the victor's] crown of life which God has promised to those who love Him.

Let no one say when he is tempted, I am tempted from God; for God is incapable of being tempted by [what is] evil and He Himself tempts no one" (James 1:12–13).

Patient endurance is a sure, protective shield, which enables us to be overcomers in our trials. Our position in Christ is both defensive and offensive. Often patience is an offensive action that accomplishes a great deal by simply *doing nothing*. Patience is also a defensive strategy, which can absorb the attacking blows of trials and the devil's darts designed to deliver death to its victims. We overcome evil with good; we need to learn to overcome impatience with patience. Truth and love are our rest (Lk. 8:15; Rom. 5:3; Heb. 6:12).

Temptation cannot come from God. Our Lord is not in the business of trying to make us fall. Neither can the Spirit of God be tempted, hence, when we walk in the Spirit, we walk not in temptation but rather we are delivered from it. The Spirit of God enables us to remain standing even in the presence of extreme pressure; it holds us up in our position of approval by God. It leads us into life abundantly as the chisel of trial transforms us into the ideal servant of the Lord (Neh. 9:21; Ps. 55:22).

✞ **OPERATION OF GRACE:** (grace warns us not to be tempted into sinning)

"But every person is tempted when he is drawn away enticed and baited by his own evil desire (lust, passions).

Then the evil desire, when it has conceived, gives birth to sin, and sin, when it is fully matured, brings forth death.

Do not be misled, my beloved brethren" (James 1:14–16).

The grace of God never entices us to commit sin. Temptation will raise its head when evil desires within us conceive and give birth to actions, which satisfy those desires. Bait is used to capture prey; bait appears appealing to the unregenerate mind. The devil baits us and draws us into error, but God loves us unto righteousness. The purpose of temptation is to cause us to go astray, and be seduced to wander out of the way of truth. Desires fulfilled outside of the bounds of God's will are desires, which mature unto death (Prov. 7:1–27). Desires fulfilled within the bounds of God's will, bring maturity into our life.

Evil desires within our soul can seize and take us captive to ungodliness. Grace warns us not to fall into the snare of error which reveals itself through wrong actions and attitudes. We are to have the mind of Christ — a mind that does not lead into error, deceit, or fraud. The anointing within us will always lead us into the abundant life found in all truth; there is no falsehood in this anointing (John 10:10). The Spirit of grace will never mislead us in our walk in Christ.

Temptation to sin is ever present. When our evil desires fall into temptation, this will lead to death, but through the renewing of our soul these evil desires will be dealt with. Grace operating in our life can curb the conception of sin, and when we fall, our Advocate of grace calls us to repentance and renews our soul in Christ. It takes God's grace to place us in righteousness, and it takes God's grace to keep us in righteousness (Ps. 143:8; Lk. 18:10–14).

✞ **POSITION OF GRACE:** (grace places us on the receiving end of God's goodness)

"Every good gift and every perfect (free, large, full) gift is from above; it comes down from the Father of all [that gives] light, in [the shining of] Whom there can be no variation [rising or setting] or shadow cast by His turning [as in an eclipse].

And it was of His own [free] will that He gave us birth [as sons] by [His] Word of Truth, so that we should be a kind of first fruits of His creatures [a sample of what He created to be consecrated to Himself]" (James 1:17–18).

The grace of God imparts the goodness of His life to us. Everything good and perfect comes only by the grace of God. It is the holy Thing, which calls us to be examples of His will and character — His goodness. Being representatives of God's goodness does not bring just ordinary, natural goodness to those around us; it brings the best and perfect, eternal goodness (Lk. 1:35, 46–55). Godly qualities are from God alone, and cannot be duplicated by man, no matter how good he tries to be.

Only humble vessels are allowed to carry such precious cargo. Goodness and perfection are only sourced from above. The light of grace shining upon an unregenerate heart has the ability to manifest the glory of God and bring perfection to a sin sick world. It is God's will to bring goodness and perfection to us, and such qualities are only accessible by being birthed by His Spirit and the Word of Truth (2 Cor. 4:7).

His gifts and goodness are only given to us to magnify Christ; they are never given to magnify ourselves. They are sourced in Jesus hanging on the cross — God Himself demonstrating His perfect love. We are called to be samples of what He created and consecrated to Himself.

✝ **OPERATION OF GRACE:** (grace calls us to cleanness, and to receive the Word)

"So get rid of all uncleanness and the rampant outgrowth of wickedness and in a humble (gentle, modest) spirit receive and welcome the Word which implanted and rooted [in your hearts] contains the power to save your souls" (James 1:21).

The grace of God calls us to an on-going salvation and deliverance from the power of wickedness in our life. Jesus is constantly working on our wholeness. God would have our attitude to be modest gentleness of spirit, which enables us to receive from Him. His word is able to heal, preserve, and make our souls whole and complete (Mk. 10:52; Lk. 8:48, 50).

It is only to a receptive, welcoming heart that the revelations of God are inborn — revealed by the Holy Spirit. Such welcomed Word, planted and rooted in a heart of good soil, will bring forth the desired, divine fruit. The Word invariably brings wholeness and healing to any receptive soul. The word of God, born of the Spirit of God, bears with it the authority of God, and when we live in the Word we walk in God's authority (John 9:1–41).

✝ **POSITION / OPERATION OF GRACE:** (grace commands action that lines up with the Word)

"But be doers of the Word [obey the message], and not merely listeners to it, betraying yourselves [into deception by reasoning contrary to the Truth].

For if anyone only listens to the Word without obeying it and being a doer of it, he is like a man who looks carefully at his [own] natural face in a mirror;" (James 1:22–23).

The grace of God calls us to be a doer of the Word, not 'a person of reason'. Reasoning can be an enemy of our faith, and can be the cause of our inaction to His word. We need to be careful of reasoning prompted by the evil one, which is designed to deceive and lead us in a path contrary to the Truth (Gen. 3:1–6).

We should submit to God when He reasons with us, and to come closer to Him and obey His word (Is. 1:18). God is manifested through action, and from our position of grace we are enabled to live out the Word by faith, not reasoning. Reasoning can spoil us (Col. 2:8).

To be a doer of the word is to manifest God. To try to make God 'reasonable' is to deceive oneself, and end up in a position, which is contrary to the will of God. Any reasoning with God will result in us conforming into His character, not to trying to change God into our character (Is. 1:18).

God's Word is creative and powerful and hence when graciously received by any heart, it will be creative and powerful, both in word and deed. Any reasoning contrary to the Truth is antichrist and cannot display Christ's character or life — the way of God.

We are always responsible for our own actions and reactions to our affairs encountered in this life. Grace does not fix blame on anyone other than our self when things go wrong in our life. The Christ-like response to any and all situations should be, "Lord, do not hold this sin against them." This is a Christ-like example of being a doer of the Word. We are called to do the same. Beloved, do not be deceived by reasoning contrary to the Truth (Prov. 26:16).

✝ **POSITION / OPERATION OF GRACE:** (grace calls us to persevere in the perfect law of liberty)

"For he thoughtfully observes himself, and then goes off and promptly forgets what he was like.

But he who looks carefully into the faultless law, the [law] of liberty, and is faithful to it and perseveres in looking into it, being not a heedless listener who forgets but an active doer [who obeys], he shall be blessed in his doing (his life of obedience)" (James 1:24–25).

The grace of God calls us to perceive and understand who we are in Christ Jesus. We are to consider attentively, our position in Christ. As we persevere in looking into the perfect law of liberty of the Gospel of Jesus Christ, we allow the grace of God to actively impart the Word into our life. To just thoughtfully observe is not enough. Thoughtful observance without action is both negligent and uncaring. Such a complacent position results in fruitlessness; it makes us unconscious to the things of the kingdom of God (John 9:40–41).

Grace draws us to fix our eyes on the Word as we walk in the steps of Jesus. It is only there that we remain in Life and can overcome the ways of the law of sin and death — the ways of world (1 Thess. 2:1–9). Just as faith without works is dead, thoughtfulness without works is also dead. The gracious blessing of God can only be realized in gracious obedience to God.

It is not good sermons that make us mature in Christ. Maturity develops only when we exercise our spiritual senses to discern the way of God before us, and do what the Word calls us to do (Heb. 5:11–14). The sacrifice of listening to the Word from the pew never replaces the active doing of the Word in our life. Thousands of hours of pew sitting does not a mature Christian make (1 Tim. 4:12). Maturity only comes through a life of obedient action.

✞ **POSITION OF GRACE:** (grace makes the poor, rich)

"Listen, my beloved brethren: Has not God chosen those who are poor in the eyes of the world to be rich in faith and in their position as believers and to inherit the kingdom which He has promised to those who love Him" (James 2:5)?

The grace of God takes those whom the world looks down upon, and places them in a position of abundance and honour. It is the lowly and afflicted who are most open to the calling of God. Whoever forgives much, loves much (Lk. 7:47). It is not poverty that makes one righteous; it is a heart that has been transformed by the Gospel of grace. Righteousness makes one fix his eyes on eternal things, not on the temporary things of the earth. Correlating earthly riches and eternal wealth is a deception, which shows ignorance of what God's righteousness truly is (Prov. 3:14; 8:10, 19; 17:16; 22:1). Grace calls us to attend to and consider the richness of our calling and walk in Christ Jesus.

Worldly riches have no attraction to a heart seeking God. How can one possibly put a monetary value on an eternal character? Even if one had all the riches of the world, he could not purchase even the smallest bit of God's wisdom. He could not even ransom a single soul with it, or pay for a single sin (Matt. 16:24–26). To equate monetary value with righteousness is to adulterate the grace of God (Prov. 19:1; 23:23; Mk. 8:36; Acts 4:32). When we peddle and present the grace of God as a means of making money, it is a direct violation of the death and resurrection of our Lord Jesus Christ (2 Cor. 12:17–18; 1 Tim. 6:5–11). We need to be careful not to set our hearts on the security of worldly wealth. The love of money is a root of all evil (Prov. 16:16; 23:23).

✞ **OPERATION OF GRACE:** (grace triumphs over judgement)

"So speak and so act as [people should] who are to be judged under the law of liberty [the moral instruction given by Christ, especially about love].

For to him who has shown no mercy the judgment [will be] merciless, but mercy [full of glad confidence] exults victoriously over judgment" (James 2:12–13).

The grace of God speaks of His mercy. Oh that we would see the vital importance of being under God's mercy. Our position in Christ is founded on mercy, and it is imperative that we respond accordingly. Just as good overcomes evil, and love overcomes hatred, mercy exults victoriously over judgment (Mk. 10:46–52). We have been freed from the judgment of God by His divine mercy, and hence we are called to be vessels of divine mercy to those around us. To deny the giving of mercy makes us a hypocrite of the highest degree, and worthy only of the judgment of God. Do not be misled my brethren, God will not be mocked (Prov. 24:17–18; Matt. 18:23–35).

Grace calls us to act as people who are to be judged under the law of liberty. Mercy liberates, both when it is exercised, and when it is received. The flow of mercy is stopped when we allow our flesh to enter into judgment. As the body of

Christ, we are destined by grace to show works of mercy. True liberty is realized only when we live as God says we should, not as our flesh demands (Matt. 5:7).

Our actions reveal our understanding of God's mercy. Our life emulates either our self-righteousness or the genuine righteousness of God (Lk. 18:9–14). Oh Lord, let my life be aglow by showing how much I owe! Just as he who has been forgiven much, loves much; he who knows much mercy, reflects the mercy he knows.

✞ **OPERATION OF GRACE:** (grace manifests faith by good works)

"So also faith, if it does not have works (deeds and actions of obedience to back it up), by itself is destitute of power (inoperative, dead).

But someone will say [to you then], You [say you] have faith, and I have [good] works. Now you show me your [alleged] faith apart from any [good] works [if you can], and I by [good] works [of obedience] will show you my faith" (James 2:17–18).

The body of Christ is not a dead, lifeless, inoperative body. It is called to operate in the word of God by the Spirit. The body of Christ is living and active and if led by the Spirit, it is able to discern and judge the thoughts and purposes of the heart of man. It is called to dwell in the purposes of God. The Spirit of God longs to commune and fellowship with His people (Rom. 1:11–12; Phil. 1:8; 1 John 1:3). It is essential to have a personal relationship with our heavenly Father, but if it is not walked out within the body of Christ, it is unfruitful. Faith in God demands a manifestation of such fellowship; it is a distinguishing mark of Christians.

If we say we love God, and yet hate our brother, we deceive ourselves; it is dead faith. Grace enables us to employ the works of God — to walk in the ways of God. Our good works should flow from a life of faith and trust in the Living God. Faith reveals God, nothing more, nothing less. As Christians, we are called to love everyone, but not necessarily the things that people say or do.

Jesus died on the cross for everyone, not just *most* of mankind. To hate anyone is to hate someone God loves. The cross of Christ and the grace of God do not allow such an attitude (Col. 3:13). It takes our re-birth in Christ to change our attitudes and actions into ways and purposes that are pure and right, enabling us to live as examples of people of faith.

✞ **OPERATION OF GRACE:** (works that spring from grace identify us as God's friends)

"You see that [his] faith was cooperating with his works, and [his] faith was completed and reached its supreme expression [when he implemented it] by [good] works.

And [so] the Scripture was fulfilled that says, Abraham believed in (adhered to, trusted in, and relied on) God, and this was accounted to him as righteousness (as conformity to God's will in thought and deed), and he was called God's friend" (James 2:22–23).

A work that is birthed from belief and trust in God is an expression of faith. Works and faith cooperate with each other. One without the other is dead. When our thoughts and deeds conform to God's will, we are known as friends of God.

The righteousness of God operating in our soul produces works that reflect God's image. Faith-inspired works fulfil Scripture and manifest the living Word. Scripture will be fulfilled — that is its destiny. Just as Jesus was destined to fulfil the Law of God for us, we now, as new creations, are the fulfilment of the word of God in our life. It is by grace that we are enabled to be examples of the divine purpose to be fulfilled both now and forever more.

✞ **POSITION / OPERATION OF GRACE:** (grace commands action)

"You see that a man is justified (pronounced righteous before God) through what he does and not alone through faith [through works of obedience as well as by what he believes]" (James 2:24).

Works of God fulfil Scripture and hence are inseparable from faith. Our works, executed by our faith is what perfects us and fulfils Scripture. Our position of grace will cause an operation of God's grace in our life, producing works of obedience that come from faith and build more faith within us (Rom. 1:17). We can never do anything to merit God's grace and we can never work our way into faith. Works of God manifest the character of God; works of man manifest the character of man.

What a man truly believes can be evidenced by what he does. We show our faith by our works. It is not our work that furnishes our faith; it is our work that reveals our faith. A work of faith is founded on humility; a work of the flesh is founded in pride. Anyone can talk the talk of righteousness, but only true faith walks the walk of righteousness. That is why Jesus said, *"But that you may know that the Son of Man has the (power of) authority and right on earth to forgive sins, He said to the paralyzed man, I say to you, arise, pick up your litter (stretcher), and go to your own house"* (Luke 5:24)! Righteousness is proven by what we do, not by what we say. Hypocrisy is to say one thing, yet do another (Matt. 6:2, 5, 16; 22:18; 23:13–35).

✝ **OPERATION OF GRACE:** (grace works through humility)

"Who is there among you who is wise and intelligent? Then let him by his noble living show forth his [good] works with the [unobtrusive] humility [which is the proper attribute] of true wisdom" (James 3:13).

The wisdom of God is simple, modest, and unpretentious; it is designed and destined to be lived out, not hidden (Matt. 5:14–16). Wisdom is revealed to a heart desiring it; it is not revealed to an unregenerate, hard heart (Prov. 1:24–33; 8:9; Matt. 13:10–14).

God's wisdom forms the *best* plans and uses the *best* means to execute them. *Best* can only be defined and sourced in God; it can only be accomplished by our reliance upon Him. It comes from having knowledge of the character of the Lord, which is learned by costly and actual experience. God has *our* best interest in mind; the world has *its* best interest in mind (Lk. 11:43; 12:22).

Wisdom is only accessible by the grace of God, when we walk in humility; it furnishes evidence and spiritual proof of our relationship with Him. Our manner of life, our conduct, and our behaviour are designed to expose to the eyes of those around us, the grace and wisdom of God. Divinely motivated deeds manifest the character of God as they display the truth of Christ through His body in all gentleness, meekness, and humility (2 Cor. 3:5–6; 6:1–10).

✝ **OPERATION OF GRACE:** (grace warns us of discord and its root)

"What leads to strife (discord and feuds) and how do conflicts (quarrels and fightings) originate among you? Do they not arise from your sensual desires that are ever warring in your bodily members" (James 4:1)?

The grace of God enables our sensual desires to become subject to the Spirit of God. The sensual, non-spiritual man does not accept or admit into his heart the things of the Spirit of God. The sensual man wrestles against flesh and blood; the spiritual man wrestles against powers, principalities, and wickedness in high places (1 Cor. 2:14–15; Eph. 6:12). It took the blood of Christ to introduce the grace of God to a sensual heart, and it takes this same blood of grace operating in our heart, to conform our soul into the image of God's dear Son.

Revelations of the Spirit of God are meaningless nonsense to the natural, carnal man; he is incapable of either knowing them or understanding them. The carnal, sensual nature of man is ever warring against the things of the Spirit; it opposes the workings of God (John 6:63; Rom. 8:4–13).

The desires of the flesh are always antagonistic to the desires of the Holy Spirit. Strife is a work of the flesh and is a sure sign of opposition to God. God hates those who sow discord among the brethren (Prov. 6:16, 19). Conflicts originating within the body of Christ are not from God. That is why divisions and factions in the body of Christ are not of God. The Holy Spirit never operates with strife within the body of Christ (1 Cor. 3:3; Gal. 5:20; Jas. 3:14–16). Beloved, there is never strife between Jesus, the Father, and the Holy Spirit. Grace teaches us to respond to strife with, "Not my will be done Lord, but Thy will be done."

† **OPERATION OF GRACE:** (grace empowers the humble)

"But He gives us more and more grace (power of the Holy Spirit, to meet this evil tendency and all others fully). That is why He says, God sets Himself against the proud and haughty, but gives grace [continually] to the lowly (those who are humble enough to receive it)" (James 4:6).

When we are friends with the world, we are enemies of God (Jas. 4:4). God loves us with a godly jealousy, which draws our heart towards His heart, causing us to desire His will for our lives. The grace of God is given more and more to us as our need arises; you cannot out-give God's grace (John 15:19; 2 Tim. 4:10; 1 John 2:15; 4:17).

Friendship with the world positions us against the things of God and we become hostile to the Holy One. Pride always places itself above what God decrees as proper, just, and right. It likes to be conspicuous and pre-eminent, with a misrepresented estimate of its own merit. It despises and treats with contempt the things of God, and hence it is hostile, hating, and opposing life defined by God (3 John 1:9–11).

Grace acknowledges God, and can only be received by a lowly, humble spirit. It is necessary for a soul to acknowledge truth in order to receive and operate in God's grace. Humility is a character of God, and it is a necessary quality for a heart, which desires to hear from God and be busy about the Father's business (John 8:37–59; 10:24–33).

† **POSITION / OPERATION OF GRACE:** (grace warns us to come clean of spiritual adultery)

"So be subject to God. Resist the devil [stand firm against him], and he will flee from you.

Come close to God and He will come close to you. [Recognize that you are] sinners, get your soiled hands clean; [realize that you have been disloyal] wavering individuals with divided interests, and purify your hearts [of your spiritual adultery]" (James 4:7–8).

The grace of God positions us in a place where we become subjects of the Almighty. It then operates in us, enabling us to draw near to God and experience His presence. It is not enough to just resist the devil; we must also draw near to God, for it is in our drawing near to God that we are cleansed and purified (Heb. 4:16; 7:19, 25; 10:22; 11:6). It is only when we are in subjection and yielded to God's grace that we are enamoured by the Almighty drawing near to us. Recognition of our need for grace is the only way for us to realize the benefit and working of grace. To declare that you do not need God's grace is to declare Jesus a loser — that His grace is in vain (1 Cor. 15:10; 2 Cor. 6:1; Gal. 2:21).

The unregenerate heart of man — the soul or mind, the wellspring and seat of our passions, desires, purposes, and endeavours — tends naturally towards spiritual adultery (Jer. 17:9). The natural man has a will and character, which normally wavers and is uncertain and doubting. The fallen nature of man is contrary to Christ (anti-Christ) (1 John 2:15–18). Divided interests are a sign of spiritual adultery. Beloved, God calls us to keep ourselves free from anything and everything that would usurp the place of God in our hearts (Is. 57:8; 1 John 5:21).

Grace enables us to walk through the valley of the fear of man and to not be affected by its talons of destruction and its taunts of degradation. The authority of God found in His kingdom is the required tool to accomplish any work, which God sets before us. To dwell in the authority of God is our Christian calling; it is vital for us to know and recognize God's authority, and not be disloyal to it (Mk. 1:22). Grace calls us to be subject to God in His kingdom, not man's kingdom.

† **OPERATION OF GRACE:** (grace calls us to right doing)

"So any person who knows what is right to do but does not do it, to him it is sin" (James 4:17).

The grace of God operating in a soul enables it to know God's way and to respond to whatever direction the Spirit leads. Grace enables us to know what is right. When we perceive something in the Spirit, we are automatically accountable to God to respond in the appropriate manner.

Discernment without action is disobedience. To know what is right and good, and then not do it is more wicked than disobedience birthed from ignorance (Prov. 24:11–12; John 19:11). *"Rejoice not when your enemy falls, and let not your heart be glad when he stumbles or is overthrown, lest the Lord see it and it be evil in His eyes and displease Him, and He turn away His wrath from him [to expend it upon you, the worse offender]"* (Proverbs 24:17–18).

The omission of a known trust and the commission of a known transgression are both spiritual violations; they are a definition of sin (Prov. 29:24).

✟ **OPERATION OF GRACE:** (grace calls us to carry out our word)

"But above all [things], my brethren, do not swear, either by heaven or by earth or by any other oath; but let your yes be [a simple] yes, and your no be [a simple] no, so that you may not sin and fall under condemnation" (James 5:12).

The grace of God simply commands us to let our 'Yes' be 'Yes' and our 'No' be 'No'. Anything other than this is rooted in evil. Swearing is something only God can do. We are unable to know our own heart and its motives (Jer. 17:9). Better we say, "No" and act accordingly, than swear, and hear the 'cock crow in condemnation' (Lk. 22:33–34, 55–62). Such action or lack thereof, brings with it a rejection and bitterness, which can only be atoned for by the blood of the Lamb. Better to look into the eyes of the Lamb of God with humility, than with broken oaths and wanton words, which are not kept. Eternity calls us to walk in humble simplicity, not self-eloquence.

✟ **OPERATION OF GRACE:** (grace empowers us in our confession of faults to one another)

"Confess to one another therefore your faults (your slips, your false steps, your offenses, your sins) and pray [also] for one another, that you may be healed and restored [to a spiritual tone of mind and heart]. The earnest (heartfelt, continued) prayer of a righteous man makes tremendous power available [dynamic in its working]" (James 5:16).

Grace calls us to acknowledge openly our faults and sins to one another (Prov. 28:13). The godly result of this is restoration and reconciliation — a full joy and celebration in the Spirit of God. The ministry of reconciliation is the calling of every Christian to one another, as well as to the world (2 Cor. 5:18).

Confession is a separator; it scrapes the dross from the silver. To the carnal man confession is seen as shame, but to the spiritual man, it is salvation and deliverance — the wisdom of God. Confession removes the fig leaf of human wisdom and replaces it with the covering from God. Confession distances us from sin and death, and draws us near to truth and life. Any lapse or deviation from truth and uprightness needs to be acknowledged and severed from our life (Lev. 5:5; Num. 5:7; Ps 32:5; 38:18; 51:3, 14).

Confession cuts the cords of corruption that fetter our soul; it frees us to be healed and restored to a holy tone of mind and heart. Grace calls us to be vessels of mutual encouragement so that our souls may be healed. Confession, bathed in prayer beckons the power of God to work in our lives to make us whole, and keep us free from error and sin. *"For the fool speaks folly and his mind plans iniquity: practicing profane ungodliness and speaking error concerning the Lord, leaving the craving of the hungry unsatisfied and causing the drink of the thirsty to fail"* (Isaiah 32:6).

It is within the context of fellowship that God's love flows and as we submit to one another, the dynamic power of confession and deliverance is manifest to us. If we walk in Light, we have fellowship with one another, and the blood of Christ cleanses us from all error and sin. Fellowship is a distinguishing mark of Christians; it is the dynamic working of God through our love and prayer one for another. Prayer heals and restores one another to a true spiritual tone. It is divine in its source and divine in its operation as it brings about the purposes of God in our life (1 John 1:5–7).

✞ **OPERATION OF GRACE:** (grace calls for repentance from sin)

"[My] brethren, if anyone among you strays from the Truth and falls into error and another [person] brings him back [to God].

Let the [latter] one be sure that whoever turns a sinner from his evil course will save [that one's] soul from death and will cover a multitude of sins [procure the pardon of the many sins committed by the convert]" (James 5:19–20).

Here the grace of God talks to brethren as sinners (1 John 1:8–10). If any Christian who strays from the Truth and falls into error and then is brought back to God, be certain that he who turns from his evil course will be saved from death in that area of his life. He will receive pardon for the many sins committed by him (2 Cor. 2:7–8). Beloved, this is the Gospel, the good news!

The truth of our faith with respect to God and the bringing forth of His purposes through Christ is the very foundation of the Christian life. Such Truth stands in opposition to the superstitions and philosophies of the Gentiles, the inventions of the Jews, and the corrupt opinions and precepts of false prophets and teachers, even found among Christians.

Grace trains us to reject all ungodliness and worldly passionate desires; it calls us to live self-controlled, upright, spiritually whole lives in this present evil time. Grace enables us to love one another — to urge, advise, encourage, warn, and rebuke with full authority — full humility and full lowliness, full of grace and mercy. *"For the law was given by Moses, but grace and truth came by Jesus Christ"* (John 1:17 KJV).

1 Peter

✝ **<u>POSITION OF GRACE</u>:** (grace is given to us in increasing abundance)

"Who were chosen and foreknown by God the Father and consecrated (sanctified, made holy) by the Spirit to be obedient to Jesus Christ (the Messiah) and to be sprinkled with [His] blood: May grace (spiritual blessing) and peace be given you in increasing abundance [that spiritual peace to be realized in and through Christ, freedom from fears, agitating passions, and moral conflicts]" (1 Peter 1:2).

The grace of God has called us to be yielding and submissive unto the Lord Jesus Christ (the Messiah). Because of our position of being *in* Christ, we are called to live our lives in obedience *to* Christ where we reap the fruit of security, safety, and prosperity. Such true fruit manifested in our life can only be obtained by being *in* Christ (Ps. 1:1–3; Is. 55:11; 3 John 1:2).

To be a chosen vessel of the Lord is no small calling, yet it does not display any pre-eminence or loftiness above others. We should present ourselves in the lowly position of being a servant-of-all. It is our carnal nature, which raises its head in judgement of a person's position and calling. It looks at the greatness of the vessel, rather than humbly accepting the equality of divine goodness, which all of God's vessels possess (2 Cor. 10:12).

A vessel of the Lord is ever increasing in grace and peace, and this process is only consummated in Christ (Prov. 4:18; Phil. 2:12–15; 2 Peter 1:19). It behoves the body of Christ to be vessels of grace and peace towards one another. Christians are called to set captives free from fear. We are to free souls from the agitating passions of the flesh; we are to break spiritual fetters leaving people unbound by the moral conflicts burning within the carnal nature (Lk. 4:16–21).

When we recognize that Christ is on the scene, He always declares to us, "Peace, be not afraid!" When Christ's love is perfected in us, we become fear-busters. It is important that we are not under the control of fear ourselves if we are ministering to someone else under the power of fear (Matt. 14:26–29). Note that Scripture does not say that the perfect power of God casts out all fear; it says that His perfect love casts out all fear. This gives us a clue as to how to approach people caught in the bondage of fear. God's power operates through His love (2 Tim. 1:7; 1 John 4:18).

✝ **<u>POSITION OF GRACE</u>:** (we have been born again by grace, to an ever-living hope)

"Praised (honoured, blessed) be the God and Father of our Lord Jesus Christ (the Messiah)! By His boundless mercy we have been born again to an ever-living hope through the resurrection of Jesus Christ from the dead" (1 Peter 1:3).

Oh, the measureless mercy and grace of God that has been bestowed upon us that we are counted as children of God. We have been born from above, become new creations in Christ (1 John 2:29; 3:1–3). We are no longer children of the world and its ways, but rather, children of God — the Way, the Truth, and the Life. We have been given an ever-living hope, and a joyful, confident expectation of eternal life with the Author of our hope, for He is now our eternal foundation and our brother (Heb. 2:11).

In Christ the power of His resurrection becomes our portion, and His grace calls us to manifest truth in a spirit of humility (Phil. 3:10–12; 1 Peter 5:5). Hatred, greed, strife, and other works of the flesh are not the works of the Spirit of grace. Beloved, as grace flows through us, those around us experience the mercy of the Almighty, not the wantonness of the world.

✝ **<u>POSITION OF GRACE</u>:** (grace has given us an imperishable, heavenly inheritance)

"[Born anew] into an inheritance which is beyond the reach of change and decay [imperishable], unsullied and unfading, reserved in heaven for you," (1 Peter 1:4).

Grace has given us an eternal possession that is forever beyond the reach of change and decay. The grace of God cannot be corrupted, defiled, or soiled. It frees us from the power of all that deforms, debases, and impairs. Grace takes our scars of corruption stamped upon us by the world and our fallen nature, and transforms us into His divine character, incorruptible, with our destiny anchored in God (1 Cor. 9:25; 1 Peter 1:23).

To take our new godly nature in Christ, and then to abuse it by living in our old carnal ways, is to do violence to the grace of God. He did not design our new born-again nature in His image to cater to the desires of our flesh. The grace of God embedded within our renewed nature enables us to do works, which are imperishable, unblemished, and do not pass away or change with time — works done in love have eternal value (1 Cor. 15:57–58). Beloved, our inheritance in God has no earthly value; it is much more valuable than even the whole world (Matt. 16:26).

✞ **POSITION OF GRACE:** (grace garrisons and secures our soul)

"Who are being guarded (garrisoned) by God's power through [your] faith [till you fully inherit that final] salvation that is ready to be revealed [for you] in the last time" (1 Peter 1:5).

The grace of God guards us until the second coming of Christ. With God watching over us, whom shall we fear? The grace of God is forever there to guard and protect us from any worldly or demonic, hostile attack on our soul. It guarantees us, through our faith, to receive our final salvation at our Lord's second coming.

Beloved, Stephen was not overcome by evil (Acts 7:57–60). He did not make a deal with the devil, call the curses of God down on those persecuting him, or pray to change his circumstances. He desired and fulfilled the Father's will by fixing his eyes on Jesus. Any negative actions on Stephen's part would have been evidence of his soul having been overcome by evil.

The shield of faith guards us from the attacks of the spirit of the world. It enables us to keep the ways of God, and not allow the ways of the world to plant seeds of doubt and fear in the good soil of our soul (Ps. 26:4–5; Matt. 21:21).

✞ **OPERATION OF GRACE:** (grace gives us a gladness now that is rooted in the future)

"[You should] be exceedingly glad on this account, though now for a little while you may be distressed by trials and suffer temptations" (1 Peter 1:6).

The grace of God allows our faith to see the blessed shores of salvation drawing closer on the horizon of life, as we encounter trials and temptations in our earthly pilgrimage. Even our whole life-time is short compared to eternity, and such revelation births within us an exceeding joy as we journey on our straight, narrow, and happy paths (Matt. 7:13–14; Heb. 12:12–13).

Christians at times may act and look like lunatics and drunkards to the carnal mind, but it is only because the world cannot see the things of God and His kingdom (Acts 2:13). Our joy is eternally founded; it can only be enjoyed by those who have responded to the call of grace on their life.

The distress of pain and grief is real and can only be conquered by endurance and long-suffering in the grace of God. It takes the peace of God, which passes our understanding to assure us that our soul is in our Saviour's arms (Phil. 4:7). Just as God's mercy triumphs over judgement, God's peace triumphs over distress. Christ makes us exceedingly glad and victorious in all situations (Phil. 4:13).

✞ **POSITION / OPERATION OF GRACE:** (grace guides us through testing for our own good)

"So that [the genuineness] of your faith may be tested, [your faith] which is infinitely more precious than the perishable gold which is tested and purified by fire. [This proving of your faith is intended] to redound to [your] praise and glory and honour when Jesus Christ (the Messiah, the Anointed one) is revealed" (1 Peter 1:7).

The genuineness of God's grace is only evidenced and manifested by the recipients of such grace. It is eternally founded; therefore it will uphold us and make us stand up-right in the tests and trials of time. Our faith is eternal and hence is outside of the limits of time (1 John 1:1–2). Faith and grace will still be active and present when the temporariness of time is dissolved. They will give the eternal One glory and honour, which He reflects back upon us. Faith and grace have eternal value for us.

Our tests and trials that we experience within the limits of time here, can never void our eternal foundation of grace. To prove eternity within the limits of time is not possible. At the second coming of Christ, even time itself will be tested and will be found wanting, to the glory and honour of God.

Our faith is so much more precious than anything on this earth. To treat grace as something less than eternally glorious is folly. Every time we catch a glimpse of eternity, the things of this earth become secondary. Beloved, the converse is also true; when we have our eyes stuck on the things of this world, the things of the kingdom of God become subordinate (Matt. 6:33; Heb. 11:13–16, 37–40).

✝ **<u>POSITION OF GRACE:</u>** (grace was intended for us, and results in inexpressible joy)

"<u>Without</u> having seen Him, you <u>love</u> Him; though you do not [even] now see Him, you believe in Him and exult and thrill with inexpressible and glorious (triumphant, heavenly) joy.

[At the same time] you receive the result (outcome, consummation) of your faith, the salvation of your souls.

The <u>prophets</u>, who prophesied of the <u>grace</u> (divine blessing) which was intended for you, searched and <u>inquired</u> earnestly about this <u>salvation</u>" (1 Peter 1:8–10).

The grace of God has opened the eyes of our understanding to see things, which the natural man cannot see. We have been positioned into an all-seeing love that is eternally consuming. This type of love can only be observed as strange or foreign to the natural man. A soul, born from above, rejoices in things unseen and hence manifests an inexpressible joy in ways, which are not understandable to the world (2 Cor. 2:14–16). Because the eyes of our understanding have been opened, we can see Jesus as truly worthy, and our desire is to anoint Him with the perfume of our praise. The revelation of Christ and His kingdom produce a soulish reaction, which is foreign to our natural understanding and ways, which we habitually operate in (Eph. 2:1–2; 1 Peter 4:4, 12).

By the Spirit, the prophets saw the grace of God, which was coming. They spoke of it by the unction of the Spirit, even sensing that it was for them. However, they could only search and inquire earnestly for it, because Jesus had not yet been born — God's grace had yet to be revealed in its entirety. Even angels long to look into the sufferings of Christ and the glories to follow. Oh, the inexpressible joy of knowing Jesus Christ, our Saviour (1 Peter 1:10–12).

✝ **<u>POSITION OF GRACE:</u>** (grace comes to us as Christ is revealed)

"So <u>brace</u> up your <u>minds</u>; be <u>sober</u> (circumspect, morally alert); set your hope wholly and unchangeably on the grace (divine favour) that is coming to you when Jesus Christ (the Messiah) is revealed" (1 Peter 1:13).

The grace of God has come, and is coming again, when our Messiah will be revealed for all to see. Such revelation commands our mind to be braced up and sober; it demands our hope to be unchangeable and fixed upon its source. Divine favour is our calling, our hope, and our destiny.

A mind that is steadied on the Saviour will not be caught unaware, and neither will it be confused by the circumstances, which come its way. An erring soul drunk on the world is not a wise soul (Mk. 13:31–37).

Morality defined by the world is ever changing and never absolute; it is controlled by the spirit that works in disobedience and rebellion (Prov. 9:12–18). A soul that is morally alert to the Spirit, sets its hope solely on the grace of God; it lives in divinely directed ways and purposes.

✝ **<u>OPERATION OF GRACE:</u>** (grace identifies the requirements of the Gospel)

"[Live] as <u>children</u> of <u>obedience</u> [to God]; do not conform yourselves to the <u>evil</u> <u>desires</u> [that governed you] in your former ignorance [when you

did not know the requirements of the Gospel]" (1 Peter 1:14).

The evil desires that govern the godless can never be used as guides to grace; they will always lead to shame (Prov. 3:35; 13:18). Compliance and submission to the God of grace is a sign that the grace of God is operating. When we walk in grace, it renews our mind and our character into the pattern prescribed by God; we become new creations in Christ. This not only occurs at the point of our salvation, it is a day to day process with the renewing of our soul. When we walk in disobedience, we eventually end up in shame and disgrace. Beloved, there is pleasure in sin for a season, but the wages paid therein is death (Rom. 6:23).

Grace identifies us as 'children of obedience' — children who do not lust or crave after what is forbidden. Grace operating in our life does not call us to remain ignorant of the knowledge of God and His will, nor to remain in moral blindness. Beloved, whatever we submit to has power over us (Rom. 6:11–23). Grace invites us to bear the Name above all names — to dwell in the Name above all names.

Ignorance of the Law was not an excuse for sin in the Old Testament (Lev. 4:2, 13); ignorance of God's will is not an excuse for sin in the New Covenant. The requirements of the Gospel are not nullified or changed by our ignorance. We are called children of obedience, not children of ignorance. As children of the Gospel, Jesus says to us, "I would not have you ignorant, brethren." (Rom. 10:3; 11:25; 1 Cor. 10:1; 12:1; 14:38; 2 Cor. 2:9–11; 1 Thess. 4:13).

✞ **OPERATION OF GRACE:** (grace nurtures us on the purity of God and calls us to separation from impurity)

"So be done with every trace of wickedness (depravity, malignity) and all deceit and insincerity (pretence, hypocrisy) and grudges (envy, jealousy) and slander and evil speaking of every kind.

Like newborn babies you should crave (thirst for, earnestly desire) the pure (unadulterated) spiritual milk, that by it you may be nurtured and grow unto [completed] salvation" (1 Peter 2:1–2).

The voice of grace calls us to put off and lay aside anything and everything that would take the place of God in our heart (1 John 5:21). Grace says, "Be done with wickedness, pretence, and deceit." As new born creations, we are to earnestly desire the pureness of God and allow such pureness to nurture our growth. With eyes fixed on Jesus and with a heart greatly desiring and panting after the pureness of God, we pursue His perfect love, which results in true increase — becoming something greater than ourselves (2 Peter 1:8).

We need to seriously look at the list here in verse one — wickedness, depravity, malignity, deceit, insincerity, pretense, hypocrisy, grudges, envy, jealousy, slander, and evil speaking. Our humble response to this call of grace is not only to give up these things, but to give up every trace of them in our life. Beloved, we cannot be very effective in the kingdom of God by carrying around even a trace scent of these things. Such rancid odour requires repentance and submission to the Spirit of grace. We need to recognize that God's grace is the only thing that can change us. Our part is to thirst for and earnestly desire God's purity. Even a trace of these qualities listed here is a sure indication of spiritual immaturity.

Beloved, if you do not see yourself as immature, you will stay right where you are — immature. Grace calls us to crave after the pure, unadulterated, undiluted, unmodified word of God to nurture our soul. Adulterated word sullies the soul, making the word of God ineffectual in our godly influence towards those around us. Untouched word touches and changes our heart and soul (2 Peter 1:8–11).

✞ **POSITION OF GRACE:** (grace gives us a taste for God)

"Since you have [already] tasted the goodness and kindness of the Lord" (1 Peter 2:3).

The grace of God gives us our sense of spiritual taste. Without this grace, the goodness of God is tasteless and even bitterly unknown. As vessels of God's grace we are called to be conveyers of the goodness and kindness of God (2 Cor. 2:14–16).

It is only through a vessel of grace that the world can taste the flavour of the Spirit, and take nourishment from the Lord (2 Cor. 1:4). The grace of God makes us fit for use; it is mild and pleasant. Grace tastes good to a soul seeking the kingdom of God; such souls find refreshment in righteousness. To the wicked, the wisdom of God is offensive and foolish, something to snub and scoff at (Prov. 1:22–33).

A soul that eats the things of the world enjoys the taste at first, but it becomes 'gravel in the mouth' (Prov. 20:17). Pleasurable impulses, which cater to the carnal nature, bring soulish bondage and death. When we follow the whims and fashions of this world, we are under the control of that demon spirit that works disobedience and rebellion towards the plans and purposes of God (Eph. 2:2; Col. 2:13–15).

✞ **POSITION / OPERATION OF GRACE:** (grace ordains us as priests and enables us to show forth the wonderful works of God)

"But you are a chosen race, a royal priesthood, a dedicated nation, [God's] own purchased, special people, that you may set forth the wonderful deeds and display the virtues and perfections of Him Who called you out of darkness into His marvellous light" (1 Peter 2:9).

The grace of God has picked us out of the garbage can of the world and placed us in His presence — a place of honour (Eph. 1:3–4). Our calling from this incredible position is one of progressively displaying and setting forth the virtues and deeds of God. Grace increasingly draws us from darkness into light (John 3:19–21; 1 John 1:5–10). We become a display of God's works and virtue. We make known the divine nature of God before all mankind — our life becomes a declaration of His desires.

There is no perfection outside of grace, and within grace, the perfection we experience is not our own — it is His (Gal. 2:20). Because of His divine nature within us, we have a position of perfection, and can thus display the divine qualities of righteousness as this perfection operates within and through our life.

We are priests of God. He sees us as special. We are distinct — God has saved us from the wrath, which is coming on the world and the sons of disobedience. We are extraordinary — God does not look upon us as He looks upon the wicked. We are unique — God made us in His image. We are new creations and He is continually renewing our souls. We are separate — God has sent us 'into the world' but we are no longer 'of the world' (John 15:17–21).

Our credential of priesthood was purchased for us by the blood of the Lamb on the cross, not by five years of Bible College. Better to revere the sweat of Jesus' brow, than idolize the sweat on men's brows (Gen. 3:19; Lk. 22:44).

✞ **POSITION OF GRACE:** (grace makes us God's special people — a people of mercy)

"Once you were not a people [at all], but now you are God's people; once you were unpitied, but now you are pitied and have received mercy" (1 Peter 2:10).

To be outside of God's grace is to be in a position of 'not a people', and 'outside' of the kingdom of the Author of pity and mercy (Rom. 9:14–26). It takes the grace of God applied to our life to make us the people of God — citizens of a holy nation (1 Peter 2:9). The experience of grace always takes place in the present; it is an operation of God that continuously occurs in the time called *now* (Heb. 3:7–8; 13:8).

Grace draws us from wretchedness to righteousness. Our claim as Christians is that we are in right relation to God; it is a claim, which is anchored in eternal truth. It is not a work of man; it is God's Sabbath work of bringing man into His rest (Heb. 4:7–11).

To an unconverted soul, the covenant of grace and mercy is not known. When a person is born-again (born-from-above) the provision of the Son is manifested to them according to the abundance of His mercy and love (Eph. 3:20). The divine regeneration within a soul becomes a continuous display of the mercy of God. You must receive God's grace to be positioned in grace; you must rest in His grace to effectively operate in it.

✞ **OPERATION OF GRACE:** (grace has made us aliens and strangers to worldly passionate desires; it calls us to proper conduct reflecting God's goodness)

"Beloved, I implore you as aliens and strangers and exiles [in this world] to abstain from the sensual urges (the evil desires, the passions of the flesh, your lower nature) that wage war against the soul.

Conduct yourselves properly (honourably, righteously) among the Gentiles, so that, although they may slander you as evildoers, [yet] they may by witnessing your good deeds [come to] glorify God in the day of inspection [when God shall look upon you wanderers as a pastor or shepherd looks over his flock]" (1 Peter 2:11–12).

Oh that we would allow the grace of God to teach us to be aliens and exiles in this world — to truly be *in the world* but not *of it*. As an alien, we require the grace of God in the daily battle of fleshy desires and passions warring against our soul. To not regard sensual urges as an enemy will result only in the embracement of such, and hence we end up becoming an enemy of God. Grace does not operate in our lives to make us lovers of the world; it operates in our hearts to make us lovers of God, and to desire to be untouched by the world (Jas. 1:27). It enables us to find joy even while being slandered for being Christ-like (John 16:1–3; Jas. 1:2).

Proper conduct must be enabled by grace in order for it to be divinely effective. Man-made works do not bear divine design, and hence cannot reveal divine purpose. Walking uprightly does not make the world love you; it makes you an object of slander. Stephen was slandered for his testimony, but in the day of inspection, he is justified before God by his accusers. Beloved, it is of vital necessity to see that Stephen was vindicated by God. Circumstances and outcomes are false gods, which can direct our lives, but even these will be brought into the light of truth on the day of inspection (Acts 8:1; 22:20).

✞ **OPERATION OF GRACE:** (grace calls us to right doing and freedom from all false motives; grace makes us servants of God)

"For it is God's will and intention that by doing right [your good and honest lives] should silence (muzzle, gag) the ignorant charges and ill-informed criticisms of foolish persons.

[Live] as free people, [yet] without employing your freedom as a pretext for wickedness; but [live at all times] as servants of God" (1 Peter 2:15–16).

The righteousness of God that hung from the cross has eternally muzzled and gagged all ignorant charges and criticisms, which can ever come our way (Col. 2:14–15). The righteousness of God that was raised from the dead, has freed us from the power of sin and death. Our faith now shields us from all the deadly darts of deception and ignorance, attempting to weaken us and discredit our completeness in Christ (Gal. 2:21). Works can never perfect grace; our works are only a reflection of His grace/faith. Grace has freed us from the power of false motivation, and released us to be servants of the Most High. Grace and truth strengthen us; self-righteous works and falsity weaken us (Col. 1:9–14).

Freedom is never found in diluted righteousness; beloved, just a little wickedness, is still wicked. A servant of God does not dabble in devilish attitudes, or employ his energies in exercising unrighteousness. Whatever we are obedient to is what we become servant to — either to righteousness, which leads to eternal life, or to unrighteousness, which results in death (Rom. 6:11–18).

✞ **OPERATION OF GRACE:** (grace calls us to patiently endure the suffering of injustice)

"[After all] what kind of glory [is there in it] if, when you do wrong and are punished for it, you take it patiently? But if you bear patiently with suffering [which results] when you do right and that is undeserved, it is acceptable and pleasing to God.

For even to this were you called [it is inseparable from your vocation]. For Christ also suffered for you, leaving you [His personal] example, so that you should follow in His footsteps" (1 Peter 2:20–21).

Our calling of grace enables us to endure injustice and suffering. Our endurance under grace is founded in the eternities; it is not just a temporary, worldly endurance, which requires the tenacity of man (Matt. 24:13; Mk. 4:17; 2 Thess. 1:4; 2 Tim. 4:5). Beloved, endurance and long-suffering is *not* an attitude of, "I'll just hang in there, and I'll be glad when this is over!"

The purpose of endurance is to allow grace to work God's character into our being. Long-suffering in the Spirit is required to get through life's temporary circumstances. Godly endurance does not look for ways to get rid of circumstances; it desires God's solution, not its own comfort. It is only by grace that we can *count it all joy* (Acts 20:24; Jas. 1:2–4). Our rest in God does not change with our circumstances; the way we look at our circumstances will change, because of our godly rest.

Grace is required to manifest God's justice. Our walk is not according to the counsel of the ungodly — demanding rights and vengeance. When we are reviled and insulted, we are not to revile or offer insult in return; when we are abused and suffer, we are not to make threats of vengeance (Ps. 1:1; Prov. 20:22; Matt. 7:12; Mk. 15:32; John 9:28; 1 Cor. 4:12; 1 Peter 2:23).

The will of the Father is that we trust Him; grace calls us to place ourselves and everything we do into the hands of Him Who judges fairly, because He can be trusted. God gets His greatest joy when He sees His children living their lives in the Truth — walking in His footsteps (3 John 1:4). The love of God is accessible to those who are trusting in Him.

✞ **POSITION OF GRACE:** (grace calls us to die to sin and live to righteousness; grace brings healing)

"He personally bore our sins in His [own] body on the tree [as on an altar and offered Himself on it], that we might die (cease to exist) to sin and live to righteousness. By His wounds you have been healed. For you were going astray like [so many] sheep, but now you have come back to the Shepherd and Guardian (the Bishop) of your souls" (1 Peter 2:24–25).

Grace draws us from darkness to light, and from sin to righteousness. It is a work, which our precious Lord and Saviour has forever completed on the cross. There is nothing, which we can do to add to His work; and there is nothing, which we can do to uphold it. All of our works of grace are a result of our belief/faith in Him.

The grip of sin has been broken over us, and there is nothing we can now do except live in His righteousness (1 Cor. 1:29–31; 2 Cor. 5:20–21; Gal. 2:21; Phil. 3:9). The drawing of our soul to God is a work of grace accomplished by Christ on the cross. The renewing of the human soul is also accomplished by grace, as we learn to submit and live in His Spirit. Grace has become the guardian of our souls; if God be for us, who can be against us (Rom. 8:31).

Jesus personally died for me, that I, personally, might die to sin and live to righteousness. Eternal healing has been provided for us in Christ Jesus. He is the Bishop and Pastor of my soul (John 10:14, 16; Heb. 13:20; 1 Peter 5:4). Let no man dare to usurp this position and think that he is doing service to God. My Pastor (Jesus) is continually working within my soul by His grace.

We find rest in His covering of righteousness, not in a man-made, man-empowered covering. There is a gift of pastor mentioned once in Scripture (Eph. 4:11); however it is never referred to as a position in any church. What is seen as the position of 'the pastor' (a person in charge of a church) simply cannot be found anywhere in Scripture. Beloved, whatever you submit yourself to, is what will control you — either the Lord Jesus Christ, or an institution. If you ever sense yourself going astray, your Pastor (Jesus) is ever there to help you; He lives within you (1 Peter 5:4). Scripture declares that you are accountable to Him and Him only (Rom. 14:12).

The duties of a shepherd are to watch for enemies attacking the sheep, to defend them, to heal the sick and wounded, and to find and save the lost. This is all done through love and the sharing of their lives together (Ezek. 34:1–31). Beloved, God so loved the world that He came as a man to share His life with us and to be the Shepherd and Guardian of our soul. The military term, 'shepherd' is a pilot who guides a partially disabled plane by flying alongside it all the way back to home and a safe landing.

✞ **OPERATION OF GRACE:** (grace commands us to love one another)

"Finally, all [of you] should be of one and the same mind [united in spirit], sympathizing [with one another], loving [each other] as brethren [of one household], compassionate and courteous (tender-hearted and humble)" (1 Peter 3:8).

The grace of God is never divisive within the body of Christ. It is the only thing, which holds the body of Christ together in unity. The Spirit of grace has brought us into oneness with God. How can it ever divide the body of Christ into parts (John 17:11, 22–23)? Division, discord, and factions are a sign of carnality, not grace (1 Cor. 3:1–4; 12:25; Rom. 16:17). Words spoken by the grace of God are righteous and true; there is nothing contrary or crooked in them. They are made plain to him who understands with his heart (spirit), and they prove themselves right by those who find the knowledge of grace, and live by it (Prov. 8:8–9; 9:4–6, 12; 25:26).

To love one another is a command, not an option for a soul living by grace. The heart that responds to the commandment of love is the heart, which manifests the will of God. Family members need not put on airs towards one another, for they know each other, and have no need of pretence. Their love is genuine (John 13:34–35).

Grace operates through our unity with each other in the Spirit. We are never called to have absolute agreement on what we believe to be right before God. Unity of the Spirit is the only thing, which will overcome differences of doctrine and belief (Rom. 14:1–23). To divide the body of Christ over doctrine is not grace; it is disgrace. There is one Holy Spirit and it will lead into all truth. Our responsibility is to remain in the unity of the Spirit. The Spirit's part is to lead and guide us into all truth (John 16:13; Eph. 4:1–16).

✞ **OPERATION OF GRACE:** (grace calls us to love even those who insult us, that we may inherit a blessing)

"Never return evil for evil or insult for insult (scolding, tongue-lashing, berating), but on the contrary blessing [praying for their welfare, happiness, and protection, and truly pitying and loving them]. For know that to this you have been called, that you may yourselves inherit a blessing [from God — that you may obtain a blessing as heirs, bringing welfare and happiness and protection]" (1 Peter 3:9).

A tongue tamed by grace is only focused on bringing life to those around it. The grace of God is not a tool of abuse; it is a channel of protection. Grace absorbs abuse, and returns life; it blots up berating, and returns with blessing; it sops up scorning, and repays with love. Grace calls us to be sanctified sponges that we may show forth the nature of God, bringing welfare, happiness, and protection to those who need it. It takes the grace of God to *never* return evil for evil (Rom. 12:17, 21; 1 Peter 4:8–10). We are best protected when we act out of love.

This does not mean that we should never correct or rebuke one another. Correction should always be designed to build up in love, using words seasoned with grace, not words of condemnation (Prov. 26:4–5).

✞ **OPERATION OF GRACE:** (grace commands us to keep our tongue free from evil, treachery and deceit)

"For let him who wants to enjoy life and see good days [good—whether apparent or not] keep his tongue free from evil and his lips from guile (treachery, deceit)" (1 Peter 3:10).

How could the mouth of Christ ever bring forth treachery, deceit or evil? Certainly not. The Grace of God, Who knew no sin, became sin for us that we might no longer live in sin. As ambassadors of Christ and ministers of reconciliation, grace calls us to keep our tongue from speaking evil (falsehood) and deceit (Jas. 1:26; 3:1–13).

Grace manifested itself on the cross that we would be empowered to follow in His steps, and die to sin (Rom. 6:2, 11). Life can only be truly attained and enjoyed within the bounds of grace. God's goodness is obvious through the eye of grace, but not always apparent to the natural eye. Good is defined by God's grace, not by man's desires. A mouth touched by the grace of God is a mouth free from foolishness (Is. 6:7; Dan. 10:16; Matt. 5:37).

✞ **OPERATION OF GRACE:** (grace commands us to turn from wickedness and eagerly pursue peace)

"Let him turn away from wickedness and shun it, and let him do right. Let him search for peace (harmony; undisturbedness from fears, agitating passions, and moral conflicts) and seek it eagerly. [Do not merely desire peaceful relations with God, with your fellow men, and with yourself, but pursue, go after them!]" (1 Peter 3:11).

The grace of God calls us to disdain wickedness — to hate evil. Grace never prompts us to do wrong; it teaches us to define what is right and wrong. It always seeks peace with God, our fellow men, and ourselves. It enables us to do right as we walk in the Spirit without fear. Grace calls us to pursue God's kingdom as a peaceful priority, not the world's compromising worry and double mindedness (Matt. 6:24–34).

When we have God's peace and a heart that desires truth, we can more clearly hear the voice of the Spirit directing our way before us. This is why the words, "Fear not!" are often spoken to us by our Saviour (Matt. 14:27; Mk. 5:36; Luke. 12:7, 32; John 6:20; Acts 18:9).

Grace calls us to not only desire the peace of God, but to eagerly pursue it. The only thing that brings peace in our life is righteousness through Christ. As we promote peace, God is not interested in us becoming unequally yoked with the world and its compromising ways (Prov. 1:10–15). God's peace is only found in the righteousness of Christ, and is to be reflected by His people.

✞ **POSITION OF GRACE:** (grace places us continually before the eyes of the Lord and guarantees that He is attentive to our prayers)

"For the eyes of the Lord are upon the righteous (those who are upright and in right standing with God), and His ears are attentive to their prayer. But the face of the Lord is against those who practice evil [to oppose them, to frustrate, and defeat them]" (1 Peter 3:12).

The grace of God places us in a position of protection found only under the eyes of the Almighty. It is through grace that we have a relationship with the Father, and it is through this same grace that He has relationship with us.

Just as oil and water do not mix, sin and grace do not mix. Grace came to the earth to deal with sin and to point mankind to righteousness. Jesus who knew no sin became sin for us, that we might be the righteousness of God in Christ. Our presence, as vessels of grace, will bring the face of the Lord to an unrighteous world, and will point them to the grace of God (2 Cor. 5:18–21). If God be for us who can be against us? If God be against us, who can be for us (Ps. 56:9; Rom. 8:31)? Eyes of grace are attentive to the needs of others and are driven by godliness, not by selfish, evil motivations (Phil. 2:1–4).

His grace is ever present to enable our eyes and ears to be always sensitive to the needs of others (Phil. 2:5–8). As vessels of grace we are given divine power to bring these needs before God, Who is always attentive to our prayers.

✞ **OPERATION OF GRACE:** (grace sometimes calls us to suffer unjustly for doing what is right)

"For [it is] better to suffer [unjustly] for doing right, if that should be God's will, than to suffer [justly] for doing wrong" (1 Peter 3:17).

It is God alone who defines justice. By grace we have entered into the justice of God — the will of God — to manifest His kingdom to the world. When we are in trouble and are battling by our own strength and understanding, we can find ourselves crying out to God and demanding whether He is for us or against us (Josh. 5:13–15). It is at times like this that we are liable to hear Him say, "Neither! Take off your shoes; you are standing on holy ground." (Ex. 3:4–5).

We need to recognize that *our* will is never holy, but rather as we stand in His presence, *His* will is always holy, just, and good. When we come to recognize that the love of God has paid the penalty for *all* our wrongdoings, it is but a small gracious step — when we are wronged — to utter, "Father, forgive them for they do not know what they are doing" (Acts 7:58–60; Col. 3:13).

Living within the will of our gracious God can at times be harsh and even painful, but it is better to hear God say, "Well done good and faithful servant!" than to hear Him say, "Adam, where are you?" (Gen. 3:8–9; Matt. 25:21–30).

✝ **POSITION OF GRACE:** (grace places us in righteousness, justification, innocence, and life)

"For Christ [the Messiah Himself] died for sins once for all, the Righteous for the unrighteous (the Just for the unjust, the Innocent for the guilty), that He might bring us to God. In His human body He was put to death, but He was made alive in the Spirit" (1 Peter 3:18).

The Grace of God from the cross of Christ has made righteousness and justification available to all mankind. The result of our position of grace is that we are reconciled to God; the purpose of this same grace working within us is to bring others into this same reconciliation with God. This is the ministry to which every Christian is called (2 Cor. 5:18).

The flesh has no part in Christ's gracious work; grace is always a work of the Spirit of God, and it is only received by faith. Christ died for sins once for all that we might be dead to sin, and not dwell in it any longer (Rom. 6:2, 11).

This work of God is a once-for-all-time deal (Heb. 10:10). It takes the grace of God to make the unrighteous righteous (2 Cor. 5:21), the unjust just (Rom. 3:24; 5:1, 9; 8:30; 1 Cor. 6:11), and the guilty innocent (Col. 2:13–14; Jude 1:24). The purpose of God's work of grace is to reconcile us to Himself so that we too might follow in His steps by the Holy Spirit.

✝ **POSITION / OPERATION OF GRACE:** (grace is required when we suffer in the flesh; it allows us to live in the will of God)

"So, since Christ suffered in the flesh for us, for you, arm yourselves with the same thought and purpose [patiently to suffer rather than to fail to please God]. For whoever has suffered in the flesh [having the mind of Christ] is done with [intentional] sin [has stopped pleasing himself and the world, and pleases God],

So that he can no longer spend the rest of his natural life living by [his] human appetites and desires, but [he lives] for what God wills" (1 Peter 4:1–2).

Grace came to us through the submissive suffering of Jesus Christ. We, as the body of Christ and having the mind of Christ, are called to let His gracious purposes equip and prepare us to carry out His will. This is pleasing to God. Thoughts and purposes that please the flesh, never work out for good. There are no short cuts in God, only the narrow path, which leads to eternal life, and beloved, it is always a joy to be found in Him (Matt. 7:13–14).

Grace has freed us from the power of the flesh by our crucifixion on the cross with Jesus (Gal. 2:20). Since we are now dead in Christ, we should not balk at suffering; we are not to let our flesh rise to control our life again (Acts 7:58–60). Jesus is our example of patient suffering (1 Peter 2:23). Whether it was with faithless disciples, or angry Pharisees, or in the Garden of Gethsemane, or dying on the cross, Jesus suffered in the flesh, and we are called to have that same attitude and mind in Christ (1 Cor. 1:10; Heb. 5:7–9). The world has no attraction or influence on a dead person. From our position of having the mind of Christ, we no longer need to waste our time with worldly passions and desires. We are free to live in the will of God.

✞ **POSITION / OPERATION OF GRACE:** (grace has made us loathsome to the world; the world will have to give an account to God)

"For the time that is past already suffices for doing what the Gentiles like to do — living [as you have done] in shameless, insolent wantonness, in lustful desires, drunkenness, revelling, drinking bouts and abominable, lawless idolatries.

They are astonished and think it very queer that you do not now run hand in hand with them in the same excesses of dissipation, and they abuse [you].

But they will have to give an account to Him Who is ready to judge and pass sentence on the living and the dead" (1 Peter 4:3–5).

Living in the lustful desires of the flesh is not the way of Christ. By grace we have been drawn out of the kingdom of darkness and placed in the kingdom of the Son (Col. 1:13). People who chronically work through the desires of the flesh like to keep company with like minds; they think it strange that someone would not desire the same delicacies they do.

What is normal to the flesh is foreign to God; what is normal to the spiritual man is foreign to the flesh. The flesh cannot comprehend the things of the Spirit. However, the spiritual man discerns all things (1 Cor. 2:14–16). The flesh demands followers, and it will abuse anyone who does not bow their knee to its wantonness. Carnality loves company and will contend and abuse those who desire to walk after the Spirit (Matt. 27:39–44). However, an accounting will be required by God (Matt. 12:36).

✞ **POSITION / OPERATION OF GRACE:** (grace causes us to find honour in humility)

"Likewise, you who are younger and of lesser rank, be subject to the elders (the ministers and spiritual guides of the church) — [giving them due respect and yielding to their counsel]. Clothe (apron) yourselves, all of you with humility [as the garb of a servant, so that its covering cannot possibly be stripped from you, with freedom from pride and arrogance] toward one another. For God sets Himself against the proud (the insolent, the overbearing, the disdainful, the presumptuous, the boastful) — [and He opposes, frustrates, and defeats them], but gives grace (favour, blessing) to the humble.

Therefore humble yourselves [demote, lower yourselves in your own estimation] under the mighty hand of God, that in due time He may exalt you" (1 Peter 5:5–6).

The grace of God calls us to submit to God's rule in our life. This does not imply that we submit to man's rule over us. Submission comes from within, not from without. It is a spiritual position founded only on humility, not dominance. Submission is found by honouring and preferring one another through the recognition of them as the body of Christ, and discerning and obeying (honouring) the Spirit of God with our words and actions towards one another. It is never over-bearing, demanding, or dishonouring; it never acts in a superior manner, because there is no superiority in Christ (Gal. 2:6).

Elders recognize the calling of the whole body of Christ as one. Their task is to guide, by exemplifying the life of Christ to fellow believers. In essence the calling of the body of Christ and the life of Christ are one and the same. Tried experience over time never makes one superior to another, but rather, it truly makes one walk in increasing humility with their life being an example for others to follow. Every Christian should be able to say to everyone else, "Do what I am doing — follow me as I follow Christ." A leader does not do different things than other Christians; he simply sets an example for others to follow (2 Thess. 3:7, 9; Heb. 13:7; 1 Peter 2:21).

It is the carnal nature, which desires hierarchal leadership as it places the priesthood of the believer into the hands of a superior, select few. Such attitude and belief results in following God vicariously; it shifts the responsibility for one's own walk in the Lord onto the shoulders of another. Such attitude never nurtures maturity; it merely caters to carnality.

We are never subject to authority, which is not sourced in God. If anyone speaks to us by the Spirit of God, we are obliged to follow after Him. Words not spoken by the Spirit of God are not to be followed after. We are responsible to discern the difference using our anointing.

When we treat authority as a position, we end up following man. When we treat authority as an operation, we follow the Spirit of God. The Greek word for authority means 'freedom of choice'. It does not mean that freedom is obtained by following a man or a system. We find freedom in Christ by choosing to follow the Spirit as He leads us in God's ways.

When we are subject to God we are automatically subject to all that is of God, and this is where true freedom is found. Such freedom is only realized when we walk and live in a way, which is free from pride and arrogance. We are called to walk humbly with our God (Micah 6:8); we are not called to idolize leaders or leadership (Gal. 2:6). This is why we do not see hierarchical leadership in the early church, and we do not see leadership as 'having power over or being victorious over the common, lay people' — this is the meaning of the Greek word 'Nicolaitans' (Rev. 2:6, 15).

The only covering a Christian is required to have is the covering of humility in Christ initiated over two thousand years ago, not the covering of some institutional organization that man has since started. Beloved, believing that our covering in Christ is not sufficient is to adulterate Scripture.

✞ **<u>POSITION / OPERATION OF GRACE</u>:** (we are not to worry when we live in grace)

"<u>Casting</u> the whole of your <u>care</u> [all your anxieties, all your worries, all your concerns, once and for all] on Him, for He <u>cares</u> for you <u>affectionately</u> and cares about you <u>watchfully</u>" (1 Peter 5:7).

We need to toss all anxiety aside — all which arises and subtly attaches itself to our life. Grace does not allow us to retain even a morsel of anxiety in our pocket; it calls for all of our life to be touched and affected by it. Grace is a completed work, and because He cares for us, it is also an ongoing work in our life. This is care, not that we care for God, but rather that He first cared for us. Grace starts with God and finishes with God. The qualities of our life that are not Christ-like should have no part in our life. If grace be for us, what can possibly be against us.

Beloved, what a blessing to know that God cares for us; He is concerned about every detail of our life. With this being the truth, why should we ever be anxious about anything (Lk. 12:22–26; Phil. 4:6–7)? His affection for us is not temporal or determined by our obedience to Him; it is eternal. His watchful eyes, which never sleep or slumber, are ever observing and ever ready to guide us on our pathway. The only time He will blink is when He takes us to be with Him (Ps. 121:3–4; 1 Cor. 15:52).

✞ **<u>OPERATION OF GRACE</u>:** (grace commands us to be vigilant and cautious)

"Be <u>well</u> <u>balanced</u> (temperate, sober of mind), be <u>vigilant</u> and <u>cautious</u> at all times; for that <u>enemy</u> of yours, the <u>devil</u>, roams around like a <u>lion</u> roaring [in fierce hunger], seeking someone to seize upon and devour" (1 Peter 5:8).

The adversary of God has been defeated by the grace of God (Heb. 2:14). Our part is to be vigilant and cautious, not anxious about our circumstances or the affairs of the future. When you hear the lion's roar and feel the lion's breath, know for certain that God's grace does not abandon us as we place our trust in His keeping power, and not our own strength and wisdom (Dan. 6:22–23; 2 Tim. 4:17).

The devil longs to draw God's people into a battle of the flesh, but we wrestle not against the flesh, and neither are our weapons carnal (2 Cor. 10:3–5). We do not need to out-roar the lion; we need only to rest in our Saviour's grace. Our hunger should *not* be of a carnal nature; it should be of a righteous nature — seeking His kingdom and His ways as first priority in our life (Matt. 6:33).

The devil comes to kill, steal, and destroy, but Jesus died and rose from the dead that we might have life and walk in it abundantly (John 10:10). Christ has defeated the devil; this was the very purpose why the Son of God was manifested (1 John 3:8).

✞ **POSITION / OPERATION OF GRACE:** (grace calls us to withstand the devil and endure the sufferings common to Christians)

"Withstand him; be firm in faith [against his onset — rooted, established, strong, immovable, and determined], knowing that the same (identical) sufferings are appointed to your brotherhood (the whole body of Christians) throughout the world" (1 Peter 5:9).

Grace operates by faith and faith alone. Even a small application of faith can withstand anything and everything, which the devil and the world can throw our way. It is not by our strength that we stand, but we are called to be firm in our faith to withstand the enemy's terrorism. It is immovable faith, which carries us through all suffering situations; it is wavering faith, which stops our manifestation of the grace of God (Eph. 4:14; Jas. 1:6).

Our comfort is founded on Jesus' sufferings and temptations. It is also a comfort in knowing that our brothers in Christ throughout the whole world are also enduring the same sufferings.

Grace is not purposed to prevent suffering; it enables us to prevail in it. Suffering appointed by God has divine motive; it is always designed to bring about that, which God intends for us — our good (Rom. 2:4; 2 Thess. 1:11). Oh, the blessing of having His purposes worked into our life. To embrace suffering at the hand of God is to die to self, and to live in grace. Walking and living in the Spirit of God guarantees that faithful suffering is set before us, and can even be counted as joy.

✞ **POSITION / OPERATION OF GRACE:** (grace completes us, establishes us securely, and strengthens us)

"And after you have suffered a little while, the God of all grace [Who imparts all blessing and favour], Who has called you to His [own] eternal glory in Christ Jesus, will Himself complete and make you what you ought to be, establish and ground you securely, and strengthen, and settle you" (1 Peter 5:10).

Never forget that it is the God of all grace Who defines how long 'a little while' is. Grace is not set nor controlled by time. Because grace is eternal, we must submit to God's timetable. Whoever has been forgiven much, loves much; whoever sets time constraints on forgiveness, loves little (Luke 7:47). A little piece of eternity is still eternal; nothing is lost in the giving of it. A piece of God's faith/love/grace the size of a mustard seed is enough to move any mountain (Matt. 17:20; 21:21).

When it comes to manifesting love, the issue is not the size or amount of love, which we manifest. The issue is the source of the love, which we manifest. Is it eternal love that we are manifesting or is it temporary/conditional love? We should never forget that God is the source of true love, and hence as it works though us, it should be unconditional and untouched by any circumstances or suffering (Jas. 2:14–17). There is nothing that can separate us from the love of Christ. There should be absolutely nothing that can separate us from our love towards one another in Christ (Rom. 8:38–39).

In Christ, it is God Himself who completes us, not we ourselves. Our suffering turns to joy as the hand of God reveals His grace operating in our life. Grace is a work often completed by suffering, where the hand of God makes us what we ought to be, grounded and established securely in Him. The fires found in suffering (the trying of our faith) is designed to burn the bands of bondage from us, leaving us free to run the race set before us, and come out of our trials without the smell of smoke, but rather with the fragrance of love and life (Dan. 3:27; 6:20–23). The lash of life's suffering is designed to remove the chaff from the kernel (Matt. 3:11–12).

✞ **POSITION OF GRACE:** (grace gives us dominion, power and rule forever)

"To Him be the dominion (power, authority, rule) forever and ever. Amen (so be it)" (1 Peter 5:11).

The grace of God places us in the position of dominion — His dominion. We are positioned in His power, His authority, and His rule. This work starts the moment you receive His grace, and it will last forever. It is from this position that we are called to allow His dominion (power, authority and rule) to operate through our life (Jude 1:25; Rev. 1:6).

2 Peter

✞ **POSITION / OPERATION OF GRACE:** (grace is perfect, all good, and it prospers us; grace and peace are multiplied in a life in Christ)

"May grace (God's favour) and peace (which is perfect well-being, all necessary good, all spiritual prosperity, and freedom from fears and agitating passions and moral conflicts) be multiplied to you in [the full, personal, precise, and correct] knowledge of God and of Jesus our Lord" (2 Peter 1:2).

The grace and peace of God are multiplied in our life by walking truthfully in our Saviour's steps. God is not interested in us being only hearers of the word; He is interested in us being doers of the word — living a life that conveys a continuous consciousness of God (Jas. 1:22). A life lived by grace is a life that will manifest His grace. A life of grace is always accompanied by peace; they are like twins. Peace is not found outside of grace. Grace precedes peace.

Grace brings us into a position of perfect well-being and then enables us to rest, free from all fears. Since all fear is cast out, we are provoked to love and good works, not to carnal passions and sin. Grace is an enabler, helping us to overcome everything hostile to the well-being of our soul. It always empowers us to live righteously; it never authorizes us to live in unrighteousness. A life that reflects His grace is a life where the knowledge of our Lord and His ways are continuously multiplied and lived out; it is a life that defines spiritual prosperity.

Our life's goal should be to find the full, personal, precise, and correct knowledge of God. All other knowledge is a waste of time, even deadly. Partial truth is not effective in the kingdom of God (Acts 4:19; 18:26; 24:22; 27:11; Rom. 3:3–4). Beware of half-truths; you may find yourself living in the wrong half.

As Christians, the correct knowledge of God is vital if we desire His plan to be fulfilled in our life (Acts 15:1–11). New Testament believers were given a set of rules of grace to follow (Acts 15:20, 24, 29; 21:25). Circumcision and tithing are not mentioned here or anywhere else in the New Testament, as Christian requirements (Gal. 2:1–3, 10–12; 5:6; 6:15; Titus 1:9–11). Christ is not interested in us following the law which requires things like circumcision and tithing (Rom. 2:28–29; Phil. 3:3; Col. 2:11). God desires one hundred percent of our heart, which includes all of our resources.

Beloved, Jesus did *not* cry out from the cross, "It is finished, except for tithing. You must give ten percent to a local church of your choice, and if you do not tithe, you are robbing God!" (John 19:28–30).

✞ **POSITION / OPERATION OF GRACE:** (grace gives us all things that are essential and suited to life; grace is personally experienced)

"For His divine power has bestowed upon us all things that [are requisite and suited] to life and godliness, through the [full, personal] knowledge of Him Who called us by and to His own glory and excellence (virtue)" (2 Peter 1:3).

Grace is the divine power of God operating within us. God imparts only things that are strong, robust and life giving. He is not in the business of giving us things of little value, weak, and ineffective. God's grace is all we need (2 Cor. 12:9). He has given us everything required for a life of righteousness — we lack nothing when we live in the grace of God. God's gift to us is indispensable and basic to all aspects of our life. It reproduces godliness.

To become thoroughly acquainted with the grace of God and to know His divinity is only possible by being in Christ. To personally know Him and the power of His resurrection is the calling of grace. It is only from this position that we come to realize and know accurately all that He has provided for us (Phil. 3:10).

Such works of God are always to His praise and glory. He Who calls us by His virtue, operates in us and manifests His glory and excellence through us. Grace calls us *by* the virtue of God, *to* the virtue of God.

✞ **POSITION / OPERATION OF GRACE:** (grace exercised, develops divine nature within us)

"By means of these He has bestowed on us His precious and exceedingly great promises, so that through them you may escape [by flight] from the moral decay (rottenness and corruption) that is in the world because of covetousness (lust and greed), and become sharers (partakers) of the divine nature" (2 Peter 1:4).

The grace of God makes us conscious of God's promises, which are meant to be applied to our life. Any promise of God is both precious and exceedingly great. It is through the means of His promises that we depart from devilish temptations and avoid greedy desires; we retire from all unrighteous unction — we hate evil (Ps. 97:10; Prov. 8:13; Amos 5:14–15). Any holy promise, personally apprehended, results in God's divine nature being imputed into our life — a life that bears fruit through our actions.

Moral decay was introduced into the world by Satan's covetousness for God's position. Just as the love of money is the root of all evil, covetousness (lust and greed) is the sin named here as the foundation for the world's moral decay and corruption (1 Tim. 6:10). As we live out His promises in our life, we are able to discern and evade the rottenness of the world, and the deception perpetrated by the devil.

✞ **POSITION / OPERATION OF GRACE:** (faith is the foundation of virtue and knowledge)

"For this very reason, adding your diligence [to the divine promises], employ every effort in exercising your faith to develop virtue (excellence, resolution, Christian energy), and in [exercising] virtue [develop] knowledge (intelligence)," (2 Peter 1:5).

The grace of God enables us to unveil divine virtues — whatever is true, whatever is worthy of reverence, whatever is honourable and seemly, whatever is just, whatever is pure, whatever is lovely and lovable, and whatever is kind, winsome, and gracious. Beloved, we need to fix our minds on these things (Phil. 4:8).

Faith exercised by the grace of God will develop virtue in our life. Virtue exercised by grace will develop experience and wisdom, resulting in a personal awareness and a testimony of God. Divine intelligence imparts an insight into our life and an acquaintance with His kingdom — a discernment and a confidential communion with God (Prov. 3:32).

✞ **POSITION / OPERATION OF GRACE:** (grace enables us to steer our character towards godliness)

"And in [exercising] knowledge [develop] self-control, and in [exercising] self-control [develop] steadfastness (patience, endurance), and in [exercising] steadfastness [develop] godliness (piety)," (2 Peter 1:6).

The grace of God enables us to exercise (to do) the knowledge of God. Because grace is not imposed upon us, we require self-control in order to do the will of God — to put His plans and purposes into effect. Just as unexercised faith results in passivity, and unexercised virtue results in a lack of God-sense, unexercised knowledge of God is a sure sign of one who is operating as a *hearer* of the word only rather than a *doer* of the word. It is only by exercising the word of God in our life that we become mature (Heb. 5:13–14). When we receive a revelation from the word of God, we receive authority to operate in that word; revelation is meant to be lived, not just looked at and talked about (Matt. 13:10–17; James 1:22–25).

The operation of self-control in our life enables us to be steadfast doers of the Word. The proving of our faith fosters endurance, steadfastness, and patience in our life (James 1:3; 1 Peter 1:7). Reverence, respect, and a godly life are the result of such steadfastness. When we attempt to take a short-cut in patience it produces and develops selfishness, covetousness, and even ungodly devotion to idolatry (Ex. 32:1, 7–8). When things do not go our way, do we tend to quickly find a substitute solution outside of God (idolatry) (1 John 5:21)?

✞ **<u>POSITION / OPERATION OF GRACE</u>:** (the goal and motivation of grace is love)

"And in [<u>exercising</u>] <u>godliness</u> [develop] <u>brotherly affection</u>, and in [exercising] <u>brotherly affection</u> [develop] <u>Christian love</u>" (2 Peter 1:7).

Ungodliness is powered by self-serving affections and hence can never result in any expression of godly love. When godliness is exercised, it opens the door to brotherly affection, and hence Christ-like love. As we allow grace to develop the character of God in our life, the inevitable result is godly love, first towards the brethren, then towards the world (John 13:35).

Exercising brotherly love is sometimes easier than loving the *unlovely*. It is easier to love and forgive those that return love, but if that is where our loves stops, we are immature and unforgiving. A mature love will love those who despitefully abuse, hate, and even kill you (Acts 7:59–60). The love of the world is not sourced in God, but rather in the lust of the flesh and the pride of life. This often causes one to operate in the fear of man. To *not* exercise godly love is to exercise hate (Matt. 5:43–44; 1 John 2:9–11, 15). God is love; hence godly love will express itself in a godly way. Worldly love expresses itself through the flesh, not the Spirit of God (Gal. 5:19–21; Col. 3:5).

Relationships that feed on and foster worldliness are not an expression of the righteous relationship we have in Christ. It is not just having a relationship, which is important; it is Christ's love (righteousness) working through us, which is vital. The world cannot comprehend God's love; hence, it has no relationship with Him. The world has its own definition of love, usually outside of the will of God (1 Cor. 2:14; Phil. 3:7–16; 1 John 5:20).

Statements like, "A loving God would never do that!" is often coming from an ignorance of who God is, who man is, and what needs to be done in order to find reconciliation. To try to define who God is or what He should be doing, using a human standard of love, is erroneous — a love defined by what we have done, rather than what God has done.

Christianity is founded on the fact that God has love for us, not that we have love for Him (1 John 4:10). All relationships must be defined by the righteousness that is founded in Christ, not on our good deeds. In order to truly come to know what a Christian is, you must personally know Christ and be led by the Spirit.

✞ **<u>POSITION / OPERATION OF GRACE</u>:** (grace produces fruitfulness; grace encourages us to terminate our relation with old sin habits)

"For as these <u>qualities</u> are yours and increasingly <u>abound</u> in you, they will keep [you] from being <u>idle</u> or <u>unfruitful</u> unto the [full personal] knowledge of our Lord Jesus Christ (the Messiah, the Anointed One).

For whoever lacks these qualities is <u>blind</u>, [spiritually] <u>short-sighted</u>, seeing only what is near to him, and has become oblivious [to the fact] that he was cleansed from his old sins" (2 Peter 1:8–9).

Godly qualities can be ours to have and experience. We are called to increase in them (be fruitful) and flourish with the character of Christ. When God's qualities predominate in our life, the result is always fruitful action. Faith, virtue, knowledge, self-control, perseverance, godliness, brotherly kindness, and love are active, fruitful characteristics of God. When we lack these things, we are blind, and hence idle and unfruitful — no matter how busy we may appear to be. Spiritual short-sightedness occurs when we cling to old habits and carnal patterns of behaviour — inattentive to what God has so graciously provided for us (2 Cor. 5:17).

Ignorance of what God has done for us entices us to wallow in old sins and be indifferent to iniquity — to muddy ourselves with misery and wretchedness. When we fail to grasp or receive what God has done for us, we end up trying to 'do our best' with the hope that this is 'good enough' for God. This attitude short-circuits repentance; it causes us to try to work out penance by the sweat of our brow. It never works godly character into our life. Jesus did not do penance for my sin; He died for my sin, and He requires that I be crucified with Him. Nevertheless, we live by our trust and faith in Him and His finished work (Gal. 2:20; 5:24–25).

✞ **POSITION / OPERATION OF GRACE:** (grace rescues us in times of trials and temptations)

"Now if [all these things are true, then be sure] the Lord knows how to rescue the godly out of temptations and trials, and how to keep the ungodly under chastisement until the day of judgment and doom," (2 Peter 2:9).

God rescues the godly and keeps the ungodly under chastisement — righteous rebuke. A righteous soul is tormented by unrighteous and wicked deeds, but it is the Lord who knows how to rescue us from such (2 Peter 2:7–8). Better off being a righteous soul troubled by unrighteousness trusting that the Lord knows how to deliver us, than being a wicked soul vexed by virtue, unable to understand (Matt. 13:14–15). We are not called to help God work out His plan by giving Him suggestions, but to submit to His plan allowing it to work effectually (eternally) in our life.

Whenever our life is in conflict with the character of God, know assuredly that He desires to change the condition of our heart (Ps. 51:10). To miss or sin against righteousness is to wrong and injure oneself (Prov. 1:24–33; 5:21–23; 6:12–15; 15:9–10, 31–32; 19:3; 21:21). Unrighteousness and righteousness both see each other as an abomination (Prov. 29:27).

✞ **POSITION / OPERATION OF GRACE:** (grace is extraordinarily patient)

"The Lord does not delay and is not tardy or slow about what He promises, according to some people's conception of slowness, but He is long-suffering (extraordinarily patient) toward you, not desiring that any should perish, but that all should turn to repentance" (2 Peter 3:9).

The grace of God is the goodness of God; it enables His people to receive and adopt His character. Long-suffering is a godly virtue; tardiness is not. Long-suffering thinks of others; tardiness is selfish — of the flesh. It is the goodness of God, which leads us to repentance. Without recognizing Christ Jesus and His provision for us, repentance does not happen. A hard, stubborn, and impenitent heart treasures up wrath for itself (Rom. 2:4–5).

Reconciliation is the object of God's goodness, and it should be the motivation of all our affairs as well. God desires all to repent, but this does not mean that all will turn and do so. God does not desire that man should sin; however, man still sins — reconciliation follows repentance (Mk. 1:15; Lk. 13:1–5; 17:1–4; Acts 2:28; 3:19; 8:22; 17:30; 26:20; Rev. 2:5, 16).

God does not desire that any should perish. If none truly perish, perishing becomes non-existent, unreal and untrue. God deals in reality and truth, and the truth is, that there are some who are going to perish (Mk. 16:16; Lk. 10:20; John 3:16; Phil. 4:3; Rev. 20:15).

✞ **POSITION / OPERATION OF GRACE:** (grace abides with God)

"But we look for new heavens and a new earth according to His promise, in which righteousness (uprightness, freedom from sin, and right standing with God) is to abide" (2 Peter 3:13).

The dwelling place of God is found in a new creation — a temple of righteousness created by Him. Original sin brought the curse — the fall of God's creation (Rom. 8:9–11, 18–23). It takes a new creation to replace that which is old. As a Christian we live *in* the world and are surrounded by the old, but we are not *of* the old. The new creation is not a work-over of the old; it is totally new, born-again from heaven above. It provides an abode of righteousness — a temple of right standing and right doing with God. We become vessels of eternal rightness with complete freedom from the power of sin (Col. 2:13–15). The expectation of such a blessed working of grace draws us to hasten and diligently exert ourselves, and be found in His character at His return (1 Cor. 9:24; 2 Cor. 3:18; Heb. 12:1–2; Phil. 3:7–16).

✞ **<u>OPERATION OF GRACE</u>:** (grace warns us of lawless activity and error; grace will grow in our life both now and to the day of eternity)

"Let me <u>warn</u> you therefore, beloved, that knowing these things beforehand, you should be on your <u>guard</u>, lest you be <u>carried</u> <u>away</u> by the <u>error</u> of lawless and wicked [persons and] fall from your own [present] firm condition [your own steadfastness of mind].

But <u>grow</u> in <u>grace</u> (undeserved favour, spiritual strength) and <u>recognition</u> and <u>knowledge</u> and <u>understanding</u> of our Lord and Saviour Jesus Christ (the Messiah). To Him [be] glory (honour, majesty, and splendour) both now and to the day of eternity. Amen (so be it)!" (2 Peter 3:17–18).

The grace of God trains us to reject ungodliness; it warns us to keep from being drawn away, snatched by sin and impaired by iniquity (Rom. 1:24; 2 Tim. 4:3; 2 Peter 3:3; Jas. 1:13–16; Jude 1:16–19). Knowing and acting on the knowledge of God keeps us on a firm foundation, free from error penetrating our life.

Discernment between truth and error is one of the most important qualities in a Christian walk. The Holy Spirit, working through the grace of God, leads and guides us into all truth (1 John 2:27). To grow in grace is to grow in spiritual authority and strength; it always takes place when we humbly rest in what God has done for us. It is not what we think we can do for God that is important; it is what He does through us (Col. 1:27).

The revelation of Christ and the working of the Spirit through His body are vital for Christian growth. Revelation of truth is what equips and empowers us with authority to accomplish what God has called us to do. To grow in grace is to increase in Christ-likeness. It is to become more and more effective in God — even as Jesus did (Lk. 2:40–52; Heb. 5:8). In order for us to become greater in God, it is necessary that *we* become less and less. There is no such thing as a great man of God; there is only a man who knows a great God. Being liked or loved by the world is not a part of our life — it is almost a sure sign of growth in carnality.

1 John

✞ **POSITION OF GRACE:** (grace is found in our fellowship with the Father and with His Son Jesus Christ)

"What we have seen and [ourselves] heard, we are also telling you, so that you too may realize and enjoy fellowship as partners and partakers with us. And [this] fellowship that we have [which is a distinguishing mark of Christians] is with the Father and with His Son Jesus Christ (the Messiah)" (1 John 1:3).

Grace enables us to enjoy fellowship with God directly and also through His people. God, lodging within us, gives us the unique experience of communing with Him through one another; something that anyone outside of Christ is incapable of enjoying. This Scripture deems fellowship to be a distinguishing mark of Christians. Therefore, it behoves us to ask God to give us an understanding heart of what this really means, and its significance in our life in the body of Christ. Beloved, true fellowship is important if we are to have an impact on the world. Is this not our calling as Christians? I do believe that if I was the devil, I would cause Christians to break fellowship — erasing their distinguishing mark before the world.

A true witness is one who has first-hand knowledge and testifies of what he has seen and heard. Our testimony is the on-going, life giving expression of our personal relationship with God (Rev. 12:11). To preach or try to live someone else's revelation does not represent a true personal testimony of the kingdom (Acts 19:13).

God is not interested in us having a vicarious relationship with Him or with other Christians (Eph. 4:14). Revelation is personal; there is nowhere in Scripture where we are encouraged to walk in or preach another's revelation. For example, Paul never preached Peter's revelation; he preached what God had shown him personally. A revelation from God does not contradict a revelation of God from someone else; they will always complement each other (Gal. 2:2). The purpose of fellowship is to share our personal experiences and revelations of God, and to enjoy being partners and partakers with Christ.

When we fellowship with the body of Christ, we are fellowshipping with the Father and with the Son, through one another; we experience the living Word together. This builds, matures, and unifies the body, drawing it closer to being of one mind and one soul (Acts 4:32). It is unfortunate for us that this is not common in the church today. Beloved, it is Messiah's plan and He is not going to change it to satisfy the whims of man.

✞ **POSITION OF GRACE:** (grace is only found in the Light; it manifests itself in fellowship and continually cleanses us)

"But if we [really] are living and walking in the Light, as He [Himself] is in the Light, we have [true, unbroken] fellowship with one another, and the blood of Jesus Christ His Son cleanses (removes) us from all sin and guilt [keeps us cleansed from sin in all its forms and manifestations]" (1 John 1:7).

The light of God is our lodging place; living in His light and truth marks our path-way and sojourn here on earth (Ps. 43:3). It is from this position of truth in Christ that we traverse trials and temptations, stride through sorrows, and hike through hard times. Jesus is not only in the Light, He is the Light. To catch the revelation of the body of Christ in fellowship is to see Jesus fellowshipping with Himself. Fellowship occurs when one piece of Jesus has communion with another piece of Jesus. It is where intimacy and joint participation partner together to become a companionship — co-workers, sharing in all things. He has confidential communion with those who love Him (Prov. 3:32; Acts 4:32–35).

Fellowship happens when we as God's people speak words given to us by the Spirit, using the Spirit's words to explain spiritual truths. In doing this, we become spiritually intimate with one another (1 Cor. 2:12–13).

Fellowship places all the vessels of Christ on a level playing field — there is no up-man-ship nor idolatrous projection upon certain people (carnal leadership). The focus is on Christ and Him alone. Positions of people matter not — pride is not entertained (Gal. 2:6). How can one person be more important than the next when standing in the presence of Jesus? How can one's gifting be more important than another's when both have their source in Jesus? The apostles had fellowship with the believers, and the believers had fellowship with the apostles and one another (Acts 2:42). There was mutual edification — a mutual building up of one another.

Fellowship is an operation of grace by the Spirit of God as it applies the cleansing blood of Christ to remove us from sin and guilt. When we are walking in the light, we are all united with one another. Fellowship dispels disunity and all other forms of carnal sin. Fellowship unifies; doctrines divide. Love unifies; deception divides.

Living in the Light does not mean that you are perfectly sinless; it means that you are living honestly, without deception or pretence. Nobody lives a sinless life (1 John 1:8); we are graciously called to walk honestly with one another (Mk. 13:5–6; 1 Cor. 3:18; Eph. 4:14–15; 5:6; 1 John 3:7).

The Living Word flows and operates upon us as we fellowship and mutually edify one another. A sure way to stifle maturity in the body of Christ is to replace fellowship with organized church services/programs. When we replace the living organism of Christ's body with an organization (a faction of the church), it retards the body of Christ to a carnal state — worldly and immature. Church divisions are founded because of worldliness (1 Cor. 1:10–12; 3:3–4); so do not be surprised when you find a lot of carnality/immaturity in its midst.

The church needs to see itself as one, and act accordingly. It needs to see the deception and desecration, which occurs when man divides the body of Christ into parts and pieces. It is not the Holy Spirit that 'calls' men to divide the body, and it is not the Holy Spirit that advertises for saints to find the 'church of your choice' or to 'find the church of your own flavour'. Church division/factions are carnally founded.

✞ **POSITION OF GRACE:** (it takes grace to recognize that we are sinners)

"If we say we have no sin [refusing to admit that we are sinners], we delude and lead ourselves astray, and the Truth [which the Gospel presents] is not in us [does not dwell in our hearts]" (1 John 1:8).

The error of not perceiving ourselves as sinners leads us away from the path of virtue, which results in actions that produce unrighteous or self-righteous fruit. A deluded mind is the result of an anti-Christ spirit working through our flesh. Note that it is not the devil that leads us astray; it is our own evil desires, passions, and lusts, which draw us away, baiting us like the proverbial carrot before the donkey (Jas. 1:13–16).

Truth is not merely words; it is always manifested by our actions and attitudes — our works (1 John 3:16–18). This is why God calls us to be *doers* of the word and not *hearers* only (Jas. 1:22). When we do not let truth live in our heart, we block ourselves from representing the Gospel. A life that is not demonstrating the Gospel is a life deluded; it has led itself astray by its own ungodly longings. It takes the grace of God for us to see ourselves as sinners, and then it takes the grace of God operating in our life to manifest the Gospel for the world to see (Prov. 24:16; 25:26; Phil 2:15–16; 1 Peter 2:9, 11–12).

The Christian life is not a life that is free from sin; it is a life that responds to sin in a godly manner — with godly remorse and repentance, allowing the cleansing nature of God to change the heart (Ps. 51:10–13). What identifies a Christian is not that he is perfect, but rather that he allows the person of Jesus to be manifest through him, and to deal with sin properly (Prov. 28:13; Jas. 5:16).

✞ **POSITION OF GRACE:** (grace continuously cleanses us from sin)

"If we [freely] admit that we have sinned and confess our sins, He is faithful and just (true to His own nature and promises) and will forgive our sins [dismiss our lawlessness] and [continuously] cleanse us from all unrighteousness [everything not

in conformity to His will in purpose, thought, and action]" (1 John 1:9).

The grace of God helps us to bear our responsibility for our sin. Confession — acknowledgment of our sin — is the path to mercy and freedom (Prov. 28:13; Jas. 5:16). When we have allowed sin to enter into our life, we need to acknowledge it fervently, without reservation or excuses. Such confession enables God's mercy to remove sin's contamination as it continues to cleanse us from all unrighteousness. To not confess, has consequences (Matt. 10:32–33; John 9:22; 12:42; Jas. 5:16; Rev. 3:5).

A deceived mind often cannot see its own sin, but at the same time it will point out that same sin in others. Such judgement is hypocritical, coming from a position of defeat and pretence of victory (Mk. 14:60–65; 1 Cor. 6:6–8). Beloved, both the beam and the mote are made of wood (Matt. 7:3). Justice coming from any position of hypocrisy will always be condemning. God's justice is never hypocritical; it is always redemptive (Rom. 3:23–26).

As God's grace operates through the Truth, it works redemption and restoration into a repentant soul (Mk. 1:14–15; 6:12; Lk. 13:1–5; Acts 2:38; 3:19). Anything not in conformity to His will in purpose, thought, and action will produce hypocritical, condemning judgement, and we need to repent of all such unrighteousness (sin) on a continuous basis (Phil. 3:13).

✝ **POSITION OF GRACE:** (grace convicts us of sin)

"If we say (claim) we have not sinned, we contradict His Word and make Him out to be false and a liar, and His Word is not in us [the divine message of the Gospel is not in our hearts]" (1 John 1:10).

When we are sinning and claim that we have not sinned, we contradict God. It takes the grace of God to see sin, and to confess it in order to be cleansed. Sin confessed for the purpose of excusing is not cleansing; it is a form of false-repentance. To be in contradiction to God is to place ourselves where we have neither the grace of God nor His power operating and accomplishing His will in our life. The Gospel is never manifested from a position where we are contradicting His Word (Acts 5:39–42). It takes the fear of God to magnify His Word (Acts 5:11–16; 19:17).

Sanctification is the process whereby God's grace works continuously in our life to remove all the falsehood, which our fleshly nature so tenaciously clings to (Heb. 12:1). When we live and move and have our being in the Light, we speak Truth, and live and practice the Gospel (Ps. 43:3).

✝ **OPERATION OF GRACE:** (grace is our Advocate)

"My little children, I write you these things so that you may not violate God's law and sin. But if anyone should sin, we have an Advocate (One Who will intercede for us) with the Father — [it is] Jesus Christ [the all] righteous [upright, just, Who conforms to the Father's will in every purpose, thought, and action].

And He [that same Jesus Himself] is the propitiation (the atoning sacrifice) for our sins, and not for ours alone but also for [the sins of] the whole world" (1 John 2:1–2).

Sin is essentially defined here as the violation of God's law (1 John 3:4). By the grace of God we have been set free from all condemnation of the Law, and we now serve God by the Spirit. However, we need to realize that neither the Spirit of God nor His grace will ever draw us into a position of violation to God's Law (sin). However, if anyone should sin, the grace of God obtained in Jesus Christ is our advocate with the Father. Grace comes from a position of righteousness and perfect conformity to the Father's will in every purpose, thought, and action. It enables us to appropriate God's will into our life. Grace will cause our will to become agreeable to His will (Prov. 16:3).

Our purpose in life becomes His purpose, our thoughts are renewed into His thoughts, and our work and actions become His work and actions. Sin should never play a part in this work. Grace has taken us out from under the dominion of sin and placed us into the kingdom of Christ (Col. 1:13).

The Grace of God so loved the world that He gave his only begotten Son, that whoever believes in Him should not perish, but have everlasting life.

There is not a sin in the whole world that the blood of Jesus has not atoned for. Whoever believes in God's Grace is not condemned; but whoever does not believe is condemned already, because he has not believed in the begotten Grace of God (John 3:15–18).

It is important for us to realize that Christ has not only atoned for all *our* sins, He has also atoned for the sins of the *whole world*. With this in mind, whenever someone sins against us, we need to realize that Jesus has atoned for that sin as well. This should take the sting out of our being offended by someone else's offense — it helps our soul heal quickly.

✝ **OPERATION OF GRACE:** (grace trains us to become better acquainted with Him through obedience to His commands)

"And this is how we may discern [daily, by experience] that we are coming to know Him [to perceive, recognize, understand, and become better acquainted with Him]: if we keep (bear in mind, observe, practice) His teachings (precepts, commandments)" (1 John 2:3).

The operation of the grace of God is progressive — an active practice. God not only wants us to grasp the knowledge of Him in our minds, He wants our very life to be permeated by His purposes, thoughts, and actions, which are revealed to and through us in Christ Jesus. Discernment does not come through head knowledge; it comes through the Holy Spirit prompting our spirit unto truth — reality. Discernment is to be exercised continuously in our life as we grow through experience (Hebrews 5:14).

To progressively perceive and recognize God's mind in purpose, thought, and action enables us to walk increasingly by His Spirit. Becoming better acquainted with God is discernible, and can be measured by how we observe and practice His teachings and commands. A habitual increase of godly practice in our life is an indicator of an increasing acquaintance with Him.

✝ **OPERATION OF GRACE:** (grace demands obedience to God's bidding)

"Whoever says, I know Him [I perceive, recognize, understand, and am acquainted with Him] but fails to keep and obey his commandments (teachings) is a liar, and the Truth [of the Gospel] is not in him" (1 John 2:4).

To know God is to bring our life into conformity to God's desires. To merely know about God does not affect heart change; He demands a personal relationship, not redundant head knowledge (John 9:29). Before we knew Christ, we were spiritually dead; we habitually walked and followed the course of this world. We lived and conducted ourselves according to the passions of our flesh. We obeyed the impulses of our flesh and the imaginings of our dark mind. Such a mind knows things about God, and yet has no acquaintance with Him (Matt. 7:22–23; Eph. 2:1–3).

Jesus, the Word of God, stood before the Pharisees and yet they had no acquaintance with Him. They undoubtedly knew the written Word and could quote it, but they had no recognition of the Living Word (1 Sam. 3:7; Jer. 23:36).

Beloved, what is important is not what comes out of our mouth, but rather what is manifested by our life in submission to God as God works through us. God is not interested in just our mouth speaking truth; He is interested in our life revealing the Truth. Even the father of lies claims that he knows God, yet the truth is not in him (Jas. 2:19).

As a Christian under grace, the prince of this world has no claim on us. The devil has nothing in common with us. There is not even one thing in us that belongs to him, and he has no power over us (John 14:30).

✝ **OPERATION OF GRACE:** (grace treasures obedience)

"But he who keeps (treasures) His Word [who bears in mind His precepts, who observes His message in its entirety], truly in him has the love of and for God been perfected (completed, reached maturity). By this we may perceive (know, recognize, and be sure) that we are in Him:" (1 John 2:5).

The grace of God draws us into entire obedience. It locates the areas where we are yet lacking, and then pours in His goodness, bringing us into a life of respectful obedience and abundance. We are called to attend to the Word carefully, taking care that we let its fullness work its work within us (1 Tim. 6:20; 2 Tim. 2:15–16). When we do so, the love of God is perfected within us. It is this work of grace that assures us of our position in Him, and it enables us to do His works. Faith without works is dead (Jas. 2:14–26).

To say that we believe the Word yet not do the word is self-deception (Lk. 21:8; 2 Tim. 3:13). It takes the Spirit of God to enable us to manifest the Word of God in our life. When we commit our ways to Him, He will cause our thoughts to become agreeable to His will, and so shall our plans be established and succeed (Prov. 16:3).

It is the followers of false religion that will kill you, thinking they are doing God a service (John 16:2–3). False religion is any 'religious' activity operating outside of the Spirit of God. It seeks to nullify or invalidate the Truth in the name of God. This can happen when we are being led by the flesh instead of the Spirit. For this purpose was the grace of God manifest, to destroy the works of the evil one — to overcome the power that desires to control our soul through our flesh (Gen. 4:7; 1 John 3:8). The Spirit of God can use the natural man to manifest the grace of God, but our sinful nature working through the flesh never will manifest God's kingdom (Gal. 5:17).

False religion appeals to the carnal eye and is at enmity towards God. Works of the Spirit cannot be comprehended by the carnal eye. For example; wearing a tie or a pretty dress to a 'church service' does not impress God in any way; in truth, it can blind the person into believing he is doing a service to God. These things can dazzle the carnal eye but they do nothing to change the heart (Rom. 2:28–29; 1 Cor. 2:14; Gal. 6:12–13; Col. 2:20–23).

Beloved, the kingdom of God is righteousness, peace, and joy in the Holy Spirit (Rom. 14:17); it is not recognized by our carnal senses. Our flesh/carnal nature can never enhance a work of the Spirit, and the Spirit never authorizes any work of the flesh, including carnal religion.

✝ **OPERATION OF GRACE:** (grace is manifested by what we do)

"Whoever says he abides in Him ought [as a personal debt] to walk and conduct himself in the same way in which He walked and conducted Himself" (1 John 2:6).

The grace of God compels us to live our life as Jesus did (1 Peter 2:21). The only requirement of a righteousness work in the kingdom of God is submission to the Spirit, not fidelity to the flesh. To abide in God is both to inhabit God and allow Him to inhabit us. Our lives should manifest such habitation. When one dwells in God, his conduct in life must be God's conduct; everything else is carnal hypocrisy.

The purpose of the Spirit is to lead and guide us into all truth (John 16:13; 1 John 2:27). The Spirit ushers us into freedom — freedom found only by allowing the grace of the cross of Christ to operate within our life. Grace calls us to do right even though many times we can suffer wrongly for choosing to walk in His truth (Matt. 13:19–23; 2 Tim. 3:12). We are to patiently bear up under unjust weight, knowing that it is to this, which we are called, because Christ also suffered on our behalf, leaving us an example so that we should follow in His steps.

✝ **OPERATION OF GRACE:** (loving our brother is a fruit of walking in the Light of grace)

"Whoever loves his brother [believer] abides (lives) in the Light, and in It or in him there is no occasion for stumbling or cause for error or sin.

But he who hates (detests, despises) his brother [in Christ] is in darkness and walking (living) in the dark; he is straying and does not perceive or know where his going, because the darkness has blinded his eyes" (1 John 2:10–11).

The grace of God never calls us to despise a work of God's reconciliation. Anyone who has been joined to God should never become an object of our hate. Evil is never overcome with evil; it is *only* overcome with good (Matt. 5:38–44; Rom.

12:9, 21). By grace, we have been delivered and saved from the hand of hate — from all who detest us and pursue us with hatred. Jesus never entertained hatred of people; He always spoke truth in love to all those He encountered. It was because of His mercy, goodness, and love that He made the grace of God available to us so that we may freely partake in it. Grace calls us to be imitators of such goodness (Matt. 5:10–12; Eph. 4:15).

When it comes to manifesting love, the issue is not the size or amount of love, which we manifest. The issue is the source of that love. Is it eternal love that we are manifesting or is it a temporary/conditional love (Jas. 2:1–4; 3:13–17)? We must never forget that God is the source of Christian love, and hence it should be unconditional and untouched by our circumstances or sufferings (1 John 3:18, 23; 4:19–21).

Light never causes a heart to stumble by drawing it into error or sin; it is darkness that causes people to stumble, not light. To those who believe on Him, Jesus is seen as the chief *Cornerstone*, but to those who are disobedient to the Word He becomes a *Stone of stumbling* (Is. 8:14; Rom. 9:32–33; 1 Peter 2:6–8). God's light reveals reality — the path of truth; any other so called 'light' is deceptive — having its origin in Satan. Therefore it is normal if people being used by him present themselves as ministers of reality/light (2 Cor. 11:13–15).

Beloved, to live a life that is not in the way of reality is to live in untruth and darkness. It makes one unable to perceive that he is straying, stumbling, and not able to see where he is going (Prov. 4:18–19). Light (honesty and truth) produces fellowship; darkness (dishonesty and deception) obstructs fellowship (Acts 5:1–5, 6–13; 1 John 1:7).

✝ **POSITION OF GRACE:** (grace has brought us into the name of God)

"I am writing to you, little children, because for His name's sake your sins are forgiven [pardoned through His name and on account of confessing His name]" (1 John 2:12).

The grace of God calls us first as babes in Christ, then as little children, then as young men, and then as fathers. As newborn babes, grace calls us to desire the sincere milk of the word that we may grow. As little children, grace calls us not to sin; it introduces us to our advocate, Jesus Christ. As young men we have overcome the wicked one. And as fathers, we have known Him that is from the beginning (1 John 2:13–14).

It is because of His name's sake that our sins are forgiven (Ps. 25:11; Rom. 10:9). God has saved us and called us with a holy calling, not according to our works, but according to His own purpose and plan, which was given us in Christ Jesus before the world began. The name of God is central to everything that ever has existed, exists now, and ever will exist. Grace has placed us into this Name (Acts 4:10–12; 9:13–16; Eph. 1:21–23; Phil. 2:5–11).

✝ **OPERATION OF GRACE:** (grace separates us from the world and its desires)

"Do not love or cherish the world or the things that are in the world. If anyone loves the world, love for the Father is not in him.

For all that is in the world — the lust of the flesh [craving for sensual gratification] and the lust of the eyes [greedy longings of the mind] and the pride of life [assurance in one's own resources or in the stability of earthly things] — these do not come from the Father but are from the world [itself]" (1 John 2:15–16).

The grace of God will not play second fiddle to idolatry. Light has no harmony with darkness. Grace demands us to give our heart and eyes jealously to attend to the ways of God. Having no gods before or besides the Grace of God is foundational to maintaining a holy life (Ex. 20:3; 23:13; Judges 10:13). The world and the carnal nature of man exist on a temporal foundation — built on the sand with a temporary existence. To love temporary things is to delight in temporary existence; this is divergent to the eternal life, which the Father has given us. Most of our ungodly responses in our life are founded in the love of the world, its things, and its ways.

Absoluteness, perfection, and purpose are only found by fixing our eyes on things eternal, not on things of this earth (Col. 3:1–2). Grace translates and delivers us from the power of worldly darkness and brings us into the Light — the kingdom of eternal grace (Eph. 1:3–5; Col. 1:13). Beloved, the lust of the flesh, the lust of the eyes and the pride of life do not come from the Father. The spirit of the world — right from the time of the Garden of Eden until now — constantly tries to redefine, pervert, and adulterate everything eternal and absolute. The spirit of the world attempts to make the commandment of God have no effect on our life (Mk. 7:13; Gal. 5:4; Rev. 22:18–19).

Temporal love tries to imitate eternal love, but the test of time always reveals its vanity. To embrace temporal love is to lose eternal love; to embrace eternal love makes temporal love secondary. God's eternal love is the only way to live victoriously as we sojourn here in these temporary tents in the midst of a wicked and perverse world (2 Cor. 4:18).

✞ **POSITION OF GRACE:** (grace performs the purposes of God in our lives)

"And the world passes away and disappears, and with it the forbidden cravings (the passionate desires, the lust) of it; but he who does the will of God and carries out His purposes in his life abides (remains) forever" (1 John 2:17).

The grace of God will never pass away or disappear. Grace working in our life makes us zealous in the pursuit of God's purposes. It will cause us to be heated with desire for heavenly things here on earth (Lk. 11:2; Phil. 1:9–11). The will and purposes of God are eternal, not temporal, hence, such works do not change with the fleeting of time — they abide forever.

Misdirected passions are fodder for our carnal nature. Grace calls us to build on the foundation of Christ using His eternal provisions. Each one's work will become obvious and will be revealed by fire. The fire of time will prove the worth of each one's work, revealing its source. If anyone's work endures, he will receive a reward; if anyone's work is burned, he will suffer loss, but he himself will be saved, but only as by fire (1 Cor. 3:10–15).

A life that is purposed on the pursuit of doing God's will, is a life, which will be driven by His grace to accomplish it. Grace calls us to carry out the plans and purposes of God in our life; all such work has eternal significance. All other work has little or no eternal value; it is of small significance.

✞ **POSITION OF GRACE:** (grace keeps our hearts in Christ Jesus — our dwelling place)

"As for you, keep in your hearts what you have heard from the beginning. If what you heard from the first dwells and remains in you, then you will dwell in the Son and in the Father [always].

And this is what He Himself has promised us — the life, the eternal [life]" (1 John 2:24–25).

The grace of God has opened our ears to hear God both now and forever; we are to respond to the eternal Living Word. The carnal man cannot recognize nor receive things of eternal nature.

Keeping things of God in our heart equips us for spiritual warfare. Note that the weapons of Christian warfare are not of carnal nature; they are not of man's device, nor are they employed by human power (John 18:3; 2 Cor. 10:4). One of our greatest weapons is prayer, which is faster than the speed of light, powerful, and effectual in Christ — able to carry us through anything (Eph. 6:10–18; Jas. 5:16).

The grace of God dwells within us, training our hearts and minds to reside in righteousness as we live our life in godliness. Grace does not call us to walk in the darkened understanding of the world, alienated from the life of God (Eph. 4:18; Col. 1:21). It calls us out of the world, and separates us from the ignorance and insensitive blindness, which the world habitually dwells in.

It is necessary for us to exercise what we have acquired in our hearts. Otherwise we stand to lose it (Lk. 19:23–26; Jas. 1:22–24). When we dwell in the truth, it will result in the truth being lived out and manifested in our life. Grace positions us and calls us to dwell in the Son and in the Father, with the promise of eternal life.

✞ **OPERATION OF GRACE**: (grace keeps us from being deceived)

"I write this to you with reference to those who would deceive you [seduce and lead you astray]" (1 John 2:26).

Misrepresentation of the Truth and the Gospel is a deadly error for any Christian to fall into. Seduction away from the thoughts and purposes of God is demonically designed to misrepresent God, and to delude the soul with false or synthetic religion. It always replaces and fabricates a false image of God, which is more pleasing and logical to the flesh. The grace of God is not always logical; it is not designed to please the flesh and its carnal ways. Any distortion of truth is at best a complete lie and will never reproduce kingdom life (Gen. 3:1–4).

We are responsible for what we believe; we can never blame distortion of truth on a false teacher, a false prophet, or even the devil himself (Gen. 3:5–8). The only significant endorsement we ever receive is from the Holy Spirit — the Anointing that resides within (John 16:13; 1 John 2:26–27). Endorsement by man or the world is not founded in the kingdom of God (John 19:10–11; Gal. 1:1). At best, man and the world can only give you a temporal, carnal endorsement — a religious certificate / a worldly authorization (1 Cor. 3:1–4).

✞ **POSITION / OPERATION OF GRACE**: (grace permanently abides within us, teaching us)

"But as for you, the anointing (the sacred appointment, the unction) which you received from Him abides [permanently] in you; [so] then you have no need that anyone should instruct you. But just as His anointing teaches you concerning everything and is true and is no falsehood, so you must abide in (live in, never depart from) Him [being rooted in Him, knit to Him], just as [His anointing] has taught you [to do]" (1 John 2:27).

The grace of God abides within and hence all godly teaching is confirmed from within — we have no need that anyone should instruct us. The body of Christ has been deluded into believing the half-truth, or lie, that we need someone to instruct us. This blindness causes its adherents to be unable to hear and hence unable to believe the truth, when Truth speaks (John 8:45).

God can use teachers to teach us, but it is the residency of the Holy Spirit within us that confirms whether a teaching is true. We are responsible for our own faith. If we believe error, it is not someone else's fault, it is our own responsibility.

Our ability to learn relies upon the anointing, which dwells within us, not upon some other person's anointing as they speak. It is the unction within us, which teaches us, not someone else's ability to teach well. One person's anointing is never designed by God to have control or authority over another person (Matt. 20:25–27; 2 Cor. 1:24). If we believe that His anointing is within us to teach us, then we can rely on the fact that whatever He teaches is always true and contains no falsehood or half-truths, which would seduce and lead us astray.

The word of God is the only word wherein the Author abides within, and promises to lead and guide you into all that He is teaching you (John 1:1; 6:63).

The unction that He has given us teaches us concerning everything. It lacks nothing and can only be experienced by Him dwelling in us, and us abiding in Him. The moment we turn aside from that anointing, we begin to believe half-truths that will cause our belief to be tossed and shaken (Is. 44:19–20). We end up living in a dysfunctional and unfruitful belief system. God has given us a strong foundation (the Rock) and the good soil of His righteousness to truly grow and mature in Him. We need to build on that foundation with precious stones, not straw. But when we believe in lies, we allow tares to be planted in our good soil. As these tares (untruths) are allowed to grow in our lives, we become less fruitful, and we soon find it difficult to hear truth (Matt. 13:18–25; John 8:43–47).

It is only the Spirit's internal unction that leads us into maturity and allows us to live a life where we do/manifest the Living Word — Christ. The grace of God teaches us to abide in and be rooted in Him. As we fellowship with one another we are knit together with every joint supplying and building itself up in love (Eph. 4:16). Fellowship is a sacred appointment; it is a distinguishing mark of Christians.

✞ **POSITION / OPERATION OF GRACE:** (grace gives us perfect confidence at His coming)

"And now, little children, abide (live, remain permanently) in Him, so that when He is made visible, we may have and enjoy perfect confidence (boldness, assurance) and not be ashamed and shrink from Him at His coming" (1 John 2:28).

To remain permanently in Him is the calling of God on every Christian's life (John 14:16; 15:4, 7). It is only when we abide in Him that we experience perfect confidence in our life. Security is a surety found only in the Spirit of God; no flesh can ever glory in His presence. God was manifest in the flesh — the flesh cannot manifest God by its own power; it takes the Spirit of God to manifest Himself through our body and soul (John 1:1, 14).

God is still manifesting Himself through us, and as we come together in fellowship, are we not making Him visible in our midst? When we boldly and confidently assemble together, we need not be ashamed of who we are — His children practicing the truth. Our works will be prompted by divine help and in complete dependence upon Him. (John 3:19–21). When we dwell (live in) the Spirit, our life becomes a bold, confident testimony of the Living Christ (Eph. 6:19–20; Heb. 4:16; 13:6).

✞ **POSITION / OPERATION OF GRACE:** (grace enables us to walk righteously in Him)

"If you know (perceive and are sure) that He [Christ] is [absolutely] righteous [conforming to the Father's will in purpose, thought and action], you may also know (be sure) that everyone who does righteously [and is therefore in like manner conformed to the divine will] is born (begotten) of Him [God]" (1 John 2:29).

The grace of God teaches us to manifest God — to be conformed to the divine will in purpose, thought, and action. Grace calls us to walk (live) in His steps — Christ is both our example and our life (Gal. 2:20). When we know for certain that our position is in absolute righteousness, it frees us to walk in that righteousness and to operate in the grace and power of God. For God has made Him to be sin for us; that we might be made the righteousness of God in Christ (2 Cor. 5:21).

Righteousness cannot be manufactured or made-up. It is something that is only imparted by believing in the work of Christ — by being born again — by receiving His life from above. He purposes us to live out a life full of grace as a representative of Christ here on earth. It is our position of righteousness that saves us — not our righteous acts. However, this being said, a position of righteousness without righteous acts is dead (Jas. 2:17–22).

✞ **POSITION OF GRACE:** (the grace of God entrusts us with his love)

"See what [an incredible] quality of love the Father has given (shown, bestowed on) us, that we should [be permitted to] be named and called and counted the children of God! And so we are! The reason that the world does not know (recognize, acknowledge) us is that it does not know (recognize, acknowledge) Him" (1 John 3:1).

The very essence of God's love has been accorded to us. The virtue and capacity of our Lord's love has been freely bestowed upon us that we may freely employ its use. Grace says, "Love I leave with you, my love I give unto you: not as the world gives, give I unto you. Let not your heart be troubled, neither let it be afraid, for the prince of the world has nothing in me, but that the world may know the love of the Father, arise, go, and even so, do" (John 14:27, 30–31 KJV paraphrased).

Beloved, as children of God, we are called to resemble our Father. The reason the world does not recognize the family of God is because it does not recognize God. As a disciple of Christ, we have been given the privilege of recognizing God, and hence, we have now been enabled to recognize the family of God and live in harmony with it. We are positioned in peace and accord with God and all of His children (1 Tim. 5:21).

Grace has granted to us all things pertaining to life and godliness and every man that follows our beloved Saviour must take up his cross and follow Him (Lk. 9:23). It is by the grace of God that He has loved us; it is by the grace of God that we are counted as the children of God; and it is by the grace of God that we alone recognize Him and His family.

✞ **<u>POSITION OF GRACE</u>:** (grace makes us God's children here and now, destined to resemble Him)

"Beloved, we are [even here and] now <u>God's children</u>; it is not yet disclosed (made clear) what we shall be [hereafter], but we know that when He comes and is <u>manifested</u>, we shall [as God's children] resemble and be like Him, for we shall see Him just as He [really] is" (1 John 3:2).

Our position of grace in God is here and now. The life of Christ is founded in the eternities and hence cannot be fully grasped here and now. Christ is the expression of the absolute, never changing, eternal God. What we are *now*, spiritually, cannot be discerned with the carnal, worldly eye. What we *will be* is rooted in what we are *now*. The world does not recognize God and His ways; it lives in temporal reality (2 Cor. 3:13–16).

The reality of truth is only found in Christ; it is only in Him that we become the children of God (John 3:3–8; 1 Peter 1:23). Our Father is God Himself and as His children we derive all our significance and being from Him. Our position in Him freely gives us our godly birth-right and inherited characteristics (Acts 20:32; Eph. 1:11–23). It is the very Spirit of God, which groans within us, giving us a longing in our soul to resemble and be like Him — as the deer pants for the water, so our soul longs after Him (Rom. 8:13–19).

✞ **<u>POSITION / OPERATION OF GRACE</u>:** (grace cleanses and purifies our souls)

"And every one who has this <u>hope</u> [resting] on Him <u>cleanses</u> (purifies) himself just as He is pure (chaste, undefiled, guiltless)" (1 John 3:3).

Godliness comes from knowing God personally. All righteous works in our life come from our position of righteousness in Christ; all other works are as filthy rags before the grace of God (Is. 64:6). The Spirit of God working within us, drawing us towards Him and His character causes us to desire to be clothed with heavenly robes (2 Cor. 5:2–4; Col. 3:10–14). For truly, as long as we are in this earthly body we cry out and long to be with the Lord (Ps. 42:1). It is our hope in Him and our resting in Him that cleanses our souls.

✞ **<u>OPERATION OF GRACE</u>:** (grace teaches us to practice righteousness)

"Boys (lads), let no one <u>deceive</u> and lead you astray. He who <u>practices</u> <u>righteousness</u> [who is upright, conforming to the divine will in purpose, thought, and action, living a consistently conscientious life] is righteous, even as He is righteous" (1 John 3:7).

The practice of grace in our life is a mark of Christ, which distinguishes us from the world. Doing what God desires is the true test of being a Christian. A Christian cannot be led astray by following the Spirit; he is only led astray by following man and the ways/spirit of the world.

Distinguishing God's ways from the ways of the world is vital to a child of God. We are called to be conformed to the image of His Son, not to be conformed to this world. In truth, we prove what the divine will of God is through our lives (Rom. 12:1–2; 2 Cor. 11:13; Rev. 2:2). We are called to follow the Spirit of God, not the spirit of the world or fallen man. Beloved, whatever we submit to is what will direct our life (Rom. 7:5–6; 8:12–14).

✞ **<u>OPERATION OF GRACE</u>:** (grace teaches us to live and love in truth and reality)

"Little children, let us not <u>love</u> [merely] in theory or in speech but in <u>deed</u> and in <u>truth</u> (in practice and in sincerity).

By this we shall come to know (perceive, recognize, and understand) that we are of the <u>Truth</u>, and can <u>reassure</u> (quiet, conciliate, and pacify) our <u>hearts</u> in His presence," (1 John 3:18–19).

The grace of God is not merely a theory or a speculation; it is the foundation of eternal reality (the person of Jesus Christ), working truth in and through our lives. Truth is not a philosophical debate; it is the reality of God's love (the person of Jesus Christ) manifesting Himself through us (John 13:33–38; 18:33–38; 19:1–11). The reality of grace is God's truth in action — God's will; the reality of Satan's domain is deception in action — disobedience to the purposes of God (John 8:44; Eph. 2:2).

Grace operates beyond the boundaries of God's natural laws, for example, Jesus and Peter walking on the water, or raising Lazarus from the dead, or Philip caught up by the Spirit. Truth is an expression of God's eternal principles, which are to be lived out in the present. They are only accessible by placing our faith in the work of Jesus Christ. They are an expression of God's character. Grace makes His eternal principles available to us as we experience His reality working in our life (Mk. 4:36–41).

Though faith and grace are intangible to the carnal man, they are the *only* divinely designed means of approaching God. They are essential in finding His perfect will, and living it out. The kingdom of God cannot be acquired by guesswork or by surmising the truth; it is only found by faith, and it is only taught to us by the Holy Spirit's anointing, which is within us (John 14:26; 1 John 2:27).

Practising love ushers us into the recognition that we are of the Truth and reassures our hearts in His presence.

✝ **OPERATION OF GRACE:** (grace is greater than self-guilt and self-condemnation)

"Whenever our hearts in [tormenting] self-accusation make us feel guilty and condemn us. [For we are in God's hands.] For He is above and greater than our consciences (our hearts), and He knows (perceives and understands) everything [nothing is hidden from Him].

And, beloved, if our consciences (our hearts) do not accuse us [if they do not make us feel guilty and condemn us] we have confidence (complete assurance and boldness) before God;" (1 John 3:20–21).

The grace of God is stronger than any condemnation or guilt, which man can possibly find himself bond by. Self-accusation, self-condemnation, and self-quilt all carry with them the weight of torment; they are never liberating. They always cater to the flesh; they are never a work of God. Attitudes like 'should have', 'would have', and 'could have' are all postures that lead one down the path of self-accusation.

Grace operates in the *now*, not in the past. Dragging ourselves into the past only ensnares and traps us into areas of self-condemnation, when we *should* be living in the *now* (1 Cor. 13:13; Gal. 2:20; Heb. 10:38; 11:1). Christ's life is only found in the now, therefore to attempt to walk in the past only causes stumbling, like looking over your shoulder while walking ahead.

The attributes of God are eternal. Anything that we do by the Spirit of God is eternal by nature and *never* needs an apology. A work of the Spirit can be convicting, but it is *never* condemning. The purpose of the cross is to redeem our acts of wrong-doing and to place our focus on right-doing (Titus 2:11–15).

Guilt is a legal position that has been forever dealt with — whether we feel it or not. Self-condemnation happens by not seeing ourselves the way God sees us. God is our ever-present help in our time of need (Heb. 4:16). God's Word — operating by the Spirit — is liberating; it sets us eternally free (John 8:36).

✝ **POSITION OF GRACE:** (grace has defeated all agents of antichrist)

"Little children, you are of God [you belong to Him] and have [already] defeated and overcome them [the agents of the antichrist], because He Who lives in you is greater (mightier) than he who is in the world" (1 John 4:4).

The grace of God is bigger than the devil and his works, and it is bigger than our flesh and its temptations. When we live in the revelation that 'we are of God', we know for certainty that 'we belong to Him'. There is nothing that can overcome or remove us from this incredible position of grace in our life. As sure as David knew that Goliath was defeated, we too can be assured that all things, which are anti-Christ are defeated and have no power or authority over us, unless it is given from above (John 16:33; 19:11; Acts 7:54–60).

The agents of anti-Christ do not like to submit to the authority of Christ living in us; however, they have no choice (Matt. 17:14–20). The spirit of antichrist does not acknowledge that Jesus Christ has come in the flesh today. As surely as Jesus was attacked and accused before He died on the cross, He is still attacked and accused today, because He sends us out even as the Father sent Him (Matt. 27:38–44).

Note that the word does *not* say, "He who lived in the past *was* greater than he who is in the world." Beloved, we carry about within us now, the Christ — the living Jesus — in these tents. The purpose that the Son of God is manifest in us, is that we may destroy the work of the evil one and his influence over our life. Our position in Christ guarantees that the agents of antichrist are defeated and overcome. Walking/living by the Spirit of God — the authority of God — is vital for a fruitful Christian life. It is not life's circumstances, which determine if we are in the victory; it is our position in Christ. Being *in Christ* is the highest authority, which anyone can possess.

✞ **POSITION OF GRACE:** (grace has birthed Christ's love in us and directs it to both the Father and to one another)

"Everyone who believes (adheres to, trusts, and relies on the fact) that Jesus is the Christ (the Messiah) is a born-again child of God; and everyone who loves the Father also loves the one born of Him (His offspring)" (1 John 5:1).

God has been birthed in His people, making them born-again children of God — born from above. Since God is love, we have His love permanently dwelling within us ready and willing to manifest the love of the Father and the Son. To say that we love God, but not love His offspring, positions us in a lie. If we say that we have fellowship with God — we love God — and yet not love our brother, we lie, and do not live in the truth.

Beloved, know that no lie is of the truth, as surely as no darkness is of the Light. We are called to test the spirits (1 John 4:1). The grace which we have received from God lives in us, and we do not need any man to teach us. The Spirit of truth will teach us all things, which pertain unto life and godliness. He is truth —He is no falsehood — and even as the Spirit has taught us, we shall live and love in Him (1 John 2:27). Grace draws us into Him, causing us to love to learn, and to learn to love.

We, as His offspring, possess the truth that Jesus is the Christ, the Messiah. We have been made His children by being born-again (born from above), by trusting in Him and His work on the cross. He has purchased us and made us His own by the grace of God (Matt. 1:21; Lk. 7:11–16; 1 Peter 2:9–12).

✞ **OPERATION OF GRACE:** (grace teaches us to love — to be obedient towards God and His ways)

"By this we come to know (recognize and understand) that we love the children of God: when we love God and obey His commands (orders, charges) — [when we keep His ordinances and are mindful of His precepts and His teaching]" (1 John 5:2).

The love of God birthed within us compels us to love one another. God's grace teaches us to renounce all ungodliness and to minister to one another in godliness. To act in love towards anyone is to respond the way God desires us to — always in obedience to His word (Col. 3:13–14).

God always stands in opposition to the world and its ways, but he never disavows His own ways, because He is faithful. Obedience towards the Word's commands is the test of love towards one another, and hence towards God. Love never negates the orders, teachings, and commands of the God of grace.

The love you portray is always manifested by the life you live — you cannot separate your life from the ministry of love that you have been called to live. When we attempt to separate our life from 'our ministry' we end up missing the operation of God's word and love in our life (Acts 5:1–2). Better a life that manifests obedience to God, than a vessel, which speaks of righteousness, yet acts in disobedience to God's ways.

✞ **OPERATION OF GRACE:** (grace teaches us to obey His commands)

"For the [true] love of God is this: that we do His commands [keep His ordinances and are mindful of His precepts and teaching]. And these orders of His are not irksome (burdensome, oppressive, or grievous)" (1 John 5:3).

By the grace of God, our new, born-again nature delights and endorses the commands, precepts, and teachings of God (Rom. 7:22). To the flesh and our carnal nature they are irksome, vexing, exasperating, wearisome, inconvenient, annoying, intolerable, and irritating; but to the Spirit of God within us, they are pure, holy, and just.

Beloved, it is not the Law of God, which proves fatal to us; it is sin that proves fatal. To continue in disobedience to God is a contradiction to the purposes and power of grace working in our life. The Law is spiritual, filled with eternal precepts spoken by God. Without the grace of God, the sin defined by Gods precepts and ordinances kills you (Rom. 7:25). The Spirit of God defines ungodliness for us, and grace teaches us to denounce sin any right to work in our life (Rom. 8:3). A life founded in God will not contradict His life-defining precepts. Grace never gives us authority to walk in disobedience to God (sin) (Rom. 7:7).

✞ **POSITION / OPERATION OF GRACE:** (grace empowers our faith to overcome the world)

"For whatever is born of God is victorious over the world; and this is the victory that conquers the world, even our faith.

Who is it that is victorious over [that conquers] the world but he who believes that Jesus is the Son of God [who adheres to, trusts in and relies on that fact]" (1 John 5:4–5)?

The world and its ways are overcome by our faith in Jesus Christ. The grace of God has positioned us in the arena of victory. It is in this place of faith that grace enables us to overcome the affinities and fashions of this world. The tendencies of this world follow the prince of the power of the air — that demon spirit that constantly works in an unbelieving heart.

Unbelief in Christ goes against the purposes of God; belief in Christ positions us and operates against the onslaught we experience from the spirit of the world (Matt. 13:58). We are *in* the world but we are not *of* the world. Grace teaches us to deny the passions of the flesh and the thoughts of the mind, which go against the purposes of God (Mk. 9:24). Grace commands our actions to be prompted by faith in Christ Jesus. Faith is grace in action. It can be visibly seen as obedience to the Word and His commands (Matt. 8:8).

✞ **POSITION OF GRACE:** (grace gives us absolute knowledge of our salvation)

"I write this to you who believe in (adhere to, trust in, and rely on) the name of the Son of God [in the peculiar services and blessings conferred by Him on men], so that you may know [with settled and absolute knowledge] that you [already] have life, yes, eternal life" (1 John 5:13).

The grace of God gives us the absolute knowledge that we are saved. Absoluteness is an eternal characteristic; it is not temporal. Grace has bestowed on us blessings and services, which eternally enrich and empower our life. Eternal knowledge comes by revelation, not logic or philosophy (Col. 2:8). This is why the world and its ways are not able to come to know God; indeed the world cannot receive the teachings and revelations of God (1 Cor. 2:14).

The god of this world blinds unbelieving hearts and minds to the affairs of God, so that they can neither discern nor receive truth (Matt. 13:18–19). It takes true repentance to strip away the veil placed on the heart and mind of unbelief. It takes revelation, not common sense or logic, to know who you are and what you have in Christ Jesus — Life eternal (Gal. 1:12).

✞ **OPERATION OF GRACE:** (grace is sovereign)

"If anyone sees his brother [believer] committing a sin that does not [lead to] death (the extinguishing of life) he will pray and [God] will give him life [yes, He will grant life to all those whose sin is not

one leading to death]. There is a sin [that leads] to death; I do not say that one should pray for that" (1 John 5:16).

The grace of God is sovereign. It is God alone who defines His grace, and God alone who enables its working. To redefine anything that God has defined is to make oneself out to be God. Grace has come to reconcile man to God — to invalidate the separation of man and God caused by original sin — "For in the day that you eat of it, you shall surely die" (Gen. 2:17; Eph. 2:1, 5).

Grace is divinely designed to teach us to deny all ungodliness, thus avoiding the fruit of sin and death in our life. Various sins under the Old Covenant required the death penalty — such sins led directly to death.

Under the New Covenant there can be sin that is done deliberately and wilfully after having received the full knowledge of the truth. Such action requires another sacrifice (beyond Jesus), of which there is none; but only a certain awful expectation of God's judgement, which will devour His enemies (Heb. 10:26–31).

There is the sin of speaking against the Holy Spirit — attributing to the devil the manifest work of the Holy Spirit — this will not be forgiven, either in this age or in the age to come (Matt. 12:31–32). Beloved, the grace of God is sovereign, and all sin must be left in the hands of our sovereign God and Saviour.

✝ **OPERATION OF GRACE:** (grace invalidates sin through repentance)

"All wrongdoing is sin, and there is sin which does not [involve] death [that may be repented of and forgiven]" (1 John 5:17).

The grace of God enables us to do right. It is sanctioned by God to keep us from sin and its consequences. Repentance and forgiveness is the absolute foundation of the Christian walk, and it cannot be tampered with. All wrongdoing is sin, and it is important to walk in God's definition of life's *do's* and *don'ts*, directed graciously by the Spirit of God. Grace never authorizes us to sin; it enables us to overcome wrongdoing with right doing — doing what the Spirit of God is saying (Gen. 4:7; Rom.12:21).

Standing in righteousness is standing in the position of God's presence. To lose one's natural life in the process of standing for righteousness is *not* wrongdoing — it is right-doing. To lose anything because of right-doing is within the bounds of righteousness.

Anything gained through wrongdoing is outside of God's will. All right-doing is accomplished by the Spirit of God, by grace. God's will operating in our life is only possible through the grace of God. It is divinely designed to accomplish the will of God, which cannot be altered. God's purposes and plans can be rejected, redefined, spoken evil of, and even mocked and hated, but the will of God always is in the hands of the Lord (Prov. 16:9, 25; 19:21; 20:24; 21:1–2).

The grace of Gethsemane — the oil press — is the place where we find and live in God's will. The oil press is not an easy place — Jesus knows that. Beloved, it is better to accompany Jesus into the place called Gethsemane, and hear Him say, "Sit ye here, while I go and pray yonder", than to be a traitor to truth — a betrayer of righteousness (Matt. 26:25, 36). It is better to be the oil of God to those around us, than to be the refuse of unrighteousness, the dung of disobedience. Grace has not called us to be thrown away, having no eternal purpose and not manifesting the purpose of God to those around us (Phil. 3:8). Seeing God's purpose for His people is the oil, which anoints us to do His word — to go into all nations, to make disciples, to baptise them, and to teach them all that Jesus has shown us (Matt. 28:18–20).

✝ **OPERATION OF GRACE:** (grace protects us from the evil one and his works — sin)

"We know [absolutely] that any one born of God does not [deliberately and knowingly] practice committing sin, but the One Who was begotten of God carefully watches over and protects him [Christ's divine presence within him preserves him against the evil], and the wicked one does not lay hold (get a grip) on him or touch [him]" (1 John 5:18).

The grace of God is divinely birthed within us to safeguard us from the evil one's works and grip. Grace walks with us so that the wicked one does not get a foothold in our life. Our resistance is not against flesh and blood, but against wickedness and its works (Eph. 4:27; 6:12; 2 Peter 3:17). Anything outside of the will of God is evil. All of creation was created by God, and it is only Him Who gives moral definition to life's purpose, its use, and its final outcome. Fallen man, created in God's image, will always come short of the plans and purposes of God.

God has redeemed man by His own hand through Christ Jesus, by His willing death on the cross (Matt. 26:36–42). Man has been given a will, created in God's image. Fallen man can now choose a new, resurrected life made available because of the resurrection power of Jesus Christ. To have this revelation and then to deliberately and knowingly act contrary to such divine wisdom is not wise. To reject the work of Christ is to reject eternal life.

God preserves us even when evil seemingly overcomes us. Stephen, when he was stoned, was preserved by God, but not overcome by evil. You can tell this by his actions and response — his works (Acts 7:60). The more we acknowledge God's grace, the more we receive it and allow it to affectively operate in our life.

✝ **POSITION OF GRACE:** (grace has delivered us from the power of the world)

"We know [positively] that we are of God, and the whole world [around us] is under the power of the evil one" (1 John 5:19).

The grace of God has placed us in the absolute victory of our Lord and Saviour, Jesus Christ. Grace teaches us to deny ungodliness — all untrue, lifeless, deadly, imitations of truth. Beloved, we are *in* the world but we are not *of* the world. In this life we are surrounded by the power of the evil-one and his followers. If we choose to follow his ways, we will miss Christ and treat the grace of God as vain — leaving a sure foothold for the devil to find place to work in our life (Eph. 2:1–2).

We need to walk in obedience to the power of grace, not to the prince of the power of the air (the world). We need to walk carefully and circumspect, with the will of God being our focal point (John 12:35–36; Eph. 5:8). Grace never calls us to walk in the careless ease of the world; it calls us to carefully keep a watchful eye, because the evil one, who is against us, is prowling about like a lion in search of souls for food (1 Peter 5:8).

When you are in the lion's den and smell the lion's breath, beloved, that is when you need to intimately know God is with you (Rom. 8:31). Jesus did not take us out of the world; He is still here walking and working through His body today, holding out the truth of His kingdom through us, to the world around us (Phil. 2:16; 1 Thess. 2:13).

✝ **POSITION / OPERATION OF GRACE:** (grace has come to lead us into our walk of eternal life)

"And we [have seen and] know [positively] that the Son of God has [actually] come to this world and has given us understanding and insight [progressively] to perceive (recognize) and come to know better and more clearly Him Who is true; and we are in Him Who is true — in His Son Jesus Christ (the Messiah). This [Man] is the true God and Life eternal.

Little children, keep yourselves from idols (false gods) — [from anything and everything that would occupy the place in your heart due to God, from any sort of substitute for Him that would take first place in your life]. Amen, (So let it be)" (1 John 5:20–21).

Knowing God is only accomplished through the grace of God and it is not a one-time experience; it is progressive. Becoming a disciple of Christ (a Christian) is the starting point. He places us in our position of eternal life, but being a Christian is a life time process. Coming to progressively know the true God and eternal life, and living out the revelation of Christ in our life, is accomplished only by the operation of grace (1 Thess. 1:9).

To know the ways of God is to know His works; you cannot separate God from His works. They are one and the same. To try to separate God from His works is to separate His life from our life. God calls us into fellowship — life together in the Spirit of God. Life is a continuous experience of the Holy Spirit in this time called *now*.

False religion separates God from His works and separates our natural life from our spiritual life. False religion divides the church and then builds its own organization around its own particular doctrine. It replaces spiritual fellowship with natural organization and its activities. Fellowship will spontaneously happen when the Spirit of God has His way in our life.

False religion separates life and ministry. Beloved, our life is our ministry. If you are living a life of deception, yet God uses you to lead people to the Lord, the true question you need to answer is, "How is your ministry (life) of deception doing?" God is only interested in your life (what you are doing); He is not interested in your ministry (what He is doing). God already knows what He is accomplishing, but He is interested in seeing you walk in His ways. Remember, just because God speaks through a donkey, does not mean that the donkey is saved (Num. 22:28; Lk. 19:40).

In truth, the only temporal place God is interested in is our bodies; and when we have worn them out — finished His purpose, run the race, completed the course set before us — He will give us new, eternal bodies (2 Tim. 4:6–8).

God operates in the *now*, hence the only important and significant time for us is *now*. The eternal place where God resides is in fellowship — in the heart, *now*. Our carnal nature desires to separate the natural life and the spiritual life because of the desire to control, rather than be controlled by the Spirit of God. All control outside of the Spirit of God is idolatry. As children of God, we must keep away from anything that would take the place of God in our hearts.

2 John

✝ **POSITION OF GRACE:** (grace causes truth to live with us forever)

"The elderly elder [of the church addresses this letter] to the elect (chosen) lady (Cyria) and her children, whom I truly love — and not only I but also all who are [progressively] learning to recognize and know and understand the Truth —

Because the Truth which lives and stays on in our hearts and will be with us forever:" (2 John 1:1–2).

Grace has written the law of God in our hearts; this is eternal Truth (Jer. 31:33; 2 Cor. 3:3; Heb. 8:8–10). Truth is progressively learned as we become better acquainted with it; it grows within us — yet it is absolute. As Christians share the truth with one another, everyone benefits. Often, like the proverbial five blind men describing an elephant as they touch different parts of it, at first truth may seem contradictory. However, revelation of truth is never contradictory; it is always complimentary (2 Peter 3:14–18).

Although we have a personal relationship with God, it is also experienced through His body, and it is never divisive or in opposition to it. Truth has the power of life embedded within it. It is never ending and always growing in hearts of good soil. Our Christian objective is not to become so godly (mature) that we are independent of God. However, just as the Father, Son, and Holy Spirit are one with each other and their existence is vitally related to each other, we are to be like minded in our relationship to Christ and His body (Heb. 11:40).

Maturity is only manifested when we are totally dependent on Jesus. The goal of maturity is to bear fruit and to bring life to those around us. Even as the Father, Son, and Holy Spirit are alive, truth is alive (John 6:63; Rev. 22:19).

✝ **POSITION / OPERATION OF GRACE:** (grace causes us to walk in truth and love)

"Grace be with you, mercy, and peace from God the Father, and from the Lord Jesus Christ, the son of the Father, in truth and love" (2 John 1:3 KJV).

"I was greatly delighted to find some of your children walking (living) in [the] Truth, just as we have been commanded by the Father [Himself]" (2 John 1:4).

The trinity of grace, peace, and truth are inseparable. Truth and peace cannot be found outside of grace — the only thing that renders us free (John 1:17; 8:32). Grace and truth came by the Prince of Peace (Is. 9:6).

Truth can only be found through grace; it is divinely designed to be the foundation of our life. Mankind fell into sin by not living in the truth; hence, he reaped the consequence of cavorting with untruth — death (separation from fellowship with God) (Gen. 2:17; 3:3–11). Only by grace can we find fellowship with God again, and have the barrier of sin broken forever (Is. 59:2; Rom 8:2–3). God offers us truth; it is our responsibility to know this truth and to live in it. This brings with it a harvest of righteousness, peace, and gladness.

✝ **OPERATION OF GRACE:** (grace guides us in our walk of love)

"And this is love, that we walk after His commandments. This is the commandment, that as ye have heard from the beginning, ye should walk in it" (2 John 1:6 KJV).

The grace of God is the operation of God's love over, in, and through our life. His commands, which are filled with life and wisdom are the guidelines for our life. They are an aroma of life to our inner man. God's first commandment is to love Him, and His second is like unto the first in that we are commanded to love our neighbour (Mk. 12:29–31). God's commandment of love is not forceful or domineering; it is founded in wisdom and as we take it to heart, it begets freedom. The operation of grace empowers us to live according to God's command of love — founded in God and furnished freely to others (1 Cor. 13:4–8). God's love requires a willing heart to respond to it, and an compliant vessel to manifest it. To be guided by God is to be guided by love, because God is love (1 John 4:16–21).

✞ **OPERATION OF GRACE:** (grace helps us to persevere in fellowship in the living body of Christ, which brings great reward)

"For many imposters (seducers, deceivers, and false leaders) have gone out into the world, men who will not acknowledge (confess, admit) the coming of Jesus Christ (the Messiah) in bodily form. Such a one is the imposter (the seducer, the deceiver, the false leader, the antagonist of Christ) and the antichrist.

Look to yourselves (take care) that you may not lose (throw away or destroy) all that we and you have laboured for, but that you may [persevere until you] win and receive back a perfect reward [in full]" (2 John 1:7–8).

We need to catch the revelation that the body of Christ is truly Christ in His body. When we fail to recognize such, we miss much of the workings of Christ both in our life and in the life of the body of Christ.

Even before God created the world it was His plan for His body to manifest Christ (Eph. 1:4–9). The most devious deed that the spirit of antichrist could do is to instigate factions in the body of Christ, causing us to lose the prize/reward of fellowship that Christ so passionately died for. We, as the body of Christ, should be diligent in labouring together, persevering to keep our full reward by continuing in the teaching of Christ and not wandering beyond it.

Walking in Truth is vital for the Christian life. We are responsible for our walk in the Lord, not someone else's walk. To delegate your personal responsibility of maturing in the Lord to another person, or organization, is a sure way to end up missing the mark (Phil. 3:10–17). Within the body of Christ there is a bond of love and care for one another, which compels us to strive forward both for the benefit of ourselves and for the body as a whole (2 Cor. 8:16–17; Phil. 1:19–20; Heb. 2:1).

✞ **OPERATION OF GRACE:** (grace does not place its blessing on works of evil)

"For he who wishes him success [who encourages him, wishing him Godspeed] is a partaker in his evil doings" (2 John 1:11).

The grace of God never teaches us to bless ungodliness; it teaches us to deny ungodliness. It leads us closer towards God and enables us to accomplish His works — works founded on love, mercy, and forgiveness. To encourage the devil and his works is not the work of grace. Grace requires us to forgive those who have been used of the devil, but we are never required to forgive the devil. I renounce him, I rebuke him; and I do not forgive, encourage, or bless his disciples of deception (1 Cor. 5:4–5; 1 Tim. 1:20; 2 John 1:9–11).

It is only by grace that we can truly know that imposters, false leaders, and deceivers actually exist; and it is only by grace that we can see and identify them for what they truly are — antagonists of Christ. To deny that Jesus Christ has come in bodily form is antichrist (1 John 2:18–22; 4:3; 2 John 1:7). To not see the body of Christ as Jesus having come in bodily form, is antichrist. Jesus is the truth, all else is antichrist.

Beloved, in truth, there are only two spiritual viewpoints in the universe — Christ and antichrist. Grace warns us to search our hearts, and to be careful that we are never treating the body of Christ (Christ) in a wrongful fashion. We are responsible to discern truth, and we are responsible for our own ignorance.

The body of Christ is walking around on the earth today in His church — Christ in bodily form. Beloved, when we do not see/respond to the body of Christ in truth, we lose and throw away most of the works of God, which can be wrought in our life (John 4:10). When we replace a revelation of Jesus Christ in our life with traditions and philosophies of men, we supplant grace and truth with worldly ways and confuse and forfeit the workings of the kingdom of God (Matt. 15:1–6).

Grace never calls us to deny or relinquish the authority that God has given us — all that He laboured for. When we are discontent with the doctrine of Christ, we lag behind or run ahead of God and attempt to make God out to be something, which He is not — something more comfortable to our personal liking (Mk. 15:25–32; 2 Peter 3:14–18; Rev. 22:18–19).

If anyone does not live this doctrine of Christ and comes to us bringing a different one, we are to neither receive nor accept that person or what he is presenting. We are not to welcome him into our house (our new inner man), to bid him the blessing of God, or to give him any encouragement in whatever he is doing for his own gospel. Grace never calls us to bless the affairs of antichrist; to do so is to partake in evil.

"He who heeds instruction and correction is [not only himself] in the way of life [but also] is a way of life for others. And he who neglects or refuses reproof [not only himself] goes astray [but also] causes to err and is a path toward ruin for others" (Prov. 10:17).

3 John

✝ **OPERATION / POSITION OF GRACE:** (grace leads us in love and truth)

"The elderly elder [of the church addresses this letter] to the beloved (esteemed) Gaius, whom I truly love" (3 John 1:1).

In this particular Scripture, John as an elder, is speaking to the church in love. As a church leader (elder) who is older (mature), he is addressing them by the Spirit of grace (Heb. 5:12–14).

Leadership in the church is seen here as operating in truth and love — imploring, not commanding; loving, not demanding; submissive, not first among equals; less than, not greater than (Phil. 2:3). Love and truth are inseparable; they are like twins in life. Any love motivated outside of truth is counterfeit love — worldly, seeking its own self-gain, and not laying down its own life for others (John 15:13).

Truth, motivated by the Spirit of God, is living truth. As we deliver such truth to one another, we ought to allow the Spirit of God to manifest His love through us. Living truth is motivated by love, therefore you cannot separate truth and love. If our communication with one another is not living, then it is dead and does not contain God's love, and it will not accomplish God's purpose. We have the Spirit (anointing) living within us to enable us to recognize the difference between the living truth and deception, which comes from the spirit of the world (Matt. 4:6).

As Christians we are able to discern living truth spoken to us, even though it may not be delivered in love. We should not judge people for failing to deliver in love; we are called to discern living truth and obey it. As vessels we sometimes do not manifest perfect love. Undiscouraged by our own inadequacy, we should always be attentive to living truth; that is where we find God's unshakable love.

✝ **OPERATION / POSITION OF GRACE:** (grace operates in truth)

"In fact, I greatly rejoiced when [some of] the brethren from time to time arrived and spoke [so highly] of the sincerity and fidelity of your life, as indeed you do live in the Truth [the whole Gospel presents].

I have no greater joy than this, to hear that my [spiritual] children are living their lives in the Truth" (3 John 1:3–4).

Grace offers us the fruit of joy as we see truth manifested in the life of others. As we walk in truth, our life becomes a testimony of Christ and it brings gladness to others (Ps. 4:7; 30:11; 45:7). Beloved, our walk in Christ is our testimony; this should never be taken lightly nor replaced by a so called 'ministry' that we believe we possess (3 John 1:9–10).

This gladness of grace expressed here ended in declaring not only joy, but the greatest of joy. There is no greater joy to be experienced than seeing truth being walked (lived) out by the members of the family of God. We, as the children of God, are identified by the family of God, which has the same eternal destiny (1 John 3:1–2). The godly characteristics that are manifested in our lives are present because of our relationship to God and the body of Christ.

✝ **OPERATION / POSITION OF GRACE:** (grace operates through godly authority; it never divides the church)

"I have written briefly to the church; but Diotrephes, who likes to take the lead among them and put himself first, does not acknowledge my authority and refuses to accept my suggestions or to listen to me.

So when I arrive, I will call attention to what he is doing, his boiling over and casting malicious reflections upon us with insinuating language. And not satisfied with that, he refuses to receive and welcome the [missionary] brethren himself, and also interferes with and forbids those who would welcome them, and tries to expel (excommunicate) them from the church" (3 John 1:9–10).

Most Christians seem to know the meaning and significance of various words used in the church today (even though these words/ideas do *not* exist in Scripture). Beloved, please bear with me as I address some of these issues because of my divine jealousy for the body of Christ (2 Cor. 11:1–2).

Church hopping is basically defined as: one who attends several different churches and is not loyal or faithful to just one. This is seen as bad and even negligent to the spiritual growth of a Christian's walk in the Lord. Church hoppers are perceived as being tossed with every wind of doctrine, never able to come into the knowledge of the truth, rebellious, and even backslidden from God.

Sheep stealing is another well-known term with negative connotations. One who steals sheep is not seen in a positive light. Sheep stealing occurs when one church draws people from another church. The losing church is usually upset, and the gaining church looks the other way, believing that these new sheep have really made a good choice. The gaining church sees the increase of these *new* believers as proof positive that God is blessing them, and that they really do have better revelation of Christ than the other church. The glory of God is seen as having left the old and now is resting on the new (1 Sam. 4:21).

Neutral ground is another term that one encounters when desiring to edify the whole body of Christ as opposed to just one piece of it. This ground is a location that is not owned by any one church in the area — so is seen as being neutral. This is a method of attracting people from different churches. Neutral ground is also seen as helping to prevent sheep stealing or the appearance of sheep stealing.

In order to help clarify where these 'problems' have originated, I offer the following scenario (fabricated from *outside* of Scripture, because all these terms originate *outside* of Scripture):

There are twenty-eight chapters in the Book of Acts. Suppose we introduce another chapter, chapter twenty-nine, and in it we see Peter coming to Corinth and starting a church. A few verses farther on, we see John coming to Corinth and starting another church too. (At the time Paul started *the* church in Corinth, it had a population of approximately 700,000 people. By today's standards, there would be approximately 700 men who would come to Corinth and start *a local church* — their church.)

Now suppose you find written a few verses farther into this chapter, that some of the people who go to Peter's church change churches and start going to Paul's church. Also, some of the people from John's church start attending Peter's church, too. If all this were truly written in the Book of Acts, it would immediately be spotted as *error*. To make the story even more ridiculous, a few verses farther on, you find that Pastor Pete turns his church over to Pastor Paul, and now Pastor Paul has it all and Pastor Pete hasn't got tweet. In fact, Pastor Pete usually does not attend his old church because he could be a threat to Pastor Paul, unless of course he is *over* Pastor Paul.

I find the ripping up of the body of Christ, revolting to my spirit and an incessant burden to my heart — it hurts the heart of God and should hurt our heart as well (1 Cor. 3:1–9).

✝ **OPERATION OF GRACE:** (grace imitates good)

"Beloved, do not imitate evil, but imitate good. He who does good is of God; he who does evil has not seen (discerned or experienced) God [has enjoyed no vision of Him and does not know Him at all]" (3 John 1:11).

The grace of God is never an initiator or an imitator of evil. God is good, and it is impossible to define anything as good or right without the authorization of God. Everything, since the creation of all things, is only defined as good, if God declares it to be good (Gen. 1:4–31). Every aspect of life has been defined by God as to whether it is good or bad — right or wrong. It is only the Creator who has the right and authority to define all of man's relationships.

Even when man plans and carries out something for evil, God's grace is totally capable of making it turn out for good (Prov. 14:22; 28:10). When our eyes are fixed on grace — no matter what circumstances we find ourselves in — we can rest content knowing that we are self-sufficient in Christ's sufficiency.

The fear of the Lord will always keep us on the path of goodness, and our circumstances will work out for our good as we walk according to the dictates of the Spirit in all of our life — albeit in times of plenty or in times of famine (Rom. 8:28). It is because of God's goodness, not our own, that we are inheritors of God's kingdom. His vindication for our sin has given us our heritage, and our new life in Christ allows Him to change us into His image (Rom. 8:29; 2 Cor. 3:18; Col. 3:10). It takes the Spirit of God to change the human character of flesh and blood. Without the Spirit of God, the best trained, educated, and groomed human cannot manifest Christ. It is not our goodness, which does this; it is the Holy Spirit that accomplishes this.

God's Word defines all that is good and right in the sight of God. It is His goodness, which gives meaning and purpose to both our life here on earth and our life in the hereafter, and it is the source and reason for our rejoicing.

Only the Lord can authorize what is acceptable in His sight; we do not possess that type of authority. Attempting to exercise such false authority would be 'legalizing' — declaring something as legal or illegal (Matt 21:23–32; Mk. 1:22). This is the type of authority that Diotrephes was attempting to operate in. It is not found in Scripture. John was calling attention to this adulteration of authority. If you replace the authority, which God has given the church, and expect the church to function properly, you are foolish indeed.

The authority of the position called 'the pastor' in the church today is not found in Scripture. Today, the 'pastor' position of authority is more like unto the C.E.O. of Wall-Mart or the C.E.O. of Canadian Tire. Because church systems believe that they are ordained of God, a person who is not faithful to a system is seen as not being faithful to Christ. In truth, to be faithful to a system is to be unfaithful to the Christ (Rom. 6:16; 16:18).

The kingdoms of this world cannot survive without their ranked positions of authority operating within their bounds of self-defined responsibilities. The kingdom of God manifested by His church does not have ranking authorities or 'bosses'. It operates only through maturity found in the Spirit of God, not in positions, which men hold. The only position of authority found in the kingdom of God and manifested through His church, is the Holy Spirit. One can only operate in authority when one moves by the Holy Spirit. This is why you never see the position of 'the pastor' mentioned in the New Testament. Pastoring is not a position; it is a gifting only manifested by the Spirit of God. Organizations need C.E.O.'s; the church needs the Spirit of Jesus Christ— full of grace and truth.

Our life is sourced in Christ. Knowing that it is He Who goes with us and will not forsake us, gives us confidence and rest in Him, no matter what the circumstances may be. Grace calls us to take heed therefore unto ourselves, that we love the Lord our God with all our heart, soul, mind, and strength (1 Cor. 3:10; 1 Tim. 4:16; 2 Peter 1:8–9, 19). To love the Lord in such a way is to love Him — His way, not our own way. This is the purpose of the renewing of our soul — to have our mind renewed into the ways and purposes of God — the very character of Christ (Rom. 12:1–3).

Wrong-doing in our life distances us from the good of the land, which the Lord has so graciously provided for us. As the Spirit of the Lord operates in our life, we gain the ability to discern good from evil. To turn from, or to neglect God's way is foolish; it causes us to shipwreck our faith and prevent God's authority from operating in our life (1 Tim. 1:19).

The hand of God is upon all those who seek Him diligently, but His power and His wrath are against all of those who forsake Him (Heb. 6:11; 12:15; Jas. 4:6; 1 Peter 5:5). God's Spirit is good to us as it leads us into the land of uprightness, through the gates of faith and repentance. God shall bring every work into judgment, including every secret thing, whether it be for good, or whether it be for evil (Eccl. 12:14; 1 Cor. 4:5). To hate evil and to love goodness establishes righteous judgment in our life, by the grace of God.

When we do what God desires, we manifest goodness in our life (Eph. 5:9). There is none good but God (Matt. 19:17). There is nothing outside of God, which can truly result in any goodness. Jesus, anointed by the Spirit of God, went about doing good — healing all oppression of the devil. This is also our calling as His disciples (Acts 10:38). All things work together for good to them that love God, to them who are living according to His purpose (Rom. 8:28).

His grace is always sufficient that we may abound unto good works (Eph. 2:10). It is by our works in the Spirit that we display our acquaintance with God and His grace, which gives us a good conscience towards Him (John 8:9; Acts 23:1; Rom. 2:15). "*Beloved, follow not that which is evil, but that which is good. He that doeth good is of God: but he that doeth evil hath not seen God*" (3 John 1:11 KJV).

Jude

✞ **POSITION OF GRACE:** (grace sets us apart for God and keeps us in His love)

"Jude, a servant of Jesus Christ (the Messiah), and brother of James, [writes this letter] to those who are called (chosen), dearly loved by God the Father and separated (set apart) and kept for Jesus Christ:" (Jude 1:1).

Grace keeps us in Christ Jesus and positions us as disciples/servants of Jesus Christ. It is never our own accomplishments that make us important in Christ. A work of God never glorifies man; it only glorifies God and is maintained by Him (Lk. 18:43; Acts 3:8–9; 4:21). A work of man must be maintained by man (Phil. 2:3, 13; 3 John 1:10). Our validation and significance come from being a servant of Christ, not a leader of men (Gal. 2:1–6). There is nothing of eternal value to be found in the works and accomplishments of carnal man.

Christ is not interested in maintaining *our* image. His grace is constantly at work within us, helping us to be changed into *His* image (Rom. 8:29; 2 Cor. 3:18; Col. 3:10). Grace working in our life builds upon the truth, that we are called (chosen) by God. In order to love one another, we need to see this same calling in all our brothers and sisters around us. The wisdom of the Holy Spirit enables us to see each other as equally chosen by God.

God has no need to submit to *our* teaching; it is we who need to humbly submit to Him. The Holy Spirit within us (His anointing) will teach us concerning all things, and what He teaches is true. Also, as we submit one to another in fellowship, the Holy spirit will give us spiritual words to express spiritual truths revealing the mind of Christ (1 Cor. 2:13–16; 1 John 2:27).

Beloved, it is dangerous for us to embellish the truth found in God's Word (Prov. 30:5–6; Rev. 22:19). God does not need us to improve His image — baby Jesus did not glow in the dark in the Bethlehem barn. By adding to His word we will actually lose an aspect of His truth, and the image we have of Him will be distorted. We need to be careful not to change God into some Hollywood image, but rather see Him for Who He really is.

Grace reveals to us that we are dearly loved by God, and it is from this position that we abound in love towards others ('abounding' is a term used to describe a flower growing from a bud to full bloom). It is His abounding grace that separates us from the world; it keeps us unspotted from the ways of this present age. It keeps worldly counsel and purpose from fouling our lives (Eph. 2:2; Jas. 1:27).

The carnal nature of man constantly compares itself with others, separating those within the body of Christ by quantities of works and accomplishments (2 Cor. 10:12). This carnality constantly strives and strains to attain to positions of authority within a hierarchy. The only hierarchy that exists in the kingdom of God is that He is God, and we are His servants. Placing yourself under any authority other than the Spirit of God is placing one's self outside of Christ's authority, wherewith we lose many of the benefits of living fruitfully in His kingdom.

The reason that we have no need for any man to teach us is because we have been separated unto God, by God, and for God (sanctified). It is He who establishes us as equals within the body of Christ, and it is He who has anointed us (1 John 2:27). He has given us the Holy Spirit, sealed in our hearts as a guarantee, that we are called, loved, and separated unto Him (1 Cor. 2:12; 2 Cor. 1:22; 1 Thess. 4:8). Grace keeps us in Christ and in fellowship with one another.

✞ **OPERATION OF GRACE:** (grace stands in opposition to perversion)

"For certain men have crept in stealthily [gaining entrance secretly by a side door]. Their doom was predicted long ago, ungodly (impious, profane) persons who pervert the grace (the spiritual blessing and favour) of our God into lawlessness and wantonness and immorality, and disown and deny our sole Master and Lord Jesus Christ (the Messiah, the Anointed One)" (Jude 1:4).

Grace never presents itself in a secret or sly manner. There is nothing deceptive about grace and truth (John 18:20). They stand in opposition to corrupt opinions and all things false. Men of pretence and deceit are motivated by their own carnal cravings and desires, which are forbidden. Such men are working on behalf of the spirit of the world and operate in worldly ways (1 Cor. 3:3–4). Grace and truth define what is forbidden, and teach us to deny all intercourse with such activities and attitudes. Only Jesus is to be our sole Master and Lord.

Perversion always operates in opposition to truth, hence good is made to look like evil and evil is made to look like good (Gen. 3:1; Is. 5:20). It is God alone who defines what is good and what is evil. He created and defined the purpose of the tree of the knowledge of good and evil (Gen. 2:17). It was the devil who perverted (stood in opposition to) the plans and purposes of God (Gen. 3:5).

Perversion is an abomination to righteousness, and righteousness is an abomination to perversion (Prov. 29:27). It is only by the grace of God that we are able to discern between righteousness and perversion; it is this same grace, which enables us to see, hear, receive, love, and obey truth.

To disown and deny our sole Master and Lord is to disown and deny our soul's Creator. Just as the devil tried to redefine truth in the Garden of Eden, all perversion attempts to do the same today. Perversion can only exist by redefining/twisting the truth and getting its disciples to perpetuate this perversion in their lives. Such action always opposes the plans and purposes of God.

Our responsibility for spiritual growth and discernment is personal; it should never be relegated to some other person. It is not acceptable to say, "The devil made me do it!" Comparing ourselves with others gives us a false sense of security (2 Cor. 10:12). Safety is never to be found in numbers; it is only found in Jesus Christ (Ps. 20:7; Prov. 14:12; 19:21; Matt. 7:13–14; 1 Cor. 15:57; 1 John 5:4). Our spiritual security is not in an organization with many members. Being a member of a faction of a church of five hundred members is not more secure than one, which has only twelve members. Our security is found *only* in Jesus Christ and knowing that we are part of His body.

✞ **OPERATION OF GRACE:** (grace makes us participants in God's salvation plan)

"[Strive to] save others, snatching [them] out of [the] fire; on others take pity [but] with fear, loathing even the garment spotted by the flesh and polluted by their sensuality" (Jude 1:23).

The grace and compassion of God compels us to strive to save souls, and to shine His light into this dark world. We are to live as the King's kids in the midst of this rebellious generation. As lights of His love, we hold out and offer to the world the Word of Life — the Gospel — the good news of God's grace towards all mankind (Phil. 2:15–16; 1 John 1:1–3). By His Spirit we show forth and manifest Him who was from the beginning. We have heard and have seen our Lord with our spiritual eyes, and it is in Him that we experience the Living Word of life.

The fear of the Lord is the beginning and lifeblood of God's Wisdom; and it is this same fear, which keeps us unspotted from the world, despising even the very garments tarnished by the lusts of the world (Ps. 97:10; Prov. 8:13; Amos 5:14–15).

✞ **POSITION OF GRACE:** (grace keeps us from stumbling, and presents us blameless)

"Now to Him Who is able to keep you without stumbling or slipping or falling, and to present [you] unblemished (blameless and faultless) before the presence of His glory in triumphant joy and exultation [with unspeakable, ecstatic delight]" (Jude 1:24).

It is only the grace of God that can preserve and reserve us for His purposes. Grace is greater than any of our faltering and floundering, our stumbling and staggering, or our sinking and succumbing.

Grace confers upon us and displays in us God's nature and character. There is no true triumphant joy, exultation, or ecstatic delight found outside of the presence and glory of God (1 Peter 4:13). Only that which is of God will be able to stand.

Our position of grace is perfect and pure; it is eternal and unchanging. It is a vital truth for every disciple to know that our Lord is able to keep us from stumbling or falling. He is the one who presents us unblemished and faultless — free from all sin (Col. 1:22; 1 Thess. 3:13).

✞ **POSITION OF GRACE:** (to the one and only gracious God)

"To the one only God, our Saviour through Jesus Christ our Lord, be glory (splendour), majesty, might and dominion, and power and authority, before all time and now and forever (unto all the ages of eternity). Amen (so be it)" (Jude 1:25).

It is only God that merits *all* glory. God's expression of grace contains His splendour, magnificence and majesty. It is Him and Him alone Who merits and gives true meaning to the words 'adoration', 'praise', and 'worship' (Ps. 35:10; 71:19; 89:8; 113:5; Rev. 4:11).

The essence and definition of dominion is God-birthed, not man-made. Beloved, all might, all power, and all authority is forever founded in Him. He who was, is, and is to come created time, and hence He alone defines all things both now and forevermore (Rev.1:4, 8; 4:8).

It is His grace that allows us to partake in His excellence and experience His lordship. It is His power and authority, which enables us to be influenced by and be participants in His kingdom, allowing us to be truly called His possession.

Grace allows us to find rest in His supremacy, His protection, His ownership, and His government over us.

Revelation

✞ **POSITION / OPERATION OF GRACE:** (grace reveals God's plans and mysteries)

"[This is] the revelation of Jesus Christ [His unveiling of the divine mysteries]. God gave it to Him to disclose and make known to His bond servants certain things which must shortly and speedily come to pass in their entirety. And He sent and communicated it through His angel (messenger) to His bond servant John," (Revelation 1:1).

The grace of God allows us to communicate with God. It is from our position of grace that we are allowed to receive revelation — divine mysteries spiritually discerned and interpreted (2 Peter 1:16–21). The revelation of Jesus Christ is the only revelation that is essential or vital for life. All other things known are only temporal and have no eternal significance. Only Christ is absolute and entirely completes and fulfils all things (Rom. 8:19–23; Phil. 3:20–21).

In Christ the veil has been removed and we now enter into the Holy of Holies, into the very presence of God, without fear of condemnation (2 Cor. 3:12–18; Heb. 10:16–22). Beloved, this is not an arrogant position; it is a humble one. *"His confidential communion and secret counsel are with the righteous (those who are upright and in right standing with Him)"* (Prov. 3:32b).

As bond servants positioned in His grace, we are privileged to have direct communication with God. Revelation comes to us because of the Holy Spirit living within us, and teaching us everything, which is true (John 16:13; 1 John 2:27). God's purposes and plans are not accessible by our own efforts or intelligence; they must be spiritually discerned, not logically determined (1 Cor. 2:12–14).

✞ **POSITION / OPERATION OF GRACE:** (grace greets us and introduces us to God's nature)

"John to the seven assemblies (churches) that are in Asia: may grace (God's unmerited favour) be granted to you and spiritual peace (the peace of Christ's kingdom) from Him Who is and Who was and Who is to come, and from the seven Spirits [the sevenfold Holy Spirit] before His throne,

And from Jesus Christ the faithful and trustworthy Witness, the Firstborn of the dead [first to be brought back to life] and the Prince (Ruler) of the kings of the earth. To Him Who ever loves us and has once [for all] loosed and freed us from our sins by His own blood," (Revelation 1:4–5).

Even though John is speaking to the seven churches here, he sees himself as a representative of Jesus Christ; therefore he is also a faithful and trustworthy witness, even as Christ is. As Christians we need to be aware of the responsibility of being witnesses for our Lord and speaking truth (Truth). When we are doing this we also identify ourselves with Christ as rulers and kings of the earth. We are called to rule over darkness; we are not to let darkness rule over us.

To speak for God, requires the grace of God. As ambassadors of Christ, we should always be able to say, *"I am speaking the truth in Christ. I am not lying; my conscience [enlightened and prompted] by the Holy Spirit bearing witness with me"* (Romans 9:1).

Because we are one with Christ, we can freely approach God and one another by His grace. This same oneness gives us freedom in fellowship with all our brothers and sisters.

Grace is a spiritual greeting that embodies eternity within it. To say, "May grace be granted to you." is not just a bunch of words; it is a spiritual greeting, which has both the power and life of God within it (Rom. 16:20, 24; 2 John 1:3). Grace is not a man-made word; it is a God-made word, and hence it is only divinely revealed. The Word, which became flesh and dwelt among us, brought grace to us. Grace is empowered and kept by the very soul of God.

Grace, as a testimony and witness of God, is by nature eternally faithful and trustworthy; it never ceases loving us, and forever frees us from the bondage of sin. As we seek nurture from the Lord, all the qualities of God's grace become the very qualities of His character infused into our life (2 Cor. 3:18).

✞ **POSITION / OPERATION OF GRACE:** (grace has made us priests of the Most High)

"And formed us into a kingdom (a holy race), priests to His God and Father — to Him be the glory and the power and the majesty and the dominion throughout the ages and forever and ever. Amen (so be it)" (Revelation 1:6).

The grace of God declares that we are priests to God Almighty (1 Peter 2:9). Beloved, this is not a work, which has been done by any effort or study on man's part. Our priesthood is not a credential bestowed upon us by an institution located on earth. We are ordained priests of our Father, without ritual, ceremony, or pomp; our ordination is founded only upon the cross of Christ. It is silly, thoughtless, and unreflecting to begin such a new spiritual life by faith, and then try to reach perfection and maturity by works done for an institution (Gal. 3:1–3). We have been commissioned to our ministry by the Lord Jesus Christ (2 Cor. 5:18).

We did not receive the Holy Spirit by any human works whatsoever; we received it by hearing, receiving, loving, and obeying the message of the Gospel of Jesus Christ.

Christians are different from all other peoples on the face of the earth — we have been purchased and especially chosen as His people. There are only two authorities in the spiritual realm — God and the devil. There are only two positions — the truth and the lie. There are only two eternities — in heaven and outside heaven. There are only two religions — Christ and antichrist.

Christians have been forever redeemed from the curse of the law — the eternal penalty of disobedience to God. No earthly or heavenly power can cause any curse to land upon us (Rom. 8:31–39; Gal. 3:11–14). By grace we are under His eternal protection. If you are not for Christ, you are against Him (Luke 11:23). The Lord Jesus Christ has made us a unique race, a kingdom — the kingdom of God, the kingdom of the Son, the kingdom of heaven, and the kingdom of Christ (Phil. 3:20; Titus 2:14).

✞ **POSITION / OPERATION OF GRACE:** (grace makes us sharers and participators of tribulation and endurance; grace witnesses and testifies of Jesus Christ)

"I, John, your brother and companion (sharer and participator) with you in the tribulation and kingdom and patient endurance [which are] in Jesus Christ, was on the isle called Patmos, [banished] on account of [my witnessing to] the Word of God and the testimony (the proof, the evidence) for Jesus Christ.

I was in the Spirit [rapt in His power] on the Lord's Day, and I heard behind me a great voice like the calling of a war trumpet,

Saying, I am the Alpha and the Omega, the First and the Last. Write promptly what you see (your vision) in a book and send it to the seven churches which are in Asia — to Ephesus and to Smyrna and to Pergamum and to Thyatira and to Sardis and to Philadelphia and to Laodicea" (Revelation 1:9–11).

We are family by and in the grace of God; we are brothers, sharers, and companions. It is within His kingdom that the body of Christ is being built up by God (Eph. 4:16). We, as parts of it, are mutually dependent upon one another. Just as our body is dependent upon our head, all in the body of Christ together are dependent upon Christ — our Head (Rom. 12:5).

The body of Christ bears witness to the Word of God and is a testimony — a spiritual proof — of the living Christ. We, as Christians, both individually and corporately, are the testimony of the Living God. We are the evidence that Jesus Christ lives. It is never a question of whether the Word of God is true; it is only a question of how well our life is in submission to the Truth (Rom. 8:1–9; Jas. 4:7).

The body of Christ has been designed by God to live 'in the Spirit'. Whether the body is sojourning in a valley of dry bones, or causing the fathers' hearts to turn to the children, or encouraging and restoring the rebellious to walk in the wisdom of the upright, or preparing a people for the coming of the Lord; we are called to live in and by the Spirit of God.

Whether we groan, are troubled, or pressed on every side, the Spirit of grace calls us to be fervent and purposed in our calling to spiritual circumcision. We are to be separate from the world, cut off from bondage to the flesh. We are to let Him dwell in us in all meekness, living in the Spirit as we edify and encourage one another in Christ (2 Tim. 2:24–26; Jas. 1:21). While engaged in such spiritual work, we will not fulfil the lusts of the flesh. Living in the Spirit causes a renewing of our mind, and causes us to pray with great supplication for all of God's people (Lk. 6:12; Col. 1:9).

The words: 'tribulation and patient endurance', are not words, which the flesh enjoys; they are only understood in the Spirit. Being in the Spirit of God is a position, which places us in God's presence. He does not require any help on our part to either put us there or to keep us there. The flesh is unreceptive to the workings of the Holy Spirit. However, the flesh does enjoy selfishness and having regard for its own interests.

Becoming a member of the body of Christ is a private thing — a personal relationship birthed by Christ. However, as an active member of the body of Christ, we are called upon to encourage and edify one another in an open manifestation of love (Acts 20:22–27; 21:8–14). Revelation that is predestined for edification of the whole body of Christ ought to be openly shared. We need to be careful of private revelation or prophesy, which can be motivated by a desire to control people (1 Cor. 14:29; Gal. 2:1–5; 2 Peter 1:20).

✝ **POSITION / OPERATION OF GRACE:** (grace allows us to meet the Holder of the keys of death, without worldly fear)

"When I saw Him, I fell at His feet as if dead. But He laid His right hand on me and said, Do not be afraid! I am the First and the Last,

And the ever-living One [I am living in the eternity of the eternities]. I died, but see, I am alive forevermore; and I possess the keys of death and Hades (the realm of the dead)" (Revelation 1:17–18).

There are times when the awesomeness of God's presence strikes us down in heart (Ex.3:4–6; Is. 13:6–8; Acts 2:37), and can even make us fall down in fear (Acts 9:3–4). As the Lord would reveal His character to us, we need to realize that we are on holy ground. It is a time of removing the things of our flesh, which separate us from His holiness (Moses was asked to remove his sandals). At such times we should not be afraid, but rather wait for Him to speak to us (John 14:27).

If the Spirit causes us to fall down, He does not require any help to either lay us down, or to keep us there. If falling at His feet is something that God is doing in our life, the Lord does not require anyone to catch us. If God can knock us down, God can catch us (Ezek. 2:1–2; Acts 9:3–4). When men's hands cause people to fall down (either by passing the tipping point or by suggestion), they require men's hands to catch them (Acts 7:40–41).

It takes God's righteous right hand to restore us to the place of healing and receive assurance from Him. It is God who reveals Himself to us; we need not be afraid when He uncovers His character and ways to us. Revelation, humbly received, always leaves a reverent fear of God in our heart. It is a complacent heart, which spurns and makes light of God's revelation. We should not think it strange when the spirit of the world (even operating through Christians) belittles and even affronts the living Word of God. A servant is not greater than his Master (Matt. 10:24–25).

Keys represent authority and accessibility. If you are outside the grace of God, you cannot see either the keys, or He who holds them. Without knowing the Key-holder personally, you are in danger of living in eternal ignorance — a position outside of God's presence. The First and the Last, the ever-living One, is the Way, the Truth, and the Life — the Lord Jesus Christ (Acts 4:10–12).

Grace calls us to see the things of God, to not be afraid, and to do what He requires of us (Micah 6:8).

✝ **POSITION / OPERATION OF GRACE:** (grace brings us back to our first love)

"To the angel (messenger) of the assembly (church) in Ephesus write: These are the words of

Him Who holds the seven stars [which are the messengers of the seven churches] in His right hand, Who goes about among the seven golden lampstands [which are the seven churches]: But I have this one charge to make against you: that you have left (abandoned) the love you had at first [you have deserted Me, your first love].

Remember then from what heights you have fallen. Repent (change the inner man to meet God's will) and do the works you did previously [when you first knew the Lord], or else I will visit you and remove your lampstand from its place, unless you change your mind and repent" (Revelation 2:1, 4–5).

The grace of God never abandons us; it is we who have the ability to abandon it. Beloved, to desert or forsake anything given to us by God is foolish. To desert the love of God is spiritual suicide — a death sentence to *His* life being manifested in *our* life. To forsake the love of God hinders deeply our life's testimony. Because God is love, it is not to our advantage to be offended by Love. Love is not just a written word; it is the Living Word meant to be lived (loved) out in our lives (John 14:21).

The only remedy for the lack of godly love is repentance — the changing of one's mind for the better, permitting the will of God to rule over our soul. If we do not see the need for change in our life, we will not be changed (Prov. 26:11; 30:12). Our recognition of where we are, and where the Lord says we should be, is necessary for repentance to do its work in our life. Repentance is not something we can work up. It occurs when we see our own need and our helplessness in accomplishing the required change (Acts 2:37).

The reality of coming to know Jesus for the first time is considered to be our 'first love' in Scripture, because it is the first time we encounter true love — God's love. Love is designed to grow in our life as we exercise it; the more we give it away, the more we find to give away. He is the never-ending, unfathomable source of our true love (Heb. 5:9; 12:2).

If we do not seek Him in our life, we are not truly seeking love. Selfishness causes us to ignore and fall away from things of God; we end up attempting to direct our own way through life (Prov. 16:25; 19:3). Selfish attitudes are the result of the fall of man, initiated in the Garden of Eden; they need to be repented of. Such attitudes were dealt with in the Garden of Gethsemane.

Our newly founded exuberance, when we first come to taste of Christ's love, is not something we are destined to 'grow out of', as we 'mature'. Our 'first love' is something that should continue to grow, and be manifest in our life; it is to be a remembrance point for our continuing on and maturing in God. Grace calls us to remember, that it is He who holds His church in His hand as He walks and works amongst us. Our maturing is not a dampening of our 'first love'; it is an embracing and enhancing of it (1 John 4:19).

✞ **POSITION / OPERATION OF GRACE:** (grace calls us to be afraid of nothing)

"To the angel (messenger) of the assembly (church) in Smyrna write: These are the words of the First and the Last, Who died and came to life again:

Fear nothing that you are about to suffer. [Dismiss your dread and your fears!] Behold, the devil is indeed about to throw some of you into prison, that you may be tested and proved and critically appraised, and for ten days you will have affliction. Be loyally faithful unto death [even if you must die for it], and I will give you the crown of life" (Revelation 2:8, 10).

Being fearless in the face of sure suffering can only be accomplished by resting in the pure faith and grace of God. We are not immune to attacks from the devil. We are not exempt from tests, trials, and afflictions perpetrated by the accuser of the brethren; grace calls us to be loyally faithful — even unto death.

Being tested and critically appraised by the spirit of the world with all its hatred and evil, is not something that is likely to be pleasant to our flesh. However, it births a joy in our spirit and a true evidence of our position of eternal salvation. As citizens of heaven, we are not to be even momentarily frightened or intimidated by anything our opponents and adversaries may throw against us. Our fearlessness is a clear sign and proof of their imminent destruction, and it is also a sure sign of our salvation (Acts 7:58–60; 1 Cor. 1:18; 2 Cor. 2:15–17; Phil. 1:28).

God has not given us a spirit of fear or timidity. He has abundantly supplied us with power, love, and a sound mind to testify for our Lord. By His grace, we share in the sufferings for the Gospel (Rom. 8:15; 2 Tim. 1:7–8). His testimony in our life is given to us by God's grace. He who died and came to life again is the source of our strength. His grace is revealed to us, that we might personally come to experience the power of His resurrection, and be transformed into His likeness (Phil. 3:10–11).

✞ **POSITION / OPERATION OF GRACE:** (grace calls us to the pure unadulterated word of God)

"Then to the angel (messenger) of the assembly (church) in Pergamum write: These are the words of Him Who has and wields the sharp two-edged sword:

Nevertheless, I have a few things against you: you have some people there who are clinging to the teaching of Balaam, who taught Balak to set a trap and a stumbling block before the sons or Israel, [to entice them] to eat food that had been sacrificed to idols and to practice lewdness [giving themselves up to sexual vice].

You also have some who in a similar way are clinging to the teaching of the Nicolaitans [those corrupters of the people] which things I hate.

Repent [then]! Or else I will come to you quickly and fight against them with the sword of My mouth" (Revelation 2:12, 14–16).

Anything that occupies or inhabits a place in our heart, which is due to God, is an idol. Such spiritual unfaithfulness to our divine Husband is truly spiritual adultery (Rev. 22:17). An idol is sometimes regarded as a harmless symbol. However, an idol will end up substituting God's authority with its own authority. An idol is not something harmless; it has power over you. Anything outside of Christ, which has power over you is an idol.

It is also important to remember that harmless symbols and memorabilia, which have no power over us are not idols. For example, the wedding ring I wear on my hand is a symbol of my marriage; it has no power to either make or dissolve my marriage. It has no power or authority over me; therefore it is not an idol.

Our authority in Christ (*exousia*) gives us freedom of choice and liberty of action. God has ordained us to operate in the authority of the Living Word (2 Cor. 10:8). The world's definition of authority is 'to rule over' or 'to lord it over', making one person subservient to another (Lk. 22:24–30). Worldly authority is usually wielded by an expert, or specialist who has been authorized, or licenced by an organization, or agency to be the 'source' of all last-word decisions to be made — a C.E.O. When we follow worldly ordained authority, we can end up in a position where we serve other gods, even while quoting the Scripture (Matt. 4:6; Mk. 7:1–13). When we believe in an idolatrous belief system, we become like the idol (Ps. 115:4–8; 135:15–18). Idols are built by man, and hence need to be defined (named), protected, and sustained by man. Beloved, the kingdom of God does not operate as such.

Whenever we desert God in such a way, we shamelessly enlarge our bed to accommodate our new love. God commands us not to have any gods before or besides Him (Ex. 20:3). As soon as we tolerate another god (a perverted truth) in our life, it will immediately blind and deafen us, and prevent us from exercising tolerance towards God. In such a state we end up walking in darkness instead of the Light (John 8:12); judging according to the flesh instead of truth (John 8:15–16); not believing the Truth (John 8:24); not recognizing God's authority (John 8:28); not walking in freedom, but rather walking in sin (John 8:31–36); not allowing His word to have place or make progress in our heart (John 8:37); not recognizing who or what authority we are serving (John 8:38–42); misunderstanding and being unable to hear and believe Him (John 8:43–45); and we end up vilifying those who bring truth to us (Prov. 29:27; John 8:46–59).

Here again, the remedy is repentance, or else we will find ourselves fighting against the Lord, and His sharp two-edged sword (Acts 5:39).

The teaching of the Nicolaitans is something, which our Lord hates; it is something, which corrupts the Lord's people (the body of Christ). The word 'Nicolaitans' comes from the Greek word: 'Nikolas' which means 'victory or power over the people'. When the church is organized to have men in ministry exercise power over common people (laity), this is practicing the teaching of the Nicolaitans. Worldly organizations need C.E.O.'s; the kingdom of God does not.

This is why you do not find any New Testament examples in Scripture of different churches in a city, each with a pastor, exercising authority over their people. This is also why you do not find one example of a person being accountable to another person. God's people are always shown to be accountable to God alone. God is not interested in having different authorities over different factions of His church. God is interested in His people exercising His authority in their lives, as they submit to one another by His Spirit. It is by God's authority that I am saved, and it is by God's authority that I live, move, and have my being.

✞ **POSITION / OPERATION OF GRACE:** (grace does not tolerate either idolatry or sexual sin)

"And to the angel (messenger) of the assembly (church) in Thyatira write: These are the words of the Son of God, Who has eyes that flash like a flame of fire, and Whose feet glow like bright and burnished and white-hot bronze:

But I have this against you: that you tolerate the woman Jezebel, who calls herself a prophetess [claiming to be inspired], and who is teaching and leading astray my servants and beguiling them into practicing sexual vice and eating food sacrificed to idols.

I gave her time to repent, but she has no desire to repent of her immorality [symbolic of idolatry] and refuses to do so.

Take note: I will throw her on a bed [of anguish], and those who commit adultery with her [her paramours] I will bring down to pressing distress and severe affliction, unless they turn away their minds from conduct [such as] hers and repent of their doings.

And I will strike her children (her proper followers) dead [thoroughly exterminating them]. And all the assemblies (churches) shall recognize and understand that I am He Who searches minds (the thoughts, feelings, and purposes) and the [inmost] hearts, and I will give to each of you [the reward for what you have done] as your work deserves." (Revelation 2:18, 20–23).

Rebellion is as the sin of witchcraft; God hates pride and arrogance (1 Sam. 15:23). The grace of God never operates out of pride; it never leads into error and falsity. Pride and arrogance come from the spirit of the world — the prince of the power of the air, the spirit that now works in the disobedient and the rebellious (Prov. 8:13; Eph. 2:1–3). Sexual sin and the serving of idols are the works of rebellion towards God's authority.

God gives time to repent, but note that it is not forever. God desires that all should come to repentance, especially Christians; however, if there is no desire found in the human heart for repentance, judgement will follow (2 Peter 3:8–12). We need to turn away from any authority and way that does not represent God. Stubbornness is as idolatry, and a heart bent on its own way instead of seeking what God desires, is a heart headed for judgement.

The remedy is repentance, or else find yourselves on the wrong side of the Lord's two-edged sword (Acts 5:1–10). There is never an excuse for sinful acts, attitudes, and mind-sets. Oh God, search my heart and see if there be any wicked way in it; purge me from my sin and make me whiter than snow — Lord I believe, help my unbelief (Ps. 51:6–7; 139:23–24).

✞ **POSITION / OPERATION OF GRACE:** (grace calls us to live by His Spirit resulting in work that meets the requirements of God)

"And to the angel (messenger) of the assembly (church) in Sardis write: These are the words of Him

Who has the seven Spirits of God [the sevenfold Holy Spirit] and the seven stars: ...

Rouse yourself, and strengthen and invigorate what remains and is on the point of dying: for I have not found a thing that you have done [any work of yours] meeting the requirements of My God or perfect in His sight.

So call to mind the lessons you received and heard; continually lay them to heart and obey them, and repent. In case you will not rouse yourselves and keep awake and watch, I will come upon you like a thief, and you will not know or suspect at what hour I will come" (Revelation 3:1a, 2–3).

It is possible for us to be performing works, which we believe are of God, yet they lack the seal of the Holy Spirit upon them. It is possible to have works, which we believe are full of life, yet are truly on the point of dying. There are many 'works of God', which start out by hearing the Word and are welcomed and accepted with joy; yet they become works of self-righteousness, which have no real root in the Living Word (Matt. 13:20–22). Such works become temporary and inconstant, lasting only for a little while, and because of affliction, trouble, or persecution they disappear with time, bearing no fruit in the kingdom of God.

People working such works often stumble and actually end up distrusting the Lord, in Whom they ought to trust and obey (Mark 14:27–31). Any work of man requires man's leadership and power to keep it going. God's perfect work is not like this; it requires only a willing heart, which hears, receives, loves and obeys the Word and Spirit of God. It is the Lord Who builds His church, not man; it is the Lord Who keeps His church, not man.

Here again, the recommended remedy is repentance, or else we will find ourselves caught unawares by the Lord.

✝ **POSITION / OPERATION OF GRACE:** (grace keeps us and gives us patient endurance)

"And to the angel (messenger) of the assembly (church) in Philadelphia write: These are the words of the Holy One, the True One, He Who has the key of David, Who opens and no one shall shut, Who shuts and no one shall open:

Take note! I will make those of the synagogue of Satan who say they are Jews and are not, but lie — behold, I will make them come and bow down before your feet and learn and acknowledge that I have loved you.

Because you have guarded and kept My word of patient endurance [have held fast the lesson of My patience with the expectant endurance that I give you], I also will keep you [safe] from the hour of trial (testing) which is coming on the whole world to try those who dwell upon the earth" (Revelation 3:7, 9–10).

When God declares that He is going to do something, He does it. He does not need us to authorize or to defend His plan. There is no one who can open what He has shut, nor shut what He has opened. There is no spiritual weapon formed against us, which can prosper. There is no word spoken against us, as an undeserved curse, which can alight (Prov. 26:2). Every tongue that rises against us in judgement shall be openly displayed as being false and in the wrong. This righteous triumph over opposition is the result of us enduring in Him and displaying our Lord's character through our life, and if need be, in our death (Is. 54:14–17).

The operative word here is *us* — the body of Christ — the church. It is not our position in a church faction, which protects us; it is our being in the body of Christ, which guarantees our vindication. The Lord does not justify error; He stands for Truth (Acts 7:56).

God is our vindication; God is our justification. The kingdom of God is not sourced in this world and its ways. The prince of the world (Satan) has no claim over us, and he has nothing in common with us (John 16:30; 18:36; Acts 7:55–60). His work is to come to kill, steal, and destroy (John 10:10; 1 John 3:8).

✞ **POSITION / OPERATION OF GRACE:** (grace exposes us and grace covers us; it calls us to repent and eat with Him)

"And to the angel (messenger) of the assembly (church) in Laodicea write: These are the words of the Amen, the trusty and faithful and true Witness, the Origin and Beginning and Author of God's creation:

So, because you are lukewarm and neither cold nor hot, I will spew you out of My mouth!

For you say, I am rich; I have prospered and grown wealthy, and I am in need of nothing; and you do not realize and understand that you are wretched, pitiable, poor, blind, and naked.

Therefore I counsel you to purchase from Me gold refined and tested by fire, that you may be [truly] wealthy, and white clothes to clothe you and to keep the shame of your nudity from being seen, and salve to put on your eyes, that you may see.

Those whom I [dearly and tenderly] love, I tell their faults and convict and convince and reprove and chasten [I discipline and instruct them]. So be enthusiastic and in earnest and burning with zeal and repent [changing your mind and attitude].

Behold, I stand at the door and knock; if anyone hears and listens to and heeds My voice and opens the door, I will come in to him and will eat with him, and he [will eat] with Me" (Revelation 3:14, 16–20).

Self-satisfaction and self-righteousness are attitudes that obstruct the work of God in our life. When we are complacent in God, we are content with the status quo – the existing state of affairs (Matt. 13:15; Acts 28:27; Heb. 5:11). In such a state, our trust is not founded in God; it is founded in the contentment of our present circumstances, and what *we* have achieved. In such a state, we do not need to exercise faith because our faith tells us that we are doing just fine — we feel we have need of nothing (Josh. 7:1–5; 22:20).

In this condition, when truth crashes into our little world, we just blame something or someone else, and insist that our own life is under control. We believe that if others would just change, then everything would be all right. In such a state, we walk in darkness and we neither see nor understand our actual condition; we are blind to our true poverty and wretchedness. We are sightless to our nakedness, and hence have no feeling of shame; our eyes of self-righteousness are blinded to the fact that we are contemptible and pathetic, as we self-define our world around us (John 8:3–11). We are unable to see that our dirty hands cannot wipe a dish clean (Matt. 23:25–26). In such a state, when the waves of adversity sweep over us, they are seen as the result of other's mistakes, instead of us seeing them as the result of our reaping the consequences of being neither cold nor hot (Acts 5:1–11).

When we refuse to walk down the narrow path of repentance, we are very foolish indeed (Prov. 1:20–33). Repentance begins when we shut our ears off to our own counsel and the counsel of the world, and turn our attention toward God's counsel. The only currency required to operate in the kingdom of God is humility; without this, you cannot find the gold of God (Lk. 18:18–23; Matt. 17:27; 1 Peter 5:5).

The things of the kingdom of God are tested and refined by the trials in our life. These weathered experiences produce and purify the character of God in us (Jas. 1:2–4). To be wealthy in Christ has nothing to do with material wealth; to be clothed by Christ has nothing to do with material clothing. It has everything to do with our spiritual covering in Christ. The nudity of Christians is not a testimony of the grace of God. It is evidence of a complacent attitude, which is unwilling to see the need of repentance and the need to make Jesus the Lord of their life. The moment we make Jesus our Lord, we are no longer naked; He covers us with the white robes of His righteousness.

Dry, cracked lives need the ointment of grace in order to bring healing and the renewed discernment required for growth in the body of Christ (Jer. 8:22). Being blind to the workings of grace leaves sin undisturbed, and in such a condition one often claims that they see, yet they are wretched, pitiable, and blind (Lk. 4:21–28; John 9:40–41). The healing salve of grace, when applied to the eyes, allows one to truly see the kingdom of God.

In the world, correction, reproof, and rebuke are seen as something negative. In Christ, these workings of grace are a blessing when we realize that they are the workings of His love (Ps. 118:18; 1 Cor. 11:32; Heb. 12:5–8). Grace encourages us to be enthusiastic, earnest, and burning with zeal. Grace never teaches us to mellow out and be complacent. The fruit of repentance is found in earnest zeal for the things of God. It is not found in the complacency of pseudo-maturity (1 Cor. 5:1–8; 2 Cor. 7:10–11; Heb. 5:11–14). Repentance is never a one-time experience for the normal Christian; it is a life-style.

It was the complacent Christians at Laodicea, who were told to repent; John did not write this letter to a people who had never known God. Grace teaches us to hear, listen, and heed the words spoken to us by the Holy Spirit. This all important lifestyle of repentance is essential if we ever desire to see kingdom doors opened in our life. A life of humble repentance brings with it a confidential communion with Him, and the required word of encouragement and healing for our life. Grace calls Christians to change, not to succumb to complacency (Prov. 24:32–34; Matt. 16:24; 25:14–30; Lk. 9:57–62; 1 Peter 5:6). Oh, how foolish it is to not be found eating with Him!

✞ **POSITION / OPERATION OF GRACE:** (grace is pronounced as a blessing on Christians)

"He Who gives this warning and affirms and testifies to these things says, Yes (it is true). [Surely] I am coming quickly (swiftly, speedily). Amen (so let it be)! Yes, come, Lord Jesus!

The grace (blessing and favour) of the Lord Jesus Christ (the Messiah) be with all the saints (God's holy people, those set apart for God, to be, as it were, exclusively His). Amen (so let it be)" (Revelation 22:20–21)!

The grace of God birthed us into Christ, setting us apart for God. As it is experienced in our life, it manifests itself to those around us by warning and testifying to words of eternal truth.

Sin took away man's love for God; sin took away man's obedience to God; sin took away man's relationship with God. Grace has restored man's relationship with God, giving us a desire to be obedient to Him. It has birthed within us, a greater love for God than even Adam and Eve could experience, and grace has empowered us to obey God to an even greater extent than Adam and Eve could enjoy.

There are many examples in history of Christian martyrs singing as they were beheaded, burned, or crucified — exemplifying the empowerment of grace. Grace has bequeathed to us a providence to be enjoyed eternally in His presence. Christians are the only people on the face of the earth who know their destiny; a destiny founded, furnished, and fixed forever by grace — **G**od's **R**ighteousness, **A** **C**hristian **E**xperience (Rev. 22:1–5). The grace of the Lord Jesus Christ be with us all. Amen.

Topical Index

A

C

D

E

G

H

I

P

R

T

U

V

Y

Z

Scripture Index

Old Testament

Genesis

Leviticus

Numbers

Exodus

Joshua

Judges

1 Samuel

1 Kings

2 Kings

1 Chronicles

2 Chronicles

Nehemiah

Job

Psalms

Acts

Ephesians

CPSIA information can be obtained
at www.ICGtesting.com
Printed in the USA
LVOW04s0138260117
522204LV00001B/1/P